Cross on the Star of David

Indiana Series in Middle East Studies
Mark Tessler, general editor

Uri Bialer

Cross
on the
Star
of
David

The Christian World in Israel's Foreign Policy, 1948–1967

Indiana University Press

Bloomington • Indianapolis

This book is a publication of

Indiana University Press
601 North Morton Street
Bloomington, IN 47404-3797 USA

http://iupress.indiana.edu

Telephone orders	800-842-6796
Fax orders	812-855-7931
Orders by e-mail	iuporder@indiana.edu

© 2005 by Uri Bialer

The paper used in this publication meets the minimum requirements
of American National Standard for Information Sciences—Permanence
of Paper for Printed Library Materials, ANSI Z39.48–1984.

Manufactured in the United States of America

Library of Congress Cataloging-in-Publication Data

Bialer, Uri.
    Cross on the star of David : the Christian world in Israel's foreign policy,
1948-1967 / Uri Bialer.
        p. cm. — (Indiana series in Middle East studies)
    Includes bibliographical references and index.
    ISBN 0-253-34647-9 (hardcover : alk. paper)   1. Catholic Church—
Foreign relations—Israel.   2. Israel—Foreign relations—Catholic
Church.   3. Church and state—Israel.   4. Christians—Government
policy—Israel.   5. Israel—Politics and government—1948-1967.
I. Title.   II. Series.
BX1629.I75B53 2005
327.56940456'34'09045—dc22   2005004485

1 2 3 4 5   10 09 08 07 06 05

contents

acknowledgments

For sowing in me the seeds of academic interest in the encounter between Jews and Christians I am indebted to my former teachers, then colleagues, Professor David Vital and Professor Amnon Linder. I am grateful to the Israeli Academy of Science for its generous research grant and moral support, which made the study possible. The Leonard Davis Institute for International Relations, the Shein Institute for Israeli Society at the Hebrew University, and the Institute for the Heritage of Ben-Gurion provided valuable financial help during its final stages. I am deeply grateful to Professor Avraham Ben Zvi, Professor Gabi Sheffer, and Professor Yaacov Bar Siman Tov for their thoughtful and perceptive comments on early drafts of the book and to Elad Van Gelder for his tireless research assistance.

Haya Galai, who skillfully translated the text from Hebrew, functioned at the same time as a shrewd critic and helped make it better. For her careful copyediting, I would like to thank Elaine Durham Otto of Indiana University Press.

My daughters, Hili, Galia, Maya, and Yael, my sons-in-law, Yigal and David, and my grandsons, Guy and Tal, all followed with loving support my obsessive preoccupation with history. But it is my spouse, Rachel, a true companion, partner, and friend for almost forty years, to whom I owe the deepest gratitude. This book is dedicated to her with love.

introduction

Personal motives for tackling a particular subject are not always fully eluci-
dated in the introduction to an academic book, although understanding of motives can give the reader an insight into the mind of the author. The seeds of
curiosity about the subject of this book were planted in my adolescence. One
of my high school history classes was devoted to the Crusades. The story fas-
cinated me, but my enthusiasm for the topic was tempered by frustration when
I was unable to answer the teacher's question about the concept of the Holy
Trinity, which was not explained in our textbook. For years I remembered her
surprised reaction at this lacuna in my knowledge and the scolding she gave
me. The familiarity I gained over the years with the Christian world did not
alleviate my sense of ignorance, nor was it remedied during my academic studies. In this regard, then, this book is an attempt to answer some of the questions I was asked some forty years ago.

However, it seems that I was not alone in my ignorance. On the eve of the
Third Millennium, Israeli high school students' knowledge of Jesus was examined in several articles. Most of the students knew nothing, not even basic
details such as when and where he was born, where he lived and preached,
when and how he died. Their ignorance is hardly surprising, since the current curriculum of the state education system refers to Jesus at best once, and
then only cursorily. The state religious education system makes no mention
whatsoever because, as the superintendent of that system has explained, "it is
impossible to ignore what Christianity did to the Jews." Professor Michael
Harsegor, a prominent historian, has stated bluntly that "the schools are still
afraid that teaching anything about Jesus would be associated with mission-
izing."[1] This being so, examination of the roots of Israel's policy toward the
Church during the early years of statehood may possibly facilitate understanding components of the national psyche that have remained at the mar-
gins of Israeli public awareness.

As a historian of international relations, my personal interest in the subject
stemmed from two additional sources: current research into developments in

the domain of international relations, and the new historiography of Israel's foreign policy during the first two decades of its existence.

In the past decade increasing attention has been paid to the growing weight in international relations of economic and political "non-government organizations." Whereas, up to the Second World War, nation-states were the almost exclusive exponents of diplomacy, supranational bodies and organizations, such as international corporations and international cultural-social organizations, have since become significantly involved and exerted influence in international politics. This involvement and influence were reinforced by developments in the media, which have created the need to address issues relating to the changing identity of the international actors in the global system, patterns of relations between them, and their differential weight. Indeed, in recent years the theoretical literature in the field has assigned an important place to these questions. Although the present study does not presume to offer a new hypothesis in the field, its focus on the relations between Israel and the Christian world, which involved a number of "supranational actors," is congruent with a general tendency in disciplinary research and provides new empirical material.

Over the past decade, research on Israeli foreign policy has also undergone an important revolution. Since the early 1980s, previously classified political documents have gradually become available, enabling a systematic and orderly approach to a large array of issues and adding new depths and breadths to previous knowledge. One can now examine political, military, social, and economic cycles of activity relating to the first decade and a half of Israel's existence by perusing state documents. Not surprisingly, most of the early works that took advantage of the new documentation dealt mainly with the Arab-Israeli conflict. The existing harvest of research, however, goes beyond that framework.[2] Although the military and political conflict with the Arab states and the Palestinians was indeed the major concern of the country's leaders from Israel's early years, they also focused on other important political issues and used Israel's foreign policy to promote the relevant goals.

We have thus seen innovative studies of the "great immigration waves" of the late 1940s and early 1950s and their political contexts; Israel's efforts to chart its course in the bipolar world of that period; the political struggle to guarantee sources of energy and economic assistance; and bilateral relations with such countries as Britain, the Soviet Union, the United States, the Federal Republic of Germany, and Spain. The new research has also contributed much to understanding the processes of foreign policy formulation, generally by focusing on certain key individuals (such as Ben-Gurion and Sharett) or on structural-organizational aspects of the Foreign Ministry and its links with the military establishment. A special contribution was the analysis of how Israel coped with the problem of "everyday security" during this period, and of the events leading up to the Sinai Campaign of 1956. Yet one of the most interesting topics in Israeli foreign policy is the country's relations with the Christian world, which has yet to be treated in the framework of the "new wave" of Israeli historiography.

This historiography asserts that the country's security problems were always the focal point of physical and political activity. Next came economic issues, and then problems of immigration. In these three spheres of activity, Israel had need of the external resources of weaponry, finances, fuel, and immigrants. This dependency generated sensitivity to the question of external recognition of the state's right to exist within the parameters of the end of the 1948 war. The main problem, from the international standpoint, was the discrepancy between the specifications of the 1947 UN resolution on the establishment of a Jewish state in the Land of Israel, and the borders and population composition of that state from early 1949. Israel was in conflict not only with the Arab world and as countries that had categorically opposed Israel's establishment, but also with many countries that had supported the UN resolution but were opposed to endorsement of the new country's gains in the war. These countries clearly had the capacity to obstruct Israel politically, economically, and demographically or, alternatively, to assist it. It is evident, then, why the fourth special area of concern of Israeli foreign policy was the attainment of international recognition and legitimacy for the reality that prevailed at the end of the 1948 war.

One of the most formidable problems that Israeli foreign policy faced from its early years was the stance of the Christian world. The attitudes of that world toward Zionism and Israel after the Second World War ranged widely, from the basic hostility and categorical nonrecognition of the Catholic Church through the general Protestant ambivalence toward Evangelical support.[3] The overall effect of questioning legitimacy was certainly detrimental to the young state's foreign relations. This was a particularly knotty problem because Christianity was the majority religion of the countries that were the chief targets of Israel's attempts to obtain. The domestic political clout of the churches varied from country to country; moreover, there was not necessarily a direct, substantial connection between the stances of the different churches and the policies of their countries toward Israel. Nonetheless, the prevailing assessment in Jerusalem from 1949 onward (in the wake of Israel's defeat in the UN on the Jerusalem question) perceived Christianity as a hostile international force, whose indirect capacity to harm Israel was considerable. The perception reflected a political reality. As a recent study of the Christian churches' attitudes toward the fledgling State of Israel put it:

> Even in 1947–1948, when the desperate circumstances of the European Jews disposed most politicians and most Church leaders to endorse the Zionist solution, there was formidable opposition. In the forefront were spokesmen of the Protestant missionary societies which had worked with creditable success among the Arab populations of the Middle East for over a century. In the United States, these were allied with anti-Zionist Jewish organizations, notably the American Council for Judaism. Then, almost immediately after the initial decisions were taken, mainstream Protestant Churches as well as the

Roman Catholic Church began to shift into the ranks of those denouncing
the new State—and eventually became overwhelmingly hostile.[4]

The sources of this hostility were mainly theological but also political. The
establishment of Israel had substantially depleted the local Palestinian Christian communities, many of whom abandoned their land or were expelled from
it in 1948 and were not allowed to return. It also created a problematic border
that separated Middle Eastern Christian communities from the Holy Land.
All these facts were a thorn in the flesh of the Catholic Church in particular
and reinforced its predisposed political support for Arab positions. The situation generated conflict inside Israel as well. A proportion, albeit small, of the
non-Jewish population of Israel were Christians, and the state held sovereignty
over several sites that were sacred to local Christians and to the entire Christian world. In addition, Israel had to cope with the phenomenon of the traditional educational-missionizing activity of Christian groups in Israel. The internal friction only intensified the Church's hostility toward Israel.

Today there exists extensive historiography on the main attitudes of the
Christian churches toward the Jews, Zionism, and the State of Israel from the
beginning of the twentieth century. The information in this literature permits
an accurate reconstruction of the attitudes of the Christian world (and especially the Catholic Church) toward Israel during the first twenty years of the
state's existence and of the resultant challenges it faced in the area of international recognition. However, most of the works dealing with the international
problems that the state confronted in this regard as well as those treating the
domestic sphere are not directly based on internal Israeli political documentation, and therefore they only provide external perspectives on Israel. The
question of how Israel itself saw the problem and grappled with it, that is, the
view "from within," remains substantially unanswered in the existing literature.
Those few works that emphasize Israeli perspectives are based on limited and
eclectic use of such documentation and deal with narrow dimensions of the
more general problem on which this book focuses.

Thus the existing literature offers no detailed and periodic analysis of the
processes of Israeli policymaking on this issue; of the main considerations involved in those processes; of the individuals and organizations that dealt with
the issue; of the techniques by which Israel sought to limit the damage incurred
by the Christian world's hostility and to strengthen what Israel viewed as positive tendencies; and of the relative role of the "Christian angle" in the Israeli
foreign policy system in that period. The overall result is a deficiency in the
historiography of an important area of Israeli foreign policy. This book seeks
to redress this deficiency by answering the above-mentioned questions as well
as by addressing other concrete problems, such as the following questions:

• How did the Jewish dimension of Israeli foreign policy influence relations
with the Christian world? What perceptions, images, and modes of relating,
rooted in the historical tradition of Jewish-Christian interactions, influenced

the policymakers in Jerusalem in formulating policy toward the Christian world after Israel gained independence, and what were the practical implications? Were the attitudes of Israel's political leadership in this area, and of the officials charged with executing policy, innocent of the kind of theological-historical baggage that certainly influenced the Christian world's policy toward Israel? In short, to what extent was Israeli policy in this field "rational"?

• How did the Israeli leadership's image of the ecclesiastical world fit into the framework of its general perceptions of the external world, and how did this image influence its basic outlook and expectations?

• How did Israel maneuver between its self-proclaimed obligation to preserve freedom of worship and religion within its borders, and its opposition as a Jewish state to the missionary activity of ecclesiastical groups? What interactions were there between its efforts to cope with this dilemma and its external relations with Christian establishments throughout the world? What were the effects and implications of the internal political dimensions of this problem vis-à-vis decisions that were partially related to foreign policy?

• In the period in question, to what extent could Israel have exploited to its advantage the lack of homogeneity within, and between, the attitudes of the main Christian streams toward the Jewish state? Was there, as in the case of relations with the Arab world for some of the time, a clandestine network of relations parallel to the official one? Can historical theses be based on "wasted opportunities"?

• How did Jerusalem assess the varying influences of ecclesiastical bodies on the foreign policy of their countries, and how were these diagnoses translated into policy prognoses in the context of those churches and countries? In other words, how did the "Christian angle" influence Israeli policy toward various countries during this period?

• Did Israeli diplomacy play a role, and if so, what role, in the gradual changes in the Catholic Church's attitude toward Judaism and the state of Israel in the early 1960s?

• How did Israel's control of church property in the country affect its diplomatic relations?

Finally, some remarks are in order about the sources that served as a basis for this book. Abundant material for analyzing Israeli policymaking with regard to the Christian world in the first two decades of statehood can be culled from archives inside and outside Israel in which documents are systematically declassified thirty years after the events they deal with. The year 1967 is considered a periodic boundary, because the Israeli takeover of East Jerusalem and the West Bank ended one era in those relations and ushered in a new one. That event undoubtedly affected the Vatican's attitude toward Israel that had begun to take shape a few years earlier. Only very meager and fragmentary use has been made so far of more than 500 files of the Department of Christian Communities in the Religious Affairs Ministry: important material that addresses an array of issues pertaining to the "internal sphere." That sphere is especially crucial because, by ruling over the Holy Land, Israel held a very important card when dealing with churches throughout the world. It is not surprising, therefore, that internal problems were discussed mainly in the relevant external contexts. The missionary activity of Christian groups was also, naturally, a sensitive internal political issue, as evidenced by other as-yet unexploited documentation of the Ministry of Religious Affairs and the Ministry of the Interior, and by minutes of the cabinet and of the Knesset's Foreign Affairs and Defense Committee, some of which (up to the mid-1950s) have only recently been opened to research. Fostering relations with the Christian world was clearly a practical endeavor on the part of Israeli diplomats. Many of the Foreign Ministry files in the State Archives deal directly with this subject, and many more touch upon it indirectly, for example, in the context of general consultations or bilateral relations with different countries (especially the Latin American countries, Italy, and the Soviet Union).

The national archives of other countries also contain relevant material that illuminates the subject from the political perspective of the respective countries and that supplies, at the same time, information on Israeli activity that cannot always be found in Israeli State Archives. Notable for its absence is Vatican archival material, which is generally made available only three-quarters of a century after the event. Other churches do not permit access to their internal correspondence. Focus on the Israeli perspective, however, naturally renders that deficiency less significant. Above all, for the reasons cited, and as is the case with every new historiographical enterprise, this book constitutes an initial research framework awaiting those who will undoubtedly follow in its tracks.

Part One

Jerusalem vs. the Vatican:
Israel's Church Diplomacy

The Sense of Threat Emerges

Pre-Independence Contacts

The question of relations with the Christian world, and in particular the Catholic Church, posed an immediate challenge to the newly born State of Israel in 1948. The complexity of the problem had first been recognized during the initial stages of discussion of the Palestine problem at the United Nations a year previously. The pre-state (Yishuv) Jewish authorities were mindful then of the urgent need to establish contact with the Vatican in order to dissuade it from adopting a public (or covert) anti-Zionist stand, which was liable to influence the attitude of various Catholic countries toward the establishment of a Jewish state. Now that the state had come into being, Israel was obliged to devote considerable effort to minimizing the potentially damaging impact of official Catholic policy, which questioned the legitimacy of Israel's gains in the 1948 war. Last but not least, it needed to resolve a number of problems relating to the Christian Holy Places and the Christian minority.

Catholic policy toward the Zionist movement and Israel was fundamentally hostile, and this enmity was grounded on theological considerations, as the leaders of the Zionist movement and the state knew only too well. Theodore Herzl, founder of Zionism, had met with Pope Pius X in Rome in January 1904 to seek his support for the fledgling Zionist movement, and the pope's comments at that meeting were well known. "The soil of Jerusalem," he said then, "is sacred in the life of Jesus Christ. As head of the Church, I cannot say otherwise. The Jews did not acknowledge Our Lord and thus we cannot recognize the Jewish people. Hence, if you go to Palestine and if the Jewish people settle there, our churches and our priests will be ready to baptize you all."[1] This statement made it abundantly clear that, as far as the Church was concerned, the Jews would not be acknowledged as Jews in their homeland and had no right to territorial and national sovereignty over the Holy Land (Terra Sancta). The Christian claim to the land was firm and abiding. The pope's response was undoubtedly rooted in the Christian theological view that the destruction of the ancient Jewish sovereign state had been irrevocable proof of the wrath of God, who had established Christianity as the universal substitute for the Jewish people and for worship in the Temple. The Church was perceived as the True Israel (*Verus Israel*).[2] Close to half a century later, Moshe Sharett, Israel's first foreign minister, was to define the Vatican's attitude toward the Jewish people and the Zionist movement as "a search for revenge for the primeval sin, and the squaring of a nineteen-century-old account."[3]

The leaders of the Yishuv received painful reminders of this adamant stand when they tried and failed to recruit the Vatican's open and public aid for Jews during World War II.[4] It is clear that under Pope Pius XII, the Church did take some covert actions to save Jews. However, this was limited to what the Church deemed feasible given the circumstances. No public statement against the Nazi policies was ever pronounced by Pius XII while there was still time to influence them. The Vatican cited a number of excuses for its refusal. One reason, however, which was rarely given frank expression—though it was only too familiar to the Zionists—was that the migration of Jewish refugees to Palestine would undermine the status of the Church in the Holy Land. For example, in May 1943 the Vatican's secretary of state, Cardinal Luigi Maglione, in an internal church document, listed a number of arguments to back up the pope's refusal to help rescue 2,000 Jewish children from Slovakia. Among the reasons he mentioned were the Vatican's nonrecognition of the Balfour Declaration and the British scheme for establishment of a National Home for the Jews, fear that the sanctity of the Holy Places would be threatened by an influx of Jews into Palestine, and the view that "Palestine is holier to Christians than to Jews."[5]

A year later, in anticipation of Winston Churchill's official visit, the Vatican State Secretariat prepared background material for the pope, which included the statement that "the Holy See has always been opposed to Jewish control of Palestine. [Pope] Benedict XV took successful action to prevent Palestine from becoming a Jewish state." Consequently, after World War II, the pope expressed strong opposition to Britain's desire to withdraw from Palestine and to leave the decision on its fate to the United Nations.[6]

At the United Nations

The Vatican's categorical rejection of the Zionist movement and its aims was evinced during the political struggle at the United Nations in 1947. Papal representatives flatly refused to support the Zionist cause and to bring influence to bear on Latin American states to do the same.[7] Finally, a day before statehood was proclaimed, *L'Osservatore Romano* published the Vatican's unequivocal assertion that "modern Zionism is not the true heir of biblical Israel. . . . Therefore the Holy Land and its sacred sites belong to Christianity, which is the true Israel."[8] Although, ideologically and strategically speaking, the papal approach to Zionism did not change after World War II, the leaders of the Yishuv fostered hopes that the Holy See would in fact accept the fait accompli of the Jewish state.

The first indication of that possibility was provided by the Vatican seven months before its establishment. For obvious reasons, from mid-1947 the Jewish Agency was interested in ascertaining the Vatican's position concerning UN plans for Palestine. It tried to promote an audience with Pope Pious XII for that purpose through Alexander Glasberg, a Paris-based Jewish-born Catholic priest who had rescued Jews during the Holocaust and who later helped illegal Jewish immigrants reach Palestine. Glasberg initially put Moshe Sneh of the Jewish Agency's Political Department in contact with the Papal Nuncio in Paris, Archbishop Angelo Roncalli, who, while serving in Istanbul during World War II, had helped Jews escape death and who, as his newly declassified diaries prove, continued to render them assistance after the war. Roncalli did not succeed in organizing an audience with the pope himself, but in early October 1947 a meeting was held with a Vatican official of the Congregation for Extraordinary Ecclesiastical Affairs. At that meeting the prelate neither committed himself to supporting a Jewish state nor expressed opposition to its establishment.[9]

In 1950, three years after the UN partition resolution, Moshe Sharett provided a vivid retrospective description of events viewed from Jerusalem:

> When, in 1947, the proposal to establish a Jewish state in the Holy Land was first broached seriously, this was a grave problem for the Vatican, which pondered what to do. Would its historical responsibility and Christian conscience permit it to compromise and allow the people which had crucified the Messiah to regain sovereign status anywhere in the Holy Land; or should the Vatican go into battle and rouse all the world's Catholic Churches against the state. The decision was taken not to wage war on the Jewish state. Proof of this is the fact that we were not aware of any intense opposition on the part of the Vatican. We knew that the Vatican was unwilling to take action on our behalf, but still it did not instruct any of the delegations to vote against us. They did, of course, vote against us, but we never felt that this was because of instructions from the Vatican as commander in chief of the campaign. Why did they decide against war? They are very practical people, but they are also doctrinarians and they said to themselves: if we launch a campaign, we are declaring war on the Jewish people who want this state. This is not a local affair, it concerns the Jewish people everywhere. There is already an international front against communism. There is a prospect of winning over the Jewish people as an ally in this front. Why set up a second front and alienate possible allies in our main battle: the war against the anti-Christ. This was the negative argument. There was also a positive argument. They said: the 29 November [1947] resolution calls for a Jewish state which is unquestionably a minus and which must be restricted in one way or another, but it also includes something positive, namely, the internationalization of Jerusalem. That signifies Christian control of Jerusalem, which signifies Vatican control of Jerusalem—this was what they theorized—and such a thing has never happened before. It happened at the time of the Crusader Kingdom in Jerusalem, but then the kingdom fell and all kinds of other elements came in. Then Turkey took over and afterwards the city came under Protestant Christian rule,

but all they had there was a church. Now, for the first time—under the UN
flag, it is true—there will be territorial rule over the Holy Places and there is
a possibility that the representative will be a Catholic. Anyone acquainted with
the history of the Vatican and the New Kingdom and the history of the conflict
between the Vatican and the emperor knows what value the Vatican attrib-
utes to territorial control. And here they saw the opportunity to consolidate
such standing . . . a kind of imperial citadel. And they said, "If one of the conditions of this dispute is that we must not fight the Jewish state, it is worth
paying the price in order to achieve what we want."[10]

Yaakov Herzog, director of the Christian Communities Division of the Ministry of Religious Affairs, was the most prominent among the Israeli officials
who dealt with this issue in the first few years of statehood. He claimed that
the Vatican's acceptance of a Jewish state was inspired by a clear political and
ideological vision:

> [The Vatican] planned the renewal of the Latin Kingdom in Jerusalem . . .
> whether in order to compensate the Catholic world for the establishment of
> a Jewish state; whether as a means of gaining political influence in the Mid-
> dle East; whether as a symbol of the fusion of Rome and Jerusalem into a doc-
> trinarian concept capable of rekindling ancient Crusader instincts and setting
> international Catholicism at the head of the struggle against the "materialist
> church"; and whether as an opportunity for settling an ancient score with the
> Greeks and Protestants in Jerusalem.[11]

Israeli experts perceived other underlying reasons for the Vatican's backing
for internationalization. As they saw it, the Vatican feared that the outcome of
the anticipated hostilities between Jews and Arabs might be Jewish control of
the Holy Places, and anticipated that, in that event, the Israeli authorities would
make "a quiet attempt . . . to liquidate any Muslim or Christian presence in the
New City of Jerusalem." It also predicted that Palestinian refugees who were
not permitted to return to their homes might find refuge in the city. Then again,
it was influenced by the pressure exerted by France and several Latin American countries to promote internationalization.[12]

However utilitarian and even Machiavellian the Vatican's reasons, this approach was naturally welcomed by the Israeli leadership. The same was true
of the Church's ostensibly neutral stand toward the Israeli-Arab dispute. In Jerusalem, it was believed in 1948 that this neutrality stemmed from uncertainty
as to the eventual outcome of the hostilities which had begun immediately after the UN resolution was passed, and from trepidation at the prospect that
two non-Christian states might rule the Holy Land. As time passed, the Israeli
authorities concluded that there was a second explanation, with graver implications.[13] They discovered that, toward the end of the British Mandate, the
Vatican, like many other international bodies, had been highly skeptical as to
the ability of the Jews to withstand an Arab onslaught. In the second week of
May 1948, the Jewish Agency informed its representative in Athens that the
Italian minister to Greece had inquired whether the Greeks would be willing
to take in a quota of Jewish refugees from Palestine after the Arab attack. It

later transpired that the source of this initiative was the Papal Nuncio. Sharett learned of this humanitarian initiative while on his way home from the United States (when his plane made a stopover in Athens). His reaction was blunt: "One way or the other, either we'll win the war or we'll be thrown into the sea— there will be no Jewish refugees from Palestine."

According to Israeli sources, the Vatican believed at the time that a Jewish victory was unlikely. What is more, the Israeli Foreign Ministry later deduced that, in early 1948, the pope had not been averse to the prospect of liquidation of Jewish sovereignty over New Jerusalem. As Herzog put it:

> The Vatican anticipated that in the tumult of war between Israel and the Arabs, the Jews of Jerusalem would be destroyed. . . . This was why the Catholic Church remained silent when the danger of annihilation hovered over the Holy Places in Jerusalem in 1948, believing that the war would end in the surrender of the Jewish population. This would leave the path open for implementation of the November 1947 resolution on the internationalization of the city and adjacent areas. The Vatican thought that if we were removed from the scene, the Christian world would easily find a way "to get along" with the Arabs in Jerusalem.

The 1948 War

There are no accessible Vatican sources that could cast light on this affair. In any event, since the Vatican's public stand on the Israeli-Arab conflict was neutral—its support for internationalization notwithstanding—it did not pose a direct and significant political challenge to the Zionist leadership immediately before the proclamation of statehood. However, several weeks after the Arab invasion of the newly founded state, Israel's leaders realized that the pope was now liable to adopt a hostile and hence potentially dangerous policy. The fierce fighting raging in Jerusalem—the focal point of Israel's strategic efforts— was placing a number of Christian institutions at risk. The fate of Christian sites outside Jerusalem was also likely to arouse international concern. Israel could not ignore one of the explicit demands of the Security Council, voiced a bare two weeks after war broke out, namely, that it take all possible steps to protect the Holy Places. Moreover, this demand constituted one of the bases for the first cease-fire initiated by the United Nations and accepted by Israel.[14]

This explains why, in the first week of fighting, Israel began to record the damage inflicted on Christian Holy Places in Jerusalem by the Arabs and to disseminate this information worldwide. The reality, however, was that the Israelis were also inflicting serious damage. Thus, for example, an Israeli intelligence agent reported on 13 June that three Benedictine monks and one member of the Franciscan Order had been arrested on Mount Zion and that, despite "strongly worded orders" from the officer in charge not to damage the church, the Israeli Defense Forces (IDF) "smashed up" the place where the holy vessels were kept.[15] A later report described in detail incidents which occurred in the Dormition Church, one of the holiest sites to Catholics, which enjoyed special papal protection and received donations from a number of Catholic countries:

> When Mount Zion was occupied by the Israeli army, all the monks residing there were removed with the exception of three who remained by permission of the Jewish army in order to guard the site and the numerous valuable objects there. These valuables were concentrated in the cellar of the church (Dormition) and valuables from other churches on Mount Zion were also taken there . . . the CO Jerusalem District gave the representatives of this church his assurance that the site would be safe from looting . . . the main problem arose after the three monks were removed, apparently on the orders of one of the commanders of Mount Zion. Before long, soldiers . . . broke into a chest in the cellar and removed some of the diamonds, gold and valuables stored there. Their value is estimated at hundreds of thousands of pounds.[16]

Several months later, the IDF frontline supply officer informed the CO Jerusalem District that "the army canteens in Jerusalem are using utensils and glasses belonging to Notre-Dame Church."[17] Christian religious institutions outside Jerusalem were also harmed. Several weeks later, the minister of religious affairs informed the cabinet in September 1948 that "monasteries in the occupied area have been damaged, defiled with feces and refuse, terrible things have been done,"[18] and the military government authorities reported in October that "irresponsible army personnel . . . have found a new game: using the headstones, crucifixes and symbols in the [Jaffa Christian] cemetery for target practice."[19]

Prime Minister David Ben-Gurion, who greatly feared the negative impact on world public opinion of such actions, issued severely worded instructions to Israeli officers: "It is your duty to ensure that the special force in charge of defending the Old City makes merciless use of machine guns against any Jews, and in particular any Jewish soldier, who tries to loot or defile a Christian or Muslim Holy Place."[20] He also intervened to revoke an order from Moshe Carmel (CO Northern Front) to expel the inhabitants of Nazareth, most of whom were Christians. The Israeli commanders were specifically ordered in July 1948 to take over and run the city smoothly and to issue severe orders against desecration of monasteries and churches.[21] The leaders of the local community were asked to send a cable to the pope reporting that "all is well with the Christian communities, and the Holy Places have not been damaged."[22] These efforts did not bear fruit. The first months of the war witnessed what Israeli officials described as "a wave of poisonous propaganda directed against us . . . in the Catholic world, based on stories of a campaign of desecration of churches which was allegedly conducted by the Israel Defense Forces. . . . They are inflating each incident of damage—however slight—caused by a handful of uncultured and irresponsible people."[23] With hindsight, Herzog grasped the logic underlying this Catholic propaganda and explained to Israeli embassies and legations abroad that

> these incidents sowed seeds of suspicion in influential Vatican circles and in other Christian centers . . . the anxieties of Vatican policymakers . . . who have recently been ousted from Eastern European countries . . . have been amplified by events in the Middle East, which they regard as the main arena for

Nuns outside the Dormition Church atop Mt. Zion in Jerusalem, December 9, 1949.
Courtesy of the National Photo Collection of the Israel Government Press Office, Prime Minister's Office. Photo D532–076. Photographer Fritz Cohen.

the defensive stand of Western culture against saboteurs from the East. Our enemies have concluded that these incidents disprove the assertion that the introduction of an additional non-Islamic element into the East is likely, to some degree, to create an equal balance of power. This equilibrium could be particularly valuable, the Vatican once thought, in light of the possible emergence of an extremist Islamic movement, the early manifestations of which are a source of serious concern to Christians.[24]

Other Israeli officials believed that the attacks on Israel were inspired by the natural tendency of Italy and France to intervene in order to protect what they perceived as Catholic interests, and in particular by France's desire to perpetuate the substantial religious and cultural rights it had enjoyed in Palestine.[25] Whatever the underlying reasons, the wave of anti-Israeli propaganda reached its height in August when Monsignor Thomas McMahon, secretary of the Catholic Near East Welfare Association and chairman of the pontifical mission in Beirut, appealed to the secretary-general of the United Nations to establish a commission of inquiry to examine the Israeli government's treatment of Israel's Christian minority.[26] For obvious reasons, such a move would have posed a clear threat to the young state.

Moreover, in the early stages of the war, Israel realized that if the recommendation to internationalize Jerusalem was not implemented, its relations with the Catholic Church would become even more problematic. The director-general of the Foreign Ministry reported that "the Catholic Church is opposed to the custody of the Holy Places [in Jerusalem] being vested in the Jews, the Protestants, the Greek Orthodox, and the Muslims—in that order."[27] As time passed without any indication that the UN would succeed in implementing its resolution, it seemed increasingly likely that the city would be partitioned between Jordan and Israel, a situation that could only prove detrimental to Vatican interests. This solution seemed imminent in the first few weeks of the war, when Count Bernadotte, the United Nations mediator, submitted his initial plan for solving the Arab-Israeli conflict.[28] It entailed what Catholic circles considered to be the surrender of Jerusalem to King Abdullah of Jordan. Not surprisingly, Cardinal Spellman of the United States was horrified at the prospect of Muslim sovereignty over Jerusalem.[29] Bernadotte therefore felt it necessary to "sell him a bill of goods, telling him that he received positive assurances from King Abdullah that a Christian governor will rule Jerusalem." According to information passed on to Sharett, the cardinal "remained adamant" and immediately wrote to the pope, pleading with him to oppose the Bernadotte plan for Jerusalem. It was clear, at this early stage, that the Catholic Church had adopted an uncompromising stand against any attempt by Israel and Jordan to establish facts in Jerusalem, thereby ruining all prospects of internationalization.

Establishing Contacts

This being so, Israel now tried to establish contact with the Vatican in order to diminish the negative political impact of this stand and to resolve various problems faced by local Christian communities since mid-1948. The simplest path of action, namely, to put out feelers to examine the possibility of Vatican recognition of Israel, appeared unfeasible at the time. Israel' requests for de jure recognition were directed only at those countries thought likely to respond in the affirmative. As Herzog wrote: "At the time, the infant state was content with the thought that the Vatican would confine itself to nonrecognition and not seek to cause harm."[30] Various mediators, including clerics in Israel and elsewhere, who tried to gauge the Vatican's policy on recognition received unequivocally negative answers. In 1948, James McDonald, while en route to Israel to take up his post as first U.S. ambassador to the new state, was received in audience by the pope to discuss Vatican relations with Israel. He proposed that the pope also receive Dr. Chaim Weizmann, the future first president of Israel, then in Switzerland on his way to Israel, in order to discuss issues pertaining to relations between the two sides. The pope not only refused to meet Weizmann but also rebuked the U.S. government for having recognized Israel while withholding diplomatic recognition from the Vatican. When McDonald attempted to point out the difference between the two cases, the pope reiterated that he would never accept Israeli sovereignty over the Holy Land. The U.S. diplomat gained the impression that the pope was reluctant to enter into a binding relationship particularly in light of his fear that Israel "will turn Communist." Since the path to Rome was blocked, the natural move was for Israel to establish political contact with the Catholic leadership in Israel. However, this too was unfeasible because of a particular set of circumstances.

The newly established state encountered several local Catholic authorities, all of them hostile. The Catholic administration in the country was headed by the Latin patriarchate in Jerusalem. It had been established in 1099 by the Crusaders, it endured until the Crusaders were defeated by the Muslims in 1291, and it was not restored until 1847. The second most important body was the Custodia Terrae Sanctae, founded in 1217 as a special branch of the Franciscan order so as to defend and protect the Holy Places that were now in Muslim hands. After suffering persecution and banishment in the thirteenth century, the Franciscans returned, and for centuries they filled the gap left by the liquidation of the Latin patriarchate of Jerusalem. The reestablishment of the latter in the nineteenth century spelled the end of the exclusive rule of the Custodia, but did not curtail its independence. The "custodian" who headed it was appointed by the Franciscan order and approved by the pope.[31]

This was not the only administrative tangle. The Catholic administration in Palestine came under the jurisdiction of the Oriental Congregation, but the Vatican also maintained a permanent observer in the region, the Delegate Apostolico, who represented the pope but had no diplomatic standing. His mission was to protect the Church's local interests and to report on the situation, and his area of jurisdiction was identical to that of the Latin patriarch; he too resided in the Old City and came under the authority of the Oriental Congregation. This meant that the Catholic priesthood in Israel was subject to the patriarch whose seat was in Arab territory and whose negative attitude toward Israel was no secret. The Custodia, which was also located in the Old City and which encompassed nineteen monasteries in Israel and more than fifty monks, was also markedly hostile to Israel. Herzog described a prominent member of the Custodia, Father Terence Kuehn, as "the chief of the inciters."[32] The Delegate Apostolico was no less antagonistic. Until the late 1950s, this position was held by Gustavo Testa, who was particularly unsympathetic to Israel partly because of the confiscation of his archive by Israelis during the 1948 war.[33] And beyond all these factors, the pro-Arab stand of most of the Catholic clerics in Palestine and later in Israel was inevitably influenced by the demographic reality.

Understandably enough, Israel tried to circumvent the unfriendly heads of the local Catholic Church by fostering ties with the second rank of the priesthood. Nor did it abandon efforts to gain access to the Vatican in order to promote its political interests. The basic objective was to dispatch a delegation for informal talks at the Vatican in order to sound out the Church's stand. According to Herzog, who was earmarked to head the delegation: "We do not intend to ask for diplomatic recognition of the State of Israel. Our objective is only to clarify the demands of the Church with regard to its authority and the activities of its various institutions inside our state. These talks may lead to rapprochement between the Vatican and Israel, but if we succeed in proving to them that Israel has no intention of restricting their existing rights—as long as the basic interests of the state are not affected—we will be content."[34] Since Israel was not in direct contact with the Vatican, third party assistance was required in setting up a meeting. This role was apparently played, in a generous and positive spirit, by the U.S. administration through the U.S. ambassador to Israel, James McDonald, and Franklin Gowen, President Truman's representative at the Vatican. The two-man Israeli delegation, which consisted of Herzog and Haim Vardi of the Ministry of Religious Affairs, spent three weeks in Rome in mid-September 1948.

During this period, they held five meetings with Vatican staff: two with Count Enrico Gleazzi, special delegate of the Pontifical Commission of the State of the Vatican City, two with Monsignor Pietro Sigismondi of the Secretariat of State of the Holy See, and one with Archbishop Valerio Valeri of the Congregation for Oriental Churches. No precise details on the talks are available in the Israel State Archives but Herzog's general report at the time and later fragmented references reveal that several aims were achieved, at least in Israel's view. First, the delegation apparently succeeded in persuading the Holy See that reports of massive attacks on Christians and damage to the Holy Places were exaggerated, if not entirely lacking in significant basis. It is not clear if the Vatican was convinced by the delegation's other message, namely, that "there is no communist influence in Israel today and it is unthinkable that the basic tenets of the state . . . should ever be abandoned to a pack of ideas which have no connection with the fundamental elements of [our] culture." In any event, at the concluding discussion, the representative of the Vatican Foreign Ministry announced that instructions had been dispatched to the

Catholic press everywhere "to refrain from publishing defamatory articles against Israel."[35] Second, it was agreed that regular relations would be established with the papal representative in Israel in order to solve the problems of the Christian communities in general. Third, the Congregation for Oriental Churches seemed readier than the State Secretariat to compromise with Israel on political questions and in particular on the question of Jerusalem.[36] Hence, as will be shown below, the meetings in Rome provided an important basis for continual contact with this central Catholic body. Fourth, the pope's representatives made it clear that the Vatican would cling to its neutral stand on the Israel-Arab dispute despite concern for the fate of the refugees and fears that the plan for internationalizing Jerusalem might not be put into effect. Herzog also hinted in his later reports at some kind of deal between the parties, the details of which remain unknown to this day. He noted that "in connection with the neutral stand of the Vatican vis-à-vis the Israel-Arab dispute, the assurance was then given (in return for certain political guarantees on our part) that they would not respond to Arab pressures to change their traditional policy."

Later references indicate Israeli willingness to give priority to the pope's interests when dealing with Christian affairs. As Sharett told the Knesset's Foreign Affairs and Defense Committee, "We are demonstrating readiness to come to a direct arrangement with the Vatican and will not support the inclination of France or any other country to become the defender of Catholicism and to set itself between the Vatican and the decisive government factors. This has brought us into conflict with [Paris]."[37] Lastly, the Israeli representatives gained the impression that Rome was ready "to strengthen certain ties" in strictly judicious fashion.[38] The pope's supreme interest in the welfare and orderly activity of the Christian church in Israel was made clear to them, and Herzog apparently provided assurances on this matter. It was also clarified that political recognition was not possible. As Herzog said later: "Such a move is dependent on the Vatican's appraisal over a period of several years of Israel's spiritual and political stability—namely, the extent to which Israel is worthy of such recognition—and on the resolution of various issues between Israel and the Vatican. We were told that we must prove—through our political conduct in general and with regard to Christian interests in particular—that we have the right to such recognition."[39]

The direct outcome of the Rome talks was McMahon's mid-December visit to Israel in order to examine the situation and, so Israel hoped, to pave the way to closer relations on the local level.[40] In the course of the visit, McMahon gave the Israelis to understand that his fears that Christian institutions had been damaged during the war had largely been confuted. On the other hand, he asked Israel to take back some of the Christian Arabs who had fled the country, weakening the local Catholic Church. At the same time, "with great circumspection," he refrained from expressing an opinion on the Jerusalem problem.[41] The outcome of the visit, which the Israelis regarded as an achievement, was the report McMahon submitted to Trygve Lie, UN secretary-general, in his capacity as personal representative of Cardinal Spellman. In it McMahon wrote that he was satisfied with Israel's attitude toward Christian institutions within its borders and was convinced of Israel's sincere desire for accommodation. He therefore withdrew his demand for a UN commission of inquiry.[42]

Disregarding the Writing on the Wall

The optimistic mood in Jerusalem was apparently enhanced by a meeting between Cardinal Tisserant, head of the Congregation for Oriental Churches and a leading Vatican authority on the Middle East, and Eliyahu Ben-Horin of the U.S. Zionist Emergency Council, who was on good terms with the heads of the Catholic Church in the United States. Ben-Horin noted that the Vatican believed that, "while reprehensible actions have taken place in the heat of [the 1948] war . . . [there is now] goodwill and understanding of the central and local [Israeli] authorities [toward the Christian communities]." As to political issues, and in particular the Jerusalem question, "their attitude will be determined finally by internal developments and international political developments, over which we have no control. Like us, they too are sitting and waiting."[43] Be that as it may, the improvement in relations with the Vatican after Herzog's visit to Rome and McMahon's visit to Israel was gratifying to the Foreign Ministry. "We should advise our representatives everywhere," Herzog declared, "that there is no need to be alarmed by every tremor of a leaf. We too are finally beginning to sense a normal political framework and to understand the relations between the center and the various peripheries, and we are in definite contact—though not yet perfect—with the center which determines church policy."[44] However, the conviction that the Catholic Church was, in effect, reconciled to the status quo in the Holy Land was not long-lived.

This conviction was first shaken when Pius XII issued his second encyclical on Palestine, *Redemptoris Nostri*, on 15 April 1949. In hindsight, it seems that this document should have eradicated all doubts as to the pope's essential stand on fundamental political questions relating to Israel. It was undoubtedly composed in response to the end of hostilities, the Israeli victory, and the danger of perpetuation of the status quo. However, it was some time before Jerusalem realized that the document was a clear proclamation of the Vatican's stand, which it would maintain as long as the "present circumstances" endured.[45]

The pope posed eight concrete demands in this public declaration, each of them representing a substantial challenge to Israel, and together they constituted a threat that could not be ignored. These were the return of the refugees; international status for Jerusalem and its environs; juridical protection under international guarantee for Holy Places elsewhere in Israel; free access to all churches; freedom of worship; the right to unlimited sojourn in the Holy Places; guaranteeing of the privileges enjoyed by Catholic institutions in Israel; and guarantees of the historic rights of Catholics to the Holy Places. Analysis of the implications of these demands explains why some Israeli policymakers thought that the *Redemptoris Nostri* posed a strategic challenge to Israel's sovereignty.

The Return of the Refugees

When the pope called for the return of refugees, it was thought in Jerusalem that he was referring not only to the Latin Arabs, whose number was relatively small, and to Greek Catholics but also to other communities and even Muslims, among whom the Catholic institutions conducted educational and missionary activities. Without this Arab infrastructure, Catholic institutions were doomed to operate in a void (as did in fact happen) and the development of Catholicism in Israel would be petrified. The Church's good relations with the Arab states were also conditional on its demand for the return of non-Christian refugees to Israel. Israel's leaders were concerned at the prospect of collaboration between the Arabs and the Catholic Church as a result of this demand. Such collaboration, based on unarguable humanitarian claims, was liable to consolidate a universal Muslim and Christian international political and religious front against Israel. In any event, acquiescence to the demand for the return of the refugees or even acceptance of the principle underlying the demand were seen as a threat to Israel's existence.

Internationalization

The establishment of an international regime in Jerusalem was understood to be the pope's minimal demand "under prevailing circumstances." These words had been reiterated several times up to 1949 in papal encyclical letters. The implications were clarified to the Jewish Agency representatives by the testimony of the Franciscan Father Simon Bonaventura before the UNSCOP Committee in 1947. If the country was to be partitioned, he said, it was essential to establish international rule in Jerusalem, because sovereignty over part or all of the country was about to be handed over to a non-Christian power. Under these circumstances, the Vatican doubted that a non-Christian government would display sympathetic and active consideration for the Christian Holy Places.[46]

At a later stage, Herzog discovered that the Vatican's uncompromising support for internationalization was based on global arguments, no less than local calculations. The Vatican, he explained, faced particularly complex global challenges in the postwar era, and it was these which dictated its stand on the Middle East and Israel. In the Middle East, the Church was observing, with growing anxiety, the national and spiritual awakening of the Arab world "from the dormancy of centuries" and particularly its increasing rejection of the alien Christian elements in its midst. The ideology of the "Muslim Brothers" was living proof of this. The overall inevitable outcome would be a religious and spiritual clash between Islam and Christianity despite the "cordial" relations between the Vatican and the Arab countries. The challenge to the standing of the Catholic Church extended beyond the Middle East and North Africa.

As Herzog saw it, the take-over of China and Eastern Europe by the Communists had been traumatic events for the Vatican, which feared that they would impair its powers in any forthcoming international religious struggle. He postulated that these existential anxieties dictated the pope's policy regarding Jerusalem and Israel. It provided him with a golden opportunity "to mobilize the psychological resistance of Christianity to 'the [global] materialistic offensive' he faced," by supplying "a historic vision to stir the devotion of its adherents." The internationalization of Jerusalem and the creation of a Christian territory there and in Bethlehem were, therefore, regarded by the Church as ideal instruments for the revival and worldwide dissemination of the ideologically and politically effective concepts first forged in the Crusader period. Such a Christian center, as Herzog saw it, could provide the Vatican with a lever for global action, which would immediately improve its precarious international standing.[47] Although he was well aware of the difficulty of uniting Islam and Christianity in the struggle against Israel, Herzog did not rule out the possibility of such a transient development. When he learned in early 1951 that the secretary of the Arab League, Azzam Pasha, had offered the pope spiritual leadership of the Middle East in return for political cooperation on the refugee problem and Jerusalem, Herzog wrote that similar deals, intended to cover up "spiritual emptiness," were frequently offered by the Arabs to "Wall Street, Rome or Moscow . . . for Rome they can add the incentive of revival of the Crusaders concepts—a union of ancient enemies in this day and age, against Israel and Jewish Jerusalem."[48]

Israel's basic rejection of internationalization, which took shape between mid-1948 and late 1949, stemmed naturally from its wartime gains and from the UN's failure to implement the scheme. The signing of the armistice agreements with Jordan, which regulated the de facto partition of the city between the two states, added a new element of inestimable importance to Israel's categorical rejection of this idea. As Walter Eytan, director-general of the Israeli Foreign Ministry, said:

> To reject de facto sovereignty (in both sectors of the city) will destroy the foundation on which our armistice agreement with Transjordan is based, thanks to which Jerusalem now enjoys peace and quiet. If the validity of this agreement is violated, before long the other armistice agreement will follow suit and with them the entire structure of de facto peace in Eretz Israel. In this manner, internationalization constitutes a grave threat to peace not only in Jerusalem but in the entire Middle East.[49]

The internationalization of the Old City alone might have been acceptable to Israel, but the pope was unlikely to accept it. The fact that places holy to Christians like Gethsemane, the Tomb of the Virgin, and the Room of the Last Supper (Coenaculum-Cenacle) were located outside the Old City walls was overshadowed by the Vatican's reluctance to discriminate against the Arabs and to demand its rights from them alone. In April 1949, the Church clarified a stand on the composition of the international administration in Jerusalem that posed several threats to Israel. It insisted that this body be made up solely of Western representatives (and none from the Eastern Bloc, which backed Israel at the time) and refused to waive the demand for Vatican representation.

Legal Protection for the Holy Places

In order to guarantee legal protection for the remaining Holy Places in Israel (and the Kingdom of Jordan), the pope proposed the establishment of an international committee with powers similar to those of Christian countries which were custodians of the Holy Places, such as Spain and France. This would have implied supervision of Nazareth, Mount Tabor, Tabgha, etc. A year after the April 1949 encyclical letter, Eytan wrote:

> One should not underestimate the importance and value of the principle of sovereignty. We cannot accept an arrangement that would remove a considerable number of sites scattered over Eretz Israel from Israeli jurisdiction. If we concede on this matter, we may eventually find extraterritorial enclaves scattered all over our state, causing us deep trouble in various ways. . . . An agreement of provisional convenience vis-à-vis Jerusalem is liable to impose a heavy burden on us and will exert continual pressure on us like the 1757 status quo. In other words, the agreement may appear expedient today, but its advantages may fade in the future, and then we will find ourselves in a predicament—a new status quo of our own doing—which we will be unable to change and which will lie heavy on us. This is one of the reasons why we cannot agree to extraterritoriality of the Holy Places in Israel, in the wider sense of this term. Even if thereby we achieve peace with the Vatican today, we are bequeathing a bitter heritage to the generations to come.[50]

Freedom of Access and Worship

No less problematic for Israel was the Vatican demand for freedom of access to the Holy Places. The practical implication was the waiving of restrictions on Arab tourism to Israel and the granting of international sureties. Freedom of worship also posed a threat, since it entailed the unrestricted right "to conduct religious processions with photographers, icons and flags, with police and state protection of the safety of the participants and the holy vessels . . . and privileges for members of the clergy."[51]

Guaranteeing of Privileges and Historic Rights

Equally hazardous was the demand for the guaranteeing privileges enjoyed by Catholic institutions, since it encompassed "extraterritorial privileges, exemption from payment of taxes and excise, freedom of education and religious preaching . . . which, if granted to one people, will have to be given to others, and if given to members of one religion, will be demanded by others as well." Many members of the Israel establishment perceived freedom of Christian education in Israel as a cultural threat of cardinal importance.[52] Moreover, there was more than met the eye to the pope's demand for guarantees of Catholic historic rights to the Holy Places. This would entail examination of the Catholic claim against the Greek Orthodox and Armenian churches, acknowledgement of Catholic rights, and amendment of the status quo in Jerusalem to the advantage of the Catholics. The overall conclusion in Israel was that the Vatican considered itself and wished to be regarded by others as a partner in the Holy Land and an active participant in shaping patterns of government there. The major threat was unquestionably the possibility that the Vatican's stand would serve as the central catalyst for international pressure, which could rob Israel of its strategic and existential gains in the 1948 war.

The Illusions of Complacence

At the beginning of December 1949 the UN, under pressure from the Vatican, ratified the plan for the internationalization of Jerusalem. In light of the developments described above, this should not have come as a surprise to Israel. However—and this is one of the most interesting facts to be learned from the newly accessible documents in the State Archives in Jerusalem—the Israeli government was totally stunned by this move. The political trauma was to have a far-reaching impact on Israel's relations with the Vatican, and hence deserves to be examined in full.

Initially, the senior political echelons in Jerusalem had not been perturbed by the *Redemptoris Nostri*, and up to June 1949, they cited two main arguments in support of their extenuating interpretation. First, Sharett claimed that the wording of a number of phrases in the document was "cautious," pointing out the absence of the word *international*, use of the term *special juridical status* for Jerusalem, the failure to mention the explicit need to return the refugees "to their homes," and the absence of the word *Arab*.[53] Consequently, at a meeting of the Foreign Affairs and Defense Committee of the Knesset in early June, Sharett said that he doubted whether the pope "is adamant about the idea of "[international] trusteeship."[54] Second, it was anticipated that even if the Vatican adhered to its official line on internationalization, it would eventually come to recognize that the scheme was unfeasible because of what Jerusalem considered to be the impossibility of implementing it and the unlikelihood that it would be passed at the 1949 meeting of the UN. Hence it was thought that the Vatican would not bring its weight to bear to ensure that the issue was placed on the agenda.

McMahon's second visit to Israel in July 1949 dispelled the first illusion. Sharett described the "very serious talk" between them:

> They regard the decision on international rule in Jerusalem as a kind of written and signed contract between the Catholic Church and the United Nations—this is the Catholic Church's commitment to the UN. They are aware that there have been serious upheavals in Israel and that, as it were, the situation has altered radically and things have been turned upside down. But they claim that after all the shocks of December 1948, the Assembly reiterated explicitly the principle of international rule over the whole of Jerusalem. In other words, a year later the Assembly reaffirmed its commitment of November 1947. They

think that matters must come to a head at this session. It was clear from all he said that they are rallying their forces for a decisive and bitter struggle over the internationalization of Jerusalem.

The focus of the confrontation, as far as the pope was concerned, was not Israel but the United Nations since Catholic objectives were global, and this viewpoint did not make things easier for the Israeli leadership. Sharett quoted McMahon as saying that

> the pope has never said a word against the State of Israel and he has neither endorsed not adopted a hostile attitude towards the State of Israel. . . . They [the Catholic Church] agreed to the partition of Palestine and the establishment of a Jewish state in the Holy Land . . . as part of a scheme guaranteeing Jerusalem . . . for the Catholic Church: they agreed to the abrogation of Christian, though not Catholic, rule over Palestine on the assumption that this would ensure Catholic hegemony over all of Jerusalem. This is one of the issues which is a matter of life and death for them. They believe that their present-day mission in the world is to combat communism which is the "anti-Christ" of our times—that is their mission: as they see it, an agreement on Jerusalem will create the opportunity to transform Jerusalem into an anti-Bolshevik bulwark in the Middle East, where the Catholic Church will be securely entrenched and from which it will disseminate its influence to other countries. . . . This is not a dispute between you and us. We understand you—you were actually willing to accept this solution from the outset, and you cooperated . . . but you were attacked and nobody came to your aid, and so if you withdraw, the dispute will be between us and the United Nations. There we cannot give in because it is a commitment. . . . And this question will come up before the summit at the next Assembly.[55]

At the same time, the "priest," as Sharett called him, had hinted that "if we do not come to an agreement with them, their influence throughout the Middle East will not be to the advantage of Israel and the Jewish communities."[56] This meeting also made a profound impression on Herzog, and in a letter to Israel's UN representative, Abba Eban, two months later, he predicted a fierce struggle with the Catholic Church.[57]

The meeting with McMahon did not, as might have been expected, lead to a radical change in Jerusalem's thinking and its exhaustive preparations for a stormy confrontation at the UN Assembly. Although the enormity of the potential threat was made abundantly clear to the Israeli Foreign Ministry, it remained deeply skeptical not only as to the pope's prospects for success in imposing international rule on the city through the UN, but also as to his readiness to participate in a political campaign promoting internationalization. This skepticism was based in part on reports of fierce internal debates within the Vatican on this issue. Prime Minister Ben-Gurion was informed at the beginning of September that

> the rift between the State Secretariat and the [Congregation for Oriental Churches] on the Jerusalem question is still in force. . . . The State Secretariat believes that internationalization of Jerusalem offers the opportunity to es-

tablish a last refuge for Christian interests in the Middle East. . . . Their fears were evoked by the plan for the unification of Islam . . . the impossibility of reviving the system of privileges which prevailed under the Turks . . . and a change of regime in Israel which could also settle the account with Christianity. On the other hand, the Oriental Congregation fears the possible isolation which could stem from curtailing of Christian rule in Jerusalem and is ready to face the danger inherent in the lack of a guaranteed center so that Christianity will not be perceived as an alien shoot in the Middle East.[58]

Another source of optimism was awareness of the manifest reluctance of the de facto rulers of the city, Jordan and Israel, to cooperate, because British and U.S. policies, in effect, ran counter to the principle of internationalization and because of the complex problems entailed in administering international rule.[59] Israel was partially successful in its political maneuvering, aimed at demonstrating that the Christian world and the Christian communities in Israel were not unanimous in their support for the pope's call for internationalization. For all these reasons, Israel was convinced that the Holy See would hesitate to bring all its weight to bear in a struggle it was liable to lose. In a letter to Eban in mid-August, Sharett wrote: "McMahon is deluding himself if he believes that the Vatican . . . will find it easy to win a two-thirds majority for its demand, which has become so anachronistic."[60] A month later, he reassured one of the heads of the American Zionist organizations, expressing the conviction that "in the end the Vatican will . . . come to see that its own interests will be better served by effective U.N supervision over the Holy Places and institutions of the Churches than by setting up of a full-blooded international regime over the whole city which cannot work."[61] Thus as he reported to Eban, Sharett was optimistic about the outcome of the imminent struggle, but feared the inevitable protracted confrontation with the Vatican that would ensue:

> I myself do not overestimate these overt and implied threats, to the extent that they relate to the struggle we face at the coming Assembly session. But the trouble is that our problematic relationship with the Vatican is not restricted to the UN Assembly, but extends in time and space far beyond it. It is a grave factor in the life of the State of Israel and is present wherever Jewish and Catholics live. . . . The source of my concern is the wider and ever-present problem and not necessarily this particular stage in the specific struggle we face."[62]

Israel's contacts with church representatives prior to the Assembly session seemed to justify this tactical complacence. Shlomo Ginosar, the Israeli minister in Rome, for example, reported at the beginning of August that in his capacity as doyen of the diplomatic corps, he had met with the Apostolic Nuncio. The meeting was out of the ordinary in light of the Vatican's nonrecognition of Israel. He gained the impression that the Vatican would not insist on internationalization of Jerusalem and would not categorically reject some other solution—such as establishment of an international body to protect the Holy Places.[63] Several weeks later, the minister reported that he had met the U.S.

ambassador to Israel, McDonald, who was then visiting Rome. McDonald told him that Cardinal Spellman intended to explain to the Vatican that it was necessary to display flexibility on the Jerusalem issue, and said that his own impression was that "the Vatican is not too confident of the success of its stand at the UN."[64] In mid-October, Herzog echoed Israel's confidence when he wrote that "if the Vatican recognizes that it has lost out [on the internationalization issue], the primary question is how to extricate its prestige from a parlous situation."[65] Sharett was less emphatic, but he too guessed, prior to the UN deliberations, that "the Vatican's stand has been greatly weakened and was not fully expressed as could be learned from the stand of the American states and France."[66] In any event, even if these assessments are taken into account, it was obviously necessary to examine the situation at close quarters. This, however, was not done until very shortly before the UN General Assembly's opening session.

The complacent mood can only partly explain the failure to act in time. Another reason was Sharett's reluctance to take action at the highest levels, as Gideon Rafael, a senior Foreign Ministry official and a sharp critic of this "ostrich policy," reported in mid-June to Maurice Fischer, Israel's minister in France:

> Since the Assembly meeting in Paris . . . I have emphasized to Moshe [Sharett] again and again that we will soon face a complicated situation with the Vatican and suggested that we establish direct contact with them . . . but I haven't succeeded in persuading him that there is serious danger from there. . . . [Recently] I have raised the Vatican question again and said that, instead of dealing with all kinds of important and non-important people, it would be better to go straight for the lion's den and to clarify our stand and our relations with Rome. At this stage as well, Moshe hesitated since he was afraid that the lion might savage us."[67]

Whether the hesitation was psychologically based, as will be analyzed below, or stemmed from political considerations, the official line was reinforced by the mid-October meeting between Fischer and Cardinal Tisserant, which confirmed, at the highest level, the belief that opinions were divided within the Vatican as regards the wisdom of supporting internationalization.[68] And yet, since Herzog was pleading for permission to reestablish contact with Vatican representatives, Sharett, albeit with considerable lack of enthusiasm, eventually approved his efforts to set up a meeting with them in Rome.[69]

In early November, Herzog arrived in the Italian capital, and over the next two weeks he succeeded in making contact with the president of the Azione Cattolica, the advocate Vittorino Veronese, who was friendly with Monsignor Giovanni Benelli, then private secretary to Giovanni Battista Montini, substitute of secretariat of state. Although Veronese did not disclose what the papal stand would be at the Assembly, he managed to convey the impression that the Vatican was not planning a political onslaught. As Sharett phrased it, "It seems to him that the Assembly will not pass a resolution, and then they can consider whether to enter into official negotiations [with Israel] or not. For the time being, they are highly appreciative of Israel's attitude toward the Catholic Church and Catholic interests within Israel, including Jerusalem."[70] In a later meeting at the U.S. State Department, Herzog told American officials that, during his talks in Rome, papal representatives had expressed appreciation for Sharett's "successful" efforts to suppress local communist influence in Nazareth.[71] The fact that Herzog had no concept of what was to occur shortly afterwards is revealed by his reference during his meeting in Washington to the possibility that the Vatican might recognize Israel, which Veronese totally dismissed.[72] Herzog apparently concluded that the Assembly would reject the draft resolution on Jerusalem and that it would then be possible to arrive at a "friendly arrangement" between Israel and the Vatican.[73] There was apparently no further contact in Rome with papal representatives until the end of the first week in December.[74]

The Strategic Surprise

In the interim, the Israeli conception had collapsed: on December 9 the United Nations ratified the November 1947 recommendation to internationalize Jerusalem. There is no way of telling to what degree the information that reached Jerusalem before early December was deliberate misinformation, intended to lull Israel's policymakers—as was generally believed later in Israel. Still it is clear that papal pressure played a major role in recruiting a majority vote for the resolution—something that the Israeli government had considered totally impossible. In a pitiable effort to dissuade the pope from supporting internationalization, Israel dispatched an emotional missive to the Holy See, which, with Sharett's approval, even included an unprecedented implied threat. This letter reflected Israel's astonishment and confusion. "The internationalization resolution will never be implemented because the population will frustrate it. On the other hand, the resolution releases us from all our commitments. . . . If they [the Catholic Church] are concerned for the basic issue and are seeking a concrete outcome and not mere demonstrative action, they must prevent the adoption of the resolution, otherwise they will be responsible for the UN's failure and will forfeit their existing gains and possible achievements in the future."[75] This message was a voice crying in the wilderness. The Vatican did not even acknowledge receipt.

These developments on the UN stage stunned the Israeli leadership for two reasons. First, they came as a total surprise to the Foreign Ministry, which had anticipated that the Assembly's deliberations would end in stalemate. Sharett explained (with a certain degree of justification) that the unexpected outcome resulted from a rare combination of circumstances in the international body, but his formal resignation (which was rejected by the prime minister) bore witness to his overwhelming sense of failure.[76] His feeling was reinforced when the Israeli government decided, against his advice and in reaction to the UN decision, to transfer its seat to Jerusalem and thereby to issue a clear challenge to the international community. Second, the vote at the Assembly was perceived as dramatic proof of two political assumptions, which were to haunt the devisers of Israel's foreign policy for years to come. One was that the UN was not reconciled to Israel's gains during the 1948 war and that the political struggle to guarantee them within the framework of the international body could be, in contrast to previous expectations, bitter and dangerous. The second was that the Vatican had placed itself at the head of the revisionist section of the international anti-Israel front that the Arab League was trying to organize, and that its ability to put an anti-Israel campaign into effective motion should not be underestimated.[77]

It should be emphasized once again in this context that, despite its long-term anti-Zionism, and despite its support for internationalization in late 1947, it was not until December 1949 that the Holy See effectively wielded its influence in order to promote an international anti-Israeli decision. The pope did not bring his weight to bear against the Zionist movement in the UN deliberations of November 1947 on statehood. According to Israeli assessments, he altered his strategy a year and a half later. "Everything that the Vatican could do in order to prevent our membership of the UN was done," Eban reported to Sharett. "All delegations were told not to vote for us, unless we provide guarantee of actual and complete internationalization [of Jerusalem]."[78] This effort, as we know, came to nothing.

Thus, the pope's active anti-Israeli role in the UN deliberations on Jerusalem provided Sharett and Ben-Gurion with their first direct experience of the political power of the Holy See. It caused both of them considerable anxiety, each in his own fashion. It also convinced them of the existence of a threefold threat, consisting of the United Nations, the international community, and the Catholic Church. Whereas, until December 1949, the Israeli authorities had been able to discount the significance of the Church's anti-Israel stand and view it as a marginal issue, they were now constantly preoccupied by the problem. The pope appeared to be the most dangerous challenge to Israeli control over West Jerusalem and, indirectly, to all of Israel's gains in the 1948 war. From now on, Israel's policy vis-à-vis the Catholic Church was, to a decisive degree, part and parcel of its political struggle to frustrate the attempts of the international community to impose international rule on Jerusalem, with all that this implied.

2

The Struggle for Jerusalem: The Papal Connection

Evaluating the Threat

The shock and deep forebodings evoked in Israel by the UN resolution on internationalization inevitably led to reappraisal of policy and to a search for political tactics centered on the Catholic Church. Some *post factum* reports tended to understate the impact and to attribute the Israeli defeat to a unique set of circumstances. It was in this spirit that Sharett described to the cabinet the situation shortly before the critical vote:

> On the eve of the decisive vote at the ad hoc committee, we calculated, and so did the Americans and so did the Arabs—and we all came to the same conclusion—that there were twenty votes in favor [of the internationalization proposal, which required a two-thirds majority] and nineteen or twenty against. The Arabs were gloomy. [Charles] Malik [the Lebanese delegate] rallied, sent a cable to the pope and said that it was rumored that the Vatican was not vitally concerned with the issue and would not care if the resolution was not passed. The pope responded in a cable and authorized Malik to convey the contents to all the delegations. This was what caused the downfall. From twenty-three votes, the number rose to thirty-five.[1]

This description notwithstanding, Sharett believed that there was a vital lesson to be learned from the circumstances exposed by the Assembly deliberations. And, indeed, subsequent discussions indicate that the Israeli authorities drew weighty political conclusions that were to guide their actions for years to come. They centered on the tactical moves that preceded the UN resolution and provided dramatic evidence of the power and technique of papal influence. As Eytan told the Knesset Foreign Affairs and Defense Committee on 12 December 1949:

> Three weeks ago one of our diplomatic representatives visited Rio de Janeiro for a meeting with the Brazilian foreign minister concerning Jerusalem. . . . At the end of the talk, the minister said . . . that Brazil would vote for the internationalization of Jerusalem, "because we must follow the instructions of

the Vatican." Our representative asked: "Why must Brazil, which exerts such tremendous influence in this part of the world and is the leader of these nations, follow Vatican instructions on an issue in which it is not involved?" The Brazilian foreign minister replied that they were indeed involved. Brazil is a vast country, but precisely because it is so large, everything is fragmentary and the only two factors that unite the country are the army and the church. Every government in Brazil, whatever its standing and political orientation, must reinforce these two factors. Brazil has asked the Vatican to appoint a third cardinal, in addition to the two incumbents, for the north of the country for purposes of internal cohesion, and they are now awaiting the Vatican's reply.

"Who would have thought," concluded the Israeli diplomat, that "because of a third cardinal, Brazil would vote for the internationalization of Jerusalem? There is nothing to be done against this: it's final."[2]

Ben-Gurion cast the net wider in his retrospective analysis of the three main causes of Israel's defeat. Russia and the Arab world were two of them. "The third force, which was possibly the crucial one this time," he said, was "the force of world Catholicism which, perhaps for very many years, has not displayed the power it now wields. They mobilized about thirty countries, and it is evident that it was only the Vatican that brought pressure to bear, because some countries altered their stand overnight. Mexico, for example, abstained on the first vote but changed its mind at the Assembly. . . . The [South] American states are developed countries but have no desire to quarrel with Catholic power on our behalf. . . . It is not easy to go against the United Nations, particularly when there are underlying religious sentiments, which will undoubtedly serve as weapons for the Vatican. They have a 2,000–year-old reckoning with the Jews." The bottom line, as Ben-Gurion saw it, was "that the Vatican does not want Israeli rule here. . . . There is a dogma which has existed for 1,800 years, and we gave it the coup de grace by establishing the State of Israel."[3] A week later, he told the cabinet bluntly that Israel "must understand that the Christian world will never become reconciled to the fact that the Holy Places are in Israeli hands."[4]

Sharett, for his part, was no less emphatic in analyzing the conflict between the Vatican and Israel, as revealed at the UN Assembly. The Vatican's actions, he thought, were defensive tactics with their own clear theological and personal logic. "The Christians are willing to tolerate Muslim rule over the Holy Sepulchre but not Jewish rule over the wretched Coenaculum. We must understand the pope's way of thinking: if he agrees to Jewish rule over the Holy Places, how will he hold his head up in the next world? There has been Muslim rule over the Holy Places for generations (but the present Pope had nothing to do with it). To agree to Jewish rule today is an entirely different matter."[5] Sharett also identified motives of historical vengeance and told the cabinet on his return from the Assembly meeting in December 1949 that "we can distance ourselves from the affair and base the course of events on familiar fundamental concepts. . . . If we adopt this method, then what occurred on 9 December 1949 was a matter of retribution, the squaring of an account concerning something that happened here in Jerusalem, if I am not mistaken, 1,916 years ago, when Jesus was crucified. In the final minutes [of the UN deliberations] I had this totally subjective feeling. I sensed that there was blood in the auditorium. I felt as if it had been stated that these Jews need to know once and for all what they did to us, and now there is an opportunity to let them feel it."[6]

Consequently, the UN resolution was a red warning light for Israel, indicating the gravity of the threat posed by the Vatican. The Israeli reaction can best be understood in wider perspective. Since the threat was external and political, there was a division of opinion on its centrality (as on other similar issues) between Israeli diplomats and the Foreign Ministry, who naturally tended to inflate its significance, and the prime minister. The key to understanding Ben-Gurion's approach, which undoubtedly influenced the official Israeli viewpoint, lies in his appraisal of the importance of this particular problem within the wide range of urgent problems facing Israel. Attention should be paid to this threat, but it was not of major importance, as he explained at a cabinet meeting on 20 January 1952:

> I am not afraid of the difficult situation at the United Nations, although I do not underestimate the importance of the events occurring there, but in the terrible situation in which we now find ourselves, we must look at the true danger, the true difficulty, and not seek imaginary or unimportant ones. . . . The difficulty does not stem from the Vatican, although the Vatican is hostile to us, not only because of Jerusalem, but because we have challenged the Catholic dogma that the Jews must be eternal wanderers because they spilt the blood of Jesus. This does not impress me, although I do not underrate the power of the Vatican. . . . The true difficulty is not this, and it must be perceived . . . the major difficulty is the twelve Arab countries. . . . For every Jew in this country, there are 44 Arabs, their territory is 575 times larger. . . . Those who direct Arab affairs think that this bloc will become a single empire. I also think so. They do not know when this will occur, but occur it will, and they have time to wait. They know a little history, they know that there was once a Christian kingdom in Palestine, it existed for two centuries, [and] they destroyed it. They have time. . . . They know that our community will never surrender [and so] . . . they know that they must annihilate it. . . . This is a terrible problem. . . . Those who now determine Arab policy will agree to make peace with us [only] if we go to Madagascar or some other place and leave the country to them.
>
> This is the problem and we cannot escape it, neither to the Vatican nor anywhere else. If this problem did not exist, the Vatican would constitute a grave problem, but as far as I am concerned, the Vatican problem is truly a children's game. . . . The Arab problem is today's main problem which calls not for action in the Vatican . . . but for wide-scale immigration and rapid development of the country. . . . When all this has been done we can take action against the Vatican's moves in America and Colombia. These matters will be determined by our actions here, they will also determine what happens to the Jews in the rest of the world. . . . This is the answer. We need to deal with foreign policy as well, but to see that as the crux of the matter is absurd.[7]

Weighing Options

Although Ben-Gurion's views had an unquestionable effect on the general trend of the discussions and decision making in Jerusalem, they could not override the understandable desire, in the wake of the UN resolution, to scrutinize the way in which the problem of the Catholic Church had been handled. Many cabinet ministers and certainly all of Israel's diplomatic representatives by no means considered the Vatican issue "a children's game." It was only natural to seek to attribute blame for the defeat, and it is also clear why the Foreign Ministry was convinced that it had been a serious mistake to assign the problem to the Ministry of Religious Affairs in May 1948. In a forthright report at the end of December 1949, Eytan wrote: "It is evident now that we did not devote sufficient thought to the problem of our relations with the Holy See and that we need to plan calculated action in this sphere. . . . We can no longer regard our relations with the Vatican as a marginal matter that can be left to the Ministry of Religious Affairs."[8] Although Sharett objected to this categorical statement and argued that "if we were not successful in this area in the past, we should not make the mistake of thinking that it was due to lack of attention on our part," he too thought it essential to rethink tactics.[9]

Israel had found itself in a new situation since the third week of December 1949, having decided to challenge the UN resolution and to transfer the seat of government to Jerusalem. The inevitable result was the creation of two interlinked spheres of hostility, the Catholic Church and the United Nations. As Eban told the cabinet in February 1950:

> In addition to the existing rift between us and the Arab states, which is the main reason for the non-regulation of our relations with the United States, there are two new points of conflict—our clashes with the UN and the Vatican. . . . Since concern for the survival of the UN and for Catholic influence are weighty factors in U.S. foreign policy, it is obvious that we cannot quarrel with the UN and the Vatican and, at the same time, retain long-term friendly relations with the U.S. government. The same is true, with certain qualifications . . . with regard to our relations with other entities such as Latin America, France, and England, if these disputes continue. It is unlikely that we can continue our quarrel with the rest of the world [at the UN] and still maintain regular relations with each country separately.[10]

The implications of a confrontation with the UN over Jerusalem were not to be regarded lightly, said Eban. "The drawback of the internationalization issue is not the danger that they may decide to implement the resolution but the danger that, because of the Jerusalem issue, a hostile international front will come into being."[11]

Herzog was more pessimistic and subsequently wrote to Reuven Shiloah, head of the Mossad (Central Institute for Intelligence and Security) that "the internationalization resolution, however abstract, provides a model, from the international point of view, which could, some day, if a suitable opportunity arises, serve as the basis for effective action to remove Jerusalem from our jurisdiction."[12] Ben-Gurion, for his part, was particularly alert to the regional strategic implications of a confrontation with the UN, and he explained to the cabinet in mid-April 1950 that "our dispute with the UN concerning Jerusalem is very grave. . . . For us, a dispute with the UN does not mean the same as it would for England or even South Africa. It could, under certain circumstances, provide the Arabs with the opportunity to seize on it and fight us."[13]

The undesirable implications of the conflict with the Catholic Church were also apparent to the Israeli leadership, as Sharett explained at length to the Knesset's Foreign Affairs and Defense Committee in early November 1950:

> The State of Israel cannot ignore this element, either in Israel or in the Middle East, since the Vatican is liable to play a part in instigating a quarrel. If the Vatican come to the conclusion that they erred in coming to a compromise with Israel in 1947, this means that they could enter into an alliance with Islam against Judaism. . . . There is a possibility of such an orientation and that would be very serious indeed. The Vatican is a worldwide force just as Judaism is. The Vatican is a global power just as Judaism is and the Vatican's decisions affect the entire world and we have felt this fact very strongly. We have received letters . . . from Jews in Ireland who are very anxious because of remarks by friends who said that we are, as it were, against the Vatican. They are living in a Catholic country and whatever the Vatican says is sacred, and how can we forget that? This is also true of Belgium, Holland, France, Canada, and the United States. The Catholic minority in the United States is five times as large as the Jewish minority.[14]

The Vatican's anti-Israeli stand was not confined to the Jerusalem question. The political platform it had presented in April 1949—linking the Jerusalem problem to the wider framework of solution of the Israel-Arab dispute in accordance with the UN recommendations of November 1947—remained unchanged. Four years later, McMahon made this abundantly clear to Herzog in particularly brusque terms, declaring that "the church is the focal point of the village. If it is robbed of its surroundings and its congregants, it loses all significance. . . . [Therefore] we will not permit you to remove the [internationalization] resolution from the general Palestinian context in order to cover it in dust and cobwebs. The range of Palestinian issues must be dealt with together." This frank demand for a certain mode of action was defined by Herzog, not without justification, as "evident compliance with the Arab standpoint."[15] Even on issues that appeared less critical, it soon became clear to the Israeli leaders that the conflict with the Vatican remained as intense as before. In January 1950, for example, the Foreign Ministry learned that papal representatives were carefully collecting information on damage to Holy Places all over Israel for reasons that could prove highly dangerous for Israel. "They do not attribute responsibility for these actions to the Israeli government or the IDF high command," Eytan explained to his counterpart in the Ministry of Defense. "They are referring to spontaneous manifestations of popular emotion which the Vatican considers to be even more serious than officially planned action. Therefore, the Vatican sees no possibility of agreeing to Israeli custody over the Holy Places."[16]

The attacks on Israel in this context, which had died down in mid-1949, were renewed at the end of that year. Moreover, in a secret talk between Sharett and "a senior personality from Vatican circles" in September 1950, the latter "dwelt on the connection between propaganda and the [political] demands of the Catholic Church and hinted that the propaganda would continue until the Church gained satisfaction."[17] The main concern of the foreign minister and the cabinet was the impact of the struggle on the future of Jerusalem. The pope's unwillingness to compromise on this question was manifest to Israel long after December 1949. In late 1953 McMahon compared the Vatican's feelings toward Israel's alternative plans for internationalizing Jerusalem to those of "a man looking into the window of his home to be told by intruders that he could have any compensation except the right of possession." This was why the papal representative "proclaimed with rising fury—'we shall fight!'"[18]

Herzog listened attentively to these militant statements and told himself that they stemmed from the depths of papal disappointment and frustration at the situation in Jerusalem since 1948.

> In 1947 Rome had succeeded in rescuing from the debris of the Protestant mandate the resurrection of the Latin Kingdom in Jerusalem, which was to be the inspiration and rallying point for the Catholic conquest of despairing humanity in the twentieth century. All was cut and dry on the rolls of the UN. Only the Jews had belied the most reliable intelligence assessments in their refusal to surrender to siege, bombardment, and starvation. [It was] *their* prophesy [which] . . . stood the test of time. The essence of his church's dogma in its relation to the Jews was being shattered before his eyes. . . . [Hence] if reality would not conform to his dreams, it would have to be destroyed.[19]

Yaacov Tsur, Israel's ambassador to Paris, for his part, read the report of McMahon's statement "with dread": "We have never before encountered such a chasm of hatred for the state of Israel," he wrote, "which is close to the most despicable kind of anti-Semitism."[20] Thus the various Israeli assessments were alike in their identification of the Vatican as the moving force behind the effort to persuade the UN to implement the internationalization resolution. Although it seemed almost impossible to translate the resolution into action, Jerusalem regarded the threat as "the weakest link in the wall of our policy, because most countries are highly sensitive to this problem."[21] It was also crystal clear to Israel from now on that the Jerusalem question was the central axis for Israel's relations not only with the Vatican but with the entire Christian world.

Defining a Political Strategy

Thus the political questions that called for urgent solutions seemed to be plain: What steps could Israel take in order to minimize the twofold conflict with the

UN and the Catholic Church? How could it confront both simultaneously? Which of them was the more dangerous, and to what extent was it worth adopting a policy of compromise toward the one in order to display intransigence toward the other? The solutions devised in late 1949 and early 1950 indicated which direction the Israel government had chosen.

As noted above, underlying Israeli policy was grounded on the conviction that the Catholic Church was the prime mover behind efforts to implement the 1949 resolution. Nonetheless, Israel chose systematically to focus its efforts on attempts to frustrate the scheme within the UN framework, by trying to persuade as many UN member-states as possible that "we cannot regard the Assembly resolution as [the world's] last word on Jerusalem."[22] At the same time, it seemed to have renounced significant attempts to minimize the conflict with the Vatican through direct negotiations. While this approach had its positive aspects, its negative side should be examined.

Recently opened documents in the Israel State Archive indicate beyond the shadow of a doubt that, from mid-1949 and for some time afterwards, the Israeli leadership was distinctly reluctant to adopt a political strategy based on direct negotiations with the pope. Axiomatic assumptions were the main cause of this reluctance: first, that Israel would never abandon its position, and second, that since there seemed very little prospect of persuading the other side because of the "blank wall in the Vatican"—any negotiations which ended in agreement would require Israeli concessions.[23] Sharett, briefing the senior staff of his ministry in the first week of 1950, said that "the question is not how to find paths to the Vatican but what to bring to the Vatican. The paths exist. The question is if there are conditions for an agreement. The Vatican has just won a tremendous victory, perhaps its greatest parliamentary victory ever. It believes that its negotiation power is very great."[24] In any event, as he told the cabinet several weeks later, describing the pope's stand: "He will never agree to permit the Holy City to be prey to the people which killed Jesus, and this is his stand to date."[25] Later, he told the same forum: "We have no prospect of influencing. . . . I am opposed to dispatching an emissary to the Vatican. . . . [The pope] will perceive it as surrender and will be adamant. . . . I do not object to contact with the Vatican, but only indirectly, so that it will not be possible to say that we are running after the Vatican."[26] One of the Foreign Ministry division heads called for even greater caution when he wrote: "In a period of 'sitting tight,' it is worth avoiding contact on other issues as well so as not to give the Vatican the impression that we are sneaking up on them."[27]

The negative operative implications of this "sneaking" were explained later by Herzog to an Israeli diplomat in London: "It is obvious to us that attempts to negotiate with the Vatican under prevailing circumstances are interpreted by them as an indication of Israeli weakness and nervousness. On the other hand, they serve as grist to the mill of Vatican pressure on various Catholic countries which have been vacillating on the Jerusalem question."[28] He wrote to the foreign minister that, in his opinion, the negotiations with the Vatican "will cause the Americans to propose a compromise between the different stands and [will create] tactical complications . . . in our relations with various Protestant organizations, with the Greeks, with the Jordanians, and even with the Russians and the English."[29]

Furthermore, the pope's intractable stand, as interpreted in Jerusalem, did not totally rule out the possibility of compromise outside the framework of bilateral negotiations with Israel. Sharett explained this point to the Foreign Affairs and Defense Committee in July 1950:

> They [the Catholic Church] won a resolution in their favor at the last Assembly. They will not forgo it of their own free will, neither will they compromise on their own initiative. [On the other hand] they remain claimants as far as the UN is concerned. If the UN changes the situation, then, morally speaking, [the church] will be free to come to a settlement with the existing authorities, but will not agree to be accomplices in such a move before the UN retreats from its stand. They will not take responsibility towards history and the Christian Church for having relinquished this prey. . . . If it depends on the UN, we will have to come to an arrangement with the UN and if that arrangement is dependent on the Vatican, we must persuade the UN to decide in our favor against the Vatican. . . . Since the Vatican is not prepared to arrive at any settlement before coming to a settlement with the UN, and since its campaign is being conducted at the UN, there is no point in our transferring it from the UN to the religious sphere, because we will then have to pay a heavier price, and it may be possible to come to an agreement with the UN at a more or less acceptable price.[30]

At the first gathering of Israeli ambassadors since independence, Sharett explained this conception more vividly. "The Vatican has no reason to discuss matters with us unless the Assembly changes its mind. If it does, the pope can explain to his Maker that he had no alternative."[31] Israeli representatives, who put out feelers in Rome at the time, confirmed this diagnosis of the pope's basic outlook and reaffirmed Israel's political line.[32] And finally, the policy was based to no small extent on a clear conception of the different significance of historical time for Israel and for the Vatican.: "Something has happened that is troubling them [the heads of the Catholic Church]," declared an Israeli diplomatic representative in Rome

> For the first time in the history of the Vatican, a new element has appeared which has proved that the conviction that "the Vatican can wait" is spurious. In the dispute with Israel the Vatican cannot wait. If it waits only one more generation and Israel remains firm, the Christian community in Israel will die a natural death, and then [the church] will no longer be able to speak in the name of and on behalf of that community. What then will be the stand [of the Catholic Church] in Israel? Will it be protecting Holy Places and stones alone?[33]

In addition to rational and logical reasons, there were other considerations underlying Israel's reluctance at that time to enter into a diplomatic dialogue with the Vatican. These were elaborated by the Israeli minister in Rome, Moshe Yishai, in 1952. In an outspoken letter to the Foreign Ministry, he recommended "no cooperation of any kind with the pope." Since this document provides insight into the opinions of a considerable number of Israeli diplomats and politicians at the time, it deserves to be quoted at length. Yishai's basic assumption, shared by many in the Israeli establishment, was that despite the changes which had taken place in the Vatican, it had not forsworn its historic ambition to be "the navel of the world both in the religious and the secular sense, with all the nations of the world as its 'loyal sons,' and kings and presidents coming to receive the pope's blessing and be anointed by him." It was not only the strategic objective that remained unchanged, he wrote. The same was true of the Vatican's fanaticism, dissimulation, and ever-readiness to act deceitfully in order to achieve its aims. To realize them, he was making use of

> fanatic Orders, which are engaged, on the one hand, in the inculcation of religious fanaticism, and on the other, in the education of whole generations of young people. These Orders are not generally prominent in the life of a state and a people, their work is done discreetly, almost clandestinely, but all of them are at the disposal of the Holy See and yield to the authority of the pope. Tremendous power is inherent in his exploitation of these Orders. They are dispersed all over the world . . . and are shrouded in total secrecy. . . . The Vatican exerts total authority over all bishops, everywhere, over the Catholic shepherds . . . and it can transform black into white and white into black—and none of the servants of religion are permitted to ponder whether this is right.

Above all, Yishai recommended that the Jewish factor not be forgotten since "all the evil committed against our people stemmed from the Vatican and its popes—throughout the centuries, from the very first and up to the second half of the present century—forced conversion, wearing badges on garments to distinguish them from the rest of the population, destruction and burning of the Talmud, payments and ransoms in order to save lives, looting of property and murder." He claimed that this historical hatred of Jews had not diminished but had found devastating expression during the Holocaust when the Church, "which has always preached supreme morality, tolerance, and love of mankind," stood aside. According to his analysis, Israel should avoid any political connection with the pope, even if it appeared to be vitally necessary.

> We must adopt a policy of "respect him but suspect him." Even if an agreement is signed, we must watch the Vatican very carefully, observe its movements . . . because we can never be sure of him . . . because the religious differences between us will always remain and will always [generate] . . . the desire to devour us and bring us under the wing of his "Divine Presence." And to this end—all's fair in his eyes. It is incumbent on us to be on constant guard and to frustrate his schemes, whether overt or hidden, whether relating to faith and religion or to politics. And when we reach an agreement, it will be even more difficult for us to be on our guard. We know today that the Vatican is against us on several issues vital to our interests. But then, when we have an agreement, his schemes will be those of a "friend," and in order to be on our guard, we will have to inscribe on our shield "Lord of the World—protect us from our friends, and we alone will protect ourselves from our enemies."[34]

This categorical refusal to "run after" the Vatican, which has been revealed for the first time in this and other newly opened documents in the Israel State Archive, reflects additional fears of Israel's foreign policymakers. For example, in a memorandum from early November 1952, Leo Kohn, an experienced and highly regarded Foreign Ministry official, opposed Israeli efforts to win official recognition to be followed by the establishment of a Vatican representation in Israel. In his opinion, such a move would "significantly strengthen the Christian Arabs in Israel. . . . They will have an ambassador of their own in Israel who will represent them with full Vatican authority and backing. Their loyalty to Israel—which is not great in any event—will certainly not be reinforced by this arrangement." He even cautioned against the negative influence a Vatican ambassador would wield on the more than correct relations Israel had established with the Greek Orthodox and Protestant communities within its borders. The ambassador's only contribution would be "to restrain the [anti-Israeli attacks of] his Franciscan monks."[35] Herzog, too, expressed strong reservations at the possibility and, in a memorandum to Eytan, wrote with British understatement: "Since there has been no public discussion whatsoever in Israel on the question of diplomatic relations with the Vatican, I cannot . . . relate to [it]. . . . Yet if the possibility is raised, internal religious and political questions will arise which will call for thorough investigation."[36]

Sharett does not appear to have shared these views, and the official Foreign Ministry policy was undoubtedly that "we are ready anywhere and anytime to exchange diplomatic representatives with the Vatican."[37] However, the documents quoted above and others challenge the prevalent assumption that it was the Vatican alone which was reluctant to enter into a political relationship with Israel. They support the claim that, to a considerable degree, particularly in the early 1950s, the reluctance was mutual.

These basic reservations notwithstanding, Israel never ceased its efforts to bring indirect influence to bear and to seek ways of easing the tension between the two sides. One of these ways involved steps to alleviate the hostility of the local churches. As Sharett wrote, "We must make sure that the Vatican offensive against us in connection to our everyday administrative conduct is as limited as possible, and if we can only manage this, it should be totally eradicated."[38] While taking positive steps toward the Christian communities in Israel, and in particular the Catholic Church, Israel also tried to convey a message to the Vatican, through the local church heads, namely, that blatantly anti-Israeli policy could prove harmful "not only to one of the parties."[39] Another tactic was aimed at exploiting the lack of accord among the various Christian churches—Israel enjoyed scant support from that direction[40]—and in certain circles within the Vatican itself, on matters vital to Israel. These two tactics were directed at the periphery and not at the heart of the Catholic front. The third tactic involved attempts to empty the internationalization resolution of its content and to divert discussions to the search for a solution of the Jerusalem problem. Israel wanted a solution that would not entail any strategic change in the situation prevailing after the 1948 war and the armistice agreement with Jordan and would also promote certain Christian interests. The achievement of this aim, by force of its nature and its built-in contradictions, required a large degree of political Machiavellism and skill at maneuvering.

Implementing Containment

Israeli policy at the UN was based on several tactics. The first approach was reflected in a series of decisions to avoid Israeli political initiative with regard to Jerusalem. Israel's dilemma reminded some Israeli diplomats of an occasion in the recent past when positive initiative rather than passivity and caution had produced positive results. As Shlomo Ginosar, Israeli minister in Rome, wrote: "Essentially, we were faced with the same fundamental problem in 1947, when several leaders of the Zionist Organization, headed by Dr. Silver, objected to any declaration on partition and insisted that we wait till final proposals were made to us 'and then we will see. . . . Meanwhile we will preserve our freedom of action.' We did not take this path: we made painful concessions and with all our might and that of our friends, we supported the compromise called partition, and it was only thanks to this that we succeeded."[41] This, however, was not the view of most Israeli diplomats and the majority of the cabinet, and the arguments against any new initiative were weighty. First, there was almost no prospect that the UN would accept an alternative Israeli scheme to replace the 1949 resolution. As Sharett phrased it, "It is a Herculean task to win a resolution controverting a previous resolution. The Arabs and the Vatican will certainly object to our proposal, and under such conditions it will be easy for numerous voters to abstain, and then our prospects of winning a two-thirds majority will be almost nonexistent."[42]

Second, since Israel had categorically rejected full territorial internationalization, any alternative proposal would necessarily have to offer positive ideas in order to appear credible. In this respect, the only possibility open to Israel from mid-1949 on was to declare itself ready to discuss functional internationalization of the Christian Holy Places in Jerusalem (all but two of which were in Jordanian territory), and this also in order to satisfy the church. Diverse operative schemes were considered. These included the appointment of a UN representative responsible for protecting the rights of Christian communities and institutions in Israel; international supervision of the Holy Places in Jerusalem; internationalization of the Christian and Jewish quarters of the Old City and the Coenaculum on Mount Zion, and extraterritorialization of the Holy Places, namely, to expropriate them from the jurisdiction of various countries and place them under international rule.[43] What all these proposals had in common was a certain degree of Israeli abdication of sovereignty. This was perceived by policymakers in Jerusalem as a grave threat to Israel's gains in the 1948 war, since it opened up the possibility of further political demands that might prove uncheckable. It would also be difficult to prevent the church from expanding its demands if Israel showed itself ready to accept these schemes. Thus when the possibility of doing just that was debated in early 1950, the Foreign Ministry discovered how great were the obstacles it faced. If supervision of the rights of religious in Israel was entrusted to the UN, it was thought in Israel, the UN representative would become "the permanent patron of the minorities in Israel, and since he will belong to a foreign country, that country will eventually gain a traditional standing."[44]

The primary assumption underlying the functional territorial proposals was that the Coenaculum on Mount Zion was the only holy site under Israeli jurisdiction. It soon became evident to Ministry of Religious Affairs experts that there was no guarantee that the churches would not try to prove that certain sites in Ein Kerem village near Jerusalem or on Mount Carmel were at least as holy, if not more. One of the surprising revelations in the State Archives documents now opened to the public is the manifest willingness in that period to contemplate the possibility of granting extraterritorial status to the Annunciation basilica in Nazareth as part of the alternative proposal. In this case as well, the future seemed to enfold significant dangers. Sharett soon realized that there were no less than three sites of that name– Latin, Greek Catholic, and Greek Orthodox. An Israeli declaration of willingness to compromise could therefore be interpreted as applying to all of them.[45]

Internationalization of the Holy Places in Jerusalem and of the Wailing Wall (to which Jewish access was actually barred despite the armistice agreement with Jordan) was more compatible with Israeli interests but was no less problematic. This was because the publicly proclaimed Israeli readiness to accept such a settlement would have been a serious contravention of Israel's understanding with Jordan within the framework of the armistice agreements. This, in its turn, would diminish the ability to maintain an effective and united Israel-Jordan front against the principle of full internationalization, and endanger the prospect of a peace treaty between them, which was a central goal of Israel at the time. Ben-Gurion was deeply affected by these considerations. When Israel decided to disregard the December 1949 UN resolution, the prime minister told his close associates that "God did well for us when he gave us Abdullah on the other side of the wall."[46] He explained to the cabinet in April 1950 that "our dispute with Abdullah is no less important than our dispute with the UN. The UN will not declare war on us on this issue and the Arabs might do so."[47] Moreover, the prime minister was one of the most radical among those who perceived the Vatican as an existential foe and not just as a temporary rival for Jerusalem. "The Vatican says to itself: on the Jerusalem issue I can wait, because this is an eternal question," he told the cabinet in January 1952. "The pope thinks in terms of millennia, but I don't know if he wants to wait and wants to allow the State of Israel to grow strong."[48]

Consequently, it was Ben-Gurion's categorical refusal to surrender any part of Israel's sovereignty within the framework of an alternative plan for Jerusalem that put a final end to the proposals discussed in early 1950 by the Foreign Ministry, some of which had been advocated by Sharett. This left only one active line of political defense open to Israel—a vaguely worded declaration of readiness to discuss an agreement between the UN and Israel on the supervision of the Holy Places. Under this agreement, Israel would undertake "a certain commitment" toward the international organization. It should be noted that this formula represented an Israeli withdrawal from the principle of "functional internationalization," which had been the public line of defense against the scheme for regional internationalization until early 1950.[49] Sharett explained the "half-full glass" theory to the Foreign Affairs and Defense Committee in July 1950:

> What was the basic flaw in the line adopted by the recent Assembly? The fact that the program is unworkable. The place is governed, and there is a population living there, and it is they who will decide whether it is workable. . . . What could persuade the governments to abandon this resolution? [The answer is] a workable proposal. And there is indeed such a proposition, which we are proposing. . . . Some people will say: it may not be enough, but what is proposed is 100 percent workable, and it is better to receive half a loaf than none at all.[50]

It was undoubtedly in Israel's political interest to expunge the 1949 resolution from the UN agenda. As Sharett put it three years later, it would

> close this breach in our international front; satisfy the Christian world in acceptable fashion in a manner accordant with our sovereignty and security; permit us to assert that we have satisfied the Christian world, including the Protestant and the Orthodox churches; open the way to a settlement between us and the Vatican (on the assumption that the above-mentioned settlement will eventually not satisfy the Vatican), open a path to recognition of Jerusalem as our capital and transfer of diplomatic legations to Jerusalem; deprive the Arabs, who attack us at every Assembly meeting, of their weapons, and deprive the State Department of the possibility of threatening us and exerting all kinds of pressure on us. This will also be good for relations between Judaism and Christianity all over the world.[51]

According to the foreign minister, time was on Israel's side as long as the UN failed to implement its scheme, but was also working against it—"Meanwhile the world is becoming accustomed to the fact that the capital is not whole. . . . Meanwhile the legations are concentrated around the Kiryah [in Tel Aviv]. . . . They are building houses and branching out and the world is becoming accustomed to that as well."[52] But this equation was clearly one-sided, as he elaborated later. "To leave the Foreign Ministry and the legations outside Jerusalem can only be a temporary arrangement, while introduction of international supervision could sabotage our independence in the long term."[53]

Israel did not harbor false hopes as to its ability to amend the internationalization resolution by proposing an alternative scheme. Its true intent, as Sharett said at a cabinet meeting in January 1951, was undoubtedly to create the impression that it was ready to compromise, "The tactic we adopted was not to appear to be initiators on this question. We are making no suggestions. Our performance should be understood in this fashion. We say: you have rights to Jerusalem. There are holy sites in Jerusalem, which belong to the whole world. If you want to exercise those rights, do so in proper fashion, and if you do, we are ready to cooperate in order to implement the scheme."[54]

The Foreign Ministry naturally devoted considerable attention to this issue. But, as in other cases, there was basic disagreement between the Ministry and the prime minister. Ben-Gurion left his colleagues very few doubts as to the vital need to arrive at a settlement with the UN on Jerusalem and the policy, which should be adopted. "Any settlement of this kind will be unfavorable to us in one way or another. It would be best if there were no settlement. . . . The problem may be eliminated, and this will happen, beyond the shadow of a doubt, not through a regular and superfluous settlement, but with time, through our actions and through very gradual acceptance at the UN, in retrospect, first of all by the countries which have no interests and later, slowly and gradually, by the others as well."[55] When it came to planning Israeli strategy on this matter, Ben-Gurion's view prevailed. Behind the vague phraseology and shrewd political evasions employed by Israeli diplomats lay the real political hope that the UN and its member-states would eventually become reconciled to the existing situation—to the deadlock, the stalemate, the non-implementation of its recommendations on internationalization.[56] In such a situation, it would be possible, Sharett thought, to close the political circle and attempt to arrive at a settlement with the Vatican. "If time passes without resolution, and other problems are solved in this period and the situation improves slightly . . . we will come forward and say that, after all, we owe a debt to the Christian world and we are ready to pay it off. When the debtor comes and says that he is willing to pay the debt, he can always achieve a more advantageous settlement."[57]

Be that as it may, for the immediate future, the development of Jerusalem and transfer of official institutions to the city were given clear priority over the waging of disputes in the UN arena. The foreign minister himself pointed out in late January 1951 to the Foreign Affairs and Defense Committee of the Knesset that "the center of gravity of this question . . . has now been shifted from the political to the practical sphere."[58] Eight months later, Herzog (who had just joined the Foreign Ministry as "special adviser on Jerusalem affairs") summed up Israeli policy by saying that it was based on fundamental awareness of the need "for the new city of Jerusalem to be detached . . . from the whole internationalization game and its tactical ramifications."[59] This conception was given practical and public expression a year later when Israel decided to transfer the Foreign Ministry to the capital. The feebleness of international reaction was seen as a highly significant affirmation of the effectiveness of Israel's strategy.[60]

Obstructing Internationalization

Israel's political strategy regarding Jerusalem, which became very clear as time passed, was essentially obstructive rather than initiatory—"a defensive and delaying fight."[61] Its central motif was avoidance of any statement or action that

was liable to draw the world's attention to the problem or to the various proposals for solution voiced at the UN from time to time. These efforts at
pacification were directed both inward and outward. Herzog reported to Israeli diplomats in November 1951 that "all sections of the Hebrew press are
faithfully fulfilling the Foreign Office's request to avoid dwelling on the Jerusalem problem or affairs relating to the Christian communities."[62] Politically
speaking, more effort was invested in forestalling undesirable developments
than in laying the foundations for desirable ones.

Several examples will suffice to illustrate this point. In early January 1951
the Jordanian government decided to appoint a commissioner for the Holy
Places in Jerusalem. The motive behind this move, which had first been contemplated by the Israeli Foreign Ministry, was apparently to demonstrate Jordanian resolve not to concede its status in the Holy City, on the one hand, and
readiness to protect Christian interests in the city, on the other.[63] Israel was
gratified at the Jordanian move as a result of which "the Vatican and its French,
Italian, and Spanish satellites may forfeit the opportunity to wield influence on
an issue which is the main pretext for their struggle for internationalization of
the city."[64] However, after internal debates, it decided not to follow in Jordan's
footsteps. Israel's calculations reflect the complexity of the problems the new
state faced and explain the choice of the obstructive approach. The appointment of an Israeli commissioner, it was argued in Jerusalem, would inevitably
lead to an official decision as to which Holy Places were under Israeli jurisdiction. By widening the interpretation of the term *Holy Places* it would create
a dangerous precedent; if it narrowed it, it would provide its enemies with
weapons. Moreover, the appointment of an Israeli commissioner could rouse
the church to make various demands. If the commissioner acceded to them, he
would win over Israel's opponents. They would, on the other hand, criticize
him severely if, instead of protecting the Holy Places, he engaged, as Herzog
wrote, in protecting Israel from the Holy Places.

> Even if there is some justification for the view that to establish facts could
> weaken Catholic opposition (rather than arousing it)—facts have already been
> established by Jordan, which rules most of the Holy Places. Fortunately others
> have done our work! If we wait quietly, either the Vatican will be forced to
> vent its wrath on Jordan alone or else it will become reconciled to the situa-
> tion and then—after a long time has lapsed—we can appoint a commissioner
> on our side as well, on the basis of the Jordanian arrangement, which will mean-
> while have won de facto recognition.[65]

It was also feared that the appointment of a Jew to supervise Holy Places
might, in itself, rouse strongly negative reactions in the Christian world, which
was accustomed "to the idea that Muslims rule the Christian Holy Places."[66] In
addition, such an appointment was liable to reinforce the conviction that some
of the Holy Places in Israel had been neglected and thereby rebut the claim of
the Foreign Ministry that they were being well cared for.[67] And finally, the problematic nature of Israeli policy vis-à-vis the churches in Israel rendered the idea

of a commissioner dangerous. As Gershon Avner, a senior Foreign Ministry official wrote, A commissioner "will not be able to overcome the difficulties, mostly of a security nature, which rule out the granting of practical concessions to Christians in Israel. . . . He will not be able to act on this matter, and as for the three or four Holy Places in Israel, there is no real problem there."[68]

Therefore, Israel confined itself to a "wait and see" policy, while considerably gratified by the Jordanian decision. This approach also explains Israel's emphatic objections to any explicit and public attempt to draw a connection between the political struggle against Jordan's refusal to permit Jewish access to the Wailing Wall and an overall international settlement on the Holy Places. Rabbi Yehuda Leib Maimon-Fishman, a former member of the cabinet, had proposed this tactic to the foreign minister in early August 1953. The rabbi was informed that

> the practical possibility of arriving at a solution to the problem . . . is highly doubtful because of Jordanian recalcitrance. As for our own attitude, in order to belie the claims of the Christian nations and to deflect their anger to the neighboring Arab countries, we are constantly proclaiming our consent to international supervision. The question is whether we are sincerely interested in such supervision, which would mean intervention in our internal affairs, even if in return we gain access to the Wailing Wall. How much more doubtful must we be as to whether, in order to gain such access, it is worth surrendering part of Mount Zion and, in general, agreeing to the establishment of an international enclave in the heart of Jerusalem which will serve as the base for the Catholic Church's craving for control.[69]

At least one of Israel's leading policymakers on the Jerusalem question was of the opinion that the Vatican was interested in the continuation of the Israel-Arab conflict. He wrote that the peace process between Israel and the Arab countries would "spell the end of the Vatican's last faint hopes concerning Jerusalem. Once the region is united and enjoying internal peace, it will move toward self-definition while rejecting foreign intervention in its internal affairs."[70] Whether this was an accurate picture or not, it is indisputable that one of the Vatican's major arguments in favor of internationalization after the signing of the armistice agreements was the possibility that the Arab-Israel hostilities might flare up again, particularly in Jerusalem, and that such a situation would physically endanger the Christian Holy Places. Israel was obliged to tackle this problem in practice for the first time after the assassination of King Abdullah in the Old City in 1951. This event seriously undermined the primary contention of Israeli and Jordanian propaganda, namely, that the existing regime in Jerusalem guaranteed peace and quiet and enabled the population to fulfill their obligations with regard to the universal nature of the city. The danger was that the assassination or any subsequent military tension in Jerusalem would serve to fuel the Vatican's anxieties as to the safety of the Holy Places "in a city divided by a 38th parallel" like that which divides North and South Korea and the implementation of the internationalization resolution. "The bullets which ripped into Abdullah's body," wrote Herzog, "promoted the Vatican's objectives, whether deliberately or not."[71] In this case as well, Israeli policy was essentially obstructive. In 1951, Israeli propaganda emphasized the stability and quiet in the city before and after the assassination and stressed that arrangements for passage of pilgrims between the two sectors of the city had been unaffected throughout that period.[72]

Two years later, after several incidents in which Jordanian troops opened fire at the Jewish sector, the Israeli security authorities in the capital were enjoined not to respond to provocation from across the Jordanian border, so as to avoid playing into the hands of the Vatican. The Jordanian government, for its part, was warned that if it did not take forceful steps to prevent recurrence of shooting incidents, "the situation will deteriorate . . . and this will mean their demise as a government." A message of reassurance was also conveyed to the Jordanians to the effect that the transfer of the Foreign Ministry to Jerusalem did not mean that Israel consented to supervision of the Holy Places.[73]

Confronting Demilitarization Plans

Israel was confronted with even more complex problems in 1952–54 as a result of various proposals for partial solutions, which Israeli intelligence believed to be indirect and tactical Vatican initiatives, aimed at promoting Vatican interests without actually abandoning the principle of full internationalization of Jerusalem.[74] The most striking of the new ideas was the transformation of Jerusalem into a demilitarized zone. The story began in summer 1952, apparently not by accident, shortly after the Israeli decision to transfer the Foreign Ministry to the capital. Rumors were rife in diplomatic circles in Rome that the Vatican was preparing a plan, to be based on the declaration of Jerusalem as a "ville ouverte"—in other words, as in the case of Paris in 1940, it would be forbidden to attack the city or to permit an armed force to enter—and on establishment of an international body to supervise the Holy Places. It also became known that the Papal State Secretariat had brought up the possibility of recognizing Israel in return for the latter's declaration of readiness to accept the plan. It should be noted that, although the Vatican never officially approved the plan, it was seriously discussed by the Italian Foreign Office at the time. It was believed in Jerusalem, as a consequence, that the proposal was a papal maneuver related to the situation prior to the seventh Assembly meeting. According to this appraisal, the Vatican feared that raising the Jerusalem issue at the Assembly would lead to the revoking of the internationalization resolution, which was why it was promoting a new trial scheme outside the UN. Israel was not required to take political action, since the idea never even reached the negotiation stage, but it did help to prepare the ground for similar schemes proposed in the coming two years, which posed problems for Israel.

According to Israeli assessments, the first such scheme was proposed in late August 1953 by Brazil in conjunction with the Vatican. It was based initially on demilitarization of the area within a radius of 25 kilometers around Jerusalem, and the establishment of small enclaves of Holy Places, which were earmarked for direct Vatican supervision.[75] The Brazilian representative who proposed the idea to the State Secretariat of the Holy See also suggested that the Christian nations convene, with the participation of Jordan and Israel, in order to sign a peace treaty. In principle, the papal emissaries responded positively. However, it was explained to the Brazilian that the Vatican was unwilling to forgo the principle of internationalization but would agree to provisional postponement of implementation on condition that demilitarization brought peace and guaranteed the safety of the Holy Places. At the beginning of October, the Brazilians conveyed a new version of the scheme to the Israeli minister in Rio de Janeiro, whereby demilitarization would be extended to a 50–kilometer radius, although no mention was made of the Holy Places. At the end of October, an updated plan was submitted to the minister, which contained the demilitarization principle and extraterritoriality of the Holy Places under Israeli jurisdiction and—an interesting innovation-specified that, in return, the Vatican would recognize the State of Israel.

It was estimated in Jerusalem that the Brazilian scheme was an authentic manifestation of that country's interest in solving the Jerusalem problem. At the same time, the Israeli Foreign Ministry was convinced that the Brazilian initiative had found a ready ear in the Vatican, which had decided to exploit it in order to sound out the interested parties, including, of course, Jordan. Underlying this belief was the awareness that the Brazilians would not have commenced a protracted clarification process without papal agreement. As far as Israel was concerned, the proposal contained a number of drawbacks, but also two positive elements—discarding of the principle of full internationalization, and, naturally, political recognition of Israel by the Vatican. A series of discussions in Jerusalem ended in a negative decision, mainly because of Israeli fears that the Vatican was mainly seeking a tactical advantage by gaining Israeli consent to demilitarization. It would exploit this consent when the time was ripe for its own purposes "possibly as a first step towards internationalization," while concomitantly "embroiling Israel in attempts to establish direct contact."[76]

McMahon's vehemently anti-Israel stand on Jerusalem and the Arab refugees, as voiced in his talks with Israeli policymakers not long after details of the Brazilian plan became known, enhanced Israeli fears that all this was a dangerous Vatican ruse.[77] Jerusalem calculated that Jordan too would reject the plan. The Israeli minister to the Brazilian capital, David Shaltiel, was asked to help bury the initiative and to convey a routine message to the local authorities to the effect that "the proposal has been given serious consideration, but more time is required to examine all its aspects." He was also instructed to transmit his own "personal proposal" to the Brazilian foreign minister that he should try to gain the signatures of Jordan, Israel, and "perhaps others as well" on a treaty that would guarantee the total immunity of the Holy Places in the event of riots or warfare. It was thought that the prospects for implementation of this proposal were nil "because it appears to us almost certain that the Vatican will not support such a treaty, since it would thereby forfeit its main propaganda card without gaining a real foothold in the city."[78] The Israeli diplomat reported two weeks later that "we have achieved our objective. We have not rejected the Brazilian proposal finally and absolutely and have provided them with the opportunity to continue their reconnoitering, which means that we gain time, although we see no prospect of their practical success."[79] This initiative ended, as Jerusalem had anticipated, with a whimper in the first quarter of 1954.

However, the demilitarization scheme was not shelved. In early May of the same year, it received renewed impetus, and this time the situation was much more dangerous for Israel. According to Israeli Intelligence, the initiative began with a Vatican request to France to take political steps to guarantee protection of the Holy Places in Jerusalem. It gathered momentum in late June and early July after shooting incidents between Jordanians and Israelis in the city, in the course of which some fifty shells fell into the Old City, two women were injured as they left the Church of the Holy Sepulchre, and the church on Mount Olives was damaged.[80] The French who traditionally displayed great concern for the Holy Places under their patronage, appealed to Israel and Jordan to withdraw their troops from the Notre-Dame church and from French Hill. In mid-July, they also proposed to Britain and the United States that the whole of Jerusalem be "neutralized or demilitarized" without undermining the principle of internationalization. The three powers agreed to establish a work group consisting of their consuls general in Jerusalem, the British military attaché in Amman, and the French military attaché in Israel. The group submitted its recommendation in early October to the effect that two demilitarized zones should be established in Jerusalem. The first was to be enclosed within two lines at a distance of one and a half kilometers on either side where the deployment of artillery and mortar would be prohibited, while the other zone, where most of the Holy Places would be located, would be subject to further prohibitions.

The plan was believed to be backed by the pope. It was made to appear to have been initiated by the UN secretary-general in order to lessen anticipated Jordanian and Israeli objections. Consequently, secrecy was an important component of the discussions. However, Israel learned of these developments from its intelligence sources before the recommendations were made public, and found ways of conveying its negative response to the French. In addition to vetoing this scheme, Israel attempted, between August 1954 and February 1955, to thwart this undesirable international action and to guarantee military calm in Jerusalem by arriving at a direct—not necessarily written—understanding on Jerusalem between Israeli and Jordanian military commanders under UN mediation. It was vital to involve the UN secretary-general in the scheme in order to impede the French initiative.

Israel's main objective was eventually achieved, even if the Israel-Jordan agreement never materialized. This Israeli initiative undoubtedly played an important part in foiling the Vatican scheme for demilitarizing Jerusalem. It is noteworthy that Israel and Jordan reached agreement in another area, which was of significant importance in the context of the efforts to foil the internationalization initiative. Since signing the armistice agreement with Jordan, Israel had been trying constantly to arrive at a settlement with that country which would ensure free passage across the Israel-Jordanian border for Christian pilgrims in the Christmas season. The main aim was to deflect the Vatican's accusations that Christian rights were being violated as a result of nonimplementation of the scheme. Jordan persisted in its refusal but eventually yielded and agreed to two-way passage at Christmas. In December 1952, Jordan agreed to grant access to Bethlehem on Christmas Eve to diplomatic representatives in Jordan and in Israel. Jerusalem regarded this as a significant achievement, a "nail in the coffin of internationalization."[81]

All this activity notwithstanding, it is obvious that it was not thanks to Israel's diplomatic efforts that the United Nations failed to translate its 1949 resolution into action. In hindsight, the UN failure in the 1950s and 1960s stemmed mainly from the practical Israeli and Jordanian objections, the operative difficulties inherent in imposing and operating an international apparatus, and the standpoint of several of the powers which played into the hands of the Israeli leadership. Several countries, however, remained consistent in their support for the pope's policy, so Israel exerted little or no influence on them. Foremost among them was Italy. Most of its ministers were Catholics who were sympathetic to the pope's perspective, and according to somewhat exaggerated Israeli assessments at that time, the cabinet's "very existence" depended to a large extent on Vatican goodwill.[82]

France's Catholic leadership could not express open reservations with regard to the internationalization scheme, for internal political reasons, but the French foreign minister assured Sharett in late December 1951 that his country would not take action on the Jerusalem question and would not join in any other initiative.[83] Sharett was justifiably skeptical with regard to this promise. When the Quai d'Orsay did, in fact, take action regarding internationalization, Israeli diplomats employed an important bargaining card, namely, the special status granted to French religious and educational institutions in Israel.[84]

Other countries, however, were more sympathetic toward Israel. For various reasons, Britain supported the status quo from the outset, and the Soviet Union followed suit shortly afterwards, even though it had voted for internationalization.[85] Nor was the internationalization proposal supported by four of the Latin American states, for various reasons.[86] And the United States, for reasons of its own, did not join in any significant effort to translate the UN resolution into action. What is more, from 1949 on, the Vatican was, in effect, reconciled to the stalemate, apparently realizing that neither it nor the UN was capable of achieving more than had already been achieved that year. What was more important for Israel, the Vatican tried to the best of its ability (and with considerable success) to forestall alternative resolutions which, however practical, constituted a retraction from the December 1949 resolution. Israel surmised that the Catholic Church "has adopted a policy of 'staying the course.' It tells itself . . . that conditions today are not conducive for implementation of that plan, but who can tell what will follow in due course as political circumstances change. The Vatican is in no hurry to forgo the advantage inherent in the internationalization scheme. . . . It can content itself meanwhile with foiling any alternative plan."[87]

The paradox, which the Foreign Ministry viewed very positively, was the papal insistence at the UN on a maximalist policy which, in effect, guaranteed stalemate and immobility, or as Herzog said, "This extremist approach is perpetuating the situation."[88] The Vatican could certainly never have regarded the Israeli qualified plan, on UN supervision over the Holy Places, as satisfactory. But the situation was undoubtedly advantageous to the Israeli Foreign Ministry "On the contrary," Sharett declared, "let them cling to the 1949 resolution, which will remain inscribed on the Tablets of the Law . . . with no possibility of implementation."[89] Herzog, for his part, cited a recent example of Zionist success to bear out this theory, when he explained to an Israeli diplomat in London that "in the end it will turn out that the Vatican's extremism was to our advantage like Bevin's [Britain's foreign minister in the late 1940s] obstinacy in his day."[90]

Propagating a Political Stand

All this could create the impression that Israel was diplomatically and politically inactive on Jerusalem. However, that was not the case. At the time, Israel's leaders were by no means as confident in their analysis of political reality as the historian can be in hindsight, knowing how the story ended. They were also worried about the alternative schemes, which were liable to prove harmful to Israel. Unsurprisingly, therefore, the newly accessible documents in the State Archives reveal that a number of additional activities were undertaken out of concern for the fate of Jerusalem and uncertainty as to the direction the United Nations would take. These activities included collecting reliable information on the standpoint of various countries, explaining the purposelessness of the 1949 scheme and other schemes, and publicizing Israeli efforts to guarantee the rights of the churches in Jerusalem as the sole feasible solution to the UN's predicament.

Efforts focused, naturally enough, on the Vatican and the other Christian denominations. As hundreds of files reveal, this was one of Israel's major diplomatic concerns in the first six years of statehood. As noted, political action centered on behind-the-scenes attempts to ensure that undesirable developments at the UN would not harm Israeli interests. For example, Israeli diplomats in Washington were informed by the Americans in September 1953 that the United States had approached the Vatican in secret in order to examine whether it would be ready to recant on the principle of full internationalization and the plan for supervision of the Holy Places. This information was leaked in order to forestall independent Israeli initiative, which might torpedo the American move. "We inquired about the details of the plan," Eban reported to the Foreign Ministry, "and we cautioned [the American diplomat] against adopting any plan without prior clarification with us. . . . [He promised] to inform us of the Vatican's reply before the United States committed itself."[91] The Vatican's categorical refusal, a month later, relegated this plan, like many others, to the dustbin of history. The archival documents provide numerous examples of this type of Israeli diplomacy, including efforts directed at British, Swedish, and Dutch schemes for solution of the Jerusalem problem.

Considerable energies were also invested in disseminating information. Whereas the political struggle to win a resolution on statehood at the UN in 1947 had been the first formative effort of the Israeli diplomatic propaganda machine, the intensive activity relating to the Jerusalem question in the 1950s was the second. Foreign Ministry documents on the propaganda campaign on Jerusalem in 1950–52 indicate that it was a unique scheme in the annals of the Ministry. A special division, established in April 1950, operated it continuously for several years. It was allocated considerable funds, recruited leading experts, and was active on the international scene. The objectives of its propaganda activities were to present Jewish Jerusalem to the world as a vital modern city, an inseparable part of the State of Israel; to emphasize the special age-old ties of the Jewish people to Jerusalem; to emphasize the situation in Jerusalem whereby most of the Holy Places were concentrated in the Old City, and to demonstrate the justice and practicality of Israel's proposals for solution.[92]

One of the most important instruments employed to this end was a publication, "Jerusalem, Living City," produced in three languages (English, French, and Spanish) which was disseminated in all the relevant countries. Tens of thousands of copies were dispatched to the political, scientific, economic, and cultural elites of those states. This was not the only publication of its kind. The Israel legation in London was responsible for a special printing and international distribution of some 10,000 copies of a book by the Reverend James Parkes, *The Jerusalem Affair*, in which he expressed full support for the Israeli stand on Jerusalem.[93] At least ten additional publications were distributed in the same way and in similar quantities. Six copies of a traveling exhibition were sent to New York, London, Buenos Aires, and Paris. The Ministry also financed and produced a regular publication in English and French entitled *Christian News from Israel* ostensibly produced by the Ministry of Religious Affairs. Its purpose was to counter Vatican attacks on issues considered to be directly connected to the Jerusalem problem.[94] It should be pointed out, however, that Israel was careful not to exploit this platform in order to engage in open polemics with the Vatican so as "not to provoke the other side to launch a vocal attack on us."[95] Here too, one can clearly identify the imprint of Herzog, who consistently recommended a circumspect political and propaganda strategy.[96]

Special diplomatic effort was devoted, however, to the Latin American bloc, and Israeli emissaries were dispatched for propaganda purposes to all the capitals of these countries.[97] As part of the "Jerusalem Campaign," several dozen prominent Catholic personalities were invited to visit Israel at the expense of the Israeli government to study the Israeli perspective firsthand. This activity was limited, for financial reasons, and hence the government was forced to turn down a number of requests to which its response was: "We are ready to receive you with open but empty arms."[98] Referring to this activity, Herzog boasted in mid-1953 that "it has never yet been the case that a Catholic who visits us . . . continues to support the internationalization proposal after he leaves."[99] Even if one could argue with this statement, the importance attributed to the campaign is unquestionable, as demonstrated by the official readiness to allocate considerable sums—in terms of that period of economic austerity—when many other vital activities of the Foreign Ministry had been suspended. As Sharett reported to the government in January 1952, "Our legations are living on deficits and charity."[100] The financial crisis and the lessening of the internationalization threat in the mid-1950s inevitably checked the momentum of this effort.[101]

Part of the general political struggle to nullify the plan for Jerusalem was a focused Israeli propaganda effort to break up the Christian pro-internationalization front. This front was composed of the Catholic bloc, several very influential Protestant blocs (including the World Council of Churches,[102] the Federal Council of Churches in the United States, and Anglican circles), and the Orthodox bloc. Although the Orthodox bloc's support for the Vatican stand wavered after the Soviet Union altered its views, the stand of the Orthodox Church in the Middle East and in Greece whose ties with the Arab countries obliged it to proceed with great caution remained unchanged. Protestant circles, some of whom were opposed to internationalization, were not unanimous in their views and bowed to no central authority. This fact played into the hands of the Israelis, who tried to stir up dissent among and between the various blocs. The endeavor necessitated taking intensive action and casting a very wide organizational and human net. This was because, beyond the main churches and the sixty-six active Protestant associations in the United States,[103] Israel was required to focus propaganda efforts on the Anglican and Scottish[104] churches, the Baptist, and Congregationalist churches in Britain, the Lutheran church in Scandinavia, and churches in Holland and Switzerland.[105]

However, in Israel of the early 1950s, there were not enough people familiar with the variations in dogma between the various Protestant churches who could have been sent abroad to work effectively among them. And, above all, the budgets were lacking. This was why, apart from sporadic activity within these groups outside Israel—conducted in the United States with the aid of Zionist organizations there,[106] and elsewhere through its diplomatic legations—Israel confined itself to fostering relations with non-Catholic churches in Israel. The objective was to win their practical assent to and official acceptance of the status quo in Jerusalem. It was plainly in the interest of these churches to prevent the promotion of Catholic interests. Moreover, they had local interests, which created obvious dependence on Israel. This explains a considerable part of Israel's achievements in this field.

A single example will serve to illustrate the pattern of this activity, which was successful to a certain degree. Immediately after the state was declared, Israel established a "highly positive relationship" with Jacobus, Coptic Orthodox archbishop for Jerusalem and the Near East. As a result of the negotiations

Foreign Minister Moshe Sharett (center) introducing an Orthodox priest to President Haim Weizmann at the Independence Day garden party at the presidential residence in Rehovot, May 13, 1951. *Courtesy of the National Photo Collection of the Israel Government Press Office, Prime Minister's Office. Photo D722–116. Photographer Hans Pinn.*

between the parties, the archbishop agreed to cooperate in the political fight against internationalization, and he appealed in a letter to Trygve Lie, the UN secretary-general. In return, the Coptic leader was awarded full compensation for damage to his private property in Haifa, an allocation of building material for the erection of a new church in Nazareth, and a permit to transfer $700 monthly to Coptic institutions in the Old City.[107] The Armenians agreed to adopt a neutral stand on Jerusalem under similar conditions, and even the Greek Orthodox Church benefited from similar deals.[108]

At the same time, pressure—not necessarily moderate—was exerted on the heads of the Catholic community in Israel to dissociate themselves from Catholic attacks on Israel. A report from Yaakov Herzog to Israeli legations abroad in mid-October 1950 left little to the imagination as regards the modes of action Israel had adopted in its negotiations with two of these leaders. "The problem was presented to Vergani and Hakim as liable to alter the government's intentions with regard to Christian refugees and its attitude toward internal developments in local Christian communities. They were also warned that there was a possibility that the government might withdraw its support for Vatican representatives as spokesmen for Christian affairs in Israel. We must take care to ensure that the atmosphere is not poisoned to the point where there is an open rift between Judaism and Catholicism, which, in the existing ideological situation in the world, could have a detrimental effect and not merely on one of the parties."[109] The Protestants were extremely apprehensive about the internationalization schemes, which, as they saw it, were liable to perpetuate Vatican rule over the Christian Holy Places. This sector, however, did not constitute particularly fertile ground for Israeli political action, whether because of the proliferation and heterogeneity of Protestant groups or because some of them supported alternative schemes to the 1949 internationalization plan, which proposed placing those areas of Jerusalem where they had a foothold under UN supervision. This support was a thorn in Israel's side.[110]

The propaganda messages which Israeli emissaries conveyed systematically and continuously in that period were that it was impossible to implement the UN resolution, and not only because of Israeli objections, and that the struggle to fill it with content would demean the international organization and could even undermine the interests of the Vatican itself. In contacts with Catholic representatives from Latin American countries after the UN resolution, Israel placed special emphasis on the risks to Vatican interests from internationalization of Jerusalem. As Herzog told the Argentinean chargé d'affaires in January 1950:

> Jerusalem is liable [in this case] to become the center of political intrigue under the guise of protection of the Holy Places. In this respect, the Russian stand is particularly dangerous, since it wants to create in Jerusalem a focus of political tension and unrest through continuation of the cold war. Russia now wants to appear as the defender of the Orthodox Church all over the world. Internationalization . . . will expand Russia's opportunities since . . . the Orthodox Church, which has vital interests in Jerusalem, lacks the backing of a strong power and could easily fall under the influence of the Russian Church. The internationalization of Jerusalem could inflate the ambition to supervise Catholic interests in such Catholic countries as France, Spain, and Italy and is liable to increase the competition between them, which would weaken the Catholic front."[111]

To conduct propaganda of this kind in those countries was no easy task as the following incident illustrates. Reporting in December 1950 on his visit to Paraguay, the Israeli minister in Chile wrote that the wife of the local foreign minister had told his wife "with great enthusiasm about the power and courage of the Holy Virgin of Caacupe [Virgencita de Caacup] . . . [and that all the] cabinet ministers were going to make a pilgrimage to Caacupe to plead with the Virgin so that there would be no more revolutions in the country. . . . In light of these remarks, there is a strange flavor to our efforts to explain the Jerusalem issue in South American countries such as Paraguay and to stress the political, economic, and cultural factors which controvert the idea of internationalization."[112] In Buenos Aires, wrote the same diplomat, "at the last minute a fierce debate was staged in the House of Representatives [under pressure from the Catholic Church] and [effective] pressure was brought to bear on the delegation at the UN after the Foreign Office took the decision [to support the Israeli stand]."[113]

Different arguments were employed against other countries, and the main assertion was that when the idea of internationalization had been broached in 1947, it was only one component of a two-pronged plan. The other component was an economic alliance between the Palestinian and the Jewish states, which was to dedicate part of its income to maintenance of an international Jerusalem. According to this argument, the minute the economic plan was shelved, the financial basis for internationalization disappeared, and the UN Assembly's revival of the idea in 1949 "was an irresponsible and frivolous act . . . based on castles in the air."[114] Another propaganda tactic emphasized the condition of the Jewish Holy Places, so as to make it clear that internationalization was not exclusively a Christian issue. The conclusion was that it was vital to ensure free access for Jews to the Holy Places within Jordanian territory, including the Wailing Wall, the Cave of the Patriarchs, Rachel's Tomb, and the Mount of Olives. Israel took care not to phrase this conclusion as a demand, in order to avoid evoking Jordanian hostility, but hinted at it and at the problems entailed, in order to undermine the arguments of the advocates of full internationalization or alternative schemes. A plainer message was conveyed to Arab diplomats, to the effect that if they raised the question of internationalization at the UN, Israel would act to divert the discussion to the question of internationalization of the Old City and international supervision of the Holy Places. In both cases "the clash will not necessarily be between Israel and the world but between the Arab states and the world."[115]

The Demise of Corpus Separatus

After investing six years of political efforts on Jerusalem, Israel's policymakers felt that they had achieved significant success. Despite the fact that the struggle for international recognition of the partition of Jerusalem continued until 1967, the Foreign Ministry manifestly considered itself victorious thirteen years previously. Israeli fears notwithstanding, the internationalization issue did not come up for direct discussion at the UN Assembly after 1950. A debate at the seventh meeting of the Assembly two years later on the proposal for direct negotiations between Israel and the Arab states demonstrated indirectly that the number of supporters of internationalization was on the decline. Foreign Ministry officials claimed that, at the time, both the Vatican and the Arabs were afraid of bringing the subject up for discussion because they were by no means confident of victory. Furthermore, in late 1954 two additional facts came to light that were viewed as a triumph, however temporary, for Israel. First, the United States and Great Britain decided to instruct their representatives to submit their letters of accreditation in Jerusalem and thus brought up to nine the number of states which had expressed de jure recognition of the situation created there six years earlier. Second, representatives of twenty-two states visited the Foreign Ministry offices in the capital to deal with various matters. Herzog's memorandum to the foreign minister in late November 1954, noting these facts, reads like a declaration of political triumph.[116]

His retrospective explanation, written a year later, which summed up the situation, was apparently accepted by most of his colleagues:

> It is a fact that, of the three problems affecting Israel's political standing—refugees, borders, Jerusalem—we have succeeded with regard to the last of them more than with the other two, in consolidating our standing. . . . Our approach [which has proved successful] was based on three types of action: a. improving relations with the Christian communities inside Israel and establishing a satisfactory framework for free access; b. discreet information activity conducted on the periphery of the Catholic world in order to reduce Vatican influence on the Jerusalem issue; c. lack of contact with the Vatican and efforts to quell the problem to the best of our ability. The fundamental difference between the Jerusalem problem and the other two is, of course, that the Arabs' main concerns are the refugee and border issues and there is identity of interests between us and Jordan on Jerusalem. Furthermore, the Vatican preferred to refrain from raising the issue and to place its trust in time, lest the UN resolution be damaged. Yet I am convinced that if we tried to arrive at a final solution of the Jerusalem problem by establishing contact with the Vatican or by other means, we would be undermining our status in the city and the process whereby the world is arriving at practical recognition of the fact that Jerusalem is Israel's capital would be delayed.[117]

Herzog did not mention several other international factors that were helpful to Israel in promoting its aims and that were responsible for the fact that by 1954 what had been perceived as one of the gravest threats to Israel in the United Nations arena, was lifted.

Whatever the reasons, in hindsight and on the basis of the archival material, one cannot help but accept Herzog's assessment as to the final outcome of protracted international pressure to impose internationalization, led by the Vatican. This pressure waned significantly in the second half of the 1950s and it was not by chance that the post of special adviser on Jerusalem affairs in the Foreign Ministry was abolished in late 1955. The achievement was unmistakable, particularly in light of the lukewarm international reaction to Israel's decision to declare Jerusalem the capital of Israel, followed by the transfer of the Foreign Ministry to Jerusalem in 1952. In this context, the fact that, despite its constant preoccupation with the Christian world in this period, Israel failed to develop specific political, propaganda and intelligence apparatuses to deal with Vatican and Christian affairs may be attributed partly to this feeling of triumph.

It significantly diminished the perception of threat and the incentive to invest organizational and financial resources in the issue. On the other hand, it is not surprising that, from the mid-1950s, the sense of relief wrought a temporary change in Israel's policy of deliberate abstention from any attempt to establish direct contact with the Vatican. It was no accident that in this period Israeli diplomacy took steps to normalize political ties. These attempts, which were to meet with scant success until 1967, will be discussed in the coming chapters.

3

At the Gates of the Vatican

"Noncontact with the Vatican"

It is indisputable that, from 1948 on, the Catholic Church refused to contemplate the establishment of formal political ties with the new state of Israel. This attitude was to change radically only decades later. Until the mid-1950s, Israel, which had strong reservations of its own on this issue for various reasons, was influenced by this uncompromising rejection and by the fierce political struggle that raged around Jerusalem. Sharett's fifteen-minute audience with the pope during his official visit to Italy in March 1952—at which the Israeli foreign minister was forced for the first time in his life to wear "a frock coat with a white tie and black waistcoat in the middle of the day"[1]—was no more than a gesture to protocol. He was greatly impressed by this unusual event and interpreted the pope's brief reference to the Christian communities in Israel as "acknowledgment of Israel as the ruler." But, in fact, the meeting was of no political significance. It was not the product of prior political contacts and had no follow-up.[2]

There were, however, certain natural mutual interests that required informal contact: the Jerusalem problem and the situation of the Christian minority in Israel. Such contacts were maintained in diverse ways: visits to Rome of Israeli delegations (in 1948, 1949, and 1950); indirect communication with leading Catholic figures and organizations in various countries; infrequent visits of senior Catholic churchmen to Israel (notably, McMahon's visits in 1948, 1949, 1951, and 1953); and contacts with Catholic clerics in Israel. It was important for Israel to ascertain the pope's motives and current policy, in particular regarding internationalization. The mutual avoidance of formal relations, particularly by the Israeli embassy in Rome, however, hindered efforts to achieve this aim. As the Israeli minister in Italy, Yishai, was advised in June 1951,

> We must realize that any approach to the Vatican on matters pertaining to Israel and other Jewish issues . . . could have widespread positive but also negative repercussions. We must do everything possible to avoid such meetings

except after very meticulous consultations and planning which take into account all possible results. . . . Generally speaking, we should not take the initiative and seek meetings . . . but we should not refuse to meet when the initiative comes from the other side . . . We should not create the impression that we are eager and willing for any opportunity for contact.[3]

The Israeli diplomat apparently had no need of this explanation and reported to his superiors that "I will not believe the Vatican even when they hint that they are ready to meet with us. They will do so when it suits their own objectives, and will be ready to do so in order to reassure us and to conceal action directed against us."[4] His replacement, Eliahu Sasson, did not agree with this qualified approach; when it seemed that he was liable to embark on diplomatic activity in order to test his own theories, the director-general ordered him "not to try to establish any contact with the Vatican." The official pretext was that "it would contravene custom for a minister accredited to the Italian government to establish relations with the Vatican,"[5] but the motive was, in fact, political—unwillingness to initiate a real dialogue. Consequently, until the mid-1950s, contacts with the Holy See in Rome, which were few and far between, took place solely on the initiative of the Vatican, almost always at the behest of the papal nuncio to the Italian government.[6] In 1950–51 an attempt was made to counteract the unreliability of intelligence appraisals by establishing a small unit at the legation, headed by Avraham Kidron, charged with the task of finding informal and clandestine avenues of contact with the Vatican. It was operative for only one year and—insofar as can be learned from recently opened Foreign Ministry files—was dissolved for unclear reasons. Within the Foreign Ministry itself, a single research division official was engaged, on a part-time basis, in collection and analysis of intelligence reports on this subject. Thus the policymakers in Jerusalem received only scraps of information from these units and from Israel's diplomatic missions. No wonder, therefore, that in April 1953 Herzog complained to Eytan about "our scant knowledge of the Vatican's thinking and actions . . . on Israel."[7]

However, those few significant items of information which reached the Ministry cast some light on the infrastructure of Vatican policymaking on Jerusalem. This information reinforced Israeli reluctance to initiate formal relations with the pope until the mid-1950s and inspired a different approach from then on. In the earlier period, the Ministry gained the impression that an internal struggle over Jerusalem policy was being waged between Acting Secretary of State Tardini and Tisserant.[8] It was thought in Jerusalem that the struggle was rooted in the character of these two men and the different positions they held in the Church hierarchy. Tisserant,

French-educated and a man of liberal tendencies, is concerned above all with the welfare of his communities in the East and their material and spiritual prosperity. His political approach is pragmatic, and since the internationalization scheme seems to have no future, he sees no point in involving overall Catholic interests in the Near East in a precarious political scheme which, by its very nature, is liable to introduce tension, whose outcome is unpredictable, into a region already fraught with political tension. The lack of discipline which characterizes Tisserant, because of his age and his personal contact with the previous Pope, could lead him, from time to time, to diverge from the general line. Tisserant also serves as a kind of prop for a certain degree of freedom of expression for senior churchmen in various places who are subject to the discipline of the church, but are well aware of the insubstantiality and impracticability of the international scheme.

As for Tardini, "his political views are influenced to no small degree by the ideological elements of Italian fascism, whose task it is to expand and consolidate the international Catholic political system. It is in this light that he regards internationalization and the tensions which have grown up around it a weighty political instrument in the Catholic world itself and in its relations with the outside world." According to Jerusalem's assessments, Tardini's views prevailed where Vatican policy on Jerusalem was concerned because they were supported by central Catholic figures (including Spellman, McMahon, and Griffin), and because the pope totally agreed with him. It was thought that, in the controversy on Jerusalem as in the debate on political ties with Israel, Tisserant was the champion and Tardini the categorical opponent "of official contacts with the State of Israel."[9] Israeli diplomats in Rome speculated in May 1951 that some of the officials of the State Secretariat, for tactical reasons, favored contact with Israel in order "to influence us with the aim of softening us and creating the impression in the world that we have relaxed our stand on Jerusalem."[10] If this was so, it was logically assumed in Jerusalem, it would be pointless and even dangerous to rely on positive information from Vatican circles as long as the political and personal circumstances in papal circles remained unchanged.

By early October 1955, however, several Israeli diplomats at least believed that, although the main actors at the Vatican had not been replaced, the time was ripe for Israeli initiative. The main advocates of this approach were Yosef Ariel, Israel minister in Brussels, Eliahu Sasson, ambassador in Rome, and Yaakov Tsur, ambassador in Paris, together with Eytan himself.[11] The three diplomats were particularly critical of the dominant policy at the Ministry. Tsur complained that "we have made no attempts at rapprochement with the Vatican in the past few years," and he went so far as to "reflect that our trouble was a Diaspora Jewish outlook."[12] The major argument for initiative was the waning of the internationalization threat at the UN. This was because "the present stalemate is not furthering our cause and will not be breached by the other side without some initiative on our part."[13]

The most fervent opponent of these arguments was, unsurprisingly, Herzog. "As one who recommended a policy of noncontact with the Vatican," he wrote in answer to the ambassador in Paris, "I permit myself to say, with due modesty, that it was not Diaspora Jewish cowardice which determined our stand but a sober view of the standpoint and the intrigues of the Vatican."[14] Herzog strongly recommended continuing the existing policy for two reasons. The first was its success:

> Since the 1949 resolution on internationalization was passed, we have chosen to act on the periphery of the Catholic world and not at its heart, and to plant information on the situation in Jerusalem. . . . This policy has already borne fruit and today it would be very difficult for the Vatican, if at all, to persuade the Catholic countries to insist on internationalization. During this period, France has changed its mind and various Catholic countries in Latin America have moderated their stand, twenty-two diplomatic representations (including the Italians) now visit the Foreign Ministry [in Jerusalem], the Guatemalan minister has moved to Jerusalem and will be followed by the Uruguayan minister. This means that time is on our side.

"Do you really think," he asked Tsur, "that we could have made such gains if we had been in contact with the Vatican without making any concessions whatsoever on Jerusalem?" Herzog believed that the answer would remain negative for the foreseeable future, and was unable even to conceive that the Vatican would abandon the internationalization principle without "gaining a foothold in the city one way or another, such as an enclave including Mount Zion." Any official contact between Israel and the Vatican, he asserted, would be exploited by the Holy See "in order to delay the process of international acceptance of Jerusalem as Israel's capital."[15]

The basic strategy that Herzog continued to recommend included, above and beyond lack of contact with the Vatican, attempts to improve relations with the Christian communities in Israel and "quiet" propaganda on the periphery of the Catholic world in order to counter the Vatican's influence there on the Jerusalem question.[16] Herzog had recently been appointed head of the U.S. Division at the Ministry for Foreign Affairs, and his views bore decisive weight so that no change in policy could be foreseen. All that remained for his critics was to put out feelers to check whether the pope was now willing to separate the Jerusalem question from the issue of political recognition of Israel. Sasson exploited his contacts at the Italian Foreign Ministry in order to receive an indirect briefing from the Italian representative at the Vatican. The Italian was surprised that "Israel has made no effort whatsoever . . . to approach the Vatican" and added that "in Vatican circles, as well, this conduct is regarded as an Israeli attempt to totally ignore the existence of the Vatican, its moral and political influence in the Catholic world, and its interests in the Holy Land." However, the bottom line was that the pope had not changed his mind.[17]

Tsur, for his part, reappraised optimistic information he received from Professor Alphonse Dupront, a renowned medieval historian, who was au fait with behind-the-scenes activity at the Vatican and had expressed his readiness to help promote political ties between the Vatican and Israel. A second, more detailed discussion with Dupront made it clear that the Vatican was not willing to establish relations with Israel without a prior settlement on Jerusalem, a fact which, in effect, put paid to the possibility of launching direct Israeli political initiative. However, Dupront suggested an alternative political plan, based on Israeli activity on the periphery of the papal center in Rome, which seemed to guarantee results in the foreseeable future. His main assertion was that influential circles in the Vatican were disposed to accept Israel's existence and to co-operate with the new state. This attitude stemmed mainly from practical considerations, especially from what was defined as "increasing apprehension" at the infiltration of communism into the Middle East, fear of the expansion of Islam, and the threat to Western influence in Asia and Africa after the Bandung conference and the establishment of the nonaligned bloc. Dupront told Tsur that these views were prevalent not only in circles closely associated with the Oriental Congregation but also among several heads of monastic orders, such as the Franciscans and the Jesuits, who had been unbending in their opposition to any attempt at rapprochement with Israel. Conversely, he claimed that since the Vatican's official stand was unlikely to change as long as the incumbent pope and the head of the State Secretariat remained in office, it would be to Israel's advantage to set up a network of friends in Catholic centers in France, Switzerland, and Germany and to establish direct contact with those cardinals who were likely to come to power after the demise of the pope.[18] There is no reference in Foreign Ministry documents to discussions of these ideas. However, Israel's indecision for over a year meant, in practice, that Tsur's suggestion had been rejected and Herzog's well-known prognosis had prevailed.[19]

Initiating a Diplomatic Move

The Sinai Campaign of 1956 and, even more so, the increasing signs of Arab rapprochement with the Soviet Union called for reappraisal of the situation. There were two direct reasons: indications of a change in papal policy and Israel's political predicament after the Sinai Campaign. When a Radio Vatican broadcast on 6 November 1956 failed to mention the internationalization of Jerusalem while acknowledging Israel's right to exist—and this at a time when it was being condemned by the UN and most of its member-nations—this was seen in Jerusalem as a new and highly significant development whose start had been discerned by Dupront a year previously.[20] The conviction that change was imminent was reinforced when the Spanish foreign minister, speaking at the UN General Assembly after the Sinai Campaign, failed to mention the "corpus separatus" and referred to the internationalization of the Holy Places as an acceptable alternative. Israel presumed that the Vatican was behind the speech, and hence it was perceived as a "drastic" withdrawal from the previous stance.[21]

At the time, in late 1956 and early 1957, Israel was the target of an unremitting political onslaught aimed at forcing it to retreat from Sinai.[22] The bitter struggle over the conditions for withdrawal, Israel's political isolation as a result of the total collapse of its strategic front with France and England, and the severe threats voiced by the United States—all these factors together generated the revolutionary idea of trying to expound Israel's point of view to the Vatican. This was to be done through direct meetings with senior papal officials, in the hope of persuading the Holy See to issue positive instructions to its representatives in various countries. It was anticipated in Jerusalem that the Soviet Union's public anti-Israel stance and its support for the radical Arab-Muslim camp would create important common denominators with the Church, which had been combating these same hostile forces for many years. Despite some previous internal dissent,[23] the Foreign Ministry began to contemplate the possibility of dispatching a senior representative on an exploratory mission to Rome in order to promote Israel's immediate political objectives and to attempt to breach the Vatican gates, politically speaking.[24]

The diplomat selected for this assignment was Maurice Fischer, at that time deputy director-general of the Ministry, who had served in the early years of statehood as minister in Paris and had succeeded Herzog as the official responsible for Christian churches when Herzog accepted a post in Washington. Unlike his predecessor, Fischer favored initiative aimed at promoting rapprochement with the Vatican. This approach, together with the personality and standing of the emissary, the preparations for the visit, and its duration, attested to what was essentially Israel's first official and significant attempt to establish formal political contact through independent action at the Vatican. Fischer arrived in Rome on 15 January 1957. His first meeting was with Cardinal Tisserant, who promised to raise the subject of Israel at his next audience with the pope. The Israeli emissary also exploited his friendship with French diplomats in order to make contact with the Vatican State Secretariat to set up a senior-level meeting. However, his request was turned down on the pretext that there was a risk of retaliatory action against Catholic institutions if word of the meeting leaked out. As an alternative, the French ambassador to the Vatican agreed to convey to Tardini a memorandum on the problem of Sharm a-Sheikh and the Gaza Strip, accompanied by Fischer's explanations. The acting head of the State Secretariat flatly refused to accept the memorandum but permitted the French diplomat to leave it on his desk.[25]

Although the official objective of the mission was not achieved, it had several by-products that at first appeared favorable to Israel. In order to breach the wall of Tardini's hostility, Fischer embarked on intensive efforts to make contact with senior churchmen and diplomats in Rome, according to a plan he had devised in Paris en route to Rome. Within ten days of his arrival he had met with more than a dozen of them, clarified Israel's situation and laid the foundations for future contacts. These achievements, however, could not obscure the fact that, formally speaking, the Israelis had been rebuffed. Fischer failed to set up a meeting with the Vatican State Secretariat, and the pope continued to adhere to his official stand. "The opening, which would enable us finally to breach the Vatican walls," was not found.[26] The concurrent (and uncoordinated) initiative of the president of the World Jewish Congress, Nahum Goldmann, also failed, although he succeeded in obtaining a brief courtesy audience with the pope.[27]

Understandably, perhaps, the bitterly disappointed Fischer tried to cloak his feelings by depicting the visit as an important milestone in some respects. First, he claimed, it had helped to formulate a new authoritative analysis of the change in the pope's approach to Israel. Crosschecking a relatively large number of sources made available to him before and during the visit enabled him to present a not entirely discouraging picture. Fischer noted that the pope's indecision with regard to recognition of the existence of a Jewish state, which had dominated Vatican thinking for the past seven years, had faded. Fischer believed that the central concept of Vatican foreign policy was "defense of the West" and that consequently "Israel must appear to be the main defensive force in the Middle East, thanks to which other Christian elements can be saved." Despite differences of opinion between the Vatican and Israel on important issues, Fischer gained the impression that the message he had received was essentially positive— Vatican support for the guaranteeing of Israel's existence. He also believed that progress could be made, however slow it might be as long as Tardini, "on whom everything depends," was the dominant figure. The operative conclusion, which echoed the Dupront plan, was that intensive efforts should be invested in developing ties with the outer circle of the Vatican and Catholic centers elsewhere. These efforts would be based on the foundations laid during the visit and on information that had not been previously available to Israel.

Fischer's impressions were obviously totally misguided. It is possible that he was overwhelmed by this first direct contact with the core of Catholic diplomacy. Officials in Jerusalem were much more skeptical. Fischer himself soon began to take a more sober view and admitted frankly to Herzog in August 1957 that he had been mistaken in assuming that the Vatican had changed its stand toward Israel and added that "the State Secretariat has concluded [in light of Middle Eastern developments] that the Arabs and the Muslims must be placated."[28]

Toward the end of 1957, the Foreign Ministry suffered a rude awakening when it received a report from Fischer on a meeting between the French ambassador at the Vatican, Roland de Margerie, and Tardini. The French diplomat, having coordinated his questions with Fischer, asked Tardini whether the Holy See had decided that the ultimate fate of Christian Lebanon was bound up with the fate of Israel and whether, as a consequence, a change in Vatican foreign policy could be expected. Tardini's emphatic reply was that Vatican policy toward Israel remained unchanged. "I have always been convinced," Tardini confided, "that there was no real need to establish that state . . . that its creation was a grave mistake on the part of the Western states and that its existence is a constant source of danger of war in the Middle East. Now that Israel exists, there is of course no possibility of destroying it, but every day we pay the price of this mistake."[29] What particularly troubled Tardini was not so much the past but the future. Israeli intelligence sources had learned that he considered war between Israel and the Arab world to be inevitable. Israel, he claimed, would initiate it by occupying the disintegrating state of Jordan. According to this scenario, the occupation would lead to an overall war of the Arab world against the Jewish state, but it would end in an Arab debacle, Israel would eventually rule all the Holy Places, and the UN would be unable to implement its scheme.[30]

Fischer's mission to Rome helped to elucidate the foreign policymaking processes of the Vatican and taught the Israelis that not only had the pope not intervened in these matters but that nobody, inside or outside the Vatican, could submit a proposal or memorandum to the pope that had not first been read and approved by the State Secretariat.[31] Hence Tardini's extreme hostility was an authoritative reflection of the Vatican's inflexible stand. Even Sasson, who had formerly criticized Herzog, was forced to admit his error and to concede that "a great deal of water will flow down the Tiber" before the pope alters his stand on Israel, so any discussion of this matter with foreign diplomats was not only "pointless" but was even liable to "further harden" the hearts of the Vatican staff.[32]

As time passed, the Israeli Foreign Ministry acknowledged the futility of its hopes that the strategic alliance between the Middle Eastern Muslim states and the Soviet Union might impel the Vatican to moderate its policy on Israel. It realized that the Catholic Church, in effect, was not only reconciled to the status quo but was even trying to strengthen its ties with the Arab world. Israel received resounding proof of this in 1958 when, despite the crisis in Lebanon and the danger that the regime would be toppled by the subversive activity of radical Arab nationalism, the pope's position on Israel did not falter. As Sasson mused in the middle of the same year,

> The Vatican believes that the Arab states are pro-Soviet as far as their independence and sovereignty is concerned and anticommunist in their private and individual lives. This explains, for example, why Abd-ul-Nasser is seeking rapprochement with the Kremlin but is strongly opposed to communism in his own republic. For these reasons, the Vatican believes that it will have a wide field of action in the Middle East and in the Asian and African continents if it can only adapt itself to the aspirations and new lives of these continents.[33]

Meeting the Pope

Jerusalem's sole hope, therefore, was that a reshuffle in the Vatican might lead to policy changes. The advanced age of the pope and the head of the State Secretariat rendered this hope realistic. The death of Pius XII in late October 1958 enabled Israeli diplomats to put their axiomatic assumptions to the test. The new pope, Angelo Giuseppe Roncalli, John XXIII, had been on good terms with Israeli representatives in Istanbul during World War II and, within the limits of Vatican policy, had assisted in the rescue of Jews.[34] He had also been on friendly terms with Maurice Fischer when they were both serving in Paris. No less significant, however, was the fact that the change of popes did not immediately result in changes in the State Secretariat. It was still headed by Tardini, now promoted from acting head to head. Moreover, his promotion to the rank of cardinal seemed likely to reinforce his standing, particularly in light of what was perceived as the pallid personality of the venerable Roncalli.[35] Although Jerusalem did not entertain high hopes in this respect, the ascension of a new pope did revive certain old expectations.[36]

At first it was feared that a public visit to Rome by a senior Israeli diplomat to sound out the situation might prove as abortive as Fischer's mission. The alternative, therefore, was to try to organize a private audience between John XXIII and his old acquaintance from Venice in the early 1950s, Israel's consul-general (honorary) in Milan, Astorre Mayer.[37] It was also hoped that Tisserant's aid could be recruited. Discreet negotiations of this kind, it was hoped in Jerusalem, would prepare the ground for change.[38] Discretion was an important element in the Foreign Ministry's plan, and Golda Meir, who in 1956 became Israel's minister for foreign affairs, asked Goldmann explicitly not to obstruct Israeli diplomatic efforts as he had in early 1957.[39] "Dear Golda," replied the president of the World Jewish Congress "you may be sure of it." Since the two had been closely acquainted for many years, it is unlikely that Golda was reassured by this message.[40]

The Israeli Foreign Service was also in need of reassurance. The ambassador in Rome described himself "as a man who has held a relatively responsible position for more than five years, observing with open eyes everything that goes on in the Vatican state which is only a few hundred meters from my office." This being so, he considered himself highly qualified to head a diplomatic mission to examine the possibility of establishing political ties with the new pope.[41] Sasson's resentment stemmed from protracted frustration caused by "the stringent ban imposed by the Ministry for years against any contact whatsoever with the Vatican and those closely associated with it," which had "hindered us from preparing the ground and from studying the true situation within the Vatican in depth and searching for suitable ways of acting when the need arises."[42] To Sasson's resentment, the task was again imposed on Fischer.

As anticipated, Tisserant cooperated and broached the question of Israel at his very first meeting with Rancalli. The cardinal, who told Fischer that his efforts to promote relations between Israel and the Vatican were "a special mission with which God had charged him," gained the impression that the pope's response was "encouraging" and that he was "ready to study the problem."[43] The cautious optimism of the Foreign Ministry was bolstered when the new pope replied to a cable of congratulation from Israeli president Yitshak Ben-Zvi.[44] Experts in Jerusalem who pored over the Latin text of the reply concluded that, although it had been sent "in accordance with protocol," it was not without political importance because of the historical precedent of dispatch of similar letters to "kings and heads of state of countries maintaining diplomatic ties with the Holy See." It was estimated that letters were not sent to countries with which the Vatican was unwilling to establish relations, so that even if it would be an exaggeration to equate it with "de facto official recognition," it symbolized "if not the offering of a hand, at least—as is the custom of priests—the offering of fingertips."[45] The fact that Sasson was invited to participate in the papal coronation in Rome certainly seemed to bear out these evaluations.[46]

Jerusalem decided, therefore, to take a risk and, before requesting an audience for Mayer with the pope, to dispatch Fischer to Rome in a second attempt within two years to overcome the Vatican's official hostility. Foreign Ministry optimism proved justified, at least in part. Immediately after Fischer's arrival

President Itzhak Ben-Zvi with the heads of the Greek Orthodox, Armenian, Coptic, Maronite, and Russian churches in Israel, September 1, 1958. *Courtesy of the National Photo Collection of the Israel Government Press Office, Prime Minister's Office. Photo D678–049. Photographer David Gurfinkel.*

in Rome on 4 February 1959, Tisserant set up an audience with the pope for him.[47] The archival material casts no light on the preparations for the meeting or the question of whether Fischer was given a "green light" while still in Israel. Yet it seems that the pope was motivated by political considerations that were sufficiently persuasive to overcome the objections of the State Secretariat. Five days later, the pope received Fischer in his official residence with great cordiality, reminisced about their "Paris days," and even asked if Fischer's wife still preferred Jeremiah to Isaiah. After handing over a gift from Israel's president, Fischer told the pope that he had come to meet him "with great emotion" because he regarded his election to the Holy See as "a sign of Divine Providence." Since the subsequent conversation led to a certain change of direction in Israel-Vatican relations, it is worth quoting Fischer's report to Meir in full:

> The Pope said that I knew him to be a man who supports anything which brings human beings closer together . . . and that he is opposed to anything which separates them. For example, he said that he was in favor of human beings accepting the Old Testament together with the New, and that he was against confrontation between the two, as if there was some conflict between them. I commented that it was the same desire to build a bridge and to unite which had brought me to him and the hope that there some progress would be made between the Vatican and the State of Israel. He replied that he hoped

that Catholics were not continuing to blame the Jewish people for the crucifixion of Jesus and that he assumed that I, in any event, had never heard any such accusation from Catholics. I agreed. He added that we, for our part, should show greater respect for the New Testament. He does not insist that we accept the New Testament, but he would like our attitude to be one of respect for the holy book of Christianity. I replied that in Israel there was a spirit of complete respect for other religions . . . and members of those religions. I told him that I had established a committee to promote understanding between the religions and gave him its manifesto. . . . He displayed interest in our activities.

I continued that I hoped that what was being done in the social sphere would have a continuation in the political area. Once again, the pope failed to pursue the subject to which I was trying to direct him and spoke about understanding between Christians and Jews. I repeated my remarks and explained plainly that the lack of official contact between the Vatican and Israel could not continue. It was unthinkable for me to leave after this conversation between us without at least the beginning of some progress. The Catholic Church and the Jewish people faced common enemies, namely, communism and atheism, and it was impossible for such natural allies to have no contact between them. The pope replied that he had great respect for me personally, that he loved my eyes, in which he could read sincerity and integrity, and that he was wholly in favor of promoting understanding. But I should understand that, despite being pope, he could not make decisions alone. Even St. Peter never made decisions without consulting the apostles. To this I replied that I understood only too well the need for consultations and that I wanted to put a concrete proposal to him, namely, that the Holy See appoint an apostolic vicar in Israel. He asked what this meant, and I explained that the role of the vicar would be to supervise Catholic affairs in Israel and to maintain contact with the Israel government. The pope asked if the apostolic representative was not sufficient. I replied that the apostolic representative was not accredited to our government. . . .

The pope reiterated that he could not make decisions on the spot. I must understand that it was necessary to study the various problems entailed and, among other issues, the problem of the Catholic Church's recognition of Israel. He did not mention the Jerusalem problem and summed up by saying: "You and I love one another. Why shouldn't we find a satisfactory solution? You may be sure that I will consider the problems you have presented with sympathy and respect." When I saw that the conversation was coming to an end, I asked again if the pope was of the opinion that I should see Cardinal Tardini, the head of the State Secretariat. His reply was positive, and I asked him to arrange the meeting for me. He promised to do so. . . . When we were about to part and when I again expressed the hope that our meeting would prove beneficial to Vatican relations with Israel, he said, "You would receive immediate satisfaction if I listened to my heart," to which I replied, "The heart is always right."

No less important than what was said at the talk was what was absent. The pope did not mention Jerusalem even once, and this fact was regarded as particularly significant by policymakers in Jerusalem.[48]

Despite the hourlong exchange of views and the very positive direction it took, Fischer was apparently taken by surprise when a meeting with Tardini was in fact scheduled. Fischer's good friend, the French ambassador to the Vatican, Roland de Margerie, "could not believe his ears" when Fischer asked him for a briefing prior to the meeting.[49] The hourlong conversation, at which Tardini displayed familiarity with the details of Fischer's career, opened with a series of complaints from the state secretary about Israel's negative attitude toward Christians in Israel and the Jerusalem problem, which, he claimed, should be solved through the establishment of a "corpus separatus." The crux of the message he conveyed was, however, positive. "We have decided," the cardinal informed Fischer, "to respond positively to your request and to appoint an apostolic vicar in Israel." He added that Israel's claim that the apostolic representative was in contact almost solely with Jordan was justified and that the new appointee "would also be in contact with your authorities." Yet he cautioned that "there will be a problem in finding a suitable bishop for this post, and it will be a delicate matter which will call for respect for the feelings of various people." He went on to clarify that "the apostolic vicar should not be regarded as the representative of the Holy See, and his appointment . . . does not mean the establishment of diplomatic relations." "Generally speaking," the cardinal stressed, apparently in order to quash any false hopes entertained by the Israeli diplomat, "diplomatic relations are maintained between countries which have commercial or other important mutual interests. Such interests do not exist between the Vatican and Israel and hence there is no need for diplomatic relations, particularly since the Catholic community is small." In conclusion, he expressed the hope that Israel would be content with "this great achievement," since "the Church is accustomed to moving slowly and here we have progressed with giant steps since the new pope took office." Fischer, who also hoped for the appointment of an Israeli representative to the Vatican, tried to extract an additional promise and asked about "common objectives . . . which call for consultations from time to time." Tardini refused to commit himself to such meetings, "since I am a very busy man," but promised to ensure that "there will always be someone responsible to talk to."[50]

Breaking No Ice

It was abundantly clear that Tardini had not changed his mind on the Jerusalem issue and particularly the question of ties with the State of Israel. During one of his talks with Cardinal Tisserant, Tardini declared without equivocation that "there is no possibility of contact or negotiations with the killers of God."[51] This was apparently why he obeyed the pope's instructions reluctantly and interpreted them in restricted fashion. In a conversation with de Margerie shortly after Fischer's return to Israel, the cardinal described the event as "a two-minute meeting between doors."[52] Fischer took a different view at the time and perceived it as a considerable achievement, implying that the Vatican had recognized Israel and had accepted the principle of political contact. Taking into account Tardini's reservations and refusal to accept the prospect of Israeli representation to the Vatican, and afraid of over-optimism, the Israeli ambassador to Paris, Yaakov Tsur, described the meeting as "breaking of the ice, but not a thaw as yet."[53] Because of the inaccessibility of Vatican documentation from that period, one can only surmise what moved the Holy See to permit this "breaking of the ice" in early 1959. Israeli appraisals naturally took into account the personality of the new pope, who had rescued Jews from the Nazis during World War II. They also referred to a range of political considerations as well as the Vatican's disappointment at the failure of its protracted attempts to approach the Muslim world (particularly after its "bitter efforts" in Lebanon) and its fear that the growth of Arab nationalism "had paved the way for the infiltration of communism."[54]

It should be pointed out, however, that some Foreign Ministry officials doubted that the mission had resulted in a meaningful volte face. Leo Kohn told the director-general that, to his mind "it would have been difficult to express the refusal to establish diplomatic relations with Israel more plainly or coldly." He also argued that the new arrangement was liable to promote Catholic rather than Israeli interests. "Until now the regular representative of the Catholic Church in Israel [Vergani] has been a priest with the rank of monsignor. . . . From now on the representative will be a bishop whose opinions will naturally carry greater weight both in his approaches to the Israeli government and in his reports to Rome. I do not presume that the new pope will send a bishop who is hostile toward us, although I have no assurance that the cardinal [Tardini] will not seek an 'objective' candidate. Nor can we be sure who will follow him. What advantage, therefore, will we gain from the new arrangement? The Church will have a serious position of power in Israel—which we ourselves demanded—and we will receive nothing in return where diplomatic relations are concerned."[55]

The lack of symmetry in this arrangement was too blatant to be ignored in Jerusalem. Moreover, Fischer's second visit to Rome in April 1959, to examine whether the Vatican intended to honor its commitments, ended in profound disillusionment, and he described it as "unfortunate." The meeting scheduled for him at the State Secretariat was cancelled shortly before it was due to take place. Fischer learned during the visit that the pope had been unable to conceal from the Arabs that his attitude toward Israel had altered somewhat. He had explained to them that this new stand did indeed represent de facto recognition of Israel, but emphatically rejected any suggestion that this development represented the beginning of diplomatic relations. The visit of a senior Israeli official to the State Secretariat might have been interpreted as diplomatic negotiations, which was why Fischer was turned down. He was obliged to make do with submitting memoranda to the State Secretariat on the Jerusalem problem and the Holy Places and on Israel's political, economic, and educational activity in Asia and Africa.[56] Only five months later, Fischer was received at the Vatican for a "cool" talk with Monsignor Antonio Samore, Tardini's deputy, and was asked, in undiplomatic terms, "to reduce the frequency" of his visits.

In the course of the visit, he submitted a letter to the pope and met with five additional Vatican dignitaries, including Tisserant, who resigned shortly afterwards, and Testa, who helped him to reappraise the situation.[57]

The assessment in Jerusalem in the wake of these events was that the Vatican's stand on Israel depended on the balance of power between two outlooks, the moral and emotional outlook of the pope, who favored rapprochement, and the political outlook, represented by Cardinal Tardini, who advocated greater circumspection in Israeli-Vatican relations to prevent the Arab countries from taking retaliatory action against Catholic elements in their midst.[58] As far as Israel was concerned, this was undoubtedly an improvement over the situation at the court of the previous pope, but hopes of some practical progress toward political recognition seemed unrealistic. This was true even though the Vatican had kept its second promise—to appoint a bishop in Israel. In mid-September, the Vatican radio announced the appointment of a bishop as general vicar in Israel of the patriarch, whose area of jurisdiction covered Israel and Cyprus and whose seat was in the Old City. The appointment of the patriarch was not rescinded, and his formal authority was untouched. However, the new appointment was carried out in accordance with the procedure for the appointment of a resident bishop. The new bishop, Pier Chiapperro, was to reside in Israel, and consequently a new diocese was to be established to bear the name of the bishop's city of residence. On arrival in Israel, the bishop chose Nazareth as his seat.[59]

While this was an important development, Israel refrained, at least outwardly, in coordination with the Vatican, from attributing political significance to the appointment. Israeli officials confined themselves to the appraisal that the appointment demonstrated the importance to the pope of the Church in Israel "and, as a consequence, his increased interest in the State."[60] These statements were not circumspect enough for Tardini, who, in a letter to Fischer, expressed his "deep regret" at the way in which the Israeli press had interpreted the appointment. "Such exaggerations are of no advantage to you or to us. Israel should learn from the Church and know how to wait: to wait does not mean to lose."[61] In mid-December, "Foreign Ministry circles" felt it necessary to announce that "there is no connection between the appointment by the pope of a patriarchal vicar with the rank of bishop and the problem of the political relations between the Vatican and Israel."[62]

Jerusalem was not content with this situation, particularly in light of what had been learned during Fischer's 1959 visit. It was not thought worth investing effort in paths of action that had been rejected in the past by the Foreign Ministry senior administration, such as initiating regular organized effort aimed at winning friends in the Vatican. This explains the new Israeli initiative that began to take shape in the middle of that year. The idea was to set up a disguised Israeli representation in Rome in the form of an "Institute for the Study of Jewish-Christian Relations," whose real assignment would be to collect precise and up-to-date information on the Catholic Church, to foster relations with key figures at the Vatican, and to supply current information on Jewish and Israeli affairs to clerics. The Foreign Ministry would place its services and guidance at the disposal of the Institute, and the Ministry of Religious Affairs agreed to lend Dr. Haim Vardi of its Christian Communities Department to stand at its head. In order to conceal the fact that Israel was behind this body, it was agreed that it would be officially presented as affiliated with the World Jewish Congress.[63]

Concomitantly, it was decided to step up contacts of Israeli diplomats with the heads of the Church in Rome. It was Fischer's opinion, accepted by the foreign minister and the prime minister, that the establishment of diplomatic relations with the Vatican was not feasible in the near future, although rapprochement was possible. In any event it was agreed that Israel would not raise the issue publicly at that time.[64] Armed with information from the Israeli embassy official in Rome who was responsible for intelligence on the Vatican, and with evaluations from Zwi Werblowsky, professor of religious studies at the Hebrew University, Fischer met again with Testa and with Cardinal Alfredo Ottaviani, secretary of the Holy Office—the tribunal of the Roman Catholic Church dealing with ecclesiastical discipline. The talk with Ottaviani was considered particularly important, since Fischer had been informed that Tardini was suffering from some unspecified disease, was having difficulty carrying out his tasks, and would probably not be able to continue.[65] However, Fischer did not succeed in bringing his plans to a successful conclusion. This time it was the Israeli ambassador in Rome who constituted the obstacle to success.

Forcing a Decision

Sasson's protracted frustration seems to have contributed to his decision to exploit Tardini's indisposition in order to advocate the institution of diplomatic relations. He hoped to do so with the active and unprecedented cooperation of Ottaviani and other central figures in the Vatican, and he was ready to play an active role in their power games. While Herzog was identified more than any other Foreign Ministry official with what could be defined as a containment strategy and Fischer was associated with attempts at rapprochement, Sasson favored an alternative method of political attack. As hinted above, he was the most severe critic of Israel's Vatican strategy, particularly as practiced by Fischer, who, in his turn, was no admirer of Sasson.[66] In a frank letter to the deputy director-general of the Foreign Ministry, Haim Yahil after the event, Sasson propounded his basic views, which he continued to uphold:

> I take issue with the assumption of our friend Fischer, which has been adopted by the Ministry administration, that through long-term rapprochement efforts, we will some day succeed in establishing diplomatic relations with the Vatican, and that until then we must be as careful as possible not to anger the Vatican, even if this requires us to make concessions here and there, and also take every care not to voice any open criticism of the Vatican for refusing to recognize us and our existence, in case, Heaven forbid, what we have to say proves displeasing to some monsignor or other. . . . I object to this assumption because I am con-

vinced that it cannot further our relations with the Vatican. Because as long as the two haters of Israel, Monsignor Semore and Cardinal Tardini, head of the State Secretariat, make the decisions, we will never achieve our goal by the methods proposed by our friend Maurice Fischer. . . . It is my conviction that we must fight these two enemies with all the means at our disposal in order to break down their resistance or, at least, to give the lie to their confidence and conviction that we are reconciled to their stand and are helping to consolidate it within the Vatican and outside it. . . . We have learned that matters in the Vatican do not proceed on the basis of pure "sanctity and morality" and that a great number of churchmen would be ready to listen to us and to assist us in our struggle, if we devote ourselves properly to this task.

We have nothing to lose by doing so because we are certain that we can go on existing for many years, many fine and pleasant years, without establishing diplomatic relations with the Vatican. What harm is there in exposing Tardini and Samore's sworn enmity from time to time? On the contrary—let them defend themselves and deny it and prove to us by deeds, and not merely by words, that we are mistaken. What harm is there, for example, in trying to explain here and there that this "holy" Vatican, which proclaims so loftily the need for love between peoples and countries—is refusing to establish relations with us. On the contrary—let them defend themselves and deny it and prove to us and to the world how mistaken we are.[67]

How did Sasson's plan develop? How did his superiors view it? How did it end, and what was its outcome? He seems to have concluded in December 1959 that vigorous action was called for in order to promote his activist outlook. His first operative idea was to make some kind of package deal with the Vatican whereby Israel would persuade Jewish organizations in the United States to support the candidacy of the Catholic John Kennedy for the presidency and in return would demand official recognition of Israel.[68]

This initiative was not supported by the Foreign Ministry, which preferred Fischer's cautious strategy and also, inter alia, because of Israel's inability to act as the spokesman of U.S. Jewry and its profound reluctance to intervene in election issues. Sasson refused to accept the prevailing orientation and very soon found a new outlet for his alternative approach. He took advantage of the independent initiative of a group of Vatican officials led by Ottaviani, who were trying, for reasons related to internal power struggles, to overcome the State Secretariat's objections to establishing diplomatic relations with Israel. Sasson's reports indicate that the Holy Office was very uneasy because of the lull in the cold war, and the growing strength of the communists, and was trying to exploit Tardini's indisposition in order to "take matters into their own hands." According to these assessments Ottaviani was doing everything in his power to achieve the appointment of a replacement for Tardini, the appointment of Samore as nuncio in Bonn and of Monsignor Angelo Dell'acqua, substitute of Secretariat of State as nuncio in Rome. The attempt to further Vatican recognition of Israel was thus only one of a wide range of subversive activities being conducted behind the backs of the State Secretariat.[69]

A representative of the group approached Sasson at the end of February with a specific request for collaboration "and also guidance on various details." Naturally enough, the Israeli diplomat seized the opportunity and, without consulting his superiors, gave the initiative the "green light." As he put it in diplomatic language, he "did not consider it desirable to tie the hands [of the representative] and to ask him to suspend his activities [since] I assume that it is in our interest for pressure to be brought to bear on the pope and the State Secretariat from within the Vatican and outside it."[70] Very soon, apparently even before the Ministry could react, Sasson reported that "the old man" [as the pope was called by the Ottaviani group] had given his "100 percent" positive response to the idea of diplomatic recognition, and that Israeli interests could now be promoted, since one of the heads of the State Secretariat was ready to cooperate against Tardini. "Our mutual intention," according to representatives of the group, was "to appoint an Israeli ambassador to the Vatican and a nuncio in Tel Aviv."[71]

From that moment on, Sasson devoted his energies to an intensive round of meetings in Rome and Milan, talks with members of the group in an attempt to coordinate activity with them, and attempts to persuade his Ministry to follow the path opened up by him and those in the Vatican he regarded as his partners. His initiatives included recommendations to involve the foreign minister and even the prime minister in attempts to persuade the people in the papal court "who are sitting on the fence."[72] Shortly afterwards, Meir reported to Ben-Gurion "that there is a prospect that the Vatican too will establish diplomatic ties with Israel." Sasson recommended Fischer for the job of representative at the Vatican, "because the pope knows him from Paris and likes him."[73]

The documents do not reveal directly how Sasson's superiors reacted to these developments. Information was compartmentalized, and in this case only Ben-Gurion, Meir, Yahil, and Fischer were in the know. Their *post factum* analyses reveal that they were very afraid of undesirable complications, which was why Fischer did his best to weigh the balance against the initiative.[74] "In the course of the campaign," the deputy director-general wrote to Sasson, "on receiving your cables, we were carried away by your enthusiasm, and despite our skepticism, we began to believe that the promised hour was at hand." Consequently, Ben-Gurion, Meir, and Yahil were reluctant to halt the initiative—particularly when they were informed of the pope's readiness to move forward—and were perhaps unable to do so because it had gained momentum. This explains why they agreed, at an advanced stage, to intervene directly by setting up a meeting for Fischer with Giuseppe Sensi, the Apostolic delegate in Jerusalem. On this occasion, Fischer officially declared Israel's intention and requested that the pope receive Sasson in audience. German Chancellor Konrad Adenauer was also asked to support the efforts.[75]

The first step was particularly problematic for the Foreign Ministry since, as Yahil wrote to Sasson, "it constituted a drastic departure from our former policy of avoidance of official requests for establishment of relations unless we know that a positive response is guaranteed, and now. . . . you felt it necessary to decide on this proposal while staging [*sic*] instructions from the Israeli government. This came as a surprise to us and made us uneasy, but we did not dare at this stage to undermine your efforts. To use a colorful phrase, you appeared to us to be walking a tightrope and we were afraid to call out to you in case you fell."[76] This makes it clear why Sasson was not ordered to put an end to his involvement in the conspiracy.

His reports contain colorful descriptions of intrigues within the Vatican around the plotting of the Ottaviani group and its various supporters and the "raging struggle between the Holy Office and the State Secretariat."[77] The Israeli diplomat discovered that "not only does one hand not know what the other is doing, but that sabotage, subversion, scheming, and lies play a central part in relations between these offices and their approach to most problems. The pope himself, despite his goodness of heart and good intentions, is to a certain degree weak-charactered and, because of his advanced age, has begun to suffer from loss of memory, which the people around him are exploiting for their own purposes."[78] As part of that same campaign of rumors, Sasson received a full report on the reasons why Samore, who was then acting head in place of Tardini, was against relations with Israel:

(a) Israel—is a delicate problem; (b) certain non-Arab but Catholic countries (allusion is to either France or Germany) are advising the Vatican not to establish relations; (c) the situation of the Catholics in Israel is very difficult, there are, for example, mixed families; (d) Israel has never made a single gesture toward the Holy See; (e) some Catholic circles want to establish relations with Israel, and a certain very senior churchman [Ottaviani] is in favor. The Pope is very sensitive to the pressure exerted on him in this regard—but there is still a long road ahead of us; (f) Israel does not have people qualified to deal with the question; (g) they have no trust in the goodwill of the man who has represented Israel so far in contacts with the State Secretariat [i.e., Fischer].[79]

Sasson tried to mollify Fischer and explained that his sources had made it clear that "when the time comes, after they win the present struggle, Ottaviani will know how to make peace between you and the State Secretariat and to turn you into one of the loyal people who is acceptable to them." Israel's ambassador in Rome also confided in his superiors that he had been embarrassed by the Ottaviani group's demand that he guarantee that Israel would appoint a certain Catholic, who was a convert from Judaism, as adviser on relations with the Vatican "now and after relations are established . . . since this is the custom in all the legations accredited to the Vatican."[80]

After weeks of strenuous effort, it seemed that the die had been cast and that on 26 April the State Secretariat would submit to the pope a positive report on Israel's request for recognition.[81] Sasson was even asked to prepare for a subsequent meeting with the pope and to prepare curriculum vitae to be submitted to the State Secretariat before the audience. A rude awakening awaited him at his meeting with the Apostolic Nuncio. The Nuncio told him that "he regretted having to say that the Vatican felt that the time was not yet ripe" for diplomatic relations with Israel and that "there is no room on our part for raising this matter with the 'old man,' the State Secretariat or any other authorized body." When the despondent Sasson asked whether this was a final refusal, the Nuncio replied that "such a possibility cannot be contemplated at this time or in the near future."[82]

Back to Normalcy

Ben-Gurion, who had always been skeptical and doubtful (to put it mildly) about ties with the pope, reacted differently to the news from Rome. In a note to Yahil, he declared bluntly that "the value of these relations has been inflated, we can survive for many years without a Vatican representative."[83] Even though there were those who shared the prime minister's views, such a resounding political "slap in the face" called for reappraisal of the issue by the Ministry. It also provided additional proof that "success has many fathers while failure has none." Sasson's superiors directed unqualified blame for the embarrassing defeat at him, although they did not deny their own formal responsibility. The diplomatic language employed by Yahil in his first cable to Sasson after the latter's meeting with the Nuncio did not mask the blunt message:

> The outcome is certainly regrettable in light of the considerable efforts invested. But from the outset we did not think that the conditions were ripe for establishment of diplomatic relations and we were working solely for improvement of relations and for closer ties. I am sorry that "our friends" succeeded in making us over-enthusiastic and that we were tempted into taking steps which were not consonant with our appraisal and our approach at the beginning of the campaign, steps which were, as has now been demonstrated, too hasty. We cannot now retract them.[84]

However, even after the event, the ambassador in Rome could see no effective alternative to the path he had recommended. Moreover, he claimed that his efforts in early 1960 had resulted in several gains. These included gaining important information that the Federal Republic of Germany had been the leading force among the most extreme opponents to Israel-Vatican relations; consolidating the Ottaviani power group, which established a precedent by openly supporting the Israeli approach; similar support by the Pontifical College Angelicum; and establishing a precedent by conducting in-depth discussions with the State Secretariat on the subject.[85] Sasson remained steadfast in his views, and his somewhat pathetic recommendations for action included exerting continuing pressure on the Holy Office so that the Nuncio would "withdraw his statement and arrange an audience for me with the Pope. If after a week or two I am not satisfied, I will send a letter to the Nuncio, reiterating what I said to him and I will present the Vatican as a state which does not keep its promises." It comes as no surprise that the Foreign Ministry did not share these views. The ambassador was asked explicitly to leave well enough alone and specifically not to blame the Nuncio for giving "a dry and insulting reply to a request from an official representative of the State of Israel," not to maintain further contact with the staff of the Holy Office and the Angelicum, and not to encourage them to wage a further struggle against the State Secretariat.[86] Sasson was thus unceremoniously divested of authority to deal with Vatican affairs in order to forestall what was feared would be further damage.[87]

It had been clear to the policymakers in Jerusalem from the beginning that this affair would hinder efforts to establish relations with the Vatican in the future. Meir reported at the end of that year that among the reasons why "there is considerable anger against Israel in the Vatican" were "the efforts of the Israeli embassy in Rome at the beginning of this year to further diplomatic relations between Israel and the Vatican by means of direct contact with the pope and circumvention of the State Secretariat."[88] The Holy See apparently decided in the wake of this affair to lower the profile of contacts with Israel, a decision reflected in various weighty political ways. For example, the State Secretariat, on instructions from the pope, severed all ties with Israel's representatives, immediately after replying in the negative to the Israeli initiative and for a considerable period afterward; and Chiapperro, the newly appointed bishop in Israel, as a result of orders he seems to have received from the State Secretariat, remained "somewhere in Israel but . . . outside [its] framework."[89]

It is also understandable why, as numerous documents indicate, the Israelis concluded that "once bitten, twice shy." For at least seven years, the Foreign Ministry followed the "Fischer line," which refrained from any intensive effort to win recognition from the Vatican and was content with a gradual improvement in relations and contacts. It took the Ministry two years, and then only after Tardini's death, before they again proposed to papal representatives, and then "with great deference," that the Holy See grant Fischer an audience.[90] This circumspect strategy was also reflected in the decision to shelve the plan for an institution for the study of Jewish-Christian relations, which had first been raised in late 1959.[91] Fischer's appointment in the summer of 1960 as ambassador in Rome, replacing Sasson, was a symbolic and significant step, particularly since, in total contrast to his predecessor, he was charged with the task of maintaining contact with the pope.

4

Theology and Diplomacy

From the last months of 1960 until the 1967 Six Days' War, Israel abstained deliberately from attempts to win de jure recognition from the Vatican. This policy was not affected by the departure of Tardini, the man regarded by Foreign Ministry officials as "a sworn enemy of Israel and the main champion of internationalization,"[1] or by Israel's assessment (which turned out to be accurate) that henceforth resolution of the internationalization issue would no longer be the precondition for diplomatic relations. Israeli efforts were now confined to exerting "polite" pressure on the Vatican to honor Tardini's undertaking regarding the political status of the Catholic bishop in Israel, and attempting to solve problems relating to the Christian minority in Israel. No effort was spared, but success was limited

In the early 1960s, Jerusalem focused on endeavors to revise the Church's anti-Jewish theological stand, in order to allay its official hostility toward Israel and improve the prospects for recognition. To this end, it exploited the intensifying pressure for change on the part of diverse forces within and outside the Church in the wake of the Holocaust.[2] While Israeli experts knew only too well that such a revision would not necessarily expedite the establishment of diplomatic relations, they naturally hoped that it would augur positive developments.

Outside the Vatican Arena

It should be pointed out that in the late 1950s the Foreign Ministry knew that activity was being conducted within the Catholic Church directed at purging Christianity of elements liable to provoke anti-Jewish sentiments. Roncalli's essentially positive approach to the subject was also well known. But, recalling the diplomatic fiasco of early 1960, Israeli officials were naturally loath to lend a hand to any official and open initiative that might cause immediate damage to the delicate fabric of relations with the Vatican. Jerusalem preferred to leave such action to bodies within and outside the Vatican and to content itself with indirect contact. This was not always possible. As will be shown below, Israel could not remain on the sidelines while other forces were embroiled in intensive efforts and was eventually drawn into much greater involvement in internal Vatican affairs than had originally been intended.

The three major forces for change were an academic who set a precedent by his involvement, elements within the Vatican with various motives for advocating theological reforms, and Jewish organizations that devoted increasing attention to the issue from mid-1960 in anticipation of the Twenty-first Ecumenical Council (an international assembly of bishops and other ecclesiastical representatives whose decisions on doctrine were considered binding on all Christians). It was to be the first Council meeting in the twentieth century and was due to discuss a range of theological subjects.[3]

The first challenge to Israel's cautious approach was the campaign launched by the French historian Jules Isaac, calling for revisions of certain Church manuals of instruction which had served for generations to inspire anti-Semitism. Isaac, whose entire family had perished in Auschwitz, had founded the Amitie Judeo-Chretienne and written a widely publicized book, *Jesus and Israel*, as his personal contribution to redressing the historical injustice inflicted on the Jewish people by Christianity. He had been received in audience by Pius XII in 1949, but nothing came of their meeting at the time. A decade later, he met with the new pope, Roncalli, who proved to be unusually open-minded on this question. At the end of the meeting which, according to a leading historian of the subject, "made history," the Holy See asked the Jewish scholar to meet with Cardinal Bea to inform him that he had decided to include the Jewish question on the agenda of the imminent Council meeting.[4] We know now that the cardinal was greatly surprised by the fact that the pope had sent an 84-year-old Jewish messenger to confide his wishes to him. Still, as confidante of the pope and one of the senior churchmen who advocated closer relations between Christians and Jews, Bea began to prepare the ground for the deliberations.[5]

These deliberations quickly centered on the highly controversial need to differentiate between the individual guilt of some Jews for Christ's death and collective guilt. Isaac's audience with the pope in the second week of June 1960 was intended to accelerate the process. In preparation for the audience, Isaac approached the Israeli embassy in Rome on his own initiative for advice on how to present the matter to the Holy See and what arguments to cite. The Israeli diplomats advised him to submit three requests: that any sentence which might be interpreted as offensive to the Jewish people be erased from manuals of instruction; that a subcommittee be established, connected to one of the relevant congregations, to examine the contents of the manuals, and that the pope make a public statement announcing that these steps were being taken. The French historian was also advised which Vatican figures were worth meeting and how each should be approached. Isaac's meeting was regarded in Israel as a partial success. The pope responded favorably to the three points, although he confided in Isaac that he was not an "absolute ruler" and that "the offices will have something to say."[6] This was a diplomatic way of saying that he was aware of major opposition within the Church to Isaac's proposals.

However, the very fact that the audience took place and the pope's response were seen by the Rome embassy as indications that the Vatican was willing, to a certain degree, to take steps to redress the historical injustice. This attitude, it was thought, "could have an indirectly positive impact on the state of relations between the Vatican and Israel." Jerusalem, however, remained wary. Fischer's informal consultant on Church affairs, Professor Zwi Werblowsky, warned that Israel should maintain a formal separation between Christian-Jewish affairs and Vatican-Israel relations. To combine the two issues might provide the "Tardini sect" with the pretext for opposing any far-reaching or demonstrative moves, even if they were confined to the former area. He recommended a guarded policy, aimed at "sweetening the pill" for the Church by stressing that Israel "does not consider action against anti-Semitism to be new initiative on the part of the Church or a significant turning point. On the contrary, we are aware that such activity has been underway discreetly for some time, and are acquainted with the successful endeavors of numerous theologians to expunge this evil and root out the errors deriving from misunderstanding of tradition."[7] The Foreign Ministry accepted this recommendation. This being so, Isaac remained alone in his efforts at this stage, without Israeli participation.

International Jewish organizations and prominent Jewish figures were not similarly hesitant in the same period, and they tried to exert pressure on the pope "to speed matters up," as Fischer said. They were divided on the question of whether to submit a memorandum to the Ecumenical Council. Orthodox Jewish bodies were against any kind of approach. Other organizations, like B'nai B'rith, the World Jewish Congress, and reform organizations were very much in favor of the initiative, and Fischer was able to report to the foreign minister in late 1960 that "we have discerned bustling activity, which is evoking negative reaction to the appeals in general and to their abundance in particular." Several Jewish organizations sent missions to Rome and submitted lengthy memoranda to the Vatican. According to Werblowsky, these documents were all commissioned from Catholic scholars rather than Jews, since no Jewish experts on this subject could be found at the time. Nahum Goldmann himself was deeply involved in a diplomatic effort to gain an audience with the pope in order to persuade him.[8]

Also active, though in less spectacular fashion, was Dr. Ernst Ludwig Ehrlich of Basel University, one of the most active members of the Judische-Christliche Verstandigung (Jewish-Christian Understanding Association) and director of the West European office of B'nai B'rith. His efforts posed yet another challenge to Jerusalem. At the beginning of October, after Fischer had urged him to include Werblowsky in any action he took, Ehrlich asked for a meeting with the Hebrew University scholar, who was then on a lecture tour of Switzerland.[9] He told Werblowsky that he had met with Cardinal Bea, who had promised "serious and proper treatment of any memorandum we submit, if [the document] is done in a proper way." Moreover, the cardinal indicated that Israel's connection with the process was welcome. The solution chosen contravened the cautious approach Fischer had recommended—the Jews were to be involved in the preparation of a memorandum that would be submitted as a "purely Catholic document, signed solely by Catholic theologians." Bea asked for a list of Jewish demands that could serve as the basis for a Church document. Werblowsky thought that this tactic offered three advantages: first, the Ecumenical Council would receive "an evenhanded and responsible document"; second, the memo would be Christian and not Jewish, formally speaking, even if, in practice, it was a joint composition; and third, it would obviate the need for Jewish delegations and memoranda. "All the hurly-burly of the Jewish organizations with Goldmann at their head will vanish in a puff of smoke and we will support Bea, who can then turn them down with a clear conscience and tell them that there is no more need for anything to be done since preparation of a basic memo is already underway." Ehrlich was ready to take up the challenge, and he invited Werblowsky to meet with him in Paris in late November in order to prepare the memo.

Werblowsky succeeded in persuading the director-general of the Foreign Ministry, Arie Levavi, to approve his participation. The recently opened files at the Israel State Archive indicate that the policymakers were uncertain whether the scheduled meeting, despite its far-reaching Jewish implications, was really a legitimate concern of the Foreign Ministry. However, hesitations were overruled by several weighty considerations: Israel was naturally anxious to be involved in this significant event, the Ehrlich-Bea plan guaranteed that Israel's involvement would be discreetly managed, and participants hoped to avert any possible damage from irresponsible initiative of international Jewish organizations. No less important was Werblowsky's assessment that the fact that the pope had not assigned the Jewish question to a special committee but to the permanent Secretariat for Christian Unity, headed by Bea, could be regarded as an invitation to discuss the Jewish theological problem within a Christian ecumenical framework. Indeed, it could be interpreted as an indirect overture by the pope. Werblowsky was also convinced that the Vatican's opposition to Israel and constant attempts to undermine Israeli policy stemmed not from realpolitik—based, for example, on the Church's interests in Arab countries—but from the deeply rooted, "almost instinctive anti-Jewish effect," which it sought to justify on both scholarly theological and political grounds. According to this view, the introduction of fundamental doctrinal revisions by the supreme ecclesiastical authority would undoubtedly impact on the political sphere.[10] These arguments eventually tipped the balance.[11] For the next few years, the Foreign Ministry was to be indirectly involved in the process, which was taking place mainly inside the Vatican.

Indirect Involvement

In the last week of November 1961, five Jews and seven Catholics were invited to attend a two-day meeting in Paris. The Catholics, all sympathetic to Bea's views, attended in full, but only two of the Jewish invitees came, Ehrlich and Werblowsky. (The two rabbis who had been invited refused to attend, and a Jewish professor from Strasbourg was unable to come.) The Israeli Foreign Ministry was directly involved in preparations for the meeting. Fischer did everything in his power to overcome the objections of the rabbis, since he was anxious to receive their informal endorsement, which was important "in light of the 'hierarchical' mentality in Rome and the misguided views prevailing in the Christian world concerning the significance and role of rabbis in the Jewish religion."[12] Their absence, however, accentuated Werblowsky's contribution to the drafting of the document produced at the meeting.[13] This document deserves to be described in full, since it was the fruits of Israel's first attempt to operate directly within the Vatican's theological policymaking circles.

The participants soon discovered that Cardinal Bea's office had already drafted the document, which was more or less complete. This meant that their role was restricted to filling in the gaps, emphasizing whatever they considered vital, raising basic problems, and proposing theological formulae for the consideration of a committee headed by the pope. The Secretariat for Christian Unity would then submit the summary of the resolutions to the plenum of the Ecumenical Council. The main point, which Werblowsky tried to bring up at the deliberations, was that the problem was not confined to random anti-Semitic statements, and hence revisions or single declarations would not solve it. What was required was an unequivocal and binding declaration by the supreme ecclesiastical body.

The Israeli scholar tried to amend four major aspects of the documents. The first related to the Church Fathers. Only those familiar with theological matters, Werblowsky believed, could appreciate the decisive role in shaping the Christian mentality played by the tradition of hatred, hostility, and anti-Jewish invective contained in the writings of the Church Fathers. This being so, it was vital to obtain a declaration of principle defining their authority in this sphere. "We took into account the fact that if the Bible is the Christian Torah, then the writings of the Church Fathers are the Catholic Talmud," wrote Werblowsky. A statement was therefore drafted that invalidated the authority of the Fathers in this area of anti-Jewish politics "without offending their dignity or undermining the value of their other theological theories." Second, a formula was proposed that did not gainsay the Christian ideal of gathering the whole world under the wing of the Church but, at the same time, emphasized the unique standing of the Jewish people and exempted them from the accepted missionary approach. Third, instead of a catalog of expressions, theories, acts, and customs that needed to be expunged or revised, the committee called for "a fundamental and systematic purge" in all areas. And finally it proposed that this purge be applied on a Church-wide basis. A clause was added to the document, calling for the extension of the pope's liturgical policy to all Catholic communities. In response to an explicit question, Werblowsky conveyed a plain and clear message (coordinated in advance with the Foreign Ministry) to the effect that Israel was "totally" opposed to the participation of Jewish observers "in any form whatsoever" in the planned Ecumenical Council.

Despite the highly positive impact of the Paris meeting and the fact that

Cardinal Bea voiced no objections to the final document, it was manifest to Israeli diplomats that the proposal was going to be revised extensively. They also
anticipated a counterattack on the part of certain ecclesiastical and theological circles in an attempt to sabotage the trend toward change.[14]

This Israeli attempt to conduct quiet and discreet activity behind the scenes
failed, because of the energetic public effort of Jewish organizations to influence
the Vatican. Goldmann, for example, tried to bring pressure to bear to revive
the plan (which had been raised unsuccessfully in 1959) to establish an institute for the study of Jewish-Christian relations in Rome, to be headed by Dr.
Haim Vardi of the Ministry of Religious Affairs. The Foreign Ministry was less
than enthusiastic at the idea, apparently fearing that too much publicity might
hamper progress.[15] Despite these reservations, thanks to Foreign Minister
Meir's support and the prior understanding that Vardi's task would be merely
"to listen," the plan was approved in late May 1962.[16]

The fears very soon proved justified. Vardi was instructed by Goldmann to
deal with all problems pertaining to the imminent Ecumenical Council in his
capacity as representative of the World Jewish Congress—and his appointment
was made public about a month before he was actually accredited.[17] At the beginning of May, *Ma'ariv* published an interview with the mysterious Joe
Golan, who was associated with Nahum Goldmann. Golan referred to Vardi's
appointment as representative of the World Jewish Congress *at* the Vatican.
Vardi himself suspected that Golan had revealed this information in order to
sabotage the appointment, which he himself had coveted since 1958. The news
item infuriated Orthodox Jewish circles in the United States and in England,
who feared the participation of a Jewish representative as an observer at the
Ecumenical Council. Whatever the motives of the opponents, the outcome was
clear and damaging from the Foreign Ministry's point of view. At the end of
the first week in July, the director-general was informed that the publicity had
incensed the Arab ambassadors to the Vatican. Shortly afterwards, word was
received from Egypt and Iraq that steps were being taken or were being threatened against Catholics there. The State Secretariat, according to Israeli
briefings, was convinced that the publicity on Vardi's appointment had been
planted as part of a "nefarious" Israeli scheme, devised in conjunction with Dr.
Goldmann, aimed at bringing in an Israeli observer "by the back door" and exploiting the Ecumenical Council in order to promote Israeli political interests.[18] According to information Fischer received, this activity "has provided
our enemy, Monsignor Samore (the spiritual heir of Cardinal Tardini) with the
opportunity of breaking his silence" and demanding that the State Secretary
veto discussion of the Jewish problem at the Council, "due to the appointment
of an Israeli government official as representative of the World Jewish Congress at the Vatican."[19]

This development occurred only a few days before the Vatican's central committee was scheduled to discuss proposals relating to the Church's attitude
toward the Jews. According to reports, which reached Israel, the incident was
"like a bolt from the blue" for those Vatican officials who were trying to pro-

mote change.[20] Bea decided to defer the plan he had been working on for so
long, and his secretary informed Goldmann that Bea "no longer wants" to see
him. A representative of an American Jewish organization who met with
"friends" at the Vatican, reported that "there has been a drastic change in the
attitude towards the Jews" and that "they mistrust us and are deeply suspicious
of our conduct." Furthermore, it was made clear to him that "at this stage, the
Vatican's doors will be barred to any Jewish representative." The same "friends
of the Jewish people" also clarified that the Jewish organizations must eschew
their plans "at this stage" and leave well enough alone until quiet was restored.
For the immediate future, it was evident that Vardi was now persona non grata
at the Vatican. Fischer refused at first to accept this bitter defeat and tried to
salvage something from the wreckage by promising the Vatican that Vardi's appointment would be cancelled and by trying to win an audience with the pope.[21]
Golda Meir refused to accept his recommendation and insisted that the appointment go through as the "legitimate" right of the Jewish organizations.[22]
She apparently felt that Israel was not to blame for the "foolish" publicity and
that the government should wait a little and then go ahead with its plans as if
nothing had happened.[23] The only concession she was willing to make was to
postpone Vardi's arrival in Rome until "things calm down." This reaction was
misguided.

Within a few days Jerusalem received disquieting reports of the pope's response to the affair, including indications that the Israeli ambassador in Rome
would find that doors previously open to him were now closed "until further
notice," and that the Vatican would not now receive those Jewish representatives or delegations which had hoped for an audience. And indeed, shortly afterwards, Fischer reported that he would be unable to obtain an audience with
the Holy See and that "fear of the Arabs is so great that the State Secretariat
has persuaded the pope that even if I come to Castel Gandolfo [a papal residence in a town carrying the same name, on Lake Albano, near Rome] incog-
nito in a taxi, some gatekeeper in the pay of the Arabs might photograph me
going in."[24] His reports were accompanied by "fervent" appeals to prevent
Vardi's departure for Rome.[25] Meir and Goldmann were finally forced to suspend Vardi's appointment and to keep him on hold "for the time being" in
Geneva or Jerusalem. The Foreign Ministry welcomed the decision in the hope
that the idea would eventually be dropped, which is what actually happened.[26]

Dashed Hopes

This decision enabled Fischer to continue his behind-the-scenes talks at the
Vatican. On the basis of his contacts he concluded that Bea remained firmly
convinced of the need to raise the Jewish question at the Ecumenical Council, but that his stand was largely dependent on the nonintervention and official
silence of Israel and the heads of the Jewish organizations.[27] The first indication of a positive trend was the invitation to Israeli representatives to attend
the opening of the Council in the second week of October 1962, which they

accepted.[28] It also appears that during these weeks, Israel's representatives in the Italian capital discovered with certainty that "the Vardi affair" had not put a stop to the basic inclination within the Vatican to introduce theological revisions that would have positive implications for the Jewish people. It was also made clear to them that Bea's group, with the approval of the pope, was continuing its struggle to bring its ideas to fruition and was unreservedly willing to cooperate with the Israel embassy in Rome. The archival documents reveal that senior Foreign Ministry officials entertained high hopes of positive development. The Israeli consul in New York was informed that such developments could have a practical political impact on attitudes toward Israel "if not on the part of the Vatican itself, then of very important secular elements that are influenced by the Vatican. In due course there could be positive repercussions even on our relations with Western Europe, including the European Community and the Common Market."[29]

These optimistic appraisals explain why the Israeli Foreign Ministry decided to launch an international public relations campaign (which was carried out in practice by international Jewish organizations in order to conceal its origins). Prominent Jews abroad were asked to organize mass petitions aimed at various senior churchmen, the text to be coordinated in advance with Bea. The message they conveyed was that "after 2,000 years of suffering and persecution which culminated in the annihilation of six million Jews during the Holocaust, the Jewish people expect the Ecumenical Council to proclaim ceremoniously that it is the duty of every Catholic to treat members of the Jewish people with respect from the social viewpoint and with tolerance for the moral and traditional values originating in the Holy Bible, which is shared by both religions."[30] Jewish leaders, who met with some sixty Catholic leaders all over the world, were asked to conceal their connection to the State of Israel.[31]

Considerable effort was also invested in curbing the "thirst for publicity" of the heads of the three leading Jewish organizations in the United States, "all of whom are anxious to save the Jewish people, each wishing it to be known that this salvation (if it is indeed achieved) should not be attributed to the activities of the other two."[32] Concomitantly, Israel tried to thwart the onslaught of Catholic circles opposed to Bea's plans. At the beginning of December 1962, for example, Fischer discovered that an anti-Semitic tract entitled *The Plot against the Church* had been distributed to all the Council Fathers. Bishops at the Vatican with whom Fischer was connected suggested to him that "it would be a good thing if [he] succeeded in exposing the source of the tract which could then serve as evidence to the public that it was issued by a circle whose views run counter to those of the pope." Representatives of the Mossad in Rome were instructed to exploit their contacts in the Italian intelligence service to discover the source.[33] Preliminary investigation uncovered the organization, which had published the tract, which was based on material in the archives of Julius Streicher (editor of the Nazi publication *Der Stürmer*) and was funded by Egypt.[34] At the second session of the Council, and at Fischer's request, a Mexican bishop (alluding to the tract) asked whether "priests and Catholic believers treat the

Pope John XXIII with Maurice Fischer (center) at a reception on the opening day of Vatican II, Sistine Chapel, Rome, October 11, 1962. *Courtesy of Chaya Fischer.*

Jews, who are the children of our mutual father Abraham, with the same sincere exemplary love bestowed by the pope, or whether, on the contrary, they exhibit subconscious anti-Semitism?"[35]

In return, Israel was asked to facilitate Christian activity in Israel in order to deprive the opponents of theological changes of one of their major weapons. In the effort to satisfy this and other requests, the Foreign Ministry tried to persuade the Israeli Habimah Theatre to postpone (until after the Council meeting) the staging of Rolf Hochhut's play *The Deputy*, which denounced Pius XII for his indifference to Nazi crimes against the Jews.[36] "The attitude of Catholics toward the Jewish people is more important than a theater's profits," Fischer wrote.[37] A Ministry official who met with the Habimah administration told them apologetically that he had not come "in order to hand down orders from above . . . because that would be unacceptable in a democratic country." However, his appeal "to their sense of civic responsibility" met with a positive response, and the theater bowed to the Ministry's recommendation in mid-May.[38] Fischer was probably exaggerating when he wrote, "It would be hard to find words to describe how appreciative the cardinal (Bea) was when he learned of the decision," although the two men were certainly on close terms. Thanks to the cooperation between them, Fischer was informed discreetly in mid-December 1962 that the pope was suffering from stomach cancer. "It was agreed" between the sides "that it is a commission of the first order to insert the Jewish question into the agenda of the second session of the Ecumenical Council while the Pope is alive."[39]

On 21 May, the committee planning the second session of the Council agreed to submit Cardinal Bea's document to the plenum. Bea's belief that "the resolution will undoubtedly be passed by a large majority" was conveyed to Meir.[40] However, rumors of the pope's deteriorating health proved to be true, and he died shortly afterwards. Advocates of change in the Vatican and in Jerusalem were uncertain as to the attitude of the new pope, Giovanni Battista Montini, Paul VI, toward the process begun by his predecessor.[41] The Foreign Ministry was therefore relieved to discover that Montini intended to carry on the process, though with greater caution.[42] Consequently, Israel persisted in attempts to make direct contact with Council Fathers all over the world, particularly in Latin America, before the Council next met in September 1963. Considerable effort was invested in preventing public statements and newspaper coverage on this activity and in avoiding any move that might be interpreted by Rome as intervention.[43] "The modest (though far from easy) task of the embassy," Fischer reported at the beginning of November, "remains to try to restrain those who, in their fondness for mediation and/or their craving for publicity, take action that is liable to prove detrimental to the interests of Jewry in general and Israel in particular."[44]

Israel's prudence was reflected in Fischer's refusal to examine the text of the proposed statement on the Jewish question "so that I won't come under suspicion if there is a leak from a source within the Church."[45] The requests that Israel maintain a low profile on all issues pertaining to the Church were less tactful. In early August Fischer wrote to the Foreign Ministry "requesting earnestly that [Meir] bring her influence to bear in order to restrain Wahrhaftig [the minister of religious affairs] and the other Orthodox elements. . . . I cannot conceive that they do not understand that the enemy of the State of Israel is Islam and that any statement by the Ecumenical Council denouncing anti-Semitism will not damage their secular and religious interests."[46] Attempts also were made to prevent Habimah from revoking its decision to postpone staging of *The Deputy*. The theater was wavering at that time because rumors that the Foreign Ministry had had a hand in the decision had roused public protest.[47]

At the beginning of November, Israel's efforts to promote its interests at the Vatican seemed to be bearing fruit. On the first of the month, no less than eighteen months since he had asked for an audience, Fischer was received by the new pope. He was frustrated by the pope's request that he keep silent about the meeting, but he complied.[48] The Vatican did not follow suit, however, and the *L'Osservatore Romano* reported on the audience on the following day. Much more significant was the publication that same week of the content of the document on the Church's change of heart with regard to the Jewish people, which was distributed to the Council Fathers by Cardinal Bea. The document emphasized two points. The first was the profound and lasting connection between the Church and the Chosen People, and the second was the fact that the individual guilt of Jewish leaders for the crucifixion of Christ could not be directed at the Jewish people as a whole, past or present. Thus it was unjust to denote this people "Christ-killers" or to regard them as "cursed by God."[49] The publication of the document raised a storm of Arab outrage.[50] Arab diplomats in Rome asked why the pope had received the Israeli ambassador and whether this meant that the Holy See was about to institute diplomatic relations with Israel. The response of a papal spokesman—to the effect that the pope received whomsoever he chose and the issue of diplomatic relations was a matter for the Holy See alone—was brought to the attention of the Israeli ambassador, who found it highly gratifying.[51] In Israel itself, reactions to the document were mixed. A cartoon by the popular Israeli cartoonist Dosh in *Ma'ariv* on 11 November showed the pope washing his hands and the heading read: "He is cleansing himself and not us." The Foreign Ministry, which was anxious to minimize the damage, asked the *Jerusalem Post* not to copy the cartoon.[52] It was less successful in its attempt to prevent the American Jewish Committee from issuing press releases applauding its own contribution to the Vatican document.[53]

Be that as it may, the Council session came as a great disappointment to Israel. Vociferous objections were raised from the outset by Council members, based on two main arguments: first, that there was no reason to confine the discussion to the Jewish people and it should be extended to other non-Christian sects, and second, that the document was liable to undermine the Catholic cause in "certain" countries. The critics included prelates from the Arab countries, led by Monsignor Alberto Gori, the Latin patriarch of Jerusalem, and representatives of the conservative bloc, including members of the papal court, the Curia. According to Israeli assessment, the pope decided eventually to postpone discussion of the Jewish issue and not to risk bringing it up for a vote.[54] Information, which reached Israel, indicated that Bea's standing had been gravely weakened by the decision.[55] Activities related to the Ecumenical Council were suspended for the time being when the pope decided, unexpectedly, in late November to include Israel in his tour of the Middle East. Moreover, from December on, Israeli activity slackened due to the protracted illness of Fischer, the only Israeli official in Rome who was conducting negotiations with the Vatican.[56] Fischer managed to schedule one more private audience at the Vatican in late May 1964 (private apparently because of the state of his health). He discovered on that occasion that the Holy See doubted that the document on the Jews would ever be ratified by the Ecumenical Council and, in any event, thought that discretion was the best policy.[57]

Heading for a Climax

In August 1964, Pope Paul issued his first encyclical letter. In Israel it was perceived as total rejection of the ideal that had inspired his predecessor and as an indication that there was little hope that the Jewish subject would be raised at the Council's next session.[58] Although this proved to be an incorrect evaluation, the impetus and sense of urgency waned. For all these reasons, the only

Israeli initiative before the September 1964 session was distribution to the participants of a Hebrew translation of the papal encyclical letter, with a foreword by Professor David Flusser of the Hebrew University.[59] The arena was now open for the more clamorous activities of Jewish organizations, but they were not the only players.[60] In the interval between the two sessions, the internal struggle within the Vatican flared up again, and the Arabs[61] and the conservative circles within the Church, including the State Secretariat, which was particularly sensitive to political considerations, did everything in their power to shelve the "Jewish document." The more judicious activities of the document's champions within the Church also continued in this period.

According to Israeli assessments, members of the drafting committee of the Secretariat for Christian Unity, which convened prior to the opening session of the Council, were perturbed and indecisive as a result of these pressures. Eventually a new text was prepared that differed from the previous text in not proposing "exoneration." It stated vaguely that the modern Jewish people should not be blamed for "what occurred with regard to the sufferings of the Messiah." It also stressed the desire of the Church "to unite the Jewish people with the Church," and omitted any explicit condemnation of anti-Semitism, merely cautioning against depiction of the Jews as a despised and outcast people. The contents of the document, which were leaked to the press before its submission to the council, evoked a wave of protest from Jews and non-Jews alike, who regarded it as a betrayal of the original objective, as presented to the Council by Pope John XXIII. The third session opened in September 1964 and immediately began to discuss the new text. While progressive circles refused to sanction the revisions, others approved of them, and there were those who demanded that the project be abandoned altogether. The latter, however, were in the minority, and it was decided to return the document to the relevant committee for rewording in the spirit of the original text. After months of heated debate, on 28 October 1965 the Council finally approved a compromise draft of what is now known as *Nostra Aetate* (In Our Times—Declaration on the Relation of the Church to Non-Christian Religions).[62] It omitted the controversial word *deicide* (killing of God) but explicitly rejected the notion that Jews were collectively guilty of Christ's death. Moreover, the Fathers proclaimed that the Jews are not "repudiated or cursed by God."

Israel renewed its behind-the-scenes activity during the Council meeting in accordance with the previous line of action. An attempt was made to restrain imprudent statements by Israeli and international Jewish sources; to maintain contact with sympathetic prelates in order to equip them with useful data and receive firsthand information; to call attention to extreme Arab political reactions against the "Jewish document" that could serve Israeli aims; to coordinate the Jewish public response with American and international Jewish organizations; to persuade prominent Catholics to send letters of support, and to ensure that Israel's president and foreign minister would not attend the premiere of *The Deputy* (its staging could no longer be postponed).[63] In August 1965, when the Council was due to finalize its discussion of the Jewish document, Israel's capacity for action within the Vatican was dealt a heavy blow by Fischer's death. He had not always shared with the Ministry information he had gathered and names of his contacts.[64] In any event, although the final version, which the pope finally succeeded in pushing through in late October, plainly condemned anti-Semitism, it was less positive on the Jewish issue than previous versions. Moreover, the Holy See himself declared in a sermon shortly before the Council took its final vote that when Christ revealed himself to the Jews they "derided, scorned and ridiculed him and finally killed him." These words generated forceful protests from Jewish leaders.[65]

All this notwithstanding, Foreign Ministry officials continued to believe that the work of four years had been crowned with success. Although the "Jewish document" was clearly theological and not political in nature and referred to the Jewish people, without mentioning the State of Israel, it was felt in Jerusalem that its very existence held out promise for Israel's foreign relations.[66] The first positive result was the expansion of direct in-depth contact between Israel and leading figures in the Catholic world. During the period when the Ecumenical Council was occupied with the "Jewish document," about 400 of its members—bishops and archbishops and some dozen cardinals—visited Israel,. They came as pilgrims, the majority with the pope's entourage, but did not steer clear of official contact with the authorities. They visited kibbutzim and non-Christian sites and thus were able to observe the Jewish State at close quarters. "A climate of understanding was created around their visits," according to an internal Foreign Ministry memorandum to diplomatic representatives abroad. "Israel is no longer 'out of bounds' and this direct contact with the upper echelons of the Church will help to break down barriers."

Moreover, according to Jerusalem, Arab opposition to the document proved that anti-Semitism was part and parcel of the Arab propaganda arsenal directed against the State of Israel. As viewed from Jerusalem, the failure of the Arab campaign provided Israel with an effective propaganda weapon. Despite the positive developments, however, there was little prospect that the proclamation would further the establishment of diplomatic relations. Although the Vatican stood firm in the face of Arab pressures, the affair clearly indicated how cautious the Holy See was on all political issues relating to Israel. But all in all, the mood in Jerusalem was optimistic because it was hoped that the document would have an impact on secular elements in Western Europe that were influenced by the Vatican and were involved in such important institutions as the European Union and the Common Market,[67] and above all, that it would influence bilateral relations with the Holy See. According to an official Foreign Ministry report, "The Vatican has its own unique methods, and it is very difficult to distinguish between religious considerations and purely political calculations: the affair of the document has proved beyond the shadow of a doubt the degree to which politics affect theology, but the reverse is also true, and it is not unlikely that the theological stand formulated in the document will affect the political relations between the Holy See and the State of Israel."[68] As events up to the late 1960s were to demonstrate, even this guarded evaluation was overly optimistic.

Recognition of a Kind

Along with the effort to bring pressure to bear behind the scenes for ratification of the Jewish document, Israel continued to work for improvement of direct political contacts with the Vatican. Several examples will suffice to illustrate. Although Fischer's first audience with the pope in early February 1959 had helped to break the ice, the achievement was limited. It was more than three years—two years after he was appointed ambassador in Rome—before he felt that the time was ripe to request another audience.[69] For eighteen months his request remained unanswered, for fear of the anticipated Arab reaction, or so he was told.[70] As noted, the audience took place only after the ascension of the new pope in early November 1963. At the meeting, the pope promised "definitely" to study the question of relations with Israel.[71]

If the pope did in fact study the issue, the results were negligible. Although the pope's acknowledgment and thanks to Israel's president who had congratulated him on his appointment was regarded by Israeli leaders as "de facto recognition," it was not a significant gesture.[72] Again, recently opened Foreign Ministry files prove that the pope's visit to the Holy Land in January 1964—which was greeted with banner headlines in the Israeli press—lacked all political significance where Israel-Vatican relations were concerned. Israel's representatives in Rome had been taken by surprise by the pope's decision, but despite their conviction that the visit could only be interpreted as public de facto recognition of Israel, it was made abundantly clear to them in Vatican circles weeks before the visit that the pope had no desire to promote such relations.[73] Paul VI wanted to visit Jordan and Israel for two reasons: first, in order to tour the Holy Places to emphasize their importance to the Vatican and the Catholic Church; second, to continue his dialogue with the Orthodox Church and to meet in Jerusalem with the ecumenical patriarch of Constantinople, Athenagoras I. This was to be the first such meeting since the rift between the Catholic and Orthodox worlds in 1054.

The pope and his entourage were careful to avoid any act with political connotations (requests for passports, requests for entrance permits or work sessions between Israeli officials and officials of the State Secretariat who accompanied the pope), and it was stressed that the visit was a pilgrimage.[74] On returning to Rome, the pope tried to disprove the impression that his visit had had political implications. His cable of thanks to President Zalman Shazar was addressed to Tel Aviv and not Jerusalem, to the regret of Israel's policymakers. At his first meeting with the Israel ambassador in Rome after his return, Paul VI made almost no reference to his visit, avoided mentioning it in the context of relations with Israel, and was clearly reluctant to take any step, however small, that might be interpreted as promoting such relations. And although he wound

Pope Paul VI replying to President Shazar's address during the official welcoming ceremony at Megiddo, January 5, 1964. *Courtesy of the National Photo Collection of the Israel Government Press Office, Prime Minister's Office. Photo D796–118. Photographer Fritz Cohen.*

up the audience by saying, "We have come a long way since you arrived in Rome," the distinct conclusion in Jerusalem was that the visit would have no impact on future diplomatic relations.

There was no change in the situation, despite Fischer's intensive labors in Rome and his regular contact with Monsignor dell'Acqua, the third most important official in the State Secretariat, with Cardinal Bea, and with Vittorino Veronese, former president of the Banco di Roma (the Vatican's financial arm), one of the most prominent figures in the Italian Catholic world, who had been Israel's liaison with the Vatican in 1949.[75] At one of their meetings, Fischer showed dell'Acqua a clipping from a French newspaper in which a Catholic cardinal stated that the Holy See was ready to establish diplomatic relations with any country that requested them. With true diplomatic tact, the monsignor explained that he could not read the clipping without his spectacles, and when the item was read out to him, he responded, "Patience, patience, the main thing is that since your arrival in Rome we have made progress and have not taken any steps backward."[76] This being so, Fischer's assessment on the eve of the pope's visit to Israel that the Holy See was a "friend" to Israel was, at best, a patent exaggeration, at least where the prospects for political action were concerned.[77]

Naturally enough, Fischer's successor in Rome, Ehud Avriel, was resigned to the view that, while it might be possible to find new points of contact with

Pope Paul VI (right) with President Zalman Shazar (center) and Cardinals Tisserant and Testa at the Mandelbaum Gate frontier post during the farewell ceremony, January 5, 1964. *Courtesy of the National Photo Collection of the Israel Government Press Office, Prime Minister's Office. Photo D797–026. Photographer Fritz Cohen.*

the pope, and it was worth investing effort in this direction, no change could be expected with regard to de jure recognition and theological issues.[78] Resounding proof of the unlikelihood of change was provided after the Six Days' War. Israel now had a vitally important political playing card, since the Holy See was largely dependent on Israel's goodwill with regard to the Christian Holy Places and the welfare of the Christian communities on the West Bank, which was now under Israeli rule. The archival material indicates plainly that after the war, the Vatican, departing from its usual custom, took the initiative, dispatched emissaries to discuss the question of diplomatic relations, and even instructed its representatives worldwide to advise against raising the Jerusalem question in international forums—but still refused to sign a bilateral agreement with Israel. This refusal may have stemmed from the Vatican's failure to arrive at a consensus with the other world churches (particularly the Greeks) or from fear of hostile Arab reaction.[79]

Hence it comes at no surprise that in the late 1960s the Israelis were not alone in their pessimistic view of the prospects for change, although there were increasing cases of discreet contacts between the sides. The British diplomatic representative at the Vatican was expressing an accepted political view when he claimed that "in the absence of any extraordinary benefit (which we do not see at the moment) to be gained from the establishment of diplomatic relations [with Israel], the Vatican will continue to prefer not to provoke the resistance of those Arab governments which have significant Christian minorities."[80] This line was followed for several more decades. It was only in 1985 that Israel was first recognized in an official Catholic document, and another decade was to pass before full diplomatic relations were established.[81]

The Domestic Scene

On the local level as well, few significant gains were recorded until 1967. As noted earlier, the Vatican kept its promise to Fischer to appoint a Catholic bishop as its official representative in Israel, and Chiapperro was in fact appointed to this post. However, as reported to the Foreign Minister in late June 1960, "he . . . has no contact with us."[82] After Chiapperro's death in mid-July 1963, Jerusalem campaigned for the appointment of a successor of higher rank who would be more sympathetic toward Israel.[83] The new appointee, to Jerusalem's disappointment, was Monsignor Hanna Kaldany, who was of lower rank than Chiapperro and who continued to address himself to the Ministry of Religious Affairs rather than the Foreign Ministry.[84]

The Foreign Ministry could, however, point to a minor formal gain in another sphere. In early December 1961, in anticipation of the replacement of the ailing apostolic representative, Monsignor Sensi, Fischer asked Monsignor dell'Acqua to change the definition of his successor's area of jurisdiction from "the Land of Israel, Transjordan, and Cyprus" to "Israel, Jordan, and the Republic of Cyprus."[85] Six months later, the Israeli ambassador was informed that his request had been approved and that the new definition would appear

Bishop Chiapperro in conversation with Arie Levavi and Maurice Fischer of the Foreign Ministry during the New Year's Eve reception at the presidential residence in Jerusalem, December 31, 1962. *Courtesy of the National Photo Collection of the Israel Government Press Office, Prime Minister's Office. Photo D678–021. Photographer Fritz Cohen.*

in the 1963 Vatican yearbook. He was warned, however, that any leakage of information was liable to thwart the plan.[86] In mid-January 1963, Fischer was shown the volume with the promised revision, which he and dell'Acqua considered to be "a modest but important" step on the road to recognition.[87] This formal revision of terms notwithstanding, the papal representation "in Jerusalem and Palestine" remained apostolic rather than diplomatic, just as it had been under the British Mandate, while the diocese, which encompassed Jordan, Israel, and Cyprus, was still headed by the Latin patriarch, whose seat was in the Old City.[88]

Relations with the Israeli authorities continued to be chilly and the contacts of the representative with the Israeli government remained cool and correct. The new apostolic representative, Zanini, who left for Israel in early May 1963, did not pay a courtesy call on Fischer before his departure and did not request an entrance visa to Israel.[89] During his two years of service in Israel, he confined his few routine contacts to the Jerusalem District Commissioner, evaded contact with the Foreign Ministry, and met with a Ministry of Religious Affairs official only twice, and then in private and not in the latter's office. He also insisted that his parting meeting in Jerusalem be held "on neutral ground," namely, in the Terra Sancta monastery.[90] The Israeli embassy in Rome was informed—

on behalf of the State Secretariat—of the appointment of his successor, Bishop Sepinski, by the secretary to the Vatican nunciature accredited to the Italian government. Israel's response to this circuitous message was somewhat pathetic. It claimed that the message indicated "a certain degree of progress, a desire not to totally ignore 'relations' [*sic!*] with Israel."[91] Israel's relations with Catholic churchmen serving locally also left little room for optimism. Officials in Jerusalem could not fail to notice at that time that prominent community heads such as Gori and Maximos, both of whom resided in Jordan, joined with other prelates in the Arab world in expressing objections to the ratification of the "Jewish document."[92]

In summary, two decades of tortuous political ties between Israel and the Vatican had brought Israel almost nothing but frustration. The pope refused adamantly to establish formal diplomatic relations, avoided drawing a political lesson from the dependence of local Catholics on the State of Israel, and was regarded in Jerusalem as a political foe.[93] And yet the energy invested in attempts to open up paths of communication to the Holy See was not entirely wasted. The sporadic contacts over a lengthy period enhanced Israel's ability to gauge the pope's modes of action and brought home to Israeli policymakers how limited were their opportunities for action within the framework of these confrontational relations. But whereas the Church enjoyed a natural and obvious advantage in the international arena, Israel held the upper hand on the local scene, as the following chapters will show.

Part Two

Christians, Christianity, and the Land in Israeli Policy

5

Missionary Activity

Converting the Jews to Christianity

One of the most important points of contact between Israel and the Christian world, which was inextricably connected to the question of Israel's foreign relations, was missionary activity. Knowledge of the basic facts on this activity in the first years of statehood is vital to understanding the perspectives of both sides and the dialogue between them.

A Christian missionary is one who carries out a mission. The duty to disseminate the religion is one of the fundamental tenets of Christianity and is fulfilled through intensive activity and the establishment of relevant institutions and organizations. Long before Israel came into being, it was considered imperative to spread the message of Christianity in the Holy Land, the cradle of that religion.[1] It should be noted that during the British Mandate, missionaries had a much wider scope for action among Arab and Christian inhabitants of the country than in later years, mostly because of the relatively large number of practicing Christians in that period. On the other hand, they encountered great difficulties in working among Jews. The secular and pioneering Jewish community regarded the churches as an alien shoot, opposed them on national grounds, and were not susceptible to religious influence of any kind, while the Orthodox community detested them for obvious reasons.

This situation changed somewhat after the establishment of the state. The Jews were now the majority and the dozens of missionary organizations, most of which remained in the country, were now faced with a sovereign Jewish community whose character was changed by the influx of hundreds of thousands of immigrants, many of them financially and socially deprived, on a scale unknown under the Mandate. On the other hand, the number of Christians and Muslims diminished significantly, and there was clear pressure from local clerics to deflect the main focus of missionary effort to the Jewish community. In the political sphere as well, there were changes that seemed to offer the potential for action. One major country recognized the State of Israel on the explicit condition that nothing be done to alter the status of their Christian institutions in Israel, which already enjoyed considerable privileges. Other countries extended more or less direct diplomatic protection to their religious institutions in the Holy Land. What is more, the establishment of Israel and the return of hundreds of thousands of Jews to their homeland provided theological validation for a certain type of missionary organization. These groups (Adventists, Pentacostalists, the Church of God, and associations of converts, mostly American) regarded the establishment of a Jewish state as fulfillment of biblical prophesies, auguring the Second Coming of Christ. They were convinced that the Jews would now convert to Christianity and acknowledge Jesus as their Messiah on the Judgment Day. As far as they were concerned, the establishment of a Jewish state was a sign of the times, indicating that the conversion of the Jews was imminent and requiring them to make every effort to expedite it.

Although missionary activity gathered momentum after 1948 for all the reasons noted above, and although Israel's religious establishment considered every priest or clergyman to be a potential missionary among the Jews, not all of them actually engaged in missionary activity. The exception were those clerics who were active among the local Arab and Christian communities—Greek Catholics, Greek Orthodox, Marronites, Armenians, Copts, and Episcopalians. Nor did the custodians of the Holy Places engage in this activity. Missionary work was confined, therefore, to two groups. The first consisted of Catholic priests who sometimes acted on an individual basis, but usually through schools, charitable bodies, medical associations, and hostels, mostly in towns with a largely Jewish population, such as Jerusalem, Jaffa, Ramla, Haifa, Acre, and Tiberias. The second group was composed of Protestants who were not affiliated to communities in Israel, whose activity was mostly missionary oriented, and who were also active in Arab villages.[2] There was a significant difference between the two groups. The Protestants publicized their activities widely in order to recruit funds abroad, and they were usually open in their efforts (the most forthright among them were the Baptists, who even attacked the religious establishment in Israel). They won considerable attention in 1962 when they established the village of *Nes Amim*, which was settled by Christians from abroad.[3]

Catholics, on the other hand, were officially instructed to refrain from convincing Jews to convert except by example. This explains why the Israeli authorities described the methods employed by Catholic institutions "in the area of *shemad* (forced conversion)" as "decent compared to those of Protestants."[4] The General Security Service, investigating the subject in the early 1960s, concluded that Catholic missionaries did not pose a threat to Jews in Israel.[5] Paradoxically enough, the Catholic Church, which constituted a significant challenge to Israel's foreign policy, posed a lesser internal threat than did the Protestants, who were usually more sympathetic to Israel's stand. It should be noted, however, that there were apparently differences of opinion among the Protestant missionary organizations after the establishment of Israel. Some of them were convinced that their prospects for success would be nil in the new Jewish state and recommended the transfer of activities to Jordan. Another apparently dominant group was not willing to concede.[6] Be that as it may, the official estimate in Israel in 1952 was that there were 200 active Catholic missionaries (out of the 700 or so individuals attached to Catholic monasteries) and a similar number of Protestants, and this out of a total of about 1,200 priests, monks, and nuns residing in Israel at the time.[7]

Missionary activity was conducted in four areas. The first of these was education. The Christian educational network shrank after the expulsion and flight of more than half a million Palestinians in 1948, some of them Christians. Under the British Mandate there had been 182 Christian schools in the country, with some 30,000 pupils in all.[8] By the early 1950s it was estimated that only fifty elementary and secondary schools remained, with 9,000 pupils, including some 1,500 Jews (the ratio remained the same). Some 500 of these were studying in boarding schools.[9] Most of the mission schools, about 25, were Catholic, with about 6,500 pupils (5,000 of them at the elementary level), 8 percent of them Jews. Prominent among them were the St. Joseph School in Jerusalem and two secondary schools in Jaffa run by the Christian Brothers and the Sisters of St. Joseph, with 250 students in all, almost all of them Jewish. There were also schools in Ramla and Acre and small institutions run by nuns. The Protestants maintained four schools, including one in Jaffa that was affiliated to the Scottish Church and one (Finnish Lutheran) in Jerusalem.[10] Most of the Jewish children in those schools were new immigrants, but some were Israel-born, mainly from the poorer sectors. What drew Jewish families to those schools? It was assumed at the time that there were several reasons: social climbing, a sincere desire to assimilate, or the superior physical conditions compared with those in Jewish schools, where children often studied in two shifts. The Christian school system also offered significant economic support to the families of its pupils. In addition to exempting them from payment of school fees, they distributed clothing and food from customs-free consignments from abroad, schools were open until the late afternoon, permitting mothers to work, and several hundred children were boarders. And finally, the pupils became fluent in English and French and thus were able to continue their studies abroad.

Some missionary activity was conducted by means of welfare payment and inexpensive medical treatment, which was a strong inducement and had been exploited as such since the turn of the century.[11] Although the number of church hospitals was considerably lower in 1948 than in the Mandate period, there were Catholic medical institutions in Jaffa, Jerusalem, and Haifa and Protestant institutions in Nazareth, Tiberias, and Jaffa. Both Catholic and Protestant organizations also gave out clothing and food collected by their supporters abroad, which were exempt from customs duty. These articles were distributed to the needy, according to a Ministry of Religious Affairs report, by "luxurious vehicles." Allocating housing was also a form of missionary activity. The mass immigration had resulted in a severe housing shortage, and several hundred thousand immigrants were living in transit camps—*ma'abarot*. Christian institutions owned buildings that had served until 1948 as hostels for pilgrims, as well as other real estate, which enabled them to offer reasonable housing conditions. Among those who exploited this opportunity, according to Ministry of Religious Affairs reports, were certain individuals who had come under the suspicion of the Israeli security authorities such as deserters, illegal immigrants, and aliens suspected of being former Nazis.

Missionary activity was also conducted directly through oral and written propaganda and through the dissemination of copies of the New Testament. In the early 1960s, six Christian bodies were thought to be engaged in such projects.[12] Israeli officials regarded some of their modes of action as particularly offensive due to the sophisticated tactics they employed. For example, the authorities were greatly concerned by the efforts of Protestant missionaries who were known to be sympathetic toward Israel and Zionism and whose methods were apt to be misleading. For example, they linked the Jewish festival of Hanukkah to Christmas, instituted prayers for the welfare of Israel's president, included in their prayer services *Hatikva* (the Israeli national anthem) and Christmas hymns in Hebrew translation, named at least one of their institutions Shomrei Shabbat (Observers of Sabbath), and produced a publication called *The Voice of Zion* with a blue-and-white border and a Shield of David at the top. The officials were also troubled by the attempts of missionary groups to reestablish contact with Holocaust survivors who had spent the war in church institutions in Europe and to help young candidates for conscription leave the country. For obvious reasons, the Israelis were less concerned about activities aimed at facilitating the emigration of converts to Christianity, Christians who were finding it difficult to adjust to life in Israel, and partners in mixed marriages. According to a Ministry of Religious Affairs report, this activity "is . . . in line with our own interest to be rid of them. . . . It would be better if they left the country."[13]

How effective was all this activity? It is very difficult, for obvious reasons, to obtain precise data beyond the number of pupils in Christian schools. The organizations never published figures and still deny access to their documents on this subject. The files now open for perusal in the State Archives give only rough estimates, partly because official reports of religious conversion were not compulsory. Moreover, according to Ministry of the Interior regulations, conversion of Jews was only recorded when they joined one of the two recognized churches (under legislation dating back to the Mandate period), the Catholic or the Orthodox. Data available to the Ministry's district commissioners in the early 1960s reveal that only a few dozen conversions had been recorded since 1948, although it is feasible that the number was actually greater. The Ministry of Religious Affairs believed that the number of conversions was in the thousands, but noted that many of those who converted officially had done so in order to facilitate their emigration and consequently, had left the country. This estimate included partners in mixed marriages, a number of whom also left the country.[14] The Foreign Ministry's estimates were somewhere in between. In 1967 the Ministry explained to the heads of Israeli diplomatic missions that there were 600 Jewish converts to Christianity in the country, and that, since 1948, "200 Jews at most, including children" had converted.[15]

It is not surprising, therefore, that even the Ministry of Religious Affairs, which naturally tended to a gloomy view of the situation, claimed in a 1963 internal (unpublished) report on the effectiveness of missionary activity that "one should not speak of mass conversion in Israel, although many hundreds of Jewish children in Christian institutions are in danger."[16] Three years later, in a frank discussion with the senior Foreign Ministry official dealing with the churches in Israel, the director-general of the Ministry of Religious Affairs, Kalman Kahana, said that he did not attribute great importance to the mission "because it has not succeeded in Israel. [He] dismissed its successes by saying 'What does it matter if 1,000 children attend mission schools?'"[17] In correspondence with other government bodies, the Ministry of Religious Affairs concealed the fact—reported to the government in March 1963—that only eleven of these children had converted to Christianity.[18] A report from the prime minister's legal adviser, to the effect that close to three-quarters of the Jewish children who attended Christian schools were enrolled in Catholic institutions "where there is no indoctrination and the Jewish pupils do not participate in religious lessons," was never distributed.[19] This explains why the prime minister, Levi Eshkol, who replaced Ben-Gurion, declared in early 1964: "There is no need to be so concerned for the Judaism of a Jewish child growing up in the atmosphere of Eretz Israel even if he attends a foreign school."[20] It was an unarguable fact that at that time only 0.2 percent of the half million Jewish pupils were attending Christian schools.[21]

Tackling the Missions

What were the implications of the various Israeli estimates? How did the government react? Which organizations and officials were involved? How did Israel's attitude toward missionary activity accord with its policy on relations with the Christian world? The newly opened archival files enable us to cast light for the first time on the characteristic features of domestic political activity and on a foreign relations issue that was acknowledged by Israel's leaders to be of considerable importance.

The Israeli authorities were first required to decide how to face Christian missionary activity shortly after independence was proclaimed, as a result of pressure from several directions. From August 1948 on, the Foreign Ministry constantly received official requests from Christian organizations and personalities all over the world for a declaration of principles and practice on this issue.[22] The heads of the Catholic Church and prominent Protestant clerics were particularly sensitive to what they regarded as obstruction of the legitimate activity of their institutions in Israel, and they made their position clear on a number of occasions to Israeli representatives. It was emphasized (particularly by Catholics) that the degree to which their representatives were permitted freedom of action would help determine their policy toward the new state. Several countries also expressed their concern, particularly France and Italy, which raised the subject a number of times in diplomatic talks. Concurrently, missionary associations in Israel itself brought pressure to bear to expand their activity with Israel's permission.[23] The question of how to deal with Christian schools was of obvious concern to the Israeli Ministry of Education, which was confronted by demands for recognition and support by some of these institutions and was obliged to give official replies that, by their very nature, involved political considerations.[24] Frequent requests by Christian clergy abroad for permission to enter Israel for open or covert missionary purposes were an additional source of pressure.[25] And finally, the question of immigration permits for mixed Christian-Jewish couples created problems that were related, however indirectly, to the question of missionary activity.[26]

The internal discussions around these issues within the Israeli establishment highlighted an often-trenchant debate on political and value issues. On the one hand, it was argued, mainly by certain Foreign Ministry officials, that Israel must grant freedom of religion and worship and maintain its character as a non-theocratic state, in line with the basic principles set out in the Declaration of Independence. This was particularly important because ecclesiastical bodies throughout the world were attacking Israel, for reasons not unrelated to the question of Jerusalem's future.[27] According to this approach, Israel should take care not to impose legal and administrative restrictions on the activities of the mission. As the Ministry's director-general pointed out, "Any interference with the activities of the missionary associations will assuredly be interpreted abroad as interference with freedom of religion as understood in the enlightened world. No country in the world restricts missionary activity, if we exclude those known as 'people's democracies,' including the People's Republic of China. Any antimissionary initiative on the part of the Israeli government will have shocking repercussions on the good name of the state."[28] In late 1953, Sharett cited additional reasons for pursuing this policy:

> Our brethren all over the world have dealings with the Catholic Church. . . . When we clash with the Church it mobilizes all its forces on radio and in the press for vicious propaganda against the State of Israel and proclaims anti-Jewish slogans, and when that happens the Jews raise an outcry. This relates not only to the Catholic Church. The mission in Israel is partly connected to the Protestant Church. We are on friendly terms with the Presbyterian and Scottish churches, who made very positive statements about our endeavors. And that was at a time when we were embroiled in a dispute with the British authorities. Even before that happened, they asked us: if a Jewish state comes into being, will you allow us to engage in missionary activity? There are a great number of progressive forces that are emphatically opposed to proselytizing and to conversion. But they will not take a positive view of an official Israeli ban on missionary activity."[29]

Levi Eshkol, when prime minister, was concerned at the prospect that "Heaven forbid, foreigners might come and conspire against our educational efforts in the Diaspora on the pretext that we are not tolerant of foreign education. We are losing more than we gain."[30]

It should be pointed out that those who supported this approach were uneasy at the thought of open missionary activity in Israel. They warned, however, against an open clash with the churches and recommended a circuitous counterstrategy—solution of the problems of social deprivation so that vulnerable sector of the population would no longer be attracted by missionary inducements. They also emphasized how limited were the successes of the mission, in order to justify their views.

The second approach was mainly upheld by Ministry of Religious Affairs officials, diplomats, other senior officials, and politicians, most of them from religious parties. It was based on the argument that the State of Israel had been established in order to preserve the Jewish people and Jewish values, against which the mission's activities were directed.[31] According to this outlook, the age-old tradition of persecution of Jews by the mission justified total restriction of its activities in Israel, however limited their scope. A draft briefing from the Ministry of Religious Affairs to the Israeli embassy in Rome, dated November 1950, stated, "On the one hand, Israel—after the departure of most of its Arab population—is no longer a suitable target for missionary activities, and on the other hand, the Israeli government is anxious for these activities to be curtailed insofar as possible and transferred to the neighboring Arab countries."[32] In a conversation with a senior Protestant clergyman from the United States in early 1953, the minister of religious affairs adviser on Christian affairs did not hesitate (in most undiplomatic fashion) to recommend that missionary organizations in Israel "suspend their activities for 100 years." "Memories of our contacts with the Christian world over two millennia," he explained, "are still fresh in our minds and, as you know, are in no way likely to evoke our respect, sympathy, or trust in the bearers of Christianity. The crucifix, which is so precious a symbol to the Christian masses and so significant even for the secular historian of Western culture, is for the Jews a symbol that arouses deeply emotional, almost subconscious pictures of horror and persecution, of intolerance and pogroms, of deliberate falsehood and false piety. Let the Jews forget! Leave them alone."[33]

Herzog was even blunter when he wrote in an internal memo in 1952: "How can the torture inflicted on the soul of the nation throughout its exile by the mission . . . be totally forgotten now that national sovereignty has been renewed? Is it [worthy] . . . to permit freedom to all those who wish . . . to undermine the basis of our spiritual and national existence? Are we black Africa?"[34] And a senior official of the Foreign Ministry asserted in an internal memo in 1952, "We should not forget that the great part of our people are devoted with all their heart and soul to tradition, to the Jewish outlook and to Jewish moral values. The moment we cooperate in any way with the Vatican and assist the Catholic world and permit freedom of action in our country, even with regard to Jews who have converted to Christianity, we are opening the gates of Jewish homes all over the world to the missionaries, who will preach to our brethren in the Diaspora and say: we are collaborating with Israel, there are Catholic Jews in Israel, what is permissible in Israel is permissible for you as well, it will be to your advantage and is no betrayal of Israel, and the road to assimilation will then be complete and open through 1,000 gateways and doors."[35] A member of the Knesset Education Committee said that as far as he was concerned, sending Jewish pupils to mission school was like "sacrificing children to Moloch."[36]

The advocates of this approach objected to the demand for caution in dealing with missionary activity and refused to differentiate between Catholic and Protestant activity in this area. Their views were formulated in an internal Ministry of Religious Affairs document at the end of January 1953: "Circumstances have taught us that every national religious community preserves its traditional-spiritual values. The Catholic nations (Italy, Spain, Latin America) provide us with an instructive example of intolerance toward Protestants. . . . On the other hand, the Protestant countries resist the infiltration of Catholicism. . . . It is the right of our renascent people to plan their own national, spiritual, and cultural future according to their own tradition and views without foreign intervention. While the tribes of Israel are gathering from the four corners of the globe and our country is preoccupied with solution of urgent material problems, we must not permit foreign elements to gain a firm foothold that will hamper the natural development of our culture. When we have a uniform language and culture, and most of our people have employment and a roof over their heads, then we can withstand any foreign influence and permit our people freely to face the spiritual test with other cultures."[37] However limited the scope of religious conversion in Israel's early years, it was perceived as a threat, justifying almost any means to eradicate it.

Accordingly, the program proposed by the religious establishment included banning the admission of missionaries into Israel; refusal to extend the right of residence of those already living there; banning the employment of Jewish teachers in Christian schools, rendering it compulsory for Jewish children to attend Jewish schools; banning use of the Hebrew language in broadcast of Christian religious services or the use of Hebrew headings and symbols that could prove misleading, plus a range of restrictions on the freedom of action of the mission.[38] This was in addition to the restrictions aimed at circumscribing Church activities in Israel. In late 1952, Shaul Colbi, who was in charge of Church affairs at the Ministry of Religious Affairs, explained the refusal to allocate building material to Christian institutions by saying that "there are enough Christian buildings and institutions in Israel and, under the circumstances created after the establishment of the state, even the existing ones are mostly superfluous."[39] In April 1950, the first director-general of the Foreign Ministry, Eytan, representing the opposite viewpoint, wrote to Ginosar, the Israeli minister in Italy:

> [In my opinion] Christian schools should be permitted full freedom of action and in any event no less than under the Mandate. But I know from experience that my views are not acceptable to the Ministry of Religious Affairs and the Ministry of Education and I am almost certain that public opinion is not in general on my side. As you know, several deeply rooted prejudices still endure in Israel against Christians and their institutions, prejudices brought here from the Diaspora. To judge by the press and conversations I have had on

this subject, public opinion would like to see Christian schools closed even if, in some cases, this will deprive children in certain neighborhoods and towns of education.[40]

The Acid Test of Freedom of Religion

The debate between these two polar approaches was acrimonious at times, but, for obvious political reasons, was mostly waged in private and was not leaked to the press. This was because it related to sensitive foreign policy issues and particularly because it resulted, in practice, in the pursuance of a policy that often contravened the official commitment to freedom of religion. The archival documents illuminate a hitherto unknown aspect of Israel's action against the natural missionary tendencies and orientation of most of the Christian groups active in Israel up to the Six Days' War. The two conflicting approaches were aired in the course of discussion of the demand for a ban on the activities of Christian missionaries.

The ban was requested by the Ministry of Religious Affairs (as well as the Ministry of Welfare, under Rabbi Yehuda Leib Levin) and the religious parties in light of missionary activity among new immigrants, but the issue was not discussed at government level until the end of 1951.[41] This was mainly because Israel was engaged in a struggle at the United Nations on the Jerusalem question, which, as Herzog put it, "ruled out any effective action to put an end to the despicable attempt of the mission to build itself up at the expense of the physical and emotional ruin rife among some of our people."[42] At the beginning of that year, the Ministry of Religious Affairs tried to introduce explicit regulations that would deny entry to missionaries, but this attempt came to nothing because of emphatic Foreign Ministry objections on political grounds.[43] The Ministry of Welfare, for its part, refused to accept this stalemate and exploited another problem relating to missionary activity in order to raise this basic and constitutional matter in the cabinet. The heads of the Ministry were particularly concerned by the requests of twelve Christian welfare bodies (the most prominent among them the Catholic Near East Welfare Association) for recognition as charitable organizations, in order to gain exemptions from payment of customs duty for their baggage.[44] Convinced that their intention was "to procure souls for Christianity," Rabbi Levin, on his own initiative and in defiance of the Foreign Ministry's stand,[45] revoked all these exemptions. In the letter to the cabinet secretary explaining this step, he claimed that "after fighting for generations with the Christian Church and its aim to convert us, and going through fire and water to sanctify the Name, and having gained our sovereignty, it is our duty not to help its emissaries in Israel to bring Jews under the wing of Christianity."[46]

This viewpoint was anathema not only to the foreign minister but also to the minister of finance, Eliezer Kaplan, although his calculations were political rather than economic. He informed the minister of welfare accordingly that if Rabbi Levin was unable, "for reasons clear to all of us, to sign a document which will grant the missionary associations exemption from customs, we have other people who are able and willing to do so."[47] It is noteworthy that legal experts thought at the time that if the plaintiffs appealed to the High Court of Justice, it would be very difficult to persuade the court that the move had been justified. The government decided therefore in late November 1951 to set up a committee, composed of representatives of the Ministries of Religious Affairs, Foreign Affairs, Education, and Justice, "to examine the activities of the missionaries in Israel and their results" and to submit its recommendations.[48] Until such recommendations were received, the government decided to maintain the status quo and continue to grant customs exemptions to missionary associations.

The committee's recommendations, submitted three months later, represented a clear defeat for the Ministries of Religious Affairs and Welfare. The committee reported that only about 600 children were attending Christian schools. Moreover, it had uncovered no evidence that missionary efforts had been crowned with success or had led to "even one conversion." Above all, the committee had received no complaints to the effect that the missionaries were employing coercive measures or other illegal means. "The reverse is true: it transpires that some of these missionaries are giving substantial help to immigrants in transit camps and to the poorer sectors of the population." Most of the committee members agreed that the "freedom of religion" guaranteed in Israel's Declaration of Independence and in the basic agenda of two governments "also entails freedom to change one's religion, and as long as there is no coercion involved in accepting or changing one's religion, not only will the government and the state, in line with its proclaimed policy, refrain from interfering, but they must permit religious education and preaching and other means of exerting influence within the framework of the law." The majority also determined that any initiative for legislation banning missionary activity would not only run counter to the government's proclaimed policy, but was also liable "to embarrass Israel in the sphere of foreign relations."[49] In positive terms, the government accepted the recommendation that the authorities must consider any request submitted by missionaries "on its merits" and in accordance with the law. Specifically, any request for exemption from customs was to be considered if the applicant was "an educational or cultural institution" in the legal definition of the term, and if this was the case, the request should not be denied merely because the applicant was a missionary. This spelled the end of the attempt to introduce constitutional amendments, which would ban or significantly restrict missionary activity.[50] The cabinet never discussed these recommendations. In this case as in others, failure to make a decision meant that the decision was negative.

The opponents of this implied decision now joined forces with other elements in efforts to put an end to missionary activity. Eighteen months later, two new draft laws were brought before the cabinet. The first was submitted by a special subcommittee on missionary activity (set up at the suggestion of the Orthodox Agudat Israel Party in May 1953), with participants from the Ministry of Education and the Ministry of the Interior. This committee decided on 2 February 1954 to recommend drafting a law banning material incentives for conversion; taking legal action against parents who sent their children to mission school thereby contravening the Compulsory Education Law, which did not recognize mission schools; and requiring prospective converts to announce their intentions in the press.[51] The committee passed these recommendations, although the foreign minister had cautioned against making them public because of the anticipated repercussions in the Catholic world. After being approached by the French embassy in Israel, the Israeli ambassador in Paris, Tsur, in a breach of diplomatic procedure, appealed directly to the prime minister in early February. He pointed out to Ben-Gurion that any attempt to undermine the cultural and religious freedom of action of Catholic institutions— of which France considered itself the protector—was liable to be interpreted "as a blow to France's vital interests." Others feared that restriction of the freedom of Catholic schools could lead to similar action against Jewish institutions and schools in Catholic countries, particularly in Latin America.[52] Avraham Harman, an experienced diplomat who became Israel's ambassador in the United States, described the proposal as "dynamite," the result of the deliberate inflation of the mission threat by the religious parliamentary opposition in the Knesset.[53]

These arguments were apparently not considered persuasive by the committee of the Knesset or by the Ministerial Committee on Internal Affairs and Services, which decided a day later to submit a draft proposal to the cabinet, calling for a ban on material inducements to conversion or the promise of such inducements.[54] The Ministry of Religious Affairs even tried to submit a draft law requiring prior announcement of any proposed conversion, thereby expanding the regulations that had prevailed under the British Mandate.[55] All these proposals were shelved and did not reach the Knesset plenum.

The subject was discussed at a cabinet meeting on 21 February 1954. The legal arguments against the law pointed out how difficult it would be to prove that, by feeding the hungry or developing social welfare, Christians were trying to encourage conversion. In other words, the law would not be able to achieve its central objective. Dov Joseph, minister for development, who was in favor of dismissing Jewish converts from the Jewish Agency and from government service, was afraid that an antimissionary law would create the impression abroad that the Israeli government was incapable of persuading Jews to retain their religion: "What kind of Israel is this?" Peretz Bernstein, minister for commerce and industry, warned against launching a war on Catholicism and advised caution, since "whoever takes a bite out of the pope dies of it." Defense Minister Pinhas Lavon recommended that the psychological aspects of the problem be ignored and that the government consider the logic of a situation in which "in a community of one and a half million, there are 400 converts." Legislation against this minor phenomenon, he said, "which has had nothing but psychological impact . . . will revive the question of the Holy Places and the internationalization of Jerusalem."

The advocates of legislation included ministers from secular parties. Prominent among them was Zalman Aranne, then minister without portfolio, who argued fervently that "Jewish converts are the fifth column within the Jewish people, the enemies of Israel." He was particularly infuriated at the "brazen audacity of many missionaries who have put the country under attack, not because the true God has been revealed for the second time but because there is a crisis here and a tendency to emigrate and they have pounced in the knowledge that now is the time to act." The minister of religious affairs, Moshe Shapira, was naturally in favor of the law, and he cautioned against "a flood of missionaries and a flood of conversions." The law "may rouse a reaction in the non-Jewish world. But there will be a very positive response within the Jewish people." And Benzion Dinur, minister of education, declared decisively that Christianity was "the enemy" and that he was in favor of the law. Political considerations finally tipped the balance, and the government decided to postpone "for the time being the decision on legislation pertaining to the mission problem." The motive underlying the negative aspect of Israel's strategy vis-à-vis the mission was later explained by Sharett to one of the leaders of the National Religious Party. "We are not overendowed with friends on the foreign front, and we should avoid leaving room for negative comment on so delicate and complex a matter as the status of Christianity in our country."[56] Israeli legations overseas were asked to reassure anyone who approached them with queries and to deny any intention to pass an antimissionary law.[57] There is no doubt that the law was shelved for some time due partly to Ben-Gurion's continuous refusal to approve antimissionary legislation. It comes as no surprise, therefore, to read a speech delivered by Rabbi Levin at the beginning of 1959 in a Knesset debate on the prime minister's office budget, in which he noted with regret that *Agudat Israel's* demand that missionary activity be banned had "come up against a blank wall."[58]

The fact that Mapai was dependent on the religious parties in order to maintain a coalition explains why the subject was raised again under Ben-Gurion's successor, Levi Eshkol. The draft bill submitted to Eshkol in the last few months of 1962 had been composed by the Knesset Committee on Internal Affairs and focused on one aspect of missionary activity.[59] According to the proposal, a minor could not be converted, nor would his or her conversion be valid unless it was carried out with the approval of both parents or a guardian, and after a court had issued an order permitting the conversion for the benefit of the minor. The draft law also stipulated that a minor could not be converted except to the religion of one or both parents. The aim was to prevent parents of a minor from converting the child without taking his welfare into consideration and without the permission of the other parent. The main objective was indubitably to reduce the effectiveness of missionary activity aimed at young children, and, not unexpectedly, the Foreign Ministry objected "on principle."[60] Levi Eshkol was apparently in favor of the law, and it was passed at a cabinet meeting on 19 May 1964.[61] The same meeting also approved a proposal to ban direct pressure on a minor to convert, the word *shidul* (pressuring, enticing) indicating that "improper" methods had been used. All the ministers from Mapai, Mapam, Ahdut ha-Avoda, and the National Religious Party supported both proposals "essentially without a debate."[62] The law was ratified in 1965.[63]

In the absence of material on the subject, it is difficult to estimate why the ministers were so ready to approve antimissionary legislation. It seems feasible that Foreign Ministry hesitations were allayed by the fact that the focus on minors made it easier to defend the law on humanitarian grounds. The Foreign Ministry, however, was behind the prime minister's rejection, two years later, of the chief rabbi's appeal for legislation against Christian missionary activity "in light of the general principle of freedom of belief, restriction of the religious propaganda conducted by each and every religion to its own community, and prevention of unjustified persuasion and solicitation."[64] Foreign Minister Abba Eban was strongly opposed to such legislation and told the minister of justice that it would have a negative impact on Israel's foreign relations.[65] The government's legal adviser asserted that the law would violate the principles of freedom of conscience and free speech in Israel.[66] These considerations won the day, and the legislation was not implemented that year.

Christian Education in a Jewish State

The other important issue in the debate on the mission was that of Christian education. The rights of Christian educational institutions in Israel were based on treaties dating back to the period of Ottoman rule. The British Mandate authorities had tried to curtail their activities, but in the end they retained the procedure laid down in Clause 16 of the Mandate. According to this procedure, these institutions did not require special permits, and they, in their turn, refused to accept the supervision of the Mandatory authorities. The schools did not submit financial reports to the authorities, and the latter had no say in the choice of teachers and the curricula. They collaborated with the authorities only on medical matters. In order to understand Israeli policy in this respect, it is necessary first to examine the legal background that enabled the state to impose restrictions on these schools. This situation was grounded on three laws—the 1933 Mandatory Education Order, the 1949 Compulsory Education Law, and the State Education Law of 1953—and on ordinances passed under these laws.[67] The Mandatory Education Order, which was not revoked during the first years of statehood, stipulated registration of all schools and official supervision of hygiene, discipline, morals, and so forth. It also introduced a system of registering teachers. The 1949 Compulsory Education Law granted the state wider scope for action. It specified that "parents of a child or adolescent of compulsory schooling age who has not yet completed his or her elementary education are obliged to ensure that the child or adolescent studies in regular manner in a recognized educational institution."

The law imposed punitive sanctions on parents who failed to do so. This meant that Israeli parents were not fulfilling their obligations under the law unless they sent their children to a "recognized educational institution." The definition of such institutions was explicit: "a. any official educational institution; b. any other educational institution which the minister declares, in a proclamation in the official government gazette, *Reshumot*, to be a recognized educational institution." The 1953 law clarified the conditions such a school must fulfill in order to win recognition. These included Ministry of Education approval of the syllabus, and educational standards of the teaching staff commensurate with the general standards prevailing in recognized Israeli schools and with the aims of state education. These aims were defined as "basing state elementary education on the values of Israeli culture and scientific achievement, and on love of the country and of the Jewish people." The objective of all these laws was to establish a network of official and recognized schools and thereby to supervise the implementation of compulsory education and the content and standard of that education. The situation in church schools in this period was significantly at odds with this legal ruling. Not one of the forty-six Christian schools was a "recognized institution," and the parents of more than 10,000 children were therefore daily breaking the law, although the authorities made no effort to bring them to justice. Moreover, a considerable proportion of those "unrecognized schools" (fourteen in all) received subsidies from the Ministry of Education and were under its supervision.

This situation was largely the outcome of a compromise between the two prevailing approaches toward Christian schools: the demand for equal treatment, recognition, and supervision for all schools irrespective of religious orientation, versus the demand for scrupulous compliance with the law, the implication of which was the elimination or considerable reduction of Christian schools. This compromise stemmed from the fact that to accept either approach in toto would have confronted the Israeli authorities with fundamental problems in those early years. To enforce the educational laws would have been a problematic move for several reasons. First, there was no law banning the existence of unrecognized schools; second, unrecognized schools were not required to ask for recognition. Third, the State of Israel had accepted the existence of various types of *heder* (religious elementary schools) of the ultra-orthodox community, which, for its part, did not recognize the State of Israel. What is more, in the early 1960s the Ministry of Education was not optimistic as to the prospects for successful enforcement. It was thought at the time that prosecution of parents who sent children to mission schools would encompass only a few dozen cases.[68] That being so, the schools themselves would be ready to pay the necessary fines. If, on the other hand, there were hundreds of cases, two particularly problematic scenarios could ensue. The school might accept the Ministry of Education demands in full—including the clause defining the "aims of state education"—while retaining its missionary orientation. This would oblige the Ministry to recognize the school, thereby enabling it to increase enrollment. Such recognition would also imply official sanction for the enrollment of Jewish children in Christian schools.

This possibility was ruled out categorically not only by the religious establishment but also by the more liberal element, who refused to force the

Teacher and student in a Roman Catholic school attached to the new church at the Arab village of Rami in the Galilee, November 10, 1962. *Courtesy of the National Photo Collection of the Israel Government Press Office, Prime Minister's Office. Photo D532–002.*

state to cross what they saw as a social and religious Rubicon.[69] This explains why official diplomatic appeals to the Foreign Ministry in 1966 to grant official recognition to French educational institutions in Israel were rejected despite the positive political impact such recognition could have had. "We have no doubt," wrote a Ministry of Religious Affairs official in an internal memorandum "that granting recognition to the French schools would make them '*kosher*' in the eyes of the Jewish public and increase the number of pupils attending them."[70] On the other hand, if the state had been urged to guarantee that Christian schools did not win recognition, it would have been obliged to impose more stringent conditions, "to harass the schools and to devise formal pretexts for withholding recognition." Such action would have had a damaging impact on Israel's foreign relations,[71] particularly since a considerable proportion of the Catholic institutions, where the bulk of the Jewish pupils were enrolled, were under the auspices of the French consulate and embassy and their freedom of action was officially guaranteed under a 1949 understanding between Israel and France.[72]

It was decided to leave the mission schools to their own devices.[73] The operative solution was formulated in late 1967 by the minister of education: "Out of consideration for the rights of non-Jewish citizens of the state, the Ministry has not refused to supervise the private schools of the Christian communities, but will exercise such supervision only with regard to schools without Jewish pupils."[74] At the same time, it is clear why this casuistic approach could not be interpreted as granting freedom to Christian schools to continue their activities without interference and impediment. Prime Minister Levi Eshkol, was undoubtedly sincere when he wrote to the chief rabbi of Great Britain in 1964 that "we share your views and regret every soul that falls into the net of the mission."[75] Faced with this complex situation, it is not surprising that the minister of education, Aranne, a nonbeliever, came to the conclusion that a solution was required, namely, "establishment of a special apparatus equipped with wide-ranging instruments that will act systematically to persuade parents to remove their children from mission schools."[76] As will be shown below, such an apparatus existed in Israel from its early years.

State Bureaucracy vs. the Church

The practical decision not to initiate antimissionary legislation and not to enforce the law in Christian schools was not the whole story. One of the most important and effective means of combating the mission was through bureaucratic control of the entry into Israel of Christian clerics, (some of whom had left during the 1948 War in the wake of the expulsion or flight of many members of their flock.) They were required to submit requests for entry permits to the Ministry of Religious Affairs, in accordance with official procedure. The Ministry's consistent opposition to missionary activity provided the main motive for the official policy, which greatly reduced their entry and essentially halted it.[77] The Ministry conducted a selective process among applicants for entry permits and granted them in very few cases, particularly at the time when the diplomatic battle over Jerusalem was at its height.[78] At the same time, it was careful not to contravene the law "and not to arouse suspicion that it was practicing discrimination on religious sectarian grounds."[79] The Ministry also successfully wielded its authority to advise on applications for the establishment of new missionary associations in Israel. In early December 1950, for example, it vetoed a request from the Christian Brothers Association, on the pretext that "missionary activity on the part of this association would lead to grave friction, clashes and scandals between members of the association and non-Christian communities, thereby disrupting the public order."[80] The Ministry did its best to curtail the freedom of movement of those missionaries already living in Israel. In mid-1952 it recommended to the Ministry of Transport that it turn down the application of a representative of the Scottish Church for an import license for a private car on the grounds that "he has no need of it," adding that "because of the new petrol rationing, there is no possibility of increasing the number of motor vehicles in Israel."[81] It should be noted that until 1951, none of these decisions were ever discussed beyond the Ministry of Religious Affairs, which took full advantage of its wide-ranging powers, which were resented by the Foreign Ministry. As pointed out at the time by the director-general of the Ministry of Immigration, which issued the entry permits, there was "a yawning chasm" between the outlooks of the two ministries.[82]

The constant bickering between these two bodies on the missionary question is frequently reflected in the State Archives documents. Herzog, then head of the Christian Communities Department of the Ministry of Religious Affairs, explained the views of his Ministry to a senior Foreign Ministry official in January 1951. "Where is it written or stated that the Israel government is obliged to open its gates to any missionary who chooses to return here. Jews who seek to enter Christian countries in order to convert Christians to Judaism will not enjoy the concessions, which they apparently want us to grant to Christian missionaries. About a year ago, the Netherlands minister submitted to the minister for religious affairs a series of queries about the attitude of the Israel government toward missionary activity. The minister promised to fulfill this request if the Dutch diplomat showed him an official announcement from the Dutch government that it had no objections to similar activities on the part of Jews among Christian citizens of the Netherlands or to the entry of Jewish emissaries for similar purposes. The Netherlands minister never came back. It is the custom throughout the world to show consideration for the unique spiritual features of each nation in light of its history." Herzog, who was born in Dublin, said he had "never heard that the Irish in New York are required to explain why Protestants in Ireland do not enjoy the same social conditions and ease as in Britain. . . . The attitude of Jews towards missionaries is inspired by matters buried deep in the Jewish soul and in the history of the Jews. . . . We will settle our controversial issues among ourselves in light of our own sentiments and not under sanctimonious pressure from others."[83]

As a result of this protracted dispute, the Ministry of Immigration received conflicting evaluations from different sources. Clear-cut procedures were required, and these were introduced in mid-February 1951 after discussions between the representatives of the relevant ministries and a representative of the Ministry of Education (which was called on from time to time to grant entry visas to Christian teachers) and the prime minister's adviser on Arab affairs. The conclusion was that, in principle, the state could not object to the entry of monks, nuns, and clerics who were connected to monasteries or other Christian institutions. At the same time, in cases of "improper missionary interference" it was decided to call the attention of the relevant diplomatic legations and church heads, and in cases of protracted missionary activity "it will be possible to indicate that the presence in Israel of this particular individual is undesirable." According to the summarizing report, "in due course" Israel would have to make public its objections to missionary activity within its borders, but "the time is not yet ripe for such an announcement" or for raising the question in the Knesset. Foreign Ministry officials were asked to explain these objections discreetly and "at a suitable opportunity" to foreign diplomats. An interministerial body was established to deal with every application for visas by missionaries.[84] Decisions on the admission of Arab monks and clerics were left exclusively to the security authorities. The Foreign Ministry believed that these recommendations ruled out future antimissionary legislation and that the establishment of this committee marked the end of the monopoly on this issue held by the Ministry of Religious Affairs. With hindsight, however, it is apparent that the committee not only failed to thwart the Ministry's consistent policy but even legitimized it, since in its recommendations, which laid the basis for bureaucratic action for years to come, it declared that missionary activity was undesirable to the Israel government.

The general attitude was clearly reflected in the administrative decisions taken in September 1952, to the effect that after the UN Assembly meeting and the scheduled transfer of the Foreign Ministry to Jerusalem, efforts should be directed at "cutting back missionary activity." Moreover, it should be established that entry visas would not be granted to missionaries unless they were coming to join a particular community that had been left without a priest or clergyman, when no member of the community was able to take over this role.[85] In other words, from now on, "for each monk who leaves, one will be permitted to enter."[86] Although this ruling was not anchored in law, in ordinances, or even in an official document, it was of enormous significance because it served as a guideline for the granting of entry visas for many years. And as a result, the number of church representatives remained at the same level for many years, lower than under the Mandate.[87] Clerics were granted temporary residence permits for no more than one year, to be reconsidered at the end of that period.[88] The committee appointed to deal with this subject applied stringent criteria to requests for permanent residence for church representatives who had been in the country for five years or more.[89]

It is unquestionable that administrative action of this kind was stepped up as a result of the rejection of antimissionary legislation, the relaxation of political tension on the Jerusalem issue, and the transfer of Herzog—one of the main advocates of an uncompromising struggle against the mission—to the Foreign Ministry in late 1951.[90] The Ministry of Religious Affairs continued to do everything in its power to contain missionary activity. For example, every application for import of copies of the New Testament was scrupulously checked. The Ministry banned such import on grounds of "a threat to local production," and examined "the ratio between the number of Christians in the country and the number of books the missionaries wish to import." It was claimed that "we must observe the golden mean: on the one hand, we must reduce to the minimum the import of missionary literature—on the other, we must forestall negative reactions on the part of those Christian countries with which we wish to live in peace."[91] The Ministry even collaborated with the Ministry of Welfare in the hope that it could reduce the attractiveness of Christian schools through imposition of administrative restrictions. An internal report from late 1966 notes that "according to the new Ministry of Welfare regulations, which prohibit the enrollment of children whose parents are not Christians, those boarding schools which are openly proselytizing, have now become cautious about accepting Jewish pupils, and their number has dropped. . . . It is not clear to what extent these regulations are legal—and it is a good thing that no Christian institution has of yet brought this issue before the courts. . . . This is thanks to our Department [on Christian Affairs,] which has persuaded several priests not to raise the problem, although we are not sure that we can continue to prevent them from so doing."[92]

It is noteworthy that in the course of the administrative battle waged by the Ministry of Religious Affairs against the mission, it often came up against the Foreign Ministry and the Ministry of the Interior as well. Its differences of opinion with the latter related to two questions.[93] The first was the problem of Christians who came to Israel for religious reasons but proclaimed that they had no intention of engaging in missionary work, and the second was the definition of such activity. The Ministry of the Interior did not refuse residence rights to such Christians on condition that they had the means to support themselves. The Ministry of Religious Affairs, on the other hand, totally denied the right of non-Jews to live in Israel, particularly since, according to their view, they were all potential missionaries. The Ministry of the Interior supported denial of permanent residence rights only in cases of aggressive missionary activity (open solicitation, distribution of food, and other material inducements), and even then, so the Ministry of Religious Affairs claimed, the Ministry of the Interior "was reluctant" to refuse or to deport individuals. The Ministry of Religious Affairs, on the other hand, claimed that religious Christian activity was "endangering the unity of the people and the public order" and called for strict action.[94] The most striking illustration of the clash between these two viewpoints related to the establishment of the Christian settlement of Nes Amim.[95]

In addition to bringing constant pressure to bear to restrict the entry of missionaries, the Ministry of Religious Affairs tried from early 1951 to obstruct attempts to persuade Jews to convert. It acted clandestinely because of foreign sensitivity to the subject and Israel's official commitment to freedom of religion. Under the supervision of its own Christian Communities Department, the Ministry began to extend regular financial aid to a public body known as the Association for Combating Foreign Education, which had gained previous experience in antimission activity.[96] It was chosen in order to conceal the link to the Ministry, since "renewed and intensified activity on the part of the Association will not be regarded as something new by Christian circles."[97] The plan of action was presented to the Ministry's director-general in mid-March:

> The people who will engage in this work [will recruit] the aid of rabbis, activists, journalists, and social workers. But, in addition to propaganda and information efforts, it will deal with cases on an individual basis. This work calls for great tact. Nevertheless, [we] anticipate that in some cases coercion will be required, such as the expulsion of missionaries who enter immigrant camps, put pressure on employers of Jews who send their children to missionary schools, etc.[98]

Forcing the Way

The Ministry also tried to promote a socioeconomic scheme targeted at those populations which were more vulnerable to missionary attention. This scheme required a government-sponsored network, and to this end the Ministry initiated the establishment of yet another organization that was to remain under cover. This was the Inter-Ministerial Committee against Missionary Activity, whose task was to coordinate antimissionary action and to obtain public funding for it, a goal it did in fact achieve.[99] An organization entitled *Keren Yeladeinu* (Our Children's Fund) was set up, and the fact that it was affiliated to the Ministry of Religious Affairs was concealed. It carried out the overt social activities aimed at thwarting the Christian mission and endeavored to enhance public awareness of the vital need for such action.[100] The Fund, whose activities are documented in dozens of thick files in the Ministry of Religious Affairs archives, was the public executive arm of the interministerial committee, which enabled it to camouflage the direct government involvement.[101] It should be emphasized that in February 1954 the government officially sanctioned this policy of combating the mission through obstructive bureaucratic activity rather than through legislation. The Foreign Ministry, which was aware of these efforts, had no basic objections to the plan to limit the achievements of the mission, but was anxious to conceal the fact that the Israeli government was involved. It should be noted, however, that several senior Ministry officials did not support it because they doubted that this activity could be kept secret.[102] It may well be that these reservations and the fact that this was essentially an internal matter explain the Foreign Ministry's decision not to attend most of the interministerial committee's meetings. This absence made it easier to steer the committee in the direction favored by the Ministry of Religious Affairs, namely, not only to focus on improving the lot of underprivileged populations, which were the official target of missionary efforts, but also to launch direct attacks on the instigators of these efforts and to campaign against them.[103]

And indeed the dynamic antimissionary work of these bodies included surveillance of public officials suspected of contacts with the mission (whose number was estimated "in the hundreds")[104] and exertion of pressure on them to sever all connections;[105] removing children from Christian institutions, sometimes by force;[106] pressuring Christian clergy to refrain from conducting marriage ceremonies between Christians and Jews [although this was not prohibited by law];[107] disseminating crude antimissionary propaganda that greatly embarrassed Israeli diplomats abroad,[108] distributing thousands of copies of the Bible at popular prices in order to compete with those "distributed by the mission in transit camps and immigrant settlements";[109] attempting to prevent public performances of Catholic liturgical music that "could be interpreted as rapprochement with Christianity,"[110] and inspection of the content of the broadcasts on Israel Radio in the time slot allotted to Christian sects in order to prevent proselytizing messages.[111] "The converts themselves," according to a report sent to the Israel Minister in Berne,

> live—and this too is self-evident—like outcasts, lepers, their lives are made difficult by rumors and their children are unpopular. Israel is a Jewish state, but it is not a theocratic state nor is it exclusively religious. Members of other religions have the right to live here, and they even enjoy equal rights. All this is well and good theoretically speaking and before the courts. But a society has a life of its own, customs of its own, and its own laws. Israeli society has its own reality, and there is no room here for converts. What can one do?[112]

This antimissionary activity, and in particular the propaganda conducted in the religious press [which was greatly concerned because the 1958 wave of immigration from Poland had included a considerable number of mixed Catholic-Jewish couples], was observed closely by church heads in Israel. Foreign ministries and church centers all over the world were briefed on this propaganda and on several physical attacks on Christian institutions.[113] The Vatican was particularly sensitive on this subject, and in the early to mid-1950s the Catholic press was strongly critical of what it considered to be Israel's reprehensible conduct toward the Church.[114] Israel's consent in late 1955 to compensate Catholic institutions for war damage[115] was not regarded by Israeli diplomats as sufficient to rectify this negative impression. A senior official reported to the head of the *Histadrut's* Political Department in early 1958 that "the most prominent clerical leaders in Israel, when they report the situation to church leaders all over the world, sometimes paint the blackest possible picture, and quote articles published in the *Mizrahi* and *Agudat Israel* press. The unavoidable conclusion is that if our national mood is judged by these articles, it can only be compared to the mood of the Spanish public in the sixteenth century."[116] Protests that reached Israel highlighted the undesirable implications of this situation, and a sympathetic French diplomat told the foreign minister in late 1964 that "a single stone hurled at the window of a Christian institution in Israel could cause more harm to French-Israeli relations than ten speeches by Nasser."[117]

These reactions forced the Foreign Ministry to adopt a defensive position and to claim that there were indeed "certain negative attitudes" toward Christians in Israel but that these did not add up to "persecution"; that Israel had not anchored antimissionary activity in law; that the activities of Christian clerics were offensive to Israel because of the high proportion of missionaries "in so small a country, and because it is insulting to be regarded as non-believers as if we were natives in one of the colonial countries"; that missionary activity was concentrated in poorer neighborhoods; and that in Muslim countries, unlike Israel, religious conversion was illegal.[118] The Ministry also issued press releases on the lives of Christian communities as evidence that Israel respected the principle of freedom of worship. In addition, it tried to restrain antimissionary expressions and activities emitted from within the Israeli bureaucracy, notably in the first half of the 1960s, when the Catholic Church was debating the "Jewish document." A unique Ministry initiative in 1958—which received the blessing of the prime minister—was the establishment, funding, and operation of the Committee for the Encouragement of Understanding between Members of all Religions in Israel and throughout the World.[119] A year previously, Maurice Fischer (then deputy director of the Foreign Ministry) had explained to the director-general of the Ministry of Education why such an organization was needed:

> [There is concern] in Christian circles both in Israel and abroad at the negative attitude which is often displayed towards Christians in Israel. You know that this subject is officially under the auspices of the Ministry of Religious Affairs, and you are also familiar with the fanatic spirit in which these matters are conducted there. . . . There is no doubt, to my mind, that not only that Ministry's emissaries are responsible for the situation. There is a prevailing mood in wide circles of the population which can only be attributed to the suffering and persecutions which the Jewish people underwent in the Diaspora,[120] but it is unjustifiable and we should certainly try to prevent its continuation into the generations to come.[121]

The U.S. consulate in Tel Aviv was convinced that there was an additional reason why the Israeli public was reconciled to the situation. "Most of the [Israeli] public have no particular interest in those anti-Christian activities of religious bodies which win headlines from time to time. Their attitude may be summed up as 'The [religious] fanatics don't only harass Christians, they also harass us.'" A senior Foreign Ministry official used more circumspect language when he reported to Israeli ambassadors in the West that "the problem is that these priests believe that freedom of religion and worship includes freedom of [open missionary] action . . . and that the police should defend them in such a way that they are able to carry them out and continue them. On the other hand, the actual situation in Israel is such that the Jewish public, both religious and non-religious, objects to such activities and regards them as provocation and the police will not easily defend the priests under these circumstances and permit them to carry on their work."[122] Whatever the reason, the committee conducted internal and external propaganda for several years, but found it difficult, on the existing evidence, to achieve its aim and was dissolved in unclear circumstances in the early 1960s.

France Stands Alone

Israeli bureaucratic measures against the mission were hedged by one significant restriction: the rights enjoyed for many years by French religious institutions were scrupulously observed. This issue, which was of great concern to the Israeli Foreign Ministry, deserves more detailed discussion. From the sixteenth century on, France had enjoyed special standing in the Ottoman Empire as the representative and patron of Christianity in general and Catholicism in particular, a role which involved, inter alia, protection of Catholic institutions. The sultans consequently granted certain privileges to French institutions, at first to places of worship and monasteries and later to schools and hospitals as well. In light of France's special status, non-French institutions also requested and were granted French patronage. As a result of their privileged status, they enjoyed certain concessions that enabled them to operate without disturbance, and their staffs were protected against the usually hostile Muslim milieu and against harassment by the local administrative authorities. In due course, these concessions were extended to fiscal privileges (which included exemption from customs duty on certain items and exemption from government and municipal taxes on real estate owned by the institutions) and concessions to schools. Because of the vagueness of certain of these arrangements and as a result of French pressure, agreements were signed between the parties in 1901 and 1913. When the Ottoman Empire broke up after World War I, France lost its status as patron of non-French institutions, but continued to be highly sensitive to the rights of its own bodies, which served as bridgehead for political and cultural infiltration that gained importance as France's strategic advantages diminished. This sensitivity was common to the political echelons and the French public at large, irrespective of political orientation or religious convictions. Although the British were unhappy about the existence of these privileges, they did not take effective steps to annul them.[123]

The great importance which France attributed to its privileges, particularly where Christian schools and medical institutions were concerned, was acknowledged by Jewish Agency emissaries in the campaign they waged at the United Nations in 1947–48.[124] Since France's political support was perceived to be vital, a Jewish Agency representative in Paris announced on 13 July 1947 that the Zionist executive intended to honor France's privileges as laid down in the international treaties it had signed with the Ottoman Empire and with Britain. The French were not content with this statement and later insisted on a signed agreement guaranteeing their rights as a condition for their recognition of Israel. From the beginning of the 1948 war, the negotiations were tense between the parties, since Israel was unwilling, for military reasons, to evacuate strongholds in the grounds of French institutions (such as the Notre-Dame monastery in Jerusalem). The French were scathing "and even insulting" in their various demands, which were submitted in full in August 1948.[125] The French consul in Jerusalem demanded privileges for "four hospitals, eighteen clinics, two hostels, three high schools, four religious seminaries, thirty-nine colleges, schools, boarding schools for girls, and orphanages with 12,000 pupils, including the pupils at Alliance Israelite schools and six convents." The Ministry of Religious Affairs official who received this list was reluctant to accept it and reported to his superiors that "in effect, they are demanding that we abandon the education of our Christian nationals to French schools," which consequently would enjoy "many more privileges than do Jewish and government schools and educational and charitable institutions."[126] It was also feared that acquiescence to the French demands would open the way to demands by other countries, with which Israel would find it hard to comply.

At the same time, Israel's hopes were dashed that France would be content with the general guarantee of interests and rights,[127] issued on 6 September 1948 by Fischer, then Israel's representative in Paris. The French demands were reiterated at meetings in Jerusalem and Paris, and it was hinted that if these demands were not met, France would not recognize the new state. The French also recommended that a formula be sought "so that the granting of privileges will not appear to be encroaching on Israeli sovereignty." It was further proposed to Israel that it accept these demands by means of an official exchange of letters similar to the correspondence between France and the Ottoman Empire in 1903.[128] While Israel was willing to commit itself to evacuating various sites and paying compensation, it did not feel it possible to accede to more barbed demands. The French insisted that Israel safeguard the rights of French institutions and exclude them from constitutional or legal changes in the future. Less problematic, as far as Israel was concerned, was the demand that in the future it grant France the same privileges it saw fit to grant to any other country or to the pope, and that it submit to the International Court for arbitration any differences of opinion on interpretation of the agreement. The Israeli foreign minister, Moshe Sharett, backed by the prime minister, declared himself ready to conduct negotiations to meet "France's justified demands," but he was unwilling to commit himself a priori to maintaining a permanent status quo for French institutions.[129] Sharett, who regarded the French demand as an attempt to "bring back the capitulation regime," was adamant in his refusal to accept the ultimatum, "which France would never have dreamed of submitting to any other country in the world."[130]

On 24 January, Fischer wrote accordingly to the French Foreign Ministry that Israel was ready to commence negotiations on French rights and promised that these would not fall short of any such privileges granted to a third party or to the pope.[131] In his reply, the secretary-general of the French Ministry of Foreign Affairs, Jean Chauvel, agreed to such negotiations. This exchange of letters came to be known as the Fischer-Chauvel agreement, although it was in fact no more than an expression of mutual willingness to negotiate.[132] Be that as it may, France decided that the positive elements in the Israeli decision had fulfilled the conditions for recognition.[133] In the end, however, the negotiations did not take place. The reason was simple—the obfuscation was convenient to both parties. Israel realized that a focused and detailed discussion of implementation of the Fischer-Chauvel agreement could have only one of two possible outcomes, both highly undesirable: to give in to the French on what the Foreign Ministry later defined as "absurd issues, just as the Turks succumbed in 1901" or "to launch a dispute with them over what is to them a matter of principle and a sacrosanct issue."[134] As for the French, they apparently found it convenient to accept the vague wording for the time being, since, in practice, their institutions continued to enjoy the same concessions and exemptions as under the Mandate; Israel avoided interference in Christian schools, and the committee that granted entry permits to Christian clerics was relatively liberal in its treatment of those coming from France because of the Fischer-Chauvel agreement. In fact, according to authoritative Israeli evaluations at the time, "French institutions actually enjoy greater concessions and privileges than ever in the past."[135]

This view was not always accepted by the French, and there were frequent disagreements, particularly in the mid-1950s during the strategic "honeymoon" between France and Israel that made it possible for Paris to exert effective pressure on Jerusalem in these areas. The Israeli ambassador in France at that time, Walter Eytan, who as Foreign Ministry director-general, had been a direct witness to the process, later told a Ministry official that Pierre Gilbert, France's ambassador to Israel in the mid-1950s, was "always very firm in defending the rights of the monasteries—and always succeeded. Who could refuse Gilbert anything? The nuns ran to him with every petty matter and he hurried to the Foreign Ministry."[136] The best proof of Israel's resolve not to enter into conflict with the French despite their growing demands was provided in 1957. In that year, the law exempting all religious, charitable, educational, and medical institutions from tax payments was rescinded. In contrast to all the other foreign religious institutions, the French continued to enjoy their traditional privileges. Israel's readiness to contravene the law in this case was influenced by political and economic calculations. The fiscal concessions, it was noted, "did not constitute an intolerable burden on the exchequer."[137] Moreover, it was easier to practice positive discrimination where French institutions were concerned since they were Catholic and hence did not constitute as great a challenge to religious circles in Israel as did the Protestants.[138] On some issues, however, Israel remained firm (for example, the French demand in 1950 for continuation of the practice introduced during the Mandate regarding the visa and residence rights of French clerics).[139] Yet the fact that the French did not insist on legal negotiations on the Fischer-Chauvel agreement suggests that they were content with the status quo.

This pattern of relationships was jeopardized in late 1963 by an affair nicknamed in internal Israeli memos "Of Pigs and Men."[140] A year previously a law

had been passed banning the raising of pigs, except in certain areas around
Nazareth and Galilee, in scientific institutions, and in public zoos.[141] The Ministry of the Interior learned in mid-October 1963 that forty pigs were being
raised in the convent of Les Filles de la Charité in Ein Karem, where several
hundred children with developmental disorders were cared for. The deputy interior minister, a member of the National Religious Party, who was to display
intensive involvement in the story, ordered the convent to rid itself of the sty
as soon as possible. The Mother Superior explained to representatives of the
Ministry that the pigs were the children's main source of food and that she could
not run the convent without them. She also told them that she refused to remove the pigsty "and would rouse the whole world" if the Israeli authorities
carried out their threats.[142] She did, in fact, alert French diplomats, who immediately briefed the Quay d'Orsay, and the subsequent discussions occupied
the attention of the Ministries of the Interior and of Religious Affairs and the
cabinet for close to five weeks, until the problem was solved. The French emphasized in their petition to the foreign minister that the order violated the
Fischer-Chauvel agreement. In Paris, the French foreign minister telephoned
the Israeli ambassador and told him "with utter seriousness and out of sincere
concern" that he had received "a warning from a senior Catholic figure concerning forty-seven pigs" and that although this was "a minor matter," it was
liable "gradually to deplete the reservoir of goodwill towards Israel which, to
his gratification, had accumulated in the past few years in ecclesiastical circles."[143] The Israel government, obliged to deal with the affair, decided to suspend the immediate implementation of the law in order to facilitate "a reasonable settlement."[144]

The Foreign Ministry understood only too well the harm which could accrue
from a new dispute with France, "for the sake of forty-seven pigs which feed
the nuns," particularly in light of the "juicy" nature of the story, which would
certainly be headlined in Catholic newspapers all over the world if it were not
nipped in the bud. As the Israeli ambassador in Paris noted, "Every French
monastery in Israel has a kind of 'main office' in France (and certainly also in
Rome). And it is only to be expected that every little issue will be inflated en
route. By the time the story about the pigs reaches Rome . . . there will be 300
of them." At the same time, for obvious reasons, the Ministry was reluctant to
exploit it in order to open a political and legal debate on the interpretation of
the Fischer-Chauvel agreement. Its prime aim was to persuade the Ministry
of the Interior to yield on the Ein Karem affair by enacting an administrative
ordinance.[145]

The Ministry of the Interior refused to do so, and the French, both in Israel and at home in Paris, also proved inflexible and unwilling to compromise
in light of the Israeli violation of the "legal and political principles of the Fischer-
Chauvel agreement." The Israeli embassy in Paris was forced to conclude that
while "this agreement was always to some extent a myth . . . where the French
are concerned it is now something of substance" and consequently "a dangerous deterioration in relations between our two countries" could ensue.[146] Meet-

ing on 27 November, the prime minister, the minister of the interior, and the acting foreign minister decided that the order to round up and destroy the Ein Karem pigs would not be carried out as long as their meat was earmarked solely for internal consumption at the convent and thus "does not constitute a danger to the Jewish inhabitants of the country."[147] This decision was to be conveyed to the French government, with emphasis on the fact that it had been taken out of consideration for the friendly relations between the parties "and not as a result of their legal claims."[148] Some time later Israel added another condition: the pigs were to be raised inside the convent and were not to be visible from outside it.[149] At the same time, Israel continued to evade formal discussion of the Fischer-Chauvel agreement. Although the Quay d'Orsay was displeased with this evasion, it apparently agreed in December 1963 that the affair was now over and done with.[150]

Although Paris was afraid that the "pig affair" reflected Israeli disregard for the agreement, time proved that this was not the case. On several occasions, Israel showed considerable flexibility in responding to French requests such as continued exemption from travel taxes for monks (in 1962 Israel revoked the exemption previously given to all clerics and foreign nationals who had paid for their tickets in foreign currency);[151] recognition of transit documents given to French clerics of Arab origin by the French consulate in Jerusalem; exemptions from customs duty on private vehicles imported by French clerics; and de facto recognition of the French school in Jaffa.[152] The French-Israeli agreement continued to restrict Israeli freedom of action even after the Six Days' War[153] and generated natural complaints by heads of other churches in Israel against what they saw as discrimination.[154] The Israeli response was that it was maintaining the status quo toward Christian communities and hence was obliged to honor the historical privileges awarded to certain communities in international treaties.[155] Practical calculations were also involved. It was clearly in Israel's interest to continue the Mandatory tradition of recognition of a specific number of Christian communities (not including the Protestants) and no more.[156]

To sum up, whereas the liberal approach prevailed in the debate on restrictive legislation against missionary activity and Christian education, it was defeated—except in the case of French religious institutions—when it came to practical measures against a wide range of other missionary activities. It should be recalled that both schools of thought, the liberal and orthodox, agreed in principle on the need for preventive measures, such as allocation of funds for underprivileged sectors at which mission efforts were targeted. The newly available files reveal that this consensus was exploited mainly by religious circles who introduced measures extending beyond social parameters. By exploiting a mostly sympathetic bureaucratic apparatus, they managed, in effect, to set obstacles in the path of missionary organizations. The overall picture is therefore complex. On the one hand, by refraining from antimissionary legislation, Israel was ostensibly honoring its commitment to religious freedom as laid down in the Declaration of Independence. However, it was far from granting this freedom to Christian missionaries. In mid-1948 the Dutch consul-general asked the prime minister if Christian missionaries were permitted to work in Israel. Ben-Gurion's reply consisted of two parts: "I said that, subject to the laws of the state, you will have total freedom to act in Israel although, I added, I hoped that if they worked among Jews, they would fail as they had done before."[157] The Israeli authorities undoubtedly encouraged this trend over the coming two decades. This fact was well known to the various churches and inevitably constituted an obstacle to Israel's diplomatic efforts to establish political ties. The archives provide abundant evidence of Catholic resentment of this policy in the early years of statehood. These documents, and others available in the U.S. National Archives,[158] also provide information on Protestant umbrage, which was naturally even stronger (and which was surveyed in a book, based on a doctoral thesis that appeared in Denmark in 1970).[159] This authoritative work, *The Church in Israel*, is an incisive indictment of Israel's antimissionary efforts, as revealed to the author mainly by Protestant clerics in Israel, and is also based on material that reached him long before Israel opened the files. These documents clearly substantiate his arguments and add perspective to them.

6

Goat and Chicken Diplomacy:
Israel and Its Christian Communities

Testing Freedom of Religion

The Christian communities in Israel and their world centers based their attitude toward the new state on two basic criteria: freedom of religious worship
and lack of discrimination. Israel's policymakers knew only too well how important it was to mitigate Christian hostility, particularly where Jerusalem was
concerned. Freedom of religion for all and safeguarding of the Holy Places
were acknowledged to be official objectives and were given official expression
in the Declaration of Independence on 15 May 1948. Among the achievements
to which Israel's leaders pointed with pride was this explicit guarantee to respect the full equality before the law of all religions. This guarantee entailed
recognition of the right of Christian communities to appoint ecclesiastical functionaries, to own property, and to maintain ecclesiastical courts with judicial
powers; recognition of Christian holidays as days of rest for the Christian population, and representation of Christian citizens in the Knesset. The state sanctioned the existence of more than fifty private schools run by the various Christian communities, and granted Christian clerics the legal authority to conduct
marriage ceremonies for members of their community.

As further examples of its respect for other religions, Israel cited the broadcasting of Christian prayer services over Israel Radio during Christian festivals; distribution of Christmas trees at Yuletide; the granting of permits to several thousand Christians to cross over to Jordan to visit Holy Places there during
Christian festivals, and the fact that Christians were allowed to join the Histadrut (Israel's General Federation of Labor). According to a 1956 internal
memo of the Christian Affairs Department of the Ministry of Religious Affairs: "The government of Israel is honoring its commitments and promises
toward the Christian world, and is doing everything in its power to guarantee
for all its citizens, irrespective of whether they are Jews or non-Jews, freedom
of religion and conscience, freedom of worship and prayer. This should come
as no surprise since thereby Israel is observing the humanitarian principles ex-

pounded by Israel's seers and prophets."[1] Israeli officials liked to contrast this situation with "the tragic plight of the Christian minority in most of the Arab countries—from Tunisia to Sudan, from Egypt to Syria." Understandably, Israel was led to believe that its efforts were bearing fruit when Pope Paul V1 declared at the end of his visit to Israel: "We note with satisfaction that our Catholic children living in this country continue to enjoy the rights and freedom which today every human being is entitled to enjoy."[2]

This declaration was not ungrounded, nor was the assertion in a recently published two-volume history of the Israeli Foreign Ministry: "Since the establishment of the state, Israel's governments have displayed a positive attitude towards the Christian churches in the country."[3] The newly accessible archival material, however, reveals that this idyllic picture disregarded the complexities of the situation and its positive and negative manifestations, which affected Israel's relations with the Church in the local and international arenas. A frank report in 1954 by the adviser on Christian affairs to the minister of religious affairs drew a far from rosy picture of Israel's relations with its Christian communities. "What is the situation after five and a half years of work and efforts?" he asked, and his reply was categorical: "Despite our concessions to the churches and the Christian communities in Israel, and despite the many benefits we have showered on them, we are now at loggerheads with almost all of them. Our relations with the Catholics are very bad, relations with the Protestants are deteriorating daily, and even the Orthodox, the Armenians, the Copts, and the Syrians have complaints and grievances which, for the time being, are not voiced out loud because these communities have no patron at the moment who is willing to do battle for them."[4] As will be shown below, the report was only a mild reflection of much more rancorous confrontations. Whereas Israel has widely publicized its achievements in this area, its problems and, in particular, its covert intentions with regard to the Christian minority have so far been largely unknown. The newly available material in the State Archives casts light on the true situation.

Handling a Minority: The Organizational Dimension

From the first, the problem of the Christian communities in Israel was bound up and interrelated with the issue of Israel's relations with world church centers. The natural administrative solution was to establish a single body to guarantee coordination of local and global interests and to enable effective utilization of methods of action. However, circumstances dictated the establishment of an alternative organizational bureaucratic solution that was to have far-reaching implications. For reasons that are insufficiently clear from the documentation, possibly also out of budgetary considerations, it was decided in the first year of statehood to concentrate all internal and external dealings with the subject in the Ministry of Religious Affairs.[5] The Foreign Ministry voiced no objections at the time. Gradually, however, and in particular after Israel's political defeat at the UN on the Jerusalem question in late 1949, the authority of the Ministry of Religious Affairs was restricted to dealings with the Christian communities inside Israel while the Foreign Ministry dealt with relations with world churches. Herzog's departure from the Ministry of Religious Affairs and transfer to the Foreign Ministry was a highly significant indication of this development.

Moreover, in practice, the affairs of the Christian communities were divided up among a considerable number of government agencies, including the Prime Minister's Office, the Ministry of Justice, the Ministry of Defense, the Ministry of the Interior, the Ministry of Immigration, the Ministry of Finance, the Government Press Office, the Tourism Office, and the General Custodian's Office, all of which, according to the director-general of the Foreign Ministry, "had a finger in the pie."[6] This decentralization was characterized not only by absence of official bureaucratic hierarchy but also by failure to establish important staff centers, such as a center for research and information, even in the Foreign Ministry.[7] This being so, it is not surprising that the adviser to the Ministry of Religious Affairs complained that his ministry's authority vis-à-vis the Christian community was "vague."[8]

This bureaucratic setup requires clarification. To a certain extent, it was only natural for the Ministry of Religious Affairs to be in charge of Christian affairs, since the Christian communities had distinct and separate interests in the religious sphere. At the same time, there was apparently hidden logic as well in this state of affairs. Israel was anxious, for obvious reasons, to lower the profile of Christian demands, and official handling by the Foreign Ministry would have created undesirable political reverberations. The same would have been true if the defense establishment or the Ministry of Justice had been assigned this task. On the other hand, the fact that the Ministry of Religious Affairs was dealing with the applications and demands of Christian sects was apparently considered to stress their solely administrative character, thereby making it easier to deal with them when the decisionmaking centers were elsewhere. As one senior official put it, "The Ministry of Religious Affairs is nothing but camouflage to pull the wool over their eyes."[9]

The results of this organizational situation were highly significant. First, despite the official and practical coordination between the Foreign Ministry and the Ministry of Religious Affairs on matters pertaining to Christian churches in Israel, formal dealings were entrusted to the latter, a fact which could only lower the political profile of ongoing discussions of the problems of these churches. Second, the proliferation of bodies dealing with Christian affairs meant that the official authority of the Ministry of Religious Affairs was not sufficiently great to satisfy the needs of the Christian population. This ministry had been established, naturally enough, mainly in order to deal with the religious Jewish population. Those sections of the Ministry, which dealt with non-Jews, were inevitably of lesser importance when it came to allocation of budgets and manpower.[10] At a cabinet meeting on 15 September 1949, the minister of religious affairs, Rabbi Fishman, threatened that if the sums he had requested for non-Jewish communities were not approved, he would inform the

U.S. ambassador in Israel that he, Fishman, was "not the minister of religions but the minister of the Jewish religion."[11] The budget of the Ministry did eventually include the sums requested, but Fishman's claim essentially was not far from the truth. The minister's adviser on Christian affairs declared, at the beginning of 1954, that "the Department has never benefited from strong organization, expansion, growth or increase in the number of problems entrusted to it, or the attention of the country's leaders. Nor has it succeeded in guiding propaganda efforts abroad and exerting positive influence. The reverse is true: its scope has gradually been reduced, its powers restricted, the best members of its staff have left, and it has been relegated to a corner as a pathetic unit deprived of tasks and influence, impatiently tolerated."[12] The fact that the Ministry was headed by the religious parties was also of some significance. Its directors-general were all religious Jews whose attitude toward the Christian community was not innocent of prejudice.

It was no accident that a rabbi served as the first head of the Christian Affairs Department, and Herzog's efforts in those early years reflected full concurrence with the Ministry's policy. This policy was explained frankly by the adviser on Christian affairs when he wrote, "Our problem is [how] to bring the situation of the churches in Israel to a standstill, or at least to slow down their progress insofar as possible . . . in a manner that will not evoke strong reactions abroad."[13] This was apparently an understatement of intent, at least according to one senior Foreign Ministry expert on the Catholic Church, who defined this anti-Christian policy as "fanatic and intolerant."[14] Even if one could argue with this statement, it indubitably helps to explain the unique situation of the Christian communities in Israel, as reflected in Ministry of Religious Affairs budgeting. The Ministry deliberately adopted a policy of total nonintervention in the financial affairs of the churches, which apparently suited the churches as well, but the result was that, in contrast to other religious groups, they received no real financial support from the state budget. The inevitable result was that the department's budget was tiny. It was earmarked in the main for preservation of Christian Holy Places, publication of information, and hosting of Christian visitors from abroad in consultation with the Foreign Ministry. Most of the department's practical work was devoted to maintaining contact with the heads of Christian communities and interministerial coordination.[15] And finally, and much more important, operatively speaking even when this ministry fostered positive action toward the Christian communities, it could not stand up to other influential administrative bodies, which formulated a policy often entirely hostile toward those communities.

Arab or Christian?

Examination of the statistics on these communities can help us understand this last point. Of an overall population of some 1,800,000 in Israel six years after independence, 192,000 were members of non-Jewish minorities: 130,000 Muslims, 18,000 Druze, and 44,000 Christians.[16] The Christian community, which had increased by 6,000 seven years later, was divided up as follows: 42 percent Greek Catholics, 32 percent Greek Orthodox, 15 percent Latin, 5 percent Maronites, 4 percent Protestants, and the remainder Armenians, Copts, and others. Close to 90 percent were urban Arabs, living in the north of the country, and 91 percent were native-born.[17] They were more highly educated and more Western in orientation than the Muslim Arab population, which was mostly rural.[18]

These data had several implications where policymakers were concerned. One of the basic and natural conceptions in dealing with minorities in general was, in contrast to the British Mandatory policy, to encourage differentiation, in particular in order to facilitate Israeli control and supervision in light of the conflict with the Arab world.[19] The fact that Israel's Arabs were categorized into Christians and Muslims could have facilitated this approach.[20] The problem was, however, that the great majority of Christians were Arabs, and the prevailing attitude of the government toward Christian Arabs was no different from attitudes toward Muslim Arabs, especially in light of the general consensus, which perceived every Israeli Arab as a potential enemy. According to the understated report issued after high-level discussions of this issue in April 1953: "Whether because of unwillingness or psychological inability, the Arab minority in Israel has not severed its spiritual and political ties with the Arab nationalist movement, and the latter continues to follow a line of rejection and resistance to Israel. . . . [The outcome is] that after five years of statehood, and despite all that has been done to bestow on the Arab minority the status of citizens with equal rights, we cannot observe . . . any fundamental psychological transformation that would lead to true integration in the state."[21]

This widely accepted diagnosis concealed the fierce debate within the Israeli establishment in the first decade of statehood as to whether the Arabs should be treated as a stable and permanent element in the state or should be encouraged to leave.[22] Ben-Gurion, who apparently favored the latter approach, which enjoyed considerable support, was emphatic in declaring that "our policy towards [the Arab minority in Israel] cannot be based on the fact that they did not inflict devastation on us. What should guide us is what they could have done if given the opportunity."[23] This being so, he informed the government, "We cannot buy the Arabs, and I am not ready to do a thing to buy them. . . . The Druze are loyal to the state not because they love the State of Israel but because of their political calculations, because they hate the Arabs. . . . But we cannot expect the Muslim Arabs who are backed by the Arab states, and the Christians, backed by the Vatican, to become loyal to the state. [Still] they are entitled to rights if they live in Israel. And as for us, we need a state where there are equal rights for all inhabitants."[24]

As a consequence of these views, the prevailing operative conception at the time as regards the Christian minority was akin to the general policy toward the Muslim Arab population. As the director of the Western Europe Division of the Foreign Ministry explained to Israel's minister in Rome: *"We are not dealing with relations with Christians but with relations with Arabs who happen to be*

Christians, and regarding whom there are certain security considerations and stringent rules."[25] "It was impossible to draw distinctions," declared Palmon in September 1949, since "all the Christian communities have testified against us before the commissions of inquiry at every possible opportunity and are no less responsible for the war of 1948 than was the Muslim community."[26] Two years later, he justified this policy, writing that "in light of the identification of the heads of the Greek Catholic community with the Supreme Arab Council in its efforts 'to throw the Jews into the sea' and to prevent the establishment of the State of Israel, it would be excessive to demand of Israel not to be suspicious of Catholics of Arab origin."[27]

The loyalty of Israel's Christian community was also not taken for granted by the heads of the Foreign Ministry, particularly since the leaders of that community resided in Arab countries and were unmistakably hostile toward the new state.[28] Important elements of church activity in Israel, particularly among the Catholics, were perceived as a very real security threat by the authorities, which invested considerable efforts in countering them. For example, an internal intelligence report from early 1951 established that

> the Catholic Church is clearly hostile towards Israel and [this attitude] is unlikely to change for the better in the future. As a concentration of foreign nationals [these clerics] constitute a threat. . . . Even if the church has no particular interest in collecting military data on Israel to assist in direct military action, the Church is certainly interested in collecting all possible information . . . in the conviction that it may some day find a use for it. We have proof of exchanges of information between certain Church personnel and various Powers, and military intelligence about Israel as "goods for barter."[29]

It should be noted in this context that only on rare occasions did clerics cooperate with Israel on security matters. The Carmelite Father Michel Safatli "collaborated with us whenever we required something from the Old City" and was the liaison with Pierre Gemayel, leader of the Falangists in Lebanon, when they tried to establish ties with Israel. In these cases, Israel remunerated those who assisted the authorities.[30]

The fundamental political need to take the demands of the Church heads in Israel into account sharpened the perception of the Christians as an enemy, at least in the eyes of the highly influential security establishment. This was mainly because of their incessant demand for partial restoration of the Mandatory status quo as regards population and property. This was regarded as "their way of waging a struggle to restore and increase their power and influence among members of their community and of their community among the Arab public."[31] The military authorities were therefore the most vehement opponents of restoring church property which had been seized during the 1948 war.[32]

Under these circumstances, the Israeli establishment took a grim view of what they perceived, for understandable reasons, as an attempt to restore the capitulation regime with the support of the Vatican and of Catholic governments all over the world. This was one of the main reasons for Israel's objections to the 1950 Swedish-Dutch compromise proposal on the internationalization of Jerusalem, which would have granted the UN local representative the authority to intervene, thereby, so Sharett believed, enabling the Christian and Muslim minorities to recruit outside support.[33] Complaining at the refusal of Monsignor Vergani and Archbishop George Hakim to attend the president's Independence Day reception in 1955, the head of protocol in the Foreign Ministry wrote that "the two *galahim* [derogatory term for priests] apparently plotted this together. . . . We have known for some time about the ambition of these two knights of the Church to enjoy the status of a foreign power, but . . . these demands should be categorically rejected."[34] This perception explains Palmon's statement that "our interests conflict with theirs. Stopping infiltration is a problem of the first order. Infiltration without supervision and permission . . . encourages the drug trade, expands the possibilities for smuggling funds and goods and the opportunity for espionage, introducing a fifth column and other criminals. And as to the return of refugees and their assets, I believe that the less is done the better."[35]

Likewise, the fact that the Arab Christian elite was more intensely involved in political activity than the Muslims served to confirm the views of many sections of the Israel establishment that they constituted a threat. The major role played by Christian Arabs in the development of the Communist movement in Israel and in Arab nationalist activity also influenced this official view.[36] The adviser on Arab affairs was therefore not alone in his negative attitude toward Christians. For understandable reasons, the Ministry of Finance was also consistent in its refusal to respond to Christian demands for compensation for damage to property. The influential custodian of abandoned property held even stronger views on this issue.[37]

The implications of this organizational setup for the Christian community were clear. In general, the Foreign Ministry's attitude toward that community, defined by the U.S. consulate in Tel Aviv as "scrupulously correct,"[38] was more positive than that of the Ministry of Religious Affairs, and other bodies, in particular the security establishment and the adviser on Arab affairs, guided and backed by the prime minister, were almost consistently hostile.[39] This reality, which, naturally enough, was not reflected in such propaganda publications as *Christian News from Israel*,[40] had a negative impact on Christian life in Israel and undoubtedly affected Israel's foreign relations. In October 1950, Ginosar, the Israel minister in Rome, wrote frankly to Sharett: "I know only too well the difficulties the Foreign Ministry faces in this area. The army has its own calculations, the minister of finance his accounts, and there are influential groups and individuals whose aims are precisely what the Christians fear: to be rid of the Arabs in Israel—whether this is said out loud . . . or whether they act in silence."[41] The following examples illustrate what lay behind some of Israel's actions and cast new light on its objectives and the measures adopted in order to achieve them.

Crossing Borders

A brief explanation is necessary in order to locate these matters in the proper context. The Christian community in Israel was largely Arab and therefore was treated according to the same parameters as the Muslim population. In the past decade, two exhaustive doctoral theses have been written on Israel's policy toward the Arab minority during its formative years, based on abundant declassified and revealing source material.[42] Israel's policy was based on military rule (until 1966), and the dissertations provide thorough analysis of the various manifestations of this policy, which consisted of exclusion of the Arab sector from national development schemes, disregard for their existence in public discourse, efforts to widen religious and sectarian divisions, their isolation from the Jewish population and exclusion from state apparatuses, limitations on establishment of Arab local authorities, economic and budgetary deprivation, massive confiscation of land, a ban on establishing political parties, and strict security control. From 1958 onward, policymakers were aware that the existence of an Arab minority was an inescapable fact, but this awareness was not translated into significant positive action.[43] The existing historical literature thus provides a more than adequate explanation why both Muslims and Christians suffered serious discrimination in the period discussed in the present book. It also helps explain why we have chosen not to go into detail on the general subject of the Arab minority in Israel at that time. The following analysis therefore relates to the hitherto neglected specific attitude and policy toward the Christian communities, which diverged somewhat from the basic parameters, noted above.

Israel was anxious to guarantee political calm within the Christian communities. For the first time in the annals of relations between the Church and the Jewish religion, the latter held the upper hand and consequently made effective use of the "carrot and stick" approach.[44] One of the more important issues on which Israel had dealings with the Christian communities was visits to Holy Places in Bethlehem and the Old City of Jerusalem at Christmas. Permission was first granted in 1949 for political motives, in order to demonstrate to the world at large that the State of Israel could act liberally toward its inhabitants and permit them freedom of worship to maintain their customs and traditions. This liberal attitude was in stark contrast to the refusal of the authorities to permit visits of Muslims to places in the Old City holy to Islam.[45]

The two sides, however, were not acting out of identical interests. The Christian communities wanted to receive as many exit permits as possible, while Israel wanted to impose limitations, mainly out of security considerations. In August 1955, Y. Landman, head of the Minorities Department in the Ministry of the Interior, informed his superiors, "I have heard from Arabs returning from such visits and from various other sources that the prime aim of the visit—prayers and worship at Christmas—has been overruled, and it has become an opportunity for family visits and meetings. Dispersed families now gather

A nun and a priest posing with policemen in Jerusalem at Christmas in 1948.
Courtesy of the National Photo Collection of the Israel Government Press Office, Prime Minister's Office. Photo D533–025.

together in Jerusalem from all over the Arab world. These meetings cause us considerable security damage."[46] Therefore, the authorities established an inflexible and restrictive quota of permits. The 4,000 Catholics living in the Haifa district were allotted a quota of 210 permits in 1955, while the overall quota for the Christian population was 2,800.[47] It should be pointed out that among the recipients were some whose passage to Jordan was coordinated in advance with the security authorities, apparently for intelligence purposes.[48]

The number of permits was much smaller than the number of applicants, and the Israeli authorities encountered quite a few attempts at fraud, such as submission of a fictitious list of Christian choirs in Israel that ostensibly wanted to participate in ceremonies in the Old City and Bethlehem.[49] Israel placed further obstacles in the path of those applicants who were granted exit permits. The requests were processed slowly, and positive replies were sent only two days before the date of departure. The decision to shroud the procedure in secrecy was security based—to prevent the Jordanian intelligence services from making prior plans and contacting relatives of the visitors in order to undermine Israeli security.[50] Beyond the security arguments, there were additional reasons for Israel's decision to restrict the free passage of Israeli Christians to the Holy Places in the Old City and in Bethlehem. The first was that the Jordanians stubbornly refused to introduce a reciprocal arrangement whereby Jews would be permitted to visit the Western Wall. In addition, the exit permits entailed allocations of foreign currency at a time when Israel was in financial straits. Accordingly, such officials as the Jerusalem district commissioner and the adviser on Arab affairs were in favor of granting only a small number of permits exclusively for diplomats and clerics.[51] The Foreign Ministry, on the other hand, advocated a liberal approach for political reasons, and while mass exits were not permitted, bureaucratic practice was largely based on this approach.[52]

Restrictions on visits to the Holy Places across the border were less intolerable for Israel's Christian minority than the fact that until 1966, all Arabs, both Christian and Muslim, lived under military government, which curtailed freedom of movement within and outside this area.[53] In 1953, for example, the Israel government allotted the 41,000 inhabitants of Nazareth (most of them Christians) only 7,500 regular exit permits. Another 20,000 temporary permits were allotted, though not for passage to areas "of security importance." The restrictions were a constant source of grievance on the part of the Christian minority.[54] In late 1950, Herzog supported in principle Patriarch Gori's request for relaxation of certain military government regulations in Nazareth. Gori had argued that the town "is distant from the borders, a town which has never fought against Israel, and is a display window for Israel-Christian relations. . . . And any improvement will bring you considerable publicity." The military authorities, however, eventually rejected the request.[55] A letter that Father Khalil Khouri of Tarshiha wrote to the prime minister and minister of religious affairs in January 1959 reflects the emotional reactions of Christian leaders toward these restrictions:

> The permit [to visit Holy Places outside and inside Israel] was denied only because I did not agree to be a Zionist in the eyes of His Excellency, the Acre district commissioner. . . . I will never keep silent about this nightmare. . . . History has known nothing like it toward men of the cloth in any of the most trying times except in the State of Israel, and it is a stamp of shame on the forehead of the State . . . in these times of freedom and progress, and particularly freedom of religion.[56]

Security considerations also prevented the replacement of European-born clerics by Arabs, since Israel consistently opposed the entry of Arabs into the country.[57] This policy, which was analyzed in the previous chapter, was the source of one of the main grievances of the Christian communities in Israel. According to the liaison officer of the Christian Communities Department of the Ministry of Religious Affairs, "This makes it very hard to organize the communities which, due to their composition, are unable to appoint clerics from outside the Arab countries."[58] Although this was a problem for the Christian establishment and the Christian communities, Israel rarely acceded to requests.[59] These requests for entry permits for Arab Christian clerics were rejected both on narrow security grounds and for wider national reasons. As the acting director of the Christian Communities Department in the Ministry of Religious Affairs explained, "I cannot be responsible for recommending the granting of permits to Arab clerics coming from the neighboring countries for limited periods, who will bring their influence to bear to encourage the irredentist aspirations of the Arab population."[60]

The following episode serves to illustrate the prevalent approach. The Latin Church in Israel was anxious to send Christian Arab boys to study at a seminary for priests in Jordan so as to train a cadre of local priests. Israel did not object to their departure; the problem was, of course, that they would be exposed to anti-Israeli propaganda abroad. It was also reasonable to assume that a large proportion of the candidates would fail and would want to return to Israel within a short period. Still the Ministry of Religious Affairs decided to respond positively, for political reasons, and the security authorities agreed reluctantly to "a one-time arrangement" on condition that "these boys will not be exposed to negative influences while in Jordan."[61]

Basing their decisions on security arguments, the adviser on Arab affairs and the defense establishment were much stricter than the Ministry of Religious Affairs and the Foreign Ministry when it came to granting exit permits to clerics. The two ministries, on the other hand, were influenced by political considerations.[62] However, the Ministry of Religious Affairs was scarcely liberal in its approach. When a Catholic priest asked for a transit visa to an Arab country in late 1953, it was denied, and a Ministry official reported, "I have seen that priest with my own eyes in civilian garb with two young women at an evening cinema performance. I have no inclination to supervise his conduct, but I would like to point out that this is somewhat strange behavior for a Catholic priest, and it serves to prove that he engages in tasks beyond his regular duties."[63]

The Israeli authorities exploited the permanent transit permits as rewards or punishments, tending to be more lenient toward Catholics than others.[64] Other Christian groups were sometimes granted concessions when this was in Israel's interest. In late 1953, for example, the authorities agreed to the request of Isidoros, Greek Orthodox metropolitan in Nazareth, that a young girl, who had completed her high school studies in Lebanon and wanted to return to her family, be permitted to enter on humanitarian grounds. When her earlier request had been rejected, she had crossed the border illegally and been caught. The reason cited for rescinding the deportation order was that Isidoros, who headed a community 6,000 strong, "needs our support in order to gain status among his flock who are exposed to nationalist Arab and communist influences. . . . It is very important for him to create the impression that he enjoys the support of the authorities, in order to overcome the resistance of Arab members of his community who have recently stopped obeying him."[65]

Another example demonstrates Israel's policy and tactics. A member of the Greek community in Ramleh was betrothed in 1947, but the war separated him from his fiancée, who remained in Jordan. He utilized the permit granted him by the Israeli authorities to visit the Old City on Christmas in order to marry her, and later applied for permission to bring her into Israel under the regulations permitting reunion of families. The authorities responded favorably, as in the case of a Greek Orthodox girl, and for similar reasons.[66] However, in another case, under similar circumstances, the request was rejected.[67]

On Freedom of Expression

The Israeli authorities also imposed restrictions on freedom of expression. The Christians in Israel did not enjoy total freedom; neither did the Muslims. In the case of Christians, however, the restrictions were brought to the attention of Church heads abroad and became a causus belli. The Israeli authorities agreed therefore to permit the heads of the Greek Catholic community a monthly radio broadcast to their flock, but insisted that all material be examined by the security authorities. On one occasion, when the material was broadcast without prior examination, the authorities threatened to stop the broadcasts if this occurred again.[68] On another occasion, the authorities discovered that the content of a planned broadcast was not strictly religious, and it was postponed "for technical reasons."[69]

Israel's sensitivity to depictions of Christian motifs in local culture and art was also offensive to Christians. This sensitivity was given musical expression in July 1954 when the Ministry of Religious Affairs demanded that the Israel Philharmonic remove all mention of Jesus and Mary from the text of Verdi's *Requiem*. The orchestra agreed, but under pressure from foreign soloists who threatened to leave the country if the text was altered, a compromise was achieved. The matter was then discussed at a cabinet meeting on 4 July. The prime minister, Moshe Sharett, supported the demand of the Ministry of Religious Affairs: "If this were a Buddhist performance or something by Confucius," he said, "where all kinds of gods of theirs were mentioned, I don't think this would arouse complexes or anger in the Jewish public . . . but we have a bloody history. It is not easy for a Jew to hear the name of Jesus; it is not the same for us as for Christians who hear the name of Moses. We are dealing here with problems of public psychology."

Sharett tried to win the cabinet over to his view by elaborating on a similar case:

> There was [also] the question of the movie *Salome* where John the Baptist and others appear. Christianity was the central theme of the movie. Jesus appears there, and it ends in a kind of appeal for the religion of Jesus. A movie like that could be regarded as a cinematographic means of encouraging conversion. The issue was discussed at the Foreign Ministry. I said that we should approach the company and tell them that it would be best if the movie were not shown in Israel. . . . From the point of view of public welfare, it would be better not to screen it. The problem of missionary activity evokes considerable emotion. To give this movie an official certificate means granting public sanction to a movie, which could have missionary content. It would be shown to audiences which have all kinds of instincts.

However, most of the ministers denounced the interference of the Ministry of Religious Affairs, which stemmed, according to Peretz Bernstein (minister of commerce and industry) from "the mentality of a persecuted people . . . who have not yet managed to break free of it."[70]

Church Building

The Christian community suffered from material restrictions as well. Although it was well aware that the construction of churches would serve as evidence of freedom of worship, the Ministry of Religious Affairs adopted a particularly tight-fisted policy in recommending permits for allocation of building materials (which were required at the time for every building project). The Ministry's motives were clearly and unmistakably expressed in internal correspondence, namely, not to permit expansion of Christian activity and insofar as possible to reduce it.[71] This policy was vividly illustrated in 1955, when the Russian Church applied to build a new church on its land between Tiberias and Migdal. The general custodian and the Foreign Ministry were opposed, as one official wrote, because "(a) We want as few churches as possible in Israel; (b) This is even more vital when it comes to this mixture of religion and communism; (c) We want to preserve the Jewish character of the Lake Galilee area; (d) In the long term we anticipate strategic danger from a tall tower under foreign supervision, located close to the border."[72] The only exception to this policy appears to be the permission granted in 1954 to build the monumental New Church of the Annunciation in Nazareth. The rather unusual decision was greatly influenced by the government wish to lend help to the Catholic anticommunist elements within the Arab population, by the desire to take advantage of the inflow of foreign currency in order to minimize the problem of unemployment in the city, and by obvious foreign policy considerations.

It should be pointed out in this context that in the pre-state period there were close to 250 churches and religious institutions (including Holy Places) in Israel. Fifty of these were no longer in use for Christian worship after 1948, because they had been destroyed or severely damaged during the fighting, because the structure had been leased or sold to Jewish institutions, or because the Arab worshippers had left.[73] It is clear, however, that the demand for repair of these buildings was a constant source of Christian grievances. The Ministry of Religious Affairs imposed restrictions on allocation of building materials for repairs to churches, even though it estimated that "it is more advantageous for us to display readiness to allocate materials to church organizations than to grant them concessions in other areas relating to security, the mission, etc."[74] On other subjects, such as the allocation of timber for building coffins, the recommendations were positive: "Since [denial of the request] could make a very bad impression . . . some journalists are very eager to do us an injury . . . and this must be prevented at all costs."[75] On the other hand, when a Christian institution applied for a permit to purchase a refrigerator, the Ministry decided that "it is able, through its contacts abroad, to obtain an electric refrigerator without our having to sacrifice the meager stock at our disposal here in Israel."[76]

A particularly sensitive issue was the neglect of churches in abandoned Arab villages. The following story casts light on the spirit in which Israeli policy was determined. In the deserted village of Ma'lul after the 1948 war, the only buildings left standing were two churches, one Greek Catholic and the other Greek Orthodox. Touring the village, Ministry of Religious Affairs officials discovered that the churches had been broken into, that there were heaps of garbage alongside the Greek Catholic church, and that the priest's house had been turned into an animal pen. Later, the churches themselves were used as cowsheds and lavatories. The head of the Greek Catholic Church in Israel, Archbishop Hakim, protested in the early 1960s against this state of affairs and appealed for government-subsidized restoration, in order to enable a Dutch priest who was working in the nearby kibbutz Ein Hahoresh to live in the priest's house and guard the church. The request was discussed at the Ministry of Religious Affairs and rejected. A report to the minister noted, "It is undesirable for a Catholic priest to settle there, where he could conduct religious propaganda in the neighboring kibbutzim. . . . There are two possibilities: (a) to clean up the buildings and stop up all apertures, or (b) to pay compensations to the villagers who have moved elsewhere in Israel, and of course to the church organizations which own the churches, and to wipe the settlement off the geographical map."[77]

It should be noted, in this context, that in the late 1940s and early 1950s, the authorities refused to provide guards for the twelve churches in abandoned Arab villages, so that, although some of them were cleaned up and closed, they were again vandalized. The solution devised for those church heads who agreed (and were defined as "pragmatic") was to pay compensation for the destroyed churches.[78] The best-known example of damage to churches occurred on Christmas Day 1951 when the Israel Defense Forces blew up houses in the abandoned village of Ikrit on the Lebanese border. The village church was damaged, and the story was widely exploited as anti-Israeli propaganda all over the world. In this case as well, compensation was paid.[79]

On Bread

Israel's efforts to prevent conflicts with Christian communities and grant them concessions on questions of religion and religious observance stemmed from political and propaganda motives, as the head of the Foreign Ministry's Press Department pointed out at the end of 1948: "These arrangements can divert international attention from the Arab sector, and at the same time emphasize Israel's desire to help Christians maintain their religious rituals."[80] Due to Israel's ambivalence, however, the concessions were granted sparingly and each case was scrupulously examined. In August 1948, representatives of the Christian community in Haifa requested a monthly allocation of 350 kilograms of wheat for ritual purposes. The official in charge of the Minorities Office in Haifa replied that since only one-tenth of the Christian population remained, "it is expedient and sufficient" to allocate them only 50 kilograms.[81] Although the country was in dire economic straits during the 1948 war, this reply should also be judged in the wider context.

In the dialogue between the Christian communities and the Israel government, the Christians were motivated by the desire to preserve the historic rights they had enjoyed since the Ottoman period while the Jews wanted to curtail these rights without suffering weighty political damage. Thus Monsignor Vergani, who was appointed representative of the Latin patriarch in Israel in January 1954, applied several times for permits for import of foodstuffs on the relatively large scale of $60,000.[82] On instructions from the Ministry of Finance, the Ministry of Trade and Industry informed the monsignor that his application had been rejected, since it had been decided to halt the import of food into Israel through institutions. Vergani threatened to publicize the affair if Israel did not accede to his request, which was based on arrangements dating back to the Ottoman period, ratified in a treaty with France in 1901, and never rescinded by the British Mandate authorities. Israeli experts argued that granting exemptions from customs duty was not analogous to granting import licenses, but a careful examination of the first Turkish agreement from the mid-nineteenth century confirmed that foodstuffs had also been exempted.

What concerned the Israeli authorities, however, was not only the legal problem involved. On the one hand, they wanted to curtail the rights enjoyed by Christian institutions because they constituted discrimination against Jewish institutions and were an unwanted legacy from the past. Jerusalem also feared that Christian institutions might exploit material inducements in order to gain political influence over Arabs and religious influence over both Arabs and Jews. On the other hand, it was thought that a scandal might result from persistent Israeli refusal, thereby "adding fuel to the flames of anti-Israeli propaganda and incitement." Beyond this, the danger existed that a Christian appeal to the High Court of Justice might end in a ruling against the state. The affair ended in compromise: it was agreed, as an exception to the rule, to grant an import license for the import of a specific quantity of foodstuffs for (several hundred) clerics, the remainder to be distributed under supervision of the Ministry of Trade and Industry, similarly to non-kosher meat at Christmas. Vergani agreed to this.

In another case, the authorities took a positive stand on a question of freedom of worship for purely political reasons. In 1962, the heads of the Abyssinian Church in Jerusalem, who had owned a chapel on Mount Zion in the fifteenth century, applied for permission to hold a prayer service on the Mount. Permission was granted and a special site was allotted. When the request was renewed a year later, it was denied by the Ministry of Religious Affairs on the pretext that "the general policy regarding Mount Zion has always been not to increase the number of sites holy to Christians. If the Abyssinians are permitted to pray there once or even twice a year, they will consider this their right and we will never be able to back out." However, weighty political calculations connected to Israel's desire for diplomatic relations with Abyssinia tipped the balance and permission was granted.[83]

Divide and Rule

The administrative organization of the Christian communities was a problematic issue. At the beginning of 1950, the prime minister's adviser on Arab affairs, Palmon, who was extremely hostile toward the Christians, suggested to the Ministry of Religious Affairs that it ask the Christian churches to appoint authorized representatives in Israel. The aim was to regulate official relations with the churches and to rectify a situation whereby some of the community heads in Palestine resided outside Israel and some resided in Israel but were not accredited by the Church to Israel.[84] Palmon did not delude himself that the proposal would be accepted but hoped that it would put the various churches on the defensive, "since they know that our attitude towards them is qualified . . . because they have no special representatives in Israel and those they have are accredited both to Israel and its enemies."[85]

Nothing came of this initiative in the end for reasons that explain an additional antichurch assumption. For administrative, theological, and historical reasons, it would have been difficult to ask those churches which had branches and representatives in Israel to appoint functionaries of equal rank to those whose seat was in the Old City or Transjordan. This was mainly because this would have implied the redivision of the historical diocese of Jerusalem and other dioceses in order to create an Israeli diocese, a move that would have been problematic for the churches involved. The fundamental Israeli motive, however, was political, as the adviser on Christian affairs explained to Palmon in June 1950: "It is not in our political interest for the 50,000 Christians living among us to be organized into respected church bodies (with patriarchates, bishops, etc.). It is better for the churches to appear to be small and unimportant units or even part of larger bodies whose center is abroad."[86]

The State of Israel felt it expedient to adopt the Mandatory procedure and to grant official recognition only to part of the Christian communities, in order to acknowledge the authority of their religious courts on certain questions of personal status and inheritance.[87] The Protestant community was marked by its absence from this group. Behind the official pretext of preservation of the status quo lurked the explicit intention to curb its activities, particularly in light of the important role of missionary activity in the community.[88] The Israeli authorities were particularly perturbed by attempts of Jews who had converted to Christianity to emphasize their affiliation to the Jewish people, unlike converts during the Mandate period, who had been anxious to assimilate into the small British community.[89] This explains why the state made it difficult for Protestant clerics to issue official marriage certificates and did not accept declarations of converts who announced that they had joined one of the Protestant churches.[90]

Practically speaking, this policy was aimed at obstructing Protestant proselytizing activity. The Protestants were incensed at this policy, and the head of the Christian Affairs Department of the Ministry of Religious Affairs was understating the issue when he reported to the director-general that "there was of course no shortage of reactions in Israel and abroad to the policy introduced by our Ministry."[91] In order to appease the community, Protestant clergymen were permitted to conduct marriage ceremonies for members of their community even though the community was not officially recognized.[92] However, in all Christian sects, clerics were barred from marrying Jewish men to Gentile women or Jewish women to Gentile men because the law prohibited marriage between Jews and non-Jews.[93] Here again, the underlying motive was undeniably antimissionary.

Compromise at the Cave of Elijah

One sphere in which there was no serious dispute between Israel and the Christian communities was the rarely raised question of the common ownership of Holy Places. The sole incident that occurred in this respect, relating to the right to worship at Elijah's Cave in Haifa, illustrates a pattern of relations that was characteristic of other spheres as well. The Carmelite monks claimed the right, deriving from an ancient tradition, to conduct a special prayer service in Elijah's Cave on Mount Carmel every 14 June. The Israeli authorities were aware that such a right had existed under the Mandate; they also knew that the service was brief and quiet and took place at a mobile "field" altar. At the time, it was not the custom for Jews to gather at the Cave at regular intervals to conduct ceremonies or prayer services as part of a known tradition. In the prestate period, the area had been under the jurisdiction of the Muslim Wakf, and the cave was guarded by a Muslim Arab who permitted people to enter in return for a small entrance fee. After statehood, "the Arab guard left," and in 1953, on the initiative of the Ministry of Religious Affairs and with its support, a committee was set up that established a Jewish synagogue on the site and brought in Torah scrolls. Because of the increased interest in the site in religious circles, a Jewish guard was hired. The latter refused to allow Carmelites to enter when they came to celebrate their traditional ritual on 14 June 1954. The Carmelites appealed to the Foreign Ministry and to the Israeli minister in Italy, demanding that their historic rights be acknowledged. Israel refused to yield, for obvious reasons but agreed to seek a compromise that would enable the Carmelites to pray there two weeks after the designated time. As for the future, it was agreed that during the Christian prayer services, a curtain would divide their prayer area from the area of the Holy Ark, leaving the question of the historic rights in abeyance.[94]

On another subject as well, the two sides came to a satisfactory arrangement. It will be recalled that the exemption from payment of customs duties was revoked for all Christian religious and charitable institutions except the French. In practice, however, a way was found to circumvent the law where the other Christian communities were concerned. New regulations required Christian institutions to submit to the Ministry of Religious Affairs receipts for customs and purchase tax. After examination, the Ministry of Finance reimbursed them by means of a special Ministry of Religious Affairs budget.[95] This policy reflected the Israeli establishment's careful avoidance of any confrontation or legal dispute with the churches on financial matters. To cite another example, in late 1962, five Christian religious institutions owed about 100,000 lira in property tax to the Jerusalem Municipality. The Foreign Ministry and the Ministry of Religious Affairs made it clear to the local authorities that they would strongly oppose any attempt to prosecute the institutions "since, in any case, nothing will come of it . . . at best, even of the court rules in our favor against those bodies, we will be unable, for political reasons, to implement the ruling, that is to say to force a sale of the property [in order to effect payment of debts]."[96] At a discussion of the problem, most of the participants were opposed to prosecution and favored waiting until the Christian institutions decided to sell these assets. The Municipality would then inform them that the necessary permits would only be issued if all debts were covered.[97]

Acrobatic Maneuvering

The state exercised caution in confiscating church land, particularly in Nazareth, in contrast to its policy toward Arab-owned land.[98] There were also differences in approach when it came to recruitment to the Israel Defense Forces. Whereas Muslim Arabs were barred from army service, Israel encouraged Christians to volunteer in order to establish a "Christian unit."[99] The maintenance of Christian cemeteries, however, was a loaded issue. In 1948, they had forty cemeteries in towns and about sixty in villages. When part of the Arab population left, Christian graves remained untended. In urban areas, there were dozens of complaints about various kinds of damage, some of which were brought to the attention of foreign legations and church heads. Between 1954 and 1957, there were twenty incidents of desecration of Christian graveyards. The Christian Affairs Department tried to deal with these complaints by bringing the police into the picture, allocating funds for repairs and erecting fences, but "only in urgent cases." The cemeteries were not guarded due to budgetary restrictions, which explains why the department director described the situation in late 1957 as "disgraceful."[100]

The ambivalence toward Christians can also be ascertained from the almost acrobatic maneuvers that the state employed in order to solve the problem of days of rest for the non-Jewish communities. In June 1951, an interministerial committee decided that non-Jewish communities should be permitted to observe their days of rest "or at least to be absent from work at times of prayer," but decided that this right "should not be publicized."[101] Thus, while Christians were permitted formally to join the Histadrut and observe the days of rest sacred to their religion, in practice their day of rest was Saturday. In 1952, Monsignor Vergani wrote that "Catholic workers working for private firms or private employers are forced to work on Sundays and holidays under threat of dismissal." Even more problematic was the situation of Jewish workers who converted to Christianity: "Each of them lives in constant fear and does not dare to confess that he is a Christian in case he loses his source of livelihood."[102]

The anti-Christian prejudice of at least part of the Israeli establishment was not confined to workers who converted, as can be learned from a little-known affair involving the IDF. As noted above, Israel permitted Christians to volunteer for military service, but converts received differential treatment. A Jew with the rank of major in the reserve forces converted to Christianity in late 1958. When this became known, he was dropped from the "tactical course" he had been attending and no longer summoned for reserve duty. This decision was apparently due to intervention of the Ministry of Religious Affairs, which had previously opposed the discharge of Jewish converts but had now changed its policy.[103] The story was brought to the attention of the Foreign Ministry when the officer decided to take the matter to court. In a letter to the chief of staff, with copies to the prime minister and foreign minister, Maurice Fischer aired his frustration. He wrote that his attempts, through the establishment of the Interfaith Committee and other activities, to prove to Christian colleagues that Israel was sincerely interested in pursuing a policy of tolerance would come to nothing if this case came to light, "since it is liable to serve as proof to our enemies that the attitude prevailing in Israel toward Christians is identical to that which prevailed in Tsarist Russia and the Germany of Wilhelm II toward the Jews, who were not allowed to serve as officers in their armies." It could also endanger the prospect of rapprochement with the Vatican that he was trying to achieve at the time.[104] A search through the State Archives and the Ben-Gurion Archives has not revealed any documentation on how the affair ended.

Lubricating Expenses

Israel tried to achieve "political quiet" with the local Christian communities by negotiating with their leaders and wielding its authority in diverse ways. The following examples will serve to illustrate: After Israel was established, the centers of the Armenian, Copt, and Syrian churches (which had very small communities in Israel) were located in the Old City of Jerusalem, although most income-bearing assets of those churches were now located in Israeli territory. Israel faced a problem when it came to transferring this income to Jordan. To do so would have contravened the foreign currency regulations that made it difficult to take money out of the country. It was also clear that the relatively advantageous official rate that the churches received for currency conversion was encouraging them to try and transfer most of their income to the Old City. On the other hand, if Israel refrained from transferring this income, these church centers would be in economic straits, since there were a large number of clerics in the Old City serving in the Church of the Holy Sepulcher and other Christian sites. It was manifest to Israel's leaders that a considerate attitude toward these churches could have weighty political implications when it came to the internationalization of Jerusalem.

Moreover, strategically speaking, Israel was then trying to win the trust of Christians in the neighboring Arab countries, particularly those who were suffering persecution, and were therefore likely to create a common front against the Muslims.[105] The latter calculations tipped the balance, and Israel exploited this transfer of currency as a means of reward or penalty.[106] It is noteworthy that until the mid-1950s Israel refused to institute a similar arrangement with the Abyssinian Church, since it had no particular political interest in that organization. When the question of political ties with Abyssinia arose in late 1954, foreign currency was allocated to the church.[107] At the same time, Israel displayed a consistently positive attitude toward the heads of the Scottish Church in Israel, which was particularly sympathetic toward Israel and cooperated fully during the political struggle on Jerusalem. Israel expressed its gratitude, inter alia, by granting the Church an exceptional exemption from land transfer fees, by approving its requests for vehicle imports, and by turning a blind eye to foreign currency transgressions.[108]

The Israeli authorities also made direct individual payments to several of the church heads, possibly on a considerable scale. This by no means insignificant fact is revealed in the newly accessible documents, although the State Archives have been careful, for obvious reasons, not to expose this aspect of the relations. This can be learned, for example, from a form confirming the decision not to declassify a document indicating that the heads of the Greek Orthodox community consistently benefited from such an arrangement.[109] And again, at a meeting in March 1963, Uri Lubrani, a senior Foreign Ministry official, proposed that "this support should not take the form of a salary, but rather subsidies for the festivals or other occasions as the Ministry has done so far. . . . It is advisable that only clerics who cooperate with us should receive subsidies." Dr. Vardi, on the other hand, was against this "selective" approach, which might "expose too many of our cards."[110]

This policy of propitiating the heads of the Christian communities in order to win their support was problematic for several reasons. One was their universal fear of the unprecedented Jewish rule over the country, and what they perceived as a threat to their traditional way of life, and services and benefits they had received from the Arab population. As a result, their attitude toward the Jewish authorities was qualified at best.[111] They were troubled, not only by what the future might hold in store, but also by what they already knew about the attitude of the Israeli authorities toward the Christian Arab population. A year after the occupation of the West Bank by Israel, a British Foreign Office expert on church affairs declared with typical British understatement that, in his experience, the Christian clergy in Israel had learned in the past twenty years that "the Israelis have very little tolerance for the traditional lifestyle of non-Jews."[112]

Another obstacle to this operative policy was the fact that for ecclesiastical administrative reasons, the borders of the patriarchates and dioceses remained unaltered after Israel was established. As a result, the church heads continued to reside in the neighboring Arab countries, a fact which guaranteed that they would be negatively predisposed toward Israel and which hampered give-and-take contacts.[113] Under these circumstances, Israel was obliged to direct its main efforts where Catholics were concerned at Antonio Vergani, the apostolic vicar in Galilee and the representative of the Latin patriarch in Jerusalem, and Archbishop Hakim, head of the Greek Catholic community in the same district.

Hakim, who was archbishop of Acre, Haifa, Nazareth, and Galilee from 1943 until 1967, was considered by politicians and political experts to be extremely hostile toward the Zionist movement and the State of Israel. References to him in internal correspondence leave no room for doubt that this was the almost unanimous official view. Notwithstanding, he was permitted to return to Israel after the 1948 war, mainly because he promised to assist Israel in the face of the Vatican's propaganda campaign at the time. In return, he was granted extraordinary permission to bring in several hundred refugee members of his flock. Confirmation of the effectiveness of this decision can be found in Kenneth Bilby's book *New Star in the Near East* (1951).[114]

The Israeli administration also employed the tactic of "controlled release" of Greek Catholic Church property in the early 1950s in order to win his cooperation.[115] Over the years Hakim enjoyed a number of benefits, including economic dispensations, since he was a shrewd businessman who owned a travel agency in Haifa specializing in pilgrimages[116] as well as companies for the development of Nazareth and the manufacture of religious artifacts and wine for export. After he was caught smuggling, police files against him were closed, and the authorities overlooked the fact that he had accumulated riches illegally by receiving fictitious gifts from Arab members of his community who had left Israel.[117] Eager to gain the willing cooperation of this man who was once defined by the Israel minister in Rome as "the unbridled monsignor,"[118] Israel tried "to satisfy him on small matters and in particular money matters."[119] Herzog used guarded language when he reported to Israeli diplomatic missions abroad in November 1951 that "we have found a way of allaying Hakim's demanding conscience."[120] Palmon was more blunt, referring to Hakim as "a viper with a vast appetite and ability to swallow who is not selective in the means he employs and has a finger in all the pies." He added, "I have absolutely no faith in this man. He will betray us at the first opportunity."[121]

Because of his status, however, Hakim had to be treated with kid gloves. The head of the Christian Communities Department in the Ministry of Religious Affairs thus objected to the proposal of the legal adviser to the government to prosecute Hakim for violating the foreign currency laws, arguing that "Hakim has many possible ways of taking revenge on us in serious fashion. No good will come of it for us if he decides to revive the poisonous propaganda against us concerning the situation of our Christian minority. . . . In every respect it is worth our while to maintain a state of relative peace with him."[122] This "peace" was totally conditional, and Hakim often offered a glimpse of his anti-Israeli views, sometimes symbolically, for example, when he refused adamantly to write his address in Hebrew on his official documents,[123] and sometimes more openly, through political action in the Arab sector, particularly during election campaigns and government crises. He was perceived by the Israeli establishment as "a political figure in religious guise," although in fact he was "a type of Arab-national leader who exploits his national struggle in order to gain

Prime Minister David Ben-Gurion meeting the Greek Catholic archbishop of the Galilee, George Hakim, at the prime minister's office in Jerusalem, January 11, 1960. *Courtesy of the National Photo Collection of the Israel Government Press Office, Prime Minister's Office. Photo D531–108. Photographer Moshe Pridan.*

leadership and riches." He was also described as "a disruptive element among Israel's Arabs and their main spokesman to the outside world," and as the standard-bearer "in the tense situation prevailing between the Catholic Church and the Israeli authorities." Moreover, for reasons apparently related to his diverse activities and his personality, a Vatican committee of control curtailed his authority in mid-1960 and restricted it to his own community, while the other Catholics in the country were now placed under the jurisdiction of the Latin Bishop Chiapperro.[124] In any event, even when Israel induced him to issue a positive statement about the official treatment of his community, he refused to permit it to be published in full.

In light of these facts, Israel's attempt to recruit Hakim in order to win over the Christian minority can scarcely be described as successful. Also unsuccessful was a significant attempt targeted at Monsignor Vergani. Organizationally speaking, he belonged to the Congregation for Oriental Churches. The head of the Congregation, Cardinal Tisserant, it will be recalled, then supported acceptance of Israel's existence and Israeli-Jordan jurisdiction over Jerusalem. Vergani who basically followed the same line was the implementer of the Church's religious policy in Israel, so that his views were considered authoritative. However, although in the late 1940s and early 1950s he tended to cooperate with the Israeli authorities to some degree, his prestige later waned in the local

Catholic establishment, mainly because of his views on Jerusalem, which were severely criticized by the Franciscans. In any event, Gori's appointment as patriarch and head of the Latin Church in Israel, Jordan, and Cyprus clearly marked the beginning of Vergani's decline.[125]

Moreover, unlike Hakim, the canny businessman, who enabled the Israeli authorities to offer economic incentives, Vergani, who was defined by the U.S. vice consul in Jerusalem as a man "spiritual in his approach" for whom "hospitals, schools, and churches in themselves are of greater significance than full coffers,"[126] was less vulnerable to material temptation. Like Hakim, he refused to express positive views on Israel's attitude toward the Christian communities.[127] Efforts to woo the Catholic community by showering benefits on its leaders were ineffective for yet another reason. As Gori said, "What is the point of the honors you bestow on me and the fair treatment of the churches when the community itself is in danger of deterioration?"[128]

The above survey, therefore, is an expansion of the recognized thesis of a prominent researcher on the Christian communities in Israel who claimed many years ago that the existence of the state transformed those communities into the weakest minority in the country.[129] The newly opened archival files corroborate the thesis that Israel practiced a policy favoring this process and that this policy, predictably, was a permanent obstacle to relations between the state and Christian organizations abroad. One of Israel's sworn enemies in the court of the Holy See in Rome, Tardini, exploited it frequently[130]—and was not alone in this.[131] However, it is important to note (and this is borne out by thousands of archival sources in Israel, the United States, and Great Britain, only some of which have been quoted here) that despite Israel's basically negative yet camouflaged attitude toward the Christian communities within its borders, which has been revealed here, it eventually succeeded in avoiding any significant conflict with the Western powers or with the Latin American countries on this issue.[132] This can be explained by two reasons: Israel's adoption of a cautious practical policy and the clear awareness of the dangerous international consequences of crossing "red lines" in handling Christian affairs in Israel, which was greatly facilitated by the abolition of the military rule of the Arab minority in 1966, and the parallel relatively late political awakening of the Muslim and Christian Arabs within Israel stemming from what they often defined as the Nakba (catastrophe) of 1948.[133] In any case it was no mean foreign policy accomplishment.[134]

7

Israel and the Question
of the Russian Ecclesiastical Assets

Real Estates in the Holy Land: Zionism vs. Christianity

One of the most complex issues between Israel and the Christian world in the early years of statehood was that of church property. The complexity stemmed from the conflict between Israel's desire to command and nationalize the bulk of the territory within its borders and the claims of the various church organizations to legal and historic rights over plots of land and a considerable number of buildings in the new state. The issue should be examined within the context of Israel's land policy as consolidated in that period.[1] The desire to acquire and nationalize territory had been an inseparable component of Zionist ideology and practice long before 1948. At the strategic level, it was postulated that land was the basis for national renaissance and that settlement of the land would determine territorial sovereignty and reinforce Israel's standing in the national conflict with the Arabs. This ideology was also based on social and economic motives and, after Israel was established, on critical planning considerations. And finally, in the immediate post-independence years, the existence of a large reserve of public land—state lands, absentee property, and enemy property—facilitated the implementation of a national strategy along these lines. Among the measures employed, which were aimed, inter alia, at dispossessing Arabs, were the confiscation of absentee property, as defined by Israel, the requisition of land whose owners were living in Israel, and discrimination against Arabs in leasing of land.[2]

In recent years this subject has engaged the interest of historians, who have extended their research on land purchase in the Mandate period to the first decade of statehood. Recent studies include a detailed description of the considerable effort invested in land purchase and an authoritative analysis of the considerable success of this strategy—from the perspective of its initiators—despite the difficulties they encountered. These included the complications entailed in dealing with church assets, some of which had been seized during the 1948 war. Israel had proclaimed loud and clear, particularly during its struggle to win UN membership in 1949, that it had no intention of confiscating church property and that it would endeavor to restore it to its owners, military circumstances permitting.[3] There was now a basic clash between Israel's overall strategy aimed at exercising control over all the land within its borders and the political constraints it faced. Moreover, this general policy was fueled by a particular religious, national, and political interest, which has been analyzed above, namely, to diminish the Christian presence in Israel. In internal correspondence, the general custodian wrote frankly: "We should take a favorable view of any activity aimed at reducing the amount of property held by the churches."[4] The ideal solution, as far as Jerusalem was concerned, was to engineer settlement with church organizations, which would minimize political damage and would imply de jure recognition by the Christian world of the new situation in Israel. This envisaged solution was totally at odds with the manifest interest of the Christian world to protect its rights and assets in the Holy Land. Consequently, Israel's path to achievement was by no means smooth.

The problems Israel faced were colored by the organizational structure and political ties of the various church organizations and their fate during the 1948 war. The legal ownership of property of the Scottish and Abyssinian churches, for example, was not challenged. However, during the hostilities, several of their sites were requisitioned by the army and were not restored to their owners or, alternatively, were seized by individual and institutional squatters because of the shortage of accommodation at the time. The buildings owned by the Roman Catholic Church were under the custody of the Vatican and various Catholic countries such as France, Italy, Spain, Austria, and Poland, who brought pressure to bear on Israel to release their assets. As a consequence, a large number of buildings were returned to their owners. In some cases, the churches agreed to lease some of their property to the Israeli authorities, and in others the negotiations dragged on for several years and were influenced by economic, military, and political considerations. This was also true of the assets of the Anglican and Greek Orthodox churches, where, in most cases, negotiations culminated in settlements while several disputes remained unresolved for many years.[5]

Some of these cases related to buildings requisitioned by the Israel Defense Forces, which, while acknowledging the church's legal ownership, refused for security reasons to vacate them. These included several buildings adjacent to the Stella Maris monastery on Mount Carmel, in which naval headquarters were housed. The differences were resolved only in the early 1960s. The Tabgha hostel, which overlooked the Syrian border, was another strategic stronghold that the IDF refused to vacate, although the building was German Catholic property that had been leased during the Mandate as a convalescent home for British officials. The trickiest case was that of the Franciscan monastery alongside the Coenaculum on Mount Zion, which remained empty after the war. For security reasons, the Franciscans were not permitted to return.

Another complicated question was that of the assets of the Greek Catholic community. Archbishop George Hakim had fled the country when Haifa was occupied by Haganah forces, and his community's assets were originally classified as absentee property and were placed under the guardianship of the general custodian. When Hakim was permitted to return, he invested great effort in gaining back his church's assets, and the bulk was returned in the 1950s. One of the more important agreements between the Israel government and the Vatican, signed in December 1955, resolved all problems relating to Roman Catholic property in Israel.[6] The assets of the Greek Orthodox, Coptic, Maronite, and Syrian-Orthodox churches constituted a problem of a different kind. They had been placed under the supervision of the general custodian of absentee property, either because the previous custodians of the assets had fled or because the central authority of that particular church was located outside Israel, for example, in the Old City.[7]

Closely connected to the property question was the issue of compensation for damage inflicted on churches during and immediately after the 1948 war. This subject preoccupied the authorities for close to a decade. The first settlements, in the early 1950s, related to the Notre-Dame de France edifice in Jerusalem, the convent of the Franciscan Sisters in Tiberias, the school of the Salesian monks in Beit Jamal, St. Anne's monastery in Haifa, and the mission house of the Latin patriarchate in Beisan. Other claims were settled only years later.[8] Since a detailed survey of the question of church assets is beyond the scope of the present study, I have chosen to elaborate on only four of the more interesting cases: the question of the "Russian property" is discussed in the present chapter, and the other three cases—the assets of the Lutheran, German Catholic, and Greek Orthodox churches—in the following one.

"Russian Property": The Mandatory Era

What was known as the "Russian property" in Palestine was unique in that it was owned by several Russian institutions, both government and ecclesiastical, which were still at loggerheads concerning ownership titles even after the termination of the British Mandate. Where Israel was concerned, the problem involved foreign relations considerations above and beyond the already thorny issue of its relations with the Christian world. Most of this Russian property had been accumulated in the nineteenth century in the course of Russia's intensive religious involvement in the Holy Land.[9] By the end of World War I, it consisted of thirty-five plots of land and various buildings, including the Russian consulate, housing, hostels, hospices, and churches. Soviet authorities estimated the value of all these assets at the time at eighteen million pounds sterling.[10] There were four official owners: the Russian government, the Russian Ecclesiastical Mission, the Palestine Orthodox Society, and Prince Alexandrovitch.

These two associations were founded in the nineteenth century and were backed by the tsarist government, which displayed great interest in the Middle East at the time. The Mission was an essentially religious institution, dedicated to the establishment of churches and monasteries, to religious worship and education. The Society was founded as a charitable and welfare institution for Russian pilgrims. Both associations purchased land in Palestine and built numerous buildings. The Mission was headed by an administration of monks and churchmen who received direct instructions from the synod in Russia. The Society was headed by a local administration whose head resided in Russia.[11] The main income of these two bodies came from donations and allocations from Russian institutions and from their property in Palestine. In addition to the assets of these institutions, Russian property had been purchased in Palestine before World War I by Prince Sergei Alexandrovitch (first president of the Orthodox Society) on behalf of the Society, but it had been registered in his name.[12] The Society controlled some 80 percent of the Russian assets in the country. The activity of the Russian Church in the Holy Land reached its peak in 1913. It then owned more than twenty schools, charitable institutions, seminaries, churches, and monasteries, and dealt with some 13,000 Russian pilgrims.[13]

Political developments in the first two decades of the twentieth century had a highly negative impact on these organizations. Shortly after the outbreak of World War I, Russia and the Ottoman Empire found themselves on opposite sides, a situation which supplied the Turkish authorities with justification for requisitioning Russian assets in Palestine. The October Revolution three years later had a damaging effect on both organizations. The flow of income was almost completely halted as was the influx of pilgrims from Russia, and despite the financial aid they received from émigrés from the Soviet Union, they had great difficulty in financing their activities in Palestine, particularly since the new Communist regime in Russia placed them in an entirely new situation. Church and state were officially separated in January 1918, and all church assets were nationalized.[14] The Soviet Union proclaimed itself the heir of the tsarist government and as a consequence claimed title to all Russian assets in Palestine.

The repressive measures adopted by the Soviet Union against the Church and the persecution of its leaders were protested by the Karlovtzi Group, which fled the USSR in 1919. This group, whose center was in Geneva, encompassed some two million White Russian émigrés.[15] Those leaders of the Society who escaped the purges unscathed fled the country, settled in Paris, and continued to manage its affairs from there.[16] The directors of the Mission and the Russian Orthodox Society in Palestine now refused to maintain any contact whatsoever with the Russian Church in the Soviet Union or with the Russian Palestine Society, established in Moscow after the Revolution as a replacement for the Orthodox Society.[17] Soviet attempts to persuade the local administrations of the Mission and the Society in Palestine to change their stand proved futile, and the rift naturally had economic repercussions.[18] The Mission and the Society were reduced to bankruptcy and were unable to function, as a consequence of which the British were forced in 1924 to appoint officials to conduct their affairs. This arrangement, which became permanent, was supervised by the Jerusalem district commissioner and was anchored in law in 1926 and

1938.[19] However, Jewish experts on the subject later claimed that this solution did not prevent "a state of [financial] chaos."[20]

The third factor that affected the status of these Russian organizations was the change in the political-constitutional and theological circumstances after the end of Ottoman rule over Palestine and the delegation of the Mandate over this territory to a Christian country. This situation was a source of both hope and concern for all the Christian communities in Palestine and for their world centers. It instilled new life in the conflicts over the Holy Places that had raged for so long, and increased the need for a mechanism to resolve these conflicts. The only solution that appeared feasible at the time was to assign the issue to an international committee of inquiry under the auspices of the League of Nations. This, however, was impossible because of the fierce controversy around the issue of the composition and powers of such a committee. Still the League did not abandon the idea, and in Article 14 of the Mandate treaty it demanded that such a committee be established.[21]

Thus, in the early 1920s, when the British were faced with the problem of how to handle disputes concerning the Holy Places in Palestine, they lacked international backing.[22] The solution eventually found was based on two operative principles. Britain engaged to maintain the status quo that had existed since the fall of the Ottoman Empire. It also guaranteed that local courts would not rule on questions relating to the status quo (lest these rulings prove incompatible with the decisions of the future League of Nations committee) and empowered the high commissioner to decide on appropriate procedure.[23] The precise legal details of British legislation on this matter as laid down in the 1924 King's Order in Council were clearer. It empowered the high commissioner to decide which issues in dispute could not be brought before Palestinian courts, but stipulated that his decision required ratification by the League of Nations. In any event, Mandatory legislation limited the possibility of changing the status quo on the Holy Places and reinforced Britain's authority to interpret that legislation and to act as the de facto administrator of Church assets, particularly since the League of Nations committee was never established. The facts indicate that throughout the British Mandate over Palestine, not a single dispute over the Holy Places was addressed to the local courts.[24]

Nonetheless, in this period the Soviet Union tried twice to challenge the status quo. In May 1923, a year after the Mandate began, it approached the British Foreign Office and claimed recognition as the heir of the tsarist government and hence ownership of these assets. This Russian claim constituted one of the main reasons why the British government enacted the 1924 administrative ordinance.[25] The Foreign Office's negative answer, conveyed in October of that year, was based on that ordinance. The Russians renewed their request two decades later, in early March 1945, again claiming title to the assets, and received the same reply. Ten days before the end of the Mandate, when it was obvious that Great Britain no longer wielded authority in this matter, the Soviet Union again submitted an official request, which this time remained unanswered.[26]

Concurrently with this diplomatic activity, the Soviet Union, having granted official recognition to the Russian Orthodox Church inside Russia, tried in 1945 to persuade the Russian Mission in Palestine to hand over its assets to the Church in Moscow. The new patriarch for Palestine and the Leningrad Metropolis were dispatched to Palestine, and various emissaries from the Soviet consuls in Beirut and Cairo visited Jerusalem for the same purpose. These efforts also proved fruitless.[27] The legal basis for Britain's consistent rejection of the Soviet Union's ownership claims was plain, but George V's government was apparently also guided by political motives: concern at the prospect of Soviet infiltration into Palestine in religious-ecclesiastical guise.[28] Explaining the background to Britain's rejection of the Soviet claims, as submitted in late 1944, Sir Arthur Dawe, the influential deputy undersecretary of the Colonial Office, wrote: "We should think twice before abandoning the interests of the [White] Russians who, irrespective of their technical status, have, in effect, been placed under British protection."[29] In 1948 a senior Foreign Office official offered an even franker explanation of what was considered in British ruling circles to be axiomatic policy: "We are trying to make it as difficult as possible for the Russians to intervene in Palestine."[30] As will be shown below, the British also tried to set up obstacles that would outlast the Mandate.[31]

Newly accessible Russian diplomatic papers indicate that the main Soviet interest in Palestine toward the end of World War II was strategic, based on the desire to establish a political foothold in the region and, in particular, to try and undermine British domination. The USSR therefore obviously attributed great weight to the possibility of taking over Russian assets in Palestine, an achievement that would strengthen their own position.[32] For example, in an internal memo in March 1945, the Soviet foreign minister was informed that it was vital to establish a consulate in Palestine in order to supervise Anglo-American policy in the region and protect the rights to Russian assets.[33] This explains the Soviet Union's persistent interest in these assets even in its political dealings with the State of Israel. This policy was in stark contrast to the Soviet Union's relative passivity on this issue during the Mandate period.

The Anglo-Soviet clash over Russian assets was only one of the problems that Israel inherited. The other unsolved issue was internal. After the establishment of the Soviet Union, there was heated controversy in the Russian community in Palestine, among both clerics and laity, on the question of its attitude toward the religious authorities of the new Communist state. The most vehement opponents of recognition of the new Russian patriarch and his authority in Palestine were members of the Orthodox community and the heads of the Mission.[34] Above and beyond their hostility toward Moscow and the fact that they naturally received backing from the British, these two groups were characterized by what Jewish Agency officials termed anti-Semitism and active support for the Arabs.[35] On the other hand, the Moscow-oriented laypeople bowed to the authority of the patriarch in Moscow and advocated transfer of Russian assets to official Soviet representatives—the assets of the Palestine Society to the Soviet government and of the Mission to the Moscow patriarch.

Israeli officials believed that this group was headed by the abbot of the Russian monastery in Ein Kerem.[36] The rift within the community made it even harder for Israel to resolve the problem. The policy that the British had pursued, namely, preservation of the status quo in line with the League of Nations treaty, was not a feasible option for the Israeli government, whose involvement had been demanded by both interested parties.[37] The conflict reached its height after Gromyko's speech at the UN General Assembly in April 1947, in which for the first time he voiced Soviet support for the establishment of a Jewish state in Palestine.[38]

Taking Over

Under these circumstances, Israel's first cabinet faced conflicting pressures. Many of the directors of the Palestine Orthodox Society had fled the country when the fighting began, and almost all those who remained were living on the Jordanian side of the border. The Society's secretary, the only member of the directorate who remained in Israel, placed himself and a large part of the Society's archives at the disposal of the Israeli authorities (the remainder was sent abroad) in order to obtain Israeli protection. This initiative incensed the Moscow-oriented group, who appealed for aid to the governments of Czechoslovakia, Poland, and Yugoslavia. With Moscow's blessing, these governments petitioned the Israeli government for a share in the supervision of the Society's assets,[39] and submitted documentation relating to the Society's ownership of property in Palestine in order to promote legislative action.[40]

The Jewish pre-state authorities had already been aware of another complicated aspect of the situation. In the last year of the Mandate, the heads of the Orthodox Society and the Russian Mission attempted to establish legal facts by handing over their property to the British. Their greatest fear was that once Israel was established, heavy political pressure would be brought to bear on them to hand over Russian assets to the Soviet Union. According to information received by the Jewish Agency intelligence service, the heads of the Mission and of the Society appealed to the Mandatory authorities in January 1948 to forestall such undesirable developments, and a two-stage tactic was devised.[41] In the first stage, a law would be enacted transferring the assets to a committee composed solely of Moscow's opponents. This committee would be authorized to lease, rent, and mortgage the property of these bodies and to delegate authority to another body or individual for no more than three years. In the second stage, the assets would be handed over for three years to the British consul-general in Palestine ("or some other British representative"), to whom the committee's authority would be delegated. In short, the Jewish authorities had discovered a scheme aimed at ensuring continued British legal control of Russian assets after Israel's establishment.

Great Britain has never granted full access to archival material that could elucidate the motives of the Mandate authorities, but it is evident they were trying to prevent Israel from transferring Russian property to the Soviet Union.[42]

In late 1947, the British had learned that, since the USSR had recognized Lebanese independence, the Lebanese government was planning to hand over the Russian assets within its borders to the Soviet Union.[43] Since it was now well-known that the USSR supported the establishment of a Jewish state, London was undoubtedly anxious to prevent a similar move on the part of Israel by enacting legislation "which will guarantee [British] administrative continuity even after May 15 1948," thereby blocking Israeli attempts to gain control of the assets.

Documents in the Israel State Archives and the Zionist Archives reveal that the Zionist leadership in Palestine resisted these attempts and tried to foil them. Yitzhak Rabinovitch, head of the Russian Department of the Jewish Agency, reported that the various attempts to thwart British initiatives included efforts to persuade the Jewish lawyer who was dealing with the assets on behalf of the Society and the Mission to postpone litigation, since "we are anxious for the property of the Russian people not to pass into the hands of the Russian pogromists from the tsarist era and their Arab associates as a result of a despicable conspiracy . . . [and since] we want to repay the Russian people for their positive attitude toward our cause."[44] In May 1948, the lawyer reported that the Mandatory authorities intended to enact a law placing Russian assets under the administration of the Orthodox Palestine Society and the Mission. When information was leaked from the printing press where the *Official Gazette* was to be printed, a unit of the Palmach (the pre-state Jewish strike force) broke into the press and confiscated all copies of the proposed law.[45] This operation prevented official publication of the law but did not affect its legal validity, since it was later printed as a separate booklet.[46] In any event, the second stage of the plan was never put into effect.[47]

Israel's support for the Soviet Union also took the form of economic assistance to the pro-Muscovite group in the local Russian community, which was no longer receiving funds from the central offices of the Mission and the Society. "We have decided," wrote Rabinovitch, "to come to the aid of our 'new friends' who are doubly afflicted as pro-Muscovites and pro-Zionists, and we have extended material and institutional aid to them to the best of our ability." It seemed clear to him that "the reactionary and anti-Semitic directors of these organizations have openly gone over to the side of the Arabs and fled the Jewish sector, and since most of the Russian property in now within the territory of the State of Israel—there is every reason to hope that the efforts of the representatives of the Russian people will be crowned with success."[48] The absence from Israel of the heads of the White Russian sector of the Mission in 1948 created a vacuum that was filled by the supporters of the "Red" church who thenceforth enjoyed de facto ownership of all church assets.[49] Israel, for its part, had no desire to exercise direct control over these assets and preferred, in May 1948, to take over the property of the Russian Orthodox Society—known as the "Russian Compound"—in the center of Jerusalem and house public institutions there.[50]

There is no extant documentation on how the Zionist executive and the Israeli authorities viewed the situation at the time, but this development appears to have served them well.[51] Israel was evidently influenced in its decisions by several factors: the anti-Zionist predilections of the heads of the Society and the Mission, most of whom had left or been transferred to Jordan and who enjoyed Jordanian support, fear of establishing facts that would perpetuate British control of the property and make it difficult for Israel to act, and what it perceived as the Soviet Union's pro-Israel line at the UN. In the aftermath of chaotic wartime conditions, the authorities were inundated with requests for aid on the part of individuals who had previously been supported by the Society, requests which could not be ignored for humanitarian reasons.

Thus, after appointing an official to deal with the subject and before strategic decisions were made at the cabinet level, Israel's first action was to extend aid to the needy and to settle the debts of the tenants of the Society's property.[52] The need for cabinet decisions became apparent after the appointment of a Russian minister in Israel, Yershov, who approached the Israeli authorities to clarify their stand on the subject.[53] Russian Mission circles also tried to sound out the Israelis.[54] In September 1948, Russian diplomatic representatives gained the impression that Israel would not hinder them if they tried to take over the property of the Mission and the Society.[55] At the first political discussions of the subject between the Russian consul and Rabinovitch, the latter reported "on the activity we have conducted in order to rescue [Russian] property and prevent its transfer to the British before [the termination of the Mandate on] 15.5."[56] And at his first meeting with Yershov, Rabinovitch explained that he was doing his best "to ensure that [Russian property] will be handed over to the Soviet Union."[57] In an additional discussion in October 1948 with a member of the Russian legation staff, "it was agreed that Russian assets in Israel are to be handed over sooner or later to a representative of the Russian people."[58] Rabinovitch's assurances, which were not grounded on any official Israeli decision, incensed the Foreign Ministry,[59] but in the absence of any counterdecision, the Russian diplomatic representatives in Israel had every reason to be optimistic. Recently opened Soviet Foreign Ministry documents indeed reveal that Russian diplomats and clerics were making practical preparations at the time to take over ownership of all the Russian assets in Israel.[60]

It was evident to the Israeli authorities at the time, however, that solution of the problem was by no means simple. On the one hand, legal experts voiced the definite opinion that the Russian Mission in Israel was still a part of the Russian Church, and that the fact that a small group of dissidents regarded themselves as the heirs of that Church, as in tsarist times, was irrelevant. This view was substantiated by the assertion of the Soviet government, which was usually perceived as the legal heir of the tsarist government, that the existing Russian Church was the direct heir of its predecessor. This being so, Israeli experts anticipated that the courts would confirm the legality of the appointment by the Muscovite patriarch of a director of the Mission in Palestine. Accordingly, all Israel had to do in order to avoid lengthy litigation and to allow the situation to take its own course was to revoke the high commissioner's order, establishing a three-member council to manage Mission property.[61]

The property of the Orthodox Society was a different story. Israeli experts believed at the time that the scant legal documentation they had received could not suffice to prove the title of the Russian Church and the Soviet government to the Society's assets. The search for further evidence would be lengthy, and there was no guarantee that it could serve as the basis for legal rulings. Underlying this legal argument was a weightier political calculation. Israel greatly feared any action that would openly transfer the considerable assets of the Orthodox Society to the Soviet Union, since, as Sharett phrased it, such action "might antagonize the Vatican, and there is no need to add fuel to the flames in these sensitive times."[62] Operatively speaking, therefore, it was expedient to accept the recommendation to rescind the high commissioner's order. At the same time, it was decided to institute temporary custody over the assets of this Society. On 2 September 1949 an ordinance was enacted accordingly, revoking all legislation of the Palestine government that had not been published in the *Official Gazette* as well as the 1926 King's Order in Council dealing with this subject.[63] It is noteworthy that Israel intended subsequently to take a further step, as the foreign minister explained to the cabinet. "After this legal aspect is settled, I intend to explain all this to the Russians in a very cordial manner and to ask them to make things easier for us in this respect. This request should of course be accompanied by our assurance that we will hand over [the Society's] property, but meanwhile they will make things easier for us by not insisting that we do so publicly—we will do it in due course."[64] The British were justified, therefore, in concluding that the Israeli moves were aimed, inter alia, at guaranteeing the support of the Soviet bloc for Israel's anti-internationalization campaign.[65]

However, the Russian legation flatly refused to accept the official part of this plan of action as conveyed by the Israeli Foreign Ministry in the first week of February 1949. The objections were mainly directed at the idea of appointing an Israeli custodian over the majority of Russian assets. In this context, the Soviet diplomats also cited the written assurance that Rabinovitch had given, on his own initiative and without official sanction, to Archimandrite Leonid to hand over the Mission's assets to him.[66] The Archimandrite, who was residing in the buildings of the Mission, was acting as its head, with Israel's approval, having been granted power of attorney by the Muscovite patriarch. Israel eventually acceded to the Russian request and abandoned the idea of custody over the Society's assets. It was also decided that an Israeli directorate would be appointed to administer those assets only with Soviet approval.[67]

In the absence of detailed minutes of the discussions, it may be assumed that Israel's readiness was inspired by wider political considerations, and above all by what it perceived as the vital need to foster good relations with the Soviet Union. According to a summary of Foreign Ministry discussions: "We will not enter into any disputes on these matters. We [also] approve Rabinovitch's action in entrusting Mission affairs to the Archimandrite Leonid. He must, of course, reformulate the acts of transfer and make it clear that he is acting in an individual capacity and not as representative of the government."[68] From now on, Israel claimed that Rabinovitch had acted not as a government official but as the representative of the Jewish Agency responsible for Russian and not Soviet property.[69] It should be noted that it was obviously in Israel's interest at the time—when it was still under obligation to accept the idea of internationalization—not to grant Rabinovitch official status.[70] In this manner, the Israeli authorities arranged for the practical transfer of assets without having to resolve legal problems that were liable to arise as a result of official transfer (which it was reluctant to implement at the time.) Concurrently, Israel began, with relative haste, to hand over to the Soviet government those assets of the tsarist government which were not in dispute.[71]

The process was completed in June 1949 when the records in the Land Registry were amended, and the Soviet government, as heir to the tsarist government, was granted title to the consulate building and two plots in Jerusalem.[72] These records, it should be noted, did not encompass all the assets that the Soviet government wanted to take over, for which the necessary legal proof was lacking.[73] Another matter not settled at this stage was the question of the property of Prince Sergei, which was claimed by the Soviet legation. The Israelis refused this request because of legal complications and problems of precedence.[74] The Soviet diplomats were not appeased by Israel's gestures and continued to voice claims "in rather aggressive fashion."[75] Israel's official reaction in 1949 was to assert that it would consent to the transfer of the Prince's assets on condition that it received Soviet confirmation that this property had in fact belonged to the tsarist government. As for the property of the Orthodox Society "it would be preferable [for its representatives] to have in their possession legal rulings and documents from the Russian government and the Soviet government proving legal continuity."[76]

It was no secret that the Soviet Union was trying to gain possession of Russian assets, and anti-Communist circles in the Russian Mission and the Orthodox Society in Israel and abroad were naturally anxious to thwart its efforts.[77] Foreign diplomatic representatives in Israel and the American press displayed a growing interest in the subject. The main concern voiced to Israeli representatives was that Communist influence was liable to infiltrate the Middle East under the cloak of the Russian Church. Apprehensive at the prospect of similar negative reaction in the Catholic world, the Israeli authorities cited significant legal arguments to justify their action and to bear out the view that "what we have here is not a choice between the Muscovite Church and descent churches elsewhere, but between the Muscovite Church and a gang of emigrants whose negative attitude towards us is undeniable."[78] Moreover, as Sharett revealed to the cabinet in early August 1949, Israel now wanted to conciliate the Soviet Union on the question of the Society's assets. When the foreign minister learned in late September that an emissary was due to arrive from Moscow equipped with legal documents to prove that the Society was not a private body but had been headed by the tsar, a Russian diplomat was informed that Israel would be ready to hand over the assets.[79] Although such documents never materialized, Israel chose to act with regard to the assets of the Society and of Prince Sergei "as if the legation owned them," and local authorities were instructed "not to take any action, without the consent of the Soviet legation, with regard to any type of Russian property."[80]

Holding On

This positive approach changed radically in late 1949, mainly because of the Soviet Union's backing for the internationalization of Jerusalem at the UN General Assembly. Sharett later told the Soviet deputy foreign minister that if the internationalization scheme had been implemented, the Soviet Union would not have received the Russian assets for whose sake Israel had "bent" the law, and they would never have gained their only territorial foothold in the Middle East. Israel tried in the following weeks to play on this theme in order to persuade the Russians to alter their stand on Jerusalem.[81] What is more, in the wake of the Soviet vote on Jerusalem, Ben-Gurion himself issued instructions to shelve the transfer process. As a consequence, Israel faced a number of ongoing administrative problems, particularly with regard to the Society's assets, which continued to be supervised by Rabinovitch.[82]

The change for the better in the Soviet Union's stand on Jerusalem in late 1950 did not affect Israeli policy. Formally speaking, Israel continued to insist that only if the Soviet Union produced the necessary legal documents could the official transfer be implemented, but in fact it had decided to halt the entire process. The reason appears to have been political rather than legal. As explained later to the Israeli minister in Moscow: "Before the UN resolution we agreed in practice to transfer all [the Russian assets]. The internationalization resolution totally altered the situation."[83] At a meeting with a Soviet diplomat in late October, the director-general of the Israeli Foreign Ministry said openly that although Israel was gratified by the change in the Soviet attitude on Jerusalem, yet "the time [for dealing with the property of the Society and of Prince Sergei] will come when a just solution to the Jerusalem problem has been fully implemented" and when the "present abnormal situation" whereby their talk was taking place in Tel Aviv and not in the capital, Jerusalem, was rectified.[84]

There was yet another factor influencing Israel's policy. In light of the government's decision of December 1949 to transfer the seat of government to Jerusalem, thereby openly rejecting the idea of internationalization, the location of Israeli administrative offices in the Russian Compound in the center of the capital was a delicate issue. The transfer of official title to property in that area to the Soviet Union was liable to lead to the demand that Israel vacate its premises there. Thus, the change in Israeli policy, of which the Russians were well aware, had a clear logic of its own.[85] The Soviet minister in Israel received instructions from Gromyko to protest to the Israeli authorities at the "delay" in dealings with the Russian assets and to stress that this issue was "entirely separate" from the Jerusalem question.[86] The legal documents that Israel had demanded in order to complete the official transfer process had not yet arrived, and the Soviet authorities were probably having trouble locating them. In any event, in internal official correspondence they gave the Israeli government no credit for the goodwill it had displayed and defined its actions as "delaying tactics" aimed at achieving political objectives.[87]

Heavy Soviet pressure forced the Israelis to tackle the subject in the second week of February 1951, and it was assigned to a committee, which submitted its recommendations two weeks later.[88] Its members were unanimous in their view that it was essential to complete the legal process of government endorsement for transfer to a representative of the Russian Church from Moscow of such Mission property which served for religious worship. On the other hand, opinions were divided on the basic issue of the property of the Society and of Prince Sergei. The majority of the committee, including representatives of the Ministry of Finance and the Ministry of Justice, were in favor of turning the clock back where Israeli policy was concerned. They argued that the Soviet claim should be rejected and that the issue should be decided by courts, despite the assurances given by the Foreign Ministry, while the latter's representatives urged that the commitments they had given should be honored. The majority view was that, legally speaking, Land Registry records could not be altered without a court ruling, since such a step was liable to infringe on the rights of bodies or individuals who did not have access to the administrative authority. Moreover, archival records obtained by the Israeli Ministry of Justice showed that the Orthodox Society had been disbanded by order of the Kerensky government in 1917 and that the Society registered in Petrograd two years later was a new organization and hence, under Israeli law, could not inherit.

In-depth examination by Israeli legal experts also revealed that while some of the Society's property had been officially registered in the Ottoman period in the name of the tsarist government in order to circumvent Turkish legal restrictions, it was, in fact, owned by the Society. The records had been partially amended in the early British Mandate period when the Society assumed legal ownership over part of the property. This probably explained why in the Mandate period the Soviet authorities had failed to prove their case in local Palestinian and Lebanese courts of law. As the legal adviser to the foreign minister later explained, "The legal arguments on which the Russians base their claims are somewhat dubious so that if the government agrees to hand over this property to the Russians it will, in effect, be giving them a gift."[89] Such a "gift" would almost certainly have encouraged the Soviet Union to demand extraterritorial status for the property, its partial or total evacuation, and exemption from municipal and government taxes.[90] This being so, the strategic argument bore considerable weight—"This property is of prime importance from both the economic and the security viewpoints. The political advantage to be gained from honoring the Foreign Ministry's promises is counterbalanced by the economic and security disadvantages of abandoning this property to the Soviets."[91]

Although this was not stated explicitly in the final discussion, the representatives of the Ministries of Justice and Finance apparently believed that the political considerations which had impelled Israel to cooperate with the Soviet Union on this issue between 1947 and 1949 were no longer relevant, and that in the absence of Soviet quid pro quo, Israel should not make serious concessions.[92] The Foreign Ministry representative emphasized the importance of honoring commitments: "We should not lay claim to riches that do not belong to us," he said. The majority recommended that Rabinovitch be assigned to deal with the matter until it was legally settled and that the legal adviser be empowered to claim the property if the court decided that there were no extant legal heirs. The Foreign Ministry, for its part, proposed that the Land Registry records be altered in accordance with the Soviet request "insofar as this is technically possible." If it proved impossible, the matter should be decided by the courts, the Soviet legation should be offered "all possible assistance," and the legal adviser should be authorized to intercede on behalf of the government in support of the Soviet claim.

On 8 March the cabinet conferred on this issue. Sharett delivered an impassioned speech, listing all the arguments in favor of restoring the Society's assets to the Russians. "We did not think it possible," he explained, "to act solely in our own interests. There are many important properties in this country which we requisitioned at a time of panic, but when the owners laid claim to them, we were obliged to return them, and we will continue to do so. This was the case with the Catholic Church, the French [ecclesiastical] property, and the Italian property." He also pointed out that in 1948, relations with the Soviet Union had been cordial and that "although the honeymoon is over . . . decency obliges us in this situation not to seem to be exploiting the estrangement in order to antagonize them and create an open conflict." He said this although well aware of the financial loss entailed in handing over the property, the implications of giving up a strategic area in the heart of Jerusalem, and the anticipated U.S. remonstrations. The cabinet debated the subject at length, but no decision was taken. Most of the ministers were strongly opposed to Sharett's prognosis, above all the prime minister, who argued that the Foreign Ministry's recommendations would lead to the creation of "a Soviet stronghold . . . a Muscovite territory in Jerusalem . . . Russian rule in Jerusalem." Israel's sovereign right was no less valid than that of the Russians, he declared, and just as the Soviet Union had nationalized the Jewish library of Baron Gunzburg,[93] Israel was entitled to take similar action regarding the Society's lay property.

The great majority supported this view but were divided on the appropriate tactic to be employed. Should the property be confiscated immediately, or should the case first be submitted to Israeli and international courts? It was agreed, almost unanimously, that if Israel lost the case, it would have no alternative but to requisition the property of the Orthodox Society. The legal adviser pointed out that

> if the Society . . . which is an integral part of the Soviet government, wins the Russian Compound in Jerusalem, the government will have no choice

> but to confiscate the property for security reasons . . . because we cannot
> allow the Russian Compound to become an extraterritorial area. . . . At some
> stage they will hand over the property to the Russian government . . . and it
> will be impossible to enter the courtyard of the "Moscobia" even in search
> of a biting dog.[94]

The government eventually decided to return the subject to the committee, in which several ministers had been co-opted, possibly because of Sharett's reservations.

The matter seemed urgent to Israel because the Russian legation in Tel Aviv continued to exert heavy pressure on the instructions of the heads of the Foreign Ministry in Moscow, who were apprehensive because of what seemed to them a drastic change in Israel's stand.[95] Their fears were not ungrounded. The government-appointed ministerial committee was not convened for more than a year.[96] Israel had obviously decided to postpone a decision and, in effect, to accept Lavon's recommendation at the March cabinet meeting to practice "official evasion." This meant, in essence, that the decision was negative, and since the legal status of the assets of the Mission, the Society, and Prince Sergei remained unchanged, Israel continued to administer them yet was unable to collect taxes on them.[97] The Soviet authorities for their part began to act behind the Society's back. They succeeded in deposing its secretary, who had been cooperating with Israel, and replaced him with an official who tried unsuccessfully, in conjunction with diplomats from the Soviet legation, to sound out possibilities for recognition of de facto changes in the status of its property.[98] The legation also exerted heavy pressure on the Greek Orthodox patriarch in Jerusalem, who, according to canonic law, was empowered to decide on the construction of new Russian churches in Israel and to sever relations with members of the "White" Russian Church. This pressure bore fruit in 1952.[99]

Terminating the Dialogue

It should be noted that one of the reasons why the Soviet authorities were greatly concerned by the failure to complete the legal transfer of property was that, under the prevailing circumstances, Israeli law, including the Tenants' Protection Act, was still applicable to property registered in the name of Soviet institutions.[100] In February 1952, Yershov raised the issue again, in particularly belligerent fashion, at a meeting with Sharett. He accused Israel of "illegal use" of Russian property and "unreasonable postponement" of its transfer to its legal owners. The foreign minister, who was apparently unable to justify the numerous delays, hinted for the first time at Israel's practical considerations, telling Yershov that "the Israeli government does not know if it has the right to resolve the difficult problem of transfer of assets" and that "some people are of the opinion that this matter should be settled by the legal authorities."[101] In any event, he promised that Israel would arrive at a decision "in the near future, possibly in April 1952," and actually assured Yershov that he would receive a definitive reply on Israeli Independence Day.[102] Yershov was not appeased. Moscow apparently knew only too well that it lacked convincing legal documentation.[103]

The Israeli Foreign Ministry was also subjected to pressure from within. In late April 1952 the government's legal adviser and the Ministry of Finance decided, apparently with the backing of the prime minister, to take administrative action that was to have far-reaching implications. It will be recalled that until then the Russian property had not been administered by an official Israeli individual or institution—Rabinovitch continued to act, ostensibly, as a private individual without official status. The law specified that if the general custodian was informed of this situation, he would be legally obliged to ask the courts to appoint a custodian. The legal adviser exploited this ruling in order to launch the legal procedure but postponed his application to the court in order to enable the Foreign Ministry to bring the issue before the cabinet .[104] Since the legal circumstances were unchanged, it is clear that this initiative reflected the government's desire to change its policy, possibly because of the persistent pressure on the part of the Russian legation as well as the Foreign Ministry's recommendation that the political solution it had proposed be combined with the legal solution recommended by the 1951 committee.[105]

The Israeli cabinet discussed the matter on 27 April 1952. It was decided that Israel would approve the transfer of that property proven incontrovertibly to have belonged to the tsarist government, but would not permit the transfer of the property of the Mission, the Orthodox Society, and Prince Sergei until this transfer was officially endorsed by Israeli courts.[106] The decision was conveyed to the Soviet minister two days later, and after several weeks the property of the Society and of Prince Sergei was placed under the guardianship of the general custodian.[107] For political reasons and for fear of damaging relations with the churches, Israel refrained at this stage from handing over Mission property to the general custodian, and left it in the custody of the Muscovite patriarch.[108] The Soviet legation's protest was confined to submission of a letter to the Foreign Ministry, claiming that the procedure had been illegal and violated official assurances. Its profound disappointment was revealed in reports to Moscow, describing the development as a clear indication of a change for the worse in Israel's attitude toward the Soviet Union.[109] When diplomatic ties between Israel and the Soviet Union were severed in early March 1953, the matter was put on hold, but Israel continued to avoid making decisions.[110] Even though relations were renewed in July, the subject was not restored to the political agenda, and nothing was done for several years.[111]

It should be pointed out that, beyond the legal technicalities, the dispute revolved around strategic considerations relating to the ownership of the property in the Russian Compound in Jerusalem. The Soviet authorities persistently claimed official title to the compound, since ownership of this land would have afforded them a significant territorial foothold in the region. They continued to argue that since the legal adviser had altered the registration of this property in 1949—from tsarist to Soviet ownership—all the property in the Russian Compound should be handed over, irrespective of whether it had been owned and maintained by the Russian government, was registered under a borrowed name, or was held by some other body. Israel, reluctant to grant the Soviet Union such a foothold, argued that a considerable part of the assets registered in the name of the Soviet government had never been owned or maintained by the Russian government, that the name of the tsarist government which appeared in the land register was merely borrowed, and that the property had been purchased using Society funds. Israel insisted that the revision of the records in 1949 did not constitute recognition of Soviet ownership of this property.[112]

The Soviet authorities refused to concede, and the issue, one of the insoluble problems in relations between the two countries, was frequently raised by Soviet diplomats in the 1950s.[113] The fact that there are no accessible Soviet documents on this subject makes it difficult to evaluate the intentions and tactics of the Russians on this matter. However, the status quo was certainly also awkward for Israel, since the unresolved status of the Russian property enabled the Soviet Union to harass the Israeli authorities and hamper them in their efforts to carry out certain activities, such as constructing a road to the Hadassah Hospital in Jerusalem through land belonging to the Russian Monastery in Ein Kerem.[114] The Russian Compound—a legal and physical enclave in Israel's capital—was a particularly troublesome problem. The dispute with the Russians also prevented the implementation of vital building plans that had been approved during the Mandate period. For political reasons it was still essential for various government offices to continue to be housed in the Russian buildings. It was now evident that nothing would come of Israel's insistence that the Soviet Union submit its claim to the courts, since it adamantly refused to do so.[115]

In early 1956, however, it appeared that Moscow was ready to discuss Israeli compensation to the Russian mission for the confiscation of some of its lands along the route of the new Hadassah road.[116] The cabinet therefore decided in April to establish a ministerial committee to examine the subject. After studying its recommendations, Jerusalem concluded that it was possible to arrive at a compromise, whereby Israel would purchase or lease these areas or part of them in return for its recognition of the USSR's formal and legal title to some of this land, and all this without recourse to the courts.[117] The USSR consented to the negotiations a week before the outbreak of the Sinai Campaign, after which all activity was suspended, both because of Soviet strategic and operative backing for the Arabs and because there was evidently no prospect of achieving a compromise under the prevailing political conditions.[118]

Toward a Deal

It was three years before Israel decided that the political circumstances had altered sufficiently to permit contact between the parties. In October 1959, the Russians had submitted a claim for compensation for damages resulting from Israel's failure to hand over the property. A couple of weeks later, the government set up a committee to study the possibility of renewing contact on the basis of the general plan consolidated in 1956. At the end of February 1960, the USSR responded positively, and negotiations were resumed; they lasted, with intervals, for five years. Israel's experts were cognizant of the legal complications entailed. The first problem was that, under Israeli law, the government was not empowered to remove property from the custody of the general custodian without a court order; the second was the possibility, however remote, that other claimants might appear and demand title to the property.

Nevertheless, Israel was increasingly ready to compromise and hoped that the Soviet Union would prove equally willing, so that a settlement could be achieved. Israel would recognize the Soviet government's claims to the property registered in its name and the name of Prince Sergei. More significant was Israel's consent to recognize the Russian Palestine Society, affiliated to the Soviet Academy of Sciences, as owner of the property registered in the name of the former Orthodox Society. Such recognition, however, would not be legally valid without the endorsement of the courts. Still Israel was ready, for its part and with the cooperation of the Russians, to initiate legal action; the courts would then instruct the general custodian to hand over the property to the Soviet Union. The USSR was called on to agree to Israel's requisition or purchase of those properties which were of vital importance for development schemes, in return for payment of an agreed sum; to sign long-term leases for government offices housed in buildings transferred to the Soviet Union by court order; and to provide guarantees to the Israeli government in the event that other claimants appeared who were able to prove their claim to the property.[119] The committee evidently disregarded assertion by legal experts that the Society's property was ownerless and hence came under the State Assets Law, because it had been instructed to make every effort to arrive at a settlement.[120] The cabinet ratified these guidelines on 22 May 1960 and decided to embark on negotiations with the Soviet authorities.

Israeli cabinet minutes from 1959 on are still classified so that information on the background to negotiations is meager and indirect. In June 1960 the first secretary at the U.S. embassy in Tel Aviv reported what he had learned from the director of the U.S. Division of the Israeli Foreign Ministry: "The motive underlying the present negotiations stems from the pressure which Mapam and Ahdut Haavoda have exerted on the government from time to time. These left-wing parties want to be sure that Israel is doing whatever it can to rectify or improve relations between the Soviet Union and Israel. The Israeli Foreign Ministry has no expectations of a positive outcome from these negotiations since neither party, as far as we know, had any compromise proposal to offer on the subject."[121] Five months later, the second secretary at the embassy quoted the deputy legal adviser to the Foreign Ministry as saying that "Israel has scant interest in entering into negotiations with the Soviet Union on the property of the former tsarist government unless it continues the status quo. . . . The Israelis do not believe that the Russians can present new legal evidence to support their claim. If they unexpectedly produce such evidence, Israel will be ready, if necessary, to take other tactical steps in order to preserve the property. These could include a purchase offer or a demand that the Soviet Union acknowledge its responsibility for the Jewish property it seized in the Baltic states."[122] Only full access to Israeli files could confirm the extent to which these internal political or tactical calculations influenced the Israeli decision.

The newly accessible documents at the Israeli State Archives also provide only incomplete information on the four years of negotiations between Israel and the Soviet Union. It appears that neither party was in a hurry to resolve the problem.[123] The details in dispute related to prices and to the property that the Russians were willing to sell.[124] Not all the property Israel was anxious to buy was included in this category, and Israel apparently consented to accept this limitation in the hope that the agreement would establish a precedent and that positive political and economic influences would ensue. The documents reveal that Israel was anxious to achieve a settlement, despite the characteristic Soviet intransigence during the negotiations which forced it to grant certain concessions. One of these was an undertaking to discount any third party claims and in such an eventuality to accept "the necessary aid from the Soviet Union."[125]

Moreover, since it seemed to the Israelis that the Soviets expected more than just to be paid for the sale, they appear to have decided that it was essential to consent to transfer at least some of the disputed Russian property to the Soviet Union in order to soften Moscow's stand. The general custodian, who negotiated with the USSR representatives, told them that he had been authorized to announce that "the Israeli government is ready to take possession, in return for payment, of the property listed . . . while the remainder of the property will be handed over to the Soviet Union."[126] The documents also reveal the disparity between the Soviet desire to achieve a settlement at the government level and the traditional Israeli view that the judiciary should decide the matter.[127] The fact that an agreement was eventually achieved indicates that Israel was no longer insisting on legal procedures, which might last for years, and now agreed to a compromise. Be that as it may, on 26 January 1964, the government approved a deal whereby it would purchase the Russian assets and pay $4.5 million in three equal annual payments, one-third in cash and the remainder in citrus and other goods.[128]

It should be pointed out that, in contrast to the impression Israel wished to create, part of the purchased property was registered in the name of the Russian Imperial government, part in the name of the Orthodox Society, and part in the name of Prince Sergei. There were properties all over Israel, but the largest part was located in Jerusalem, including the Compound, which housed what were known as the "Russian buildings," which was the focus of Israeli concern.[129] It was highly significant that the USSR agreed to the official transfer to Israel of property which, according to Israel's interpretation at the time, was not registered as owned by the Soviet Union, and that Israel accepted this procedure.[130] Both sides tried to conceal these facts in 1964, and the director-general of the Foreign Ministry was then informed that when the required announcement about the agreement was published, it would list the plots by

Russian Ambassador Mikhail Bodrov and Foreign Minister Golda Meir signing
the Israeli-Russian agreement of sale of Russian property in Israel, October 7, 1964.
*Courtesy of the National Photo Collection of the Israel Government Press Office, Prime
Minister's Office. Photo D774–007. Photographer Moshe Pridan.*

number without specifying the names of the registered owners or the exact location of the property.[131] Circumspection was waived only a quarter of a century later when *Ma'ariv*'s political commentator was allowed to discuss the subject in a book on Israeli-Soviet relations. He declared categorically that under
the 1964 agreement, the property of the Orthodox Society was transferred to
the Palestine Archeological Society, affiliated to the Soviet Academy of Sciences, and that from then on the main source of dispute between the Soviet
Union and Israel was the plot in King George Street in the heart of Jerusalem,
which remained under Russian ownership, and Prince Sergei's property, which
was still administered by the general custodian.[132] It is noteworthy that the Mission property was not on the agenda of these discussions, and Israeli archival
files cast no light on the matter.

Once agreement had been reached in 1964, tedious negotiations were conducted on various details. The Soviet government refused to permit its representative to sign the agreement and requested that the general custodian, Haim
Kadmon, do so on its behalf. The motive behind this unusual request, which
is not explained in the extant documents, was apparently reluctance to permit
a Soviet representative to sign an agreement in Jerusalem transferring Russian
property to a foreign government. Although the Israelis were taken aback by
the request, they acceded when it transpired the signature would be legally bind-

ing.[133] The agreement was duly signed on 7 October 1964 and, as anticipated, evoked strong protests on the part of the Russian Orthodox Society in Paris and the Russian Church in New York. In a memorandum to Prime Minister Eshkol, they stated that the Soviet Union had had no title to the property it had sold and had no right to hand it over to Israel. "White" Russian church circles threatened to institute legal proceedings, but for unknown reasons they failed to do so.[134]

This agreement can only be understood fully in its wider context. The two sides arrived at an understanding at the height of their political efforts to mend their diplomatic relations which had been characterized by acute conflict since the Sinai Campaign.[135] The property deal was perceived in Israel (and by British and American diplomats serving there)[136] as a limited expression of Soviet goodwill and readiness to make concessions. Two years later, Dov Satat, the Israel ambassador in Warsaw, who had been involved in the negotiations, claimed that "there were some who feared that this issue would exacerbate relations, and I happened to think otherwise and often reiterated my opinion that, if we remained adamant despite years of pressure and refused to hand over the property, they would be forced to accept our conditions, and that was what happened."[137] It is clear, at the same time, that in Israel's eyes the agreement was of no great political significance. This was in contrast to the situation in the late 1940s and early 1950s, when both sides had attributed considerable political importance to the subject. Israel's diplomatic approach to Russian property in the period under discussion was therefore undoubtedly bound up with its political relations with the Soviet Union. The suspension of the process resulted from Israel's reaction to Moscow's conduct in 1949 and 1956 and the subsequent estrangement. Its renewal in the early 1960s was connected, to a certain extent, to the thaw in relations between the two countries.

Unfinished Business

In any event, the 1964 agreement was merely an interlude in the diplomatic efforts. Contacts between the sides on Russian property were to continue for decades and still await their historian. It should be noted that at the time of the negotiations in the early years of statehood, the "Red" Church of the Soviet Union had been under total control of the political authorities. The influence of the "White" Russian Church, whose leaders resided in Europe, had waned considerably, and the same was true of the director of the Palestine Orthodox Society, who did not reside in Israel. Hence, there is no documentary evidence of strong pressure on their part on the Israeli government in the 1950s and early 1960s, although they objected strongly to its actions. Nor is there any indication of effective intervention by the Western powers or by ecclesiastical bodies. In the final analysis, at least up to 1967, the affair can be defined as a political problem between two sovereign states, Israel and the Soviet Union, relating to the legacy of certain religious bodies.

The situation became more problematic in 1967, when Israel occupied East

Jerusalem and the West Bank, as the two rival Russian churches came under its rule and immediately commenced legal action aimed at dispossessing one another. The Israeli stand on this question was described, in an internal memo, as "disinclination to help a church whose center is in Moscow to solve its problems or to overcome its rivals. . . . We must leave ourselves a free hand to act in either direction."[138] These efforts of the rival churches continued through the 1990s following the renewal of diplomatic relations between Israel and the Soviet Union and after the USSR was dissolved.[139] The registration of Russian property was one of the central issues raised by the Russian foreign minister during his visit to Israel in March 1995.[140] The scant press coverage of the subject, which was probably a reflection of Israel's political sensitivity, provides no detailed information. At the present time, so it appears, three problems are still unresolved: the status of property of the Mission or the "Red Church" located outside Jerusalem; the fate of the "Sergei Building" in Jerusalem, and the post-1990 Russian government's request to register in its name property formerly registered to the Soviet Union.[141]

The following chapter is devoted to complications of another kind that faced the Israeli government in its dealings with Greek Orthodox, Lutheran, and German Catholic property.

8

Land in the Shadow of the Cross: German Lutheran, Catholic, and Greek Orthodox Property in Israel

"Enemy Property"

In Israel's efforts to ensure control of all the land within its borders, one of its main targets was "enemy property." The property of the Lutheran Church was included in this category. The Israeli apparatus dealing with this subject was based, both legally and administratively, on British experience in Mandatory Palestine from November 1939 onward. At the time an ordinance was enacted, empowering the high commissioner to transfer the assets of nationals of countries at war with Great Britain into the custody of the custodian of enemy property, until the signing of a peace treaty. This category naturally included the property of German nationals. The assets of Christian organizations, on the other hand, were earmarked for immediate release.[1] In late 1947, when the establishment of a Jewish state appeared imminent, and in light of Zionist efforts to purchase some of this property,[2] pressure was brought to bear on the British to release German assets, which included 46,000 dunams (1 dunam is a quarter of an acre) of land then held by the custodian. The British government took steps to release this property so as to forestall its appropriation by the future state and so that Germans still residing in Palestine, and in particular the Templars, would not be exposed (as the high commissioner phrased it) "to the mercies of the future Israeli government, whose attitude towards all Germans— including families who have lived peacefully in Palestine for close to a century— [is dictated] more by emotion than by logic."[3] One of the British measures entailed cancellation of all the transfer directives, but the counterdirective was never published in the *Official Gazette*, so the Israeli government was later able to claim that it was not obliged to recognize it.

After the state was established, Israel took several steps aimed at de facto and legal requisition of most of the German land. These included transferring it to the Israeli custodian of enemy property, obtaining special transfer orders from the courts, invalidating old powers of attorney submitted by German lawyers, confiscating assets without paying the maximum compensation stipulated by Israeli law, and—having no choice in the matter as will be shown below—conducting negotiations with property owners with an eye to purchase. The overall objective was to obtain control of tens of thousands of dunams of land by, among other means, temporary custody of the assets as a surety for future Israeli claims against Germany and German nationals. A law enacted by the Knesset in early 1950 prohibited the release of German property and its restoration to its owners. Israel's approach was undoubtedly influenced by the unmistakably pro-German sentiments displayed by the majority of the German Protestant community in Palestine during World War II (of which the British too had been mindful).[4] Another significant factor was the wide-scale exodus of Germans that began in the 1930s, considerably reducing the demand for the services of the Lutheran Church.[5] For obvious political reasons, however, Israel adopted Mandatory legal procedures and excluded ecclesiastical assets from the law. In these circumstances, it negotiated for more than two years with the German Lutheran Church regarding Lutheran property.

These negotiations were launched on the initiative of the Lutheran World Federation, operating from Geneva. The German Lutheran Church asked this body to take action to prevent "this property from falling into alien hands," and in August 1949 the Federation submitted an official request for the release of more than 8,000 dunams of church-owned property.[6] The Israeli land administrators naturally viewed this initiative, whose precise aims and tactics were ascertained by Israeli intelligence, as a threat. What was of particular concern to Israeli officials was the Federation's stand on the strategically placed Syrian Orphanage in Jerusalem, known as the Schneller compound. This 335–dunam area had been classified in the Mandate period as "enemy property" and was seized by the Israel Defense Forces during the 1948 war. In internal discussions by Foreign Ministry's officials in late 1949, the blatant anti-Semitism of the director of the orphanage was noted, which had led him in 1938 to decide to sell the property to prevent it from falling into the hands of "stinking Eastern European Jews with low moral standards,"[7] and move his center of action to the Mar Elias monastery south of Jerusalem. The outbreak of war put an end to this plan.

Generally speaking, the Israelis were troubled by the possibility that important sections of the nonecclesiastical German assets would be classified as places of worship in order to facilitate their release. The prevalent opinion was that since the Lutheran Church was a "nationalist-religious-German" body and had never been granted official recognition under Mandatory law, its assets could be treated as if they belonged to a private and public company rather than to a religious body; this being so, they would not be eligible for release and could eventually be taken over. In this context, the Israelis thought, with some justification, that it would be easier to negotiate with the German Lutheran Church, which had few followers in Israel, than with an international church association whose directors included Swedes, Norwegians, Americans, and Germans. Thus Israel's first move was to attempt to prevent the Federation from intervening, and the second, to expedite the temporary de facto takeover of most of the Lutheran property, partly by means of lease contracts, particularly in the Schneller compound.[8]

The first part of this scheme was not easily implemented, since it was vital for Israel to rally opposition to the December 1949 UN resolution on Jerusalem. It so happened that among those who had raised objections to that resolution were several of the heads of the Lutheran World Federation in the United States, and it was in Israel's interest not to antagonize the Federation on controversial issues. Moreover, Israeli policymakers were also aware that a law was being drafted authorizing the minister of finance to release the assets of German religious, educational, and charitable institutions, in line with the policy laid down in the early years of statehood and with the statements made abroad by Israeli diplomatic representatives. The enactment of this controversial law had been delayed, thereby making it possible to shelve the matter for the time being. To justify the delays, the Israeli authorities cited both the Federation's failure to produce documents granting it power of attorney on behalf of the Lutheran Church and the anticipated legislation on German property.[9] However, Israel was unable to evade negotiations altogether for political reasons largely connected to the international struggle around Jerusalem that it was waging at that time with the Catholic Church. Sharett thus told Kaplan that "it is important for us—if this is only possible—to conciliate the Lutheran Church, to some extent, in order to prevent a united and consolidated Christian front against us."[10] The foreign minister was obliged to agree to negotiate with an Federation representative who was scheduled to visit the country in February 1950.[11]

Negotiating with the Lutherans

An internal document of the Lutheran World Federation, which fell into the hands of Israeli intelligence, indicated what the Lutherans hoped to achieve and partially explains the dynamics of the negotiations.[12] Beyond the desire to clarify the possibility of achieving "successful settlements" that would enable leasing, sale, or exchange of the property, the Lutheran World Federation's actions were guided by a basic hypothesis: "Since Israeli public opinion will not permit missionaries of German nationality to renew their activity in Israel, [and since] the services of Lutheran orphanages, schools, hospitals, and churches can only be provided effectively by a German staff . . . we should seek an agreement for transfer of the value of the assets to other parts of the Holy Land where Christian missionary activity is accepted and possible." Strategically speaking, this implied that the Federation was resigned to the cessation of Lutheran activity in Israel. Hence the challenge Israel faced in these negotiations was much less daunting than in the case of other churches. Tactically speaking, the Federation's objective was to sell the property so that the significant questions, as far as it was concerned, were to discover which Lutheran property could be won from Israel and, of course, the conditions for this sale.

The first issue was critical, since only a small proportion of the Lutheran property was devoted to religious worship, a category that Israel was under obligation to release. Naturally enough, the Lutherans were anxious to include all their property within this category. When their representatives visited Israel in January and February 1950 to sound out the situation, they discovered that Israel's basic stand conflicted with their interests. The Israeli officials stressed that no practical action could be taken until completion of the legislation process in the Knesset, which would enable the authorities to exclude German ecclesiastical property from the category of "enemy property." It was explained that discussion of this legislation was due to take into account the question of the frozen assets of German Jewish communities and that in any event the entry of German missionaries would not be permitted, "even though we are aware that not all the German Protestant clergy were Nazis." At the same time, the Israelis were undoubtedly making every effort to protract the discussions. The fact that they discovered that the Federation's approach was "extremely practical" and that it was not likely to insist on the right to renew Lutheran activity naturally raised hopes in Jerusalem.[13]

Israel's delaying tactics, such as the demand for legal documents proving the Lutheran claim, and the decision to render the continuation of the discussions conditional on the conclusion of the financial negotiations with the British, which also encompassed the question of enemy property in Mandatory Palestine, also seemed to serve their aim.[14] Moreover, it was clear to the Israelis that the Federation was on firm legal ground, but they insisted, nonetheless, on what they considered to be the overriding moral consideration. To emphasize this point, the Israelis arranged for the delegation to meet with Holocaust survivors in kibbutzim that had been established on Lutheran land.[15] Jerusalem delaying tactics seemed to be bearing fruit, and the U.S. ambassador in Israel was advised accordingly that there was no need for his intervention, since "Israel is ready to discuss the problem seriously."[16]

Israeli optimism was short-lived. On their return to Geneva, the Lutheran Federation representatives took two steps that proved beyond the shadow of a doubt that they were going to reject Israel's stand. They threatened Israeli diplomats that if they did not receive a clearer commitment than they had received during their visit, they would side against Israel on the Jerusalem question. They also succeeded in recruiting the U.S. delegate to the UN, who in February 1950 lent his support for the Lutheran Federation's demands.[17] A day later, Israel's UN representative, Abba Eban, heatedly defended Israel's right to refuse to return property to those responsible for the Holocaust. However, he also expressed willingness to negotiate on questions relating to enemy property. The uniquely scathing tone of his response was influenced by Israel's fear of a U.S. recommendation to the effect that the UN Trusteeship Council be empowered to rule on matters relating to property in Jerusalem. As a result, the Federation apparently had second thoughts, and its representative assured Eban that he would "put his trust in negotiations with us and not in international pressure."[18]

However, Israel continued to fear the harmful impact of such pressure, in light of the imminent struggle at the UN Assembly.[19] Such pressure could cause economic damage, since Israel was liable, in this event, to forfeit that part of the property which was possibly salvageable through negotiations, and also because of the UN Trusteeship Council resolution calling for restoration of church property to its previous owners or to trustees of the same religion. Israel was also liable to lose out on the deal for the return of Jewish property as a result of Lutheran pressure on the German government. In the local sphere, Israel might be forced to agree to less favorable conditions because development schemes for the capital were being delayed due to uncertainty as to the fate of such pivotal areas as the Schneller compound.[20] For these reasons it seemed expedient to abandon the delaying tactics and, indeed, in mid-June, Israel asked the Lutheran Federation to agree to immediate negotiations.[21] A month later, contacts were established between the sides in Israel, and talks were scheduled for September.[22] As part of the effort to solve the problem, the Foreign Ministry did everything in its power to ensure that the relevant law would be passed before that date, and it was enacted in July 1950.[23] Israel wanted to exploit the authority granted to the minister of finance under the law for immediate release of the Lutheran church buildings, but stipulated that income-bearing assets would not be released. Active "charitable institutions," on the other hand, would be released "down to the very last one," not into German hands but into those of trustees of the same religious denomination who were neither Germans nor former collaborators with Nazi Germany. The Lutheran Federation, for its part, would provide assurances that no further claims would be made with regard to the property and that the released assets would be purchased or exchanged for frozen Jewish property in Germany.[24]

Israel's agreement in principle to negotiations was obviously based on fear of antagonizing the Christian world, but it was equally anxious to protract the negotiations as far as possible. Its representatives explained frankly that "Israel's reckoning with German is more weighty than all other reckonings."[25] In addition to its proclaimed reluctance to compromise with regard to property which had not served for religious purposes—a significant stumbling block in relations between the parties—it raised new demands concerning property it had already agreed to release.[26] The Lutherans insisted that these assets be handed over to their Federation. The negotiations bogged down due to these differences of opinion, the lack of progress on other details of the return of German-Jewish property, and the death in late 1950 of the chairman of the Israeli delegation, but the stalemate served Israeli interests.[27] In mid-1951, as the date of the UN Assembly approached, the Israelis decided that it was inadvisable to drag out the discussions, and the matter was brought before the cabinet.[28] It decided at the end of the first week of April 1951 to return the Lutheran churches in Jaffa, Haifa, and Waldheim village (or their value); as regards the rest, it insisted on its right not to release them but, "in light of political considerations," to arrive at a monetary compensation settlement.[29] Israel planned to offer the Lutherans a half million Israeli pounds (and was ready to go up to a million) for all their assets, and to pay this sum "insofar as possible" from the aforesaid frozen Jewish property in Germany.[30]

Clinching a Deal

It should be noted that the value of the assets defined as returnable and eligible for compensation (property that had been used exclusively and practically for religious, educational, and charitable purposes) was approximately 1.5 million Israeli pounds, with a market value of at least twice that sum. This means that Israel was ready to pay the Lutherans between one-sixth and one-third of their value.[31] The proposal was dispatched to the Lutheran World Federation with an offer for further negotiations in Geneva, apparently in order to guarantee freedom from political pressures and the influence of anti-German public opinion in Israel.

The negotiations began in the first week in May, lasting several weeks, and the agreement signed on 29 August 1951 constituted a manifest, even total, victory for Israel. It was the first agreement between Israel and any Christian church that openly and officially recognized the new political circumstances in Israel.[32] Moreover, in concrete terms the Lutherans declared themselves willing to cease all missionary efforts in Israel and, in essence, all other activity as well—an important achievement as far as the Israelis were concerned.[33] At a relatively early stage in the negotiations, the Lutherans waived their demand for the return of all property in kind and confined their claim to two churches. Moreover, they agreed to provide assurances that the restored property would not be sold or transferred for fifteen years, that no German nationals would be employed without authorization from the Israeli authorities, and, since the property was leased at the time, that the lease would continue. Israel, for its part, agreed to compensate them financially for the rest of the property.[34] This being so, the main issue was its monetary value. The Lutheran World Federation demanded 5.7 million Israeli pounds but eventually agreed to accept slightly more than one-tenth of this sum—650,000 pounds—on the basis of the official value of the property before World War II. Moreover, Israel gained from the fact that the Lutherans agreed to accept a large part of this sum in Iraqi dinars, paid from frozen Jewish assets in Iraq (this plan never materialized).[35] The idea was to earmark this money for the settlement of Arab refugees in the Middle East. This was a clear indication of the Lutherans' resolve to transfer their missionary activities elsewhere. As far as Israel was concerned, this was an incontrovertible victory, not only where the Lutherans were concerned but also in the wider context of its relations with the rest of the Christian world.

This achievement can be attributed largely to the basic weakness of the Lutheran Church in Israel and the defensive stand of the Lutheran World Federation. According to several internal Lutheran documents obtained by Israeli intelligence before the negotiations began, the Federation was resigned to the fact that Israel's moral and political arguments would eventually prevail over their own legal counterarguments and that, in the wake of the Holocaust, Israel would never countenance the renewal of significant German-Lutheran activity within its borders, even if faced with international pressure. This assessment was undoubtedly accurate. The intractability of Israel's stand was demonstrated, interestingly enough, by the technique it adopted in dealing with the formal aspects of property transfer after the agreement was signed. It chose to leave the Lutheran property in the hands of the custodian of enemy property so that, ostensibly, it was not purchased directly from the Germans but released from the custodian who sold it to the Development Authority. This step was taken deliberately in order to forestall anticipated public criticism of the purchase of assets from Germans.[36] Second, the Israelis discovered that the Federation was keen to arrive at an agreement and even to pay a high price, for reasons of its own, above all because this body, being largely American, aspired to dominate the German Lutheran Church, and also because it was convinced that to insist on specific conditions would rule out the possibility of an agreement.[37] The Federation wanted to expedite the negotiations and to complete them before the Israel-German negotiations on the reparation agreement reached a successful conclusion. They suspected that if ecclesiastical assets were included in the general negotiations, the compensation for all or most of the Lutheran property would remain in the possession of the German government and would never reach the churches.

Israel, too, was interested in a separate settlement because only in this case would it have a good chance of influencing the evaluation of church property and fixing the sum to be deducted from the total reparations.[38] On the tactical level, the Israeli representatives took the Lutherans by surprise during the negotiations when they presented evidence that the German owners of the property which was not earmarked for return in kind had planned to sell it to Jews before the war at a low price. This made it easier for Israel to establish 1939 as the determining date for evaluation.[39] However, in light of the course of the concurrent negotiations with Bonn on reparations, Israel eventually gave up the idea of making use of frozen German Jewish property. Whatever the reasons, Israel succeeded, in effect, in taking possession of the Lutheran property, paying much less than its actual value, doing so by means of an official agreement that constituted recognition of the new political realities in Israel, and obtaining the consent of a Christian church to reduce its presence there and, in essence, to cease all activities. Although the Lutherans were left with a bitter aftertaste, the affair was a big step forward on Israel's path through the maze of relations with the Christian world.[40]

Targeting the Dormition and Tabgha

Although negotiations on the German Catholic assets, which were also classified as "enemy property," were more complicated than dealing with German Lutheran assets, Israel again considered the outcome a success.[41] The former, which were then registered in the name of the archbishop of Cologne, included the Dormition Church on Mount Zion in Jerusalem, the Schmidt School in Jerusalem, a building in Haifa that housed ten stores, and a hostel, farm, and small church at Tabgha on the Sea of Galilee shore. The Dormition and Tabgha, which were of strategic importance, were requisitioned by the IDF when the monks had abandoned them during the 1948 war. The Schmidt School and the Haifa properties were taken over by the Israeli authorities and put to use. In 1949, honoring its public statements and commitments, Israel permitted a Benedictine presence in those properties devoted to religious worship: the Dormition church and monastery[42] and the Mosaic Church in Tabgha. Some of this property was still occupied by the army—the hostel at Tabgha and buildings around the Dormition—and the income from several of the buildings was transferred to the custodian of the German property.[43] This change, which did not affect the legal status quo, sparked a political campaign that involved (in contrast to the Lutheran affair) not only the two directly interested parties but also representatives of the local monasteries, the German government, and the Vatican.

It was clearly in Israel's interest if not to take control of this property (particularly the Mount Zion area and Tabgha) then to guarantee its continued military presence there. Mount Zion was a vital lookout point, as had been demonstrated during the fighting with Jordan in 1948 when Israeli units took up positions there. Israeli control of this spot also ensured free access for Jews to "David's Tomb."[44] IDF presence at Tabgha guaranteed control of sections of the Tiberias–Rosh Pina road that were of strategic significance during combat with Syria. To achieve an agreement perpetuating this presence, and thereby implying recognition, however partial, of the new status quo, would be a political triumph for Israel. And finally, the Israeli authorities were also trying to curtail German Catholic activity both because of their general attitude toward Christian activity in Israel and because of their adamant opposition to reconsolidation of the German Christian presence.

Nonetheless, until mid-1951, Jerusalem was reluctant to start negotiations with the German Catholics while still negotiating with the Lutherans. It feared, with some justification, that the German Catholics' greater bargaining skills would adversely affect negotiations with the Lutherans.[45] Moreover, at least in the short run, it was to Israel's advantage to exercise de facto control over the assets. The Israeli authorities were also naturally reluctant to risk exacerbating the tension with the Catholic Church, which was then at its height because of the internationalization question, particularly since 1950 was a "Holy Year" when Israel was expected to be inundated with pilgrims.[46] The other parties involved, however, had nothing to gain from continuation of the status quo. The first of these, naturally enough, was the archbishop of Cologne, whose assets were at risk, and not only because of the establishment of the State. Since the severing of ties with Germany during World War II, supervision of this property by German Benedictines had become more lax. This was an additional source of conflict between the Vatican and this group which, according to Israeli assessments, aspired to a certain degree of independence (barring non-German clerics from their institutions) that was unacceptable to the Holy See.[47] This being so, the pope exploited the weakness of the German Benedictines in the Holy Land from 1939 on in order to assign administration of the Dormition, one of the holiest sites to Christians, to an international Benedictine group that was apparently set up for this purpose. This group was headed by Father Leo Rudloff, an American of German origin, whose aim was to take charge of the remaining German Catholic assets and who naturally also owed allegiance to the Holy See.[48] His extremely anti-Israeli views, which on one occasion impelled Israel to consider declaring him "persona non grata," did not disturb the Vatican.[49]

The tension was heightened after 1948. Officials in Jerusalem believed that the pope planned to win Israeli recognition of his ownership of the assets of the archbishop of Cologne, on the grounds that all Catholic property belonged to the Catholic Church.[50] For political reasons, this demand was not conveyed to Israel directly but through Monsignor Vergani, who in November 1950 asked Israel's consent for the transfer of the archbishop's property in Haifa to the Greek Catholic trust in that district, and threatened to go to court if his request was denied.[51] De facto or legally sanctioned takeover of German Catholic property by the Vatican would certainly have ruled out negotiations with Israel for the sale or lease of all or part of the property. Hence Israel naturally attempted to dissuade Vergani from carrying out his threat.[52] This was also the worst possible scenario for the archbishop of Cologne, who, similarly to the Lutherans, was aware of Israel's attitude toward the activities of German clerics within its borders. Consequently, from late April 1951, in light of the progress made in negotiations with the Lutherans, both Israel and the archbishop were interested in launching discussions on the assets. It was evident to both sides that a successful outcome depended on both resolving problems and thwarting Vatican attempts to prevent it.[53]

Adenauer vs. the Pope

In the negotiations that began in Cologne in July 1951, Israel had several aims in mind. It proposed that Jewish community property in Cologne be handed over to the Church by the Jewish community (which, for its part, would be compensated by the Israel government) while Catholic property would be given to Israel (the hostel and farm at Tabgha, the Schmidt School, and the stores in Haifa). As for the Dormition Church, Israel offered to assist in its renovation and in payment of Catholic debts in return for consent to a settlement. These proposals were conveyed to the archbishop's representatives, who accepted them after prior clarifications with the Jewish community in Cologne concerning their property.[54] Because of the sensitive nature of the talks, and in order to obscure the political implications of the negotiations, the formal Israeli negotiator was a Jewish National Fund representative who was accompanied by Israel's general custodian. The official version was that he was in Germany in order to negotiate with the Lutherans.[55]

Kadmon, the general custodian, reported that the other party believed that the standing of the German Catholic Church would not be undermined by exchange of property and compromise, "because this is already a lost cause. . . . The reverse is true. The settlement will give them back some of their capital and enable them to reinforce those positions remaining in Israel, such as the Dormition."[56] He continued, "From the memorandum [they submitted] I learned that there are totally conflicting views on German church property in Israel. The people from Cologne are interested in rescuing their capital or part of it. Their stand apparently derives from the conviction that they need to adapt to the new conditions in Israel and to draw conclusions from the new situation. The clerics in Israel are interested in 'holding on to their positions' . . . because of Rome's exhortation 'to preserve all church positions in Israel' apparently in the hope that the political circumstances will change."[57] According to the Israelis, the archbishop had concluded that "for Rome the Dormition is a matter of principle, and without a reasonable solution of this question, it is doubtful if [the pope] will consent to a partial settlement."[58]

In fact, no such consent was given. The Vatican, which plainly objected to the negotiations, succeeded in torpedoing an understanding between the two parties. Toward the end of May, the Israeli press reported that, by papal order, the Dormition now belonged to the Holy See and was under the personal supervision of the pope, through his local representative, Monsignor Gustavo Testa. This move was apparently motivated by fear that the German archbishop might relinquish ownership of the building to the State of Israel.[59] In December 1951, Father Rudloff exploited the temporary vacation of the Tabgha hostel by the IDF in order to move in, thereby creating a scandal; this action was probably coordinated with the Catholic Church.[60] In any event, the Holy See made no secret of its intentions, and on 22 December Radio Vatican broadcast a fierce attack on the Israeli government for not acknowledging the Vatican's supreme ownership of the German Catholic property in Israel, and leveled grave accusations at Israel concerning the Dormition Church.[61]

Additional evidence of coordination between the Vatican and the local clergy was provided at the end of January when Vergani's lawyer again threatened to resort to legal action if the stores in Haifa were not handed over to him.[62] In the legal wrangle between Vergani (and the Vatican) and Israel on the property registered in the name of the archbishop of Cologne, Vergani cited the Codex Juris Canonici, under which the property was not considered German and the universal nature of the Catholic Church was acknowledged. Israel argued that, under international law, the laws of the country where the property was located took precedence over the Canonic Codex. Moreover, even according to the Codex, the Holy See was not the true owner of the property but merely "the supreme supervisor."[63] Israeli pressure on Vergani eventually persuaded him that such a move would be considered as "hostile action," and he never carried out his threat.[64] At the same time, the Vatican's resolute stand prevailed both in Jerusalem and in Cologne, and the negotiations were put on hold. The stormy debate on the question of reparations from Germany then raging in Israel also affected Israel's attitude toward renewal of the negotiations.[65] The archbishop's representatives, who were scheduled to arrive in Israel in April 1952, were asked "because of the atmosphere created here in light of the decision on reparations negotiations" to postpone their visit or to relocate the negotiations to some site abroad.[66] The German Catholics refused, however, to countenance a long delay, and at the beginning of July, the archbishop of Cologne took a drastic step in order to force Israel's hand by suing for the return of German Catholic property in Haifa.[67]

What actually altered the basic parameters of the negotiations and facilitated their completion was the intervention of the Federal Republic of Germany. During the reparations negotiations, Germany demanded an official evaluation of the sum to be paid in compensation for total German assets in Israel (including the property of the Catholic Church) and its inclusion in the agreement. Israel surmised that this demand was initiated by representatives of the Templars, who had left the country before the establishment of the State, and of the Australian government, which had taken in most of them.[68] The vital importance of the reparations agreement for Israel explains the government's assent; the agreement signed on 10 September 1952 specified that the parties would enter into negotiations with the aim of arriving at an agreed settlement. Shortly afterwards, the Germans officially requested "the return" of the property registered in the name of the archbishop with special emphasis on Bonn's interest in early release of the Dormition. Under these circumstances there were now three official partners to the negotiations, and the implications were far-reaching. First, technically speaking, Israel faced a situation that required Jerusalem to do its utmost so as not to endanger major economic and political achievements, which were dependent on German goodwill. Second, Germany's pivotal position in the negotiations also enabled it to influence the archbishop's policy. However, Germany's Catholic government wielded enough political and moral clout to accept an agreement on German ecclesiastical property even if the contract itself and its content were unacceptable to the Vatican. This proved to be the case in the course of the negotiations in the last few months of 1953.

Israel's representatives were instructed to agree, if there were no alternative, to pay compensation for lay property belonging to the church. If that proved impossible, they were to return it in kind while obtaining long-term leases and consent to release "Holy Places," excluding the Dormition, "which is not to be released until there is lasting peace with the Arab countries."[69] The negotiations, held in several stages, culminated in an agreement on 30 November. The Dormition Church was to be released, but the restrictions imposed in the area by the IDF were to remain in force "until the state of [military] emergency in Israel ends." Israel also undertook to repair damage to the roof of the church. As for Tabgha, it was agreed that the area north of the Tiberias–Rosh Pina road would be sold to the State of Israel. The Mosaic

Church and an area of 140 dunam around it were to be earmarked for use by
the archbishop of Cologne. The remainder of the land was to be at the free
disposal of the Israel government until the "state of emergency" ended. The
government guaranteed to pay an annual sum for use of this property. Agreement was also reached for the purchase of the plot and buildings in Haifa and
the Schmidt School in Jerusalem. In financial terms, Israel was to pay the German government a half million marks from the reparations funds, and another
140,000 Israeli lira would be paid to the abbot of the Mount Zion monastery.[70]

It should be noted that Israel did not succeed in obtaining the lease for
Tabgha, and the status of Mount Zion was legally problematic since, in both
places, Israel's right to maintain a military presence was confined to states of
emergency, a term which was naturally open to numerous interpretations. According to later Israeli assessments, the Germans were swayed by Israeli arguments mainly because they had been backed by proof that ecclesiastical presence at Tabgha and Mount Zion constituted a security and intelligence threat
to Israel.[71] Israel did not, however, succeed in significantly reducing the Benedictine presence in the two released churches, nor was the financial settlement
as clearly advantageous to Israel as in the Lutheran agreement. However, Israel did succeed in perpetuating the status quo on the number of Benedictine
monks on Mount Zion, restricting their movement in accordance with the
army's instructions, and ensuring access to Jewish sites through the Dormition area.[72] The political gain was considered far more significant this time. It
was thought that since the German government regarded the settlement as
fair, "this will help to improve the political climate toward us in Germany. An
agreement has been arrived at with the Catholic Church in Germany which
strengthens the State of Israel in its political struggle with the Catholic world.
It reinforces our stand in Jerusalem, acknowledges our military needs there,
and confirms our possession of Mount Zion not by coercion but by contract
between a government headed by a devout Catholic and the Catholic Church
itself."[73]

This last statement requires elucidation and qualification. The Vatican was
undoubtedly involved, albeit indirectly, in one way or another, in the various
stages of the negotiations through its contacts with the German government,
with the archbishop of Cologne, and with Father Rudloff.[74] Israel knew only
too well how incensed the Church was at the idea of an agreement and that it
had tried to pressure the Bonn government into postponing the contacts.[75] Policymakers in Jerusalem discovered after the event that the Vatican had been
particularly vexed by the fact that despite its involvement and its known views
on the subject, the agreement had been signed without its prior approval.[76]
The Vatican's efforts proved fruitless in light of the understanding between
the Israeli and German government and the endorsement of the archbishop
of Cologne. The pope's response after the signing revealed that he was not
reconciled to the situation. He ordered Rudloff not to accept the 140,000 Israeli
lira that he was due to receive, and he refused "to recognize this agreement."[77]
In the end, however, Rudloff agreed to accept the money without requesting

Konrad Adenauer, chancellor of the Federal Republic of Germany, visiting the Church of Tabgha on the Sea of Galilee, May 7, 1966. *Courtesy of the National Photo Collection of the Israel Government Press Office, Prime Minister's Office. Photo D808–055. Photographer Fritz Cohen.*

or receiving the sanction of the Holy See, whether because he himself had participated in the early negotiations in Paris, because the archbishop had already received the first payment, because there was no effective way of retracting an intergovernment agreement, or because the funds were earmarked for assistance to Benedictine institutions in Israel. Rudloff apparently changed his attitude toward Israel when he realized that the agreement was an accomplished fact. Another reason for his acquiescence was his hope that the Dormition would become the most important Catholic center in West Jerusalem, to no small degree at the expense of the Franciscans who had exploited their domination of Catholic Holy Places in order to accumulate large sums of money. Be that as it may, Israel felt that it had confronted the Vatican with a fait accompli, and the Holy See, as in other cases in the past, accepted the logic of the situation which, in this event, was to Israel's advantage.[78] It should be noted that the affair was not widely exposed at the time, and the precise details of the agreement were not published in Israel. This was mainly because the Germans were highly sensitive to possible negative reactions in the Vatican and in Jordan. The agreement was therefore classified as "secret" in Israel for at least a decade.[79]

The Greek Orthodox Predicament

No less significant was the secrecy shrouding contacts on property between Israel and the Greek Orthodox Church. One of the inevitable results of this secrecy, which was maintained for decades, is the dearth of archival material on the subject. Both parties brought to the negotiations the extensive experience they had been acquiring since the early days of the British Mandate. The Greek Orthodox Church had amassed considerable assets, mainly in Jerusalem, since the Byzantine period. Most of them were bought in the nineteenth century, when its financial situation improved dramatically due to the wide-scale pilgrimage movement and the support it received (from 1784 on) from tsarist Russia, then the protector of the Orthodox Church in the Ottoman Empire. These two sources of income were almost entirely liquidated in the first two decades of the twentieth century, in the wake of the 1904 Russian-Japanese war, and mainly after the Communist rise to power in Russia.[80] The decentralized nature of the Greek Orthodox ecclesiastical organization, which reduced the prospect of financial aid from sister churches within and outside the Holy Land, as well as internal strife, further exacerbated the crisis and reduced the Church almost to bankruptcy.[81] As a result, in the early 1920s the Mandate authorities compelled the Church to sell part of its assets in order to cover debts. This move engendered Zionist initiative that culminated in the purchase of some 122 dunams of Greek Orthodox property in the affluent Jerusalem Rehavia quarter, 67 in the Mamilla commercial district and Ben-Yehuda Street, and 147 in the Talpiyot quarter.[82] Although the scope was modest, this land was in prime locations, as various studies have shown, and its acquisition furthered the development and expansion of Jewish Jerusalem in the Mandate period.[83]

For this reason, the Greek Orthodox readiness to sell ecclesiastical property to Jews was heavily criticized by the Catholic Church.

The underlying reasons for the renewal of the negotiations for land purchase between the State of Israel and this church were similar, although the circumstances differed. The 1948 war, which led to the partition of Palestine, was a traumatic period for the local Greek Orthodox Church. The community was split in two, some 60,000 in Jordan and only about 6,000 in Israel. This separation greatly debilitated the Jerusalem patriarchate whose area of jurisdiction had covered the entire country until 1948. The fact that the patriarch himself continued to live in the Old City of Jerusalem implied a certain degree of alienation from the Israeli sector of the community. But, above all, this Church was in dire economic straits, and even the sale of property during the Mandate period had not solved its financial problems. Furthermore, while the Antiochian patriarchate had agreed after 1945 to accept Soviet subsidies due to the USSR's renewed political and religious involvement in the region, the head of the Greek Orthodox Church in Palestine in the 1940s apparently refused to accept such aid because of his pro-Western orientation.[84] This being so, the only source of income remaining to the Church was rent from property, estimated by the Jewish Agency in 1940 at close to 21,000 dunams, most of which was agricultural. The urban property was concentrated in Jerusalem, Haifa, and Jaffa.[85]

The delineation of the border between Israel and Jordan after the war and the territorial disconnection between the areas which had formerly composed Mandatory Palestine created a complex situation for the Greek Orthodox patriarch of Jerusalem. Close to 90 percent of the patriarchate's property, some of it previously leased out, was now under Israeli control, but for obvious reasons most of its activity and expenditure was now confined to Jordan.[86] Thus the patriarchate's income from leasing out property in Israel (mostly in Jaffa) amounted to 22,000 pounds sterling annually, while expenditure in Jordan was twice that.[87] Israel had occupied a large proportion of this property during and after the war and exploited the fact that the Church's head resided permanently in an enemy country in order to classify these assets as "abandoned property."[88] This fact, and the stringent foreign currency regulations of the time, made it easy for Israel to refuse to permit transfer of rent to Jordan, thereby benefiting an enemy country.[89] The income of the Greek Orthodox Church had therefore shrunk by some 70 percent, according to the estimates it submitted to the UN Conciliation Committee in December 1949.[90] Even if these estimates were exaggerated, there is no doubt that the Church suffered considerable losses that were not just monetary.[91] Israeli experts were fully cognizant of the inability of the Greek Orthodox community to compete, mainly for financial reasons, with the relatively rapid revival of Catholic institutions. One of the consequences, it was reported, was that in 1950 more than half the families in the Greek Orthodox community were sending their children to Franciscan schools. Finally, it should be recalled that in contrast to the Catholic Church, which naturally enjoyed the massive backing of the Vatican and the political support of the countries in whose name some of its assets were registered, the Greek Orthodox Church was condemned to political isolation. Its natural ally, Greece, was by no means a great power, and its relations with Israel were characterized by stalemate.[92]

The documents reveal that in the first years of statehood Israel made every effort to exploit this predicament in two ways. First, it tried to compel the Greek Orthodox community to adopt a publicly pro-Israeli stand in the dispute on internationalization of Jerusalem. Second, it tried to compel them to sell their assets, particularly in Jerusalem, which were vitally needed—in light of this dispute and of the operative decisions taken in late 1948, and formally ratified only a year later—to consolidate Jerusalem's status as the capital of Israel and to expedite its development.[93] It should be pointed out that while most of the land in Jerusalem was in Jewish hands in 1947, the most important tracts of land were controlled by Muslims and Christians, among whom the Greek Orthodox Church was prominent.[94]

The first action taken by Israel was in the political sphere. For two years of continuous contacts with representatives of the Greek Orthodox Church in Israel, Jordan, and Greece, from September 1949 on, Israel conveyed an unequivocal message, namely, that it would adopt a positive stand on property of the churches (release it from the "abandoned property" category and agree to transfer rent to the Old City) in return for their opposition to the internationalization scheme. It also tried, without marked success, to exert pressure on the Greek government, its anti-Israel policy notwithstanding (it had voted against the establishment of Israel in November 1947), to support Israel's stand on internationalization.[95]

The documents do not give a full picture of the contacts between the parties, but they reveal that the Greek Orthodox patriarch of Jerusalem was strongly opposed to the internationalization scheme mainly because of his fear of Vatican domination of the city, a fear which Israel exploited blatantly.[96] He was also apparently troubled by the prospect of Soviet occupation of the Greek Orthodox Church in Jerusalem, although this did not prevent him from approaching the Soviet legation in Tel Aviv in 1950 and trying to recruit its aid against international pressure for internationalization of Jerusalem.[97] In any event, he obviously preferred to see the Holy City partitioned between Israel and Jordan,[98] and in secret talks, Israel tried to extract from him public expressions of support. The patriarch refused for self-evident reasons, and this helps explain why Israel chose to "wield the stick" with regard to the release of the patriarchate's assets. Perhaps the main reason was the decision to make Jerusalem the capital and accelerate the process of transfer of government institutions to the city. It was because of this change in policy, which began in 1949 and gained momentum after the General Assembly's decision on internationalization in December, that the Israeli government wanted to gain possession of several centrally located and important Greek Orthodox land reserves in Jerusalem.[99] Israeli pressure also took the form of refusal to transfer funds to the Old City and the freezing of a Church account in the sum of 75,000 Israeli lira in Barclays Bank.[100]

Striking a Deal with the "Yevoni"

Both sides appeared to be entrenched in their positions. However, the fact that the Jerusalem question was liable to be raised again at the next Assembly meeting forced them to give ground toward the end of 1950, thereby opening the way to an agreement on the future of the property. Negotiations held in September and October 1950 culminated in an agreement.[101] The patriarch sent a cable to the UN secretary-general specifying his views on the Jerusalem issue (the text to be coordinated with the Israelis), recommending that a distinction be drawn between the discussion of the religious character of the Holy City and its secular administration, and arguing that religious interests could best be served by an interdenominational international committee that would guarantee access to the Holy Places in consultation with Jordan and Israel.[102] This cable, which represented support for Israel's stand, was intended as the basis for further action, as defined by Herzog: "If King Abdullah agrees, the Greek Orthodox Church can rally considerable support from the Orthodox nations. This can only be to our benefit. It could serve as pressure on the Swedes and the Dutch to reduce outside intervention. And if, this time, the Jerusalem issue remains unresolved, UN records will note differences of opinion among the guardians of the Holy Places . . . and this breach may prove to our advantage in the future."[103]

Moreover, the Greek representatives at the negotiations promised to bring all their influence to bear on the patriarch to spur him to "additional open and secret positive action on the Jerusalem problem." The patriarch's cable marked a reversal of the Greek Orthodox official policy on Jerusalem, and roused the concern of community members who feared the reaction of other circles within the Church, particularly in Egypt and Greece, who had consistently supported internationalization. They assumed that Abdullah of Jordan would also be chagrined by their contacts with Israel. This being so, the patriarch expected and received a reward for his change of policy. This took the form of a guarantee by Israel's general custodian to release all Greek Orthodox property in Israel over the coming year, including Jerusalem, and Ministry of Finance consent to permit transfer of 1,500 pounds sterling monthly to the Old City for the coming six months. The patriarch was alarmed at the prospect that Israeli moves were liable to widen the rift between him and the Greek Orthodox Church in Israel, thereby undermining his status. The Israeli authorities were in fact contemplating the establishment of a separate ecclesiastical authority for the Greek Orthodox community in Israel, thereby eliminating the need for transfer of income to Jordan. The underlying intention was obviously to obtain the patriarch's cooperation by threatening to establish such a rival local authority. This explains why he requested and obtained Israel's assurance that it "would not act in order to undermine the standing of the patriarchate within the Greek Orthodox communities in Israel."[104]

As far as Israel was concerned, the agreement was aimed mainly at improving its position in the political struggle at the UN, but it was also essential in the context of its plan to purchase Greek Orthodox land. The two sides had been conducting hard-line negotiations on this subject all this time. In Israeli eyes, the promise to release assets and to transfer funds to Jordan was the "carrot" in the negotiations. The Greek Orthodox community, for its part, however, was expected to be accommodating. Files in the State Archives do not provide details on the negotiations, but British files indicate that it was the Israeli "stick" that decided the matter.

In the course of the negotiations, which were conducted in practice by representatives of the Jewish National Fund, Israel brought heavy pressure to bear on the patriarchate to sell its Jerusalem property at one-third of its declared value at the end of the Mandate period.[105] The synod in East Jerusalem debated the matter in December 1950, and eleven of the seventeen members recommended that the Israeli proposal be accepted. The patriarch, who objected vehemently, regarded this as a vote of no confidence and submitted his resignation, which led the synod to rescind its decision. The Israeli representatives, who apparently regarded this development as a violation of an (unwritten) obligation, reacted strongly. They threatened that Israel would retract its commitment to transfer income from Greek Orthodox property to the Old City, and added that if their demands were not met they would confiscate this property. However, in light of the written guarantee it had given, Israel did not follow through on this threat. Israel continued to transfer funds, and it released part of the Greek Orthodox assets.[106] Confiscation of property, it was feared, would antagonize Communist members of the Greek Orthodox community in Israel and provide them with a political trump card, and the patriarch, encouraged by international support, would adopt a harder line. The negotiations continued for several months without results, as a senior Israeli official reported: "Today you've finished with this lot and tomorrow they slip out of your hand and new ones arrive to fill the vacuum."[107]

The talks were still going on during the first visit of the Greek Orthodox patriarch Temelis Timotheos to Israel in April 1951. Herzog's colorful report on this event leaves little to the imagination.

> The serious rift within the synod in the past few years. . . . has obliged Timotheos to adopt a cautious and hesitant approach which he is apparently exploiting as a natural tactic in order to create the impression of unity. His followers sit around him and from time to time he throws angry glances at each side as if to demand their support for the truth and shrewdness of his remarks. This round of mutual glances attests to the fact that the synod is holding a mute meeting. And the scales of the historical legacy are tipped this way or that by means of a telepathic storm. . . . Representatives of both camps frequently went out into the hotel corridor in order to exchange "casual remarks" with the Jewish National Fund mediator.[108]

The patriarch tried to gain time by asking what the Jordanian monarch and the Greek authorities thought about the property deal, but he was reluctant to proceed even when he was reassured as to their positive attitude.[109] Two months then lapsed, in which "the old man [Timotheos] is taking a conservative stand and has frozen the vital issue."[110] The patriarch was apparently under pressure from members of his community in Amman, Beirut, and Athens not to sell the property. Herzog, who had conducted a discreet campaign in the United States to recruit funding for future purchases, referred to the postponement as "a natural digestive process," but he was very concerned. In internal correspondence he wrote: "Now I understand better why the term *Yevoni* [Greek] was given such a clear [negative] connotation by our forefathers."[111] In October, Israel's unrelenting pressure bore fruit. The threat that finally won the day was its uncompromising demand for payment of 140,000 Israeli liras in tax on the patriarchate's land in Jerusalem, a sum the latter was unable to recruit, since its frozen account in Barclays Bank contained only half that sum, and because Israel, having transferred 9,000 pounds sterling to the patriarchate's account in Jordan, as promised, had ceased transferring funds.[112] Under the agreement signed on 6 November 1951, the Church leased to Israel 104 dunams in the area between the YMCA building and King George Boulevard, Talbiyeh and the Rose Garden for a period of ninety-nine years.[113] The rent was to be paid in three installments. This settlement did not solve all of the patriarchate's monetary problems, since Israel was to pay in foreign currency only in the first two years.[114]

Nine months later, however, a second agreement was signed, whereby the patriarchate leased out 405 dunams in Jerusalem to Israel for a period of ninety-nine years, and this time it was stipulated that most of the payments would be sent abroad because of the large amount of foreign currency involved. The agreement was also the fruit of continued Israeli pressure on the Greek Orthodox Church for payment of property taxes.[115] In the preliminary discussions, the patriarchate's representatives expressed the wish that the negotiations take place within the framework of transfer for Jewish "religious purposes" so as to enable them to justify the agreement and counter the "dangerous" criticism leveled at them by "the Mufti's people in the Old City concerning their contacts with us on Jerusalem political issues and the consequences of these contacts on land deals."[116] It is unclear whether Israel acceded to this request. Be that as it may, the official Israeli signatories were Jewish National Fund representatives. After the first agreement was signed, Israel consented to release Greek Orthodox property in Israel that had been classified as "abandoned property" but in a manner that guaranteed Israeli administration of part of it for an unspecified period. This was because the patriarchate had been asked to present documents proving ownership of the property—most of which had apparently been mislaid—in order to complete the process.[117] Whatever the reason, not all the property was released, and several properties were still occupied at the beginning of 1955.[118] Israel profited from the returned assets, since the Greek Orthodox Church had undertaken to honor the leases signed when the property was under the administration of the general custodian, who had fixed particularly low rents.[119]

Israel's foreign minister expressed his satisfaction in a personal letter to the minister of the interior, in which he wrote, "We invested an eternity of tremen-

Foreign Minister Abba Eban with Greek Orthodox Patriarch Benedictus during a reception for Christian church leaders at the presidential residence in Jerusalem, December 28, 1967. *Courtesy of the National Photo Collection of the Israel Government Press Office, Prime Minister's Office. Photo D679–052. Photographer Fritz Cohen.*

dous effort in these negotiations and in preparing the ground inside the Church for implementation of the transfer. When the forces of light prevailed within the church the time was ripe for resolution."[120] The political gain was, of course, more important than the financial aspect. The first agreement was considered to be a great achievement. Herzog reported to Israeli diplomats abroad that "it has opened up the way to wide-scale economic development of the center of the city, thereby strengthening our political position there, since these areas surround the former Arab quarters and even pass through them. As a result of this agreement, our cooperation with the Greek Orthodox patriarchate where Jerusalem is concerned has become even closer."[121] Gratification was even greater after the second agreement, which it was hoped (in vain, so it turned out) would pave the way to diplomatic contacts with Greece.[122] Seven years later, desire for a Greek connection was one of the main reasons why Israel consented to restore the Mount Zion church to the Greek Orthodox community.[123] It should be pointed out that one of Israel's undeclared aims in its relations with the local Christian communities was to eradicate missionary activity. Unlike the Catholics and Protestants, the Orthodox community did not seek converts, and in this respect was not in conflict with the authorities. This explains why this issue was never raised in Israeli internal consultations during the negotiations.[124]

From all this, it is understandable why Israel's policymakers were satisfied with the outcome of their efforts in the realm of ecclesiastical property. They had succeeded in taking over Lutheran property and eradicating the Lutheran presence in Israel, in safeguarding security interests where German property was concerned and purchasing some of it, and in gaining possession of particularly important areas in Jerusalem from the Greek Orthodox Church (for much less than their market value). These agreements not only reduced the friction between these churches and Israel; they also represented recognition by all three churches of the major components of the post-1948 Israeli reality. The land agreements supplied the international political seal of approval, which was one of Israel's main objectives at the time, and facilitated Israel's struggle against those, including the Vatican, which were in no hurry to do the same.

Epilogue: On Viewing
the Enemy and Bridge Building

In 2002, the Israeli Ministry of Foreign Affairs published a weighty two-volume survey that summarized and analyzed various aspects of the first fifty years of Israeli foreign policy.[1] Two chapters were devoted to relations with the Christian world. The first, written by Nathan Ben-Horin, dealt with a specific period and a single church. The second offered a retrospective view of the entire period in the context of the Christian world as a whole. The central thesis of this chapter, written by Moshe Aumann, a diplomat who had been directly involved in the subject for several years, is that "the Christian church began to move, deliberately and convincingly, and very gradually in the direction of contrition and repentance, setting itself the aim of eradicating the hatred and anti-Semitism which had inflicted so much suffering on the Jewish people." This information was aimed at the general public, in order to achieve what the author considered a crucial objective. This change of direction, Aumann argued, required the cooperation of both sides if it was to endure. His self-evident conclusion was that the Jewish people, for their part, must stop cultivating and nurturing consciousness of their historical reckoning with Christianity even though, "emotionally speaking, this view is both valid and logical."

The present book surveys Israel's relations with the Christian world in the first years of statehood from Jerusalem's viewpoint, and demonstrates not only that this consciousness was deeply rooted and intense but also that it had a strong impact on a whole range of political decisions. Israel's qualified attitude to pilgrim-tourists in the early years, for example, was partly based on objective considerations but was also unquestionably influenced by this outlook. The year 1950 had been designated a Holy Year by the Catholic Church, and multitudes of pilgrims were expected to visit the tombs of St. Peter and St. Paul and to receive the pope's blessing.[2] Such events had taken place every twenty-five years throughout the nineteenth and twentieth centuries (excluding 1875). It was believed in Israel that the Catholic Church intended to turn 1950 into a mass demonstration and that some 5 million pilgrims would visit Rome. One of the proclaimed objectives of this Holy Year, not surprisingly in light of political events in the Middle East, was organization of a propaganda campaign in defense of the Holy Places in the Holy Land. To this end, many of the pilgrims were directed to visit there, in order to demonstrate (as the pope wrote in his encyclical letter known as *Redemptoris Nostri*) the "inseparable link between the city of the tombs of the Apostles and the city of the tomb of the Messiah." The Israeli authorities calculated in mid-1949 that approximately 100,000 pilgrims could be expected in Israel in 1950, a troubling prospect. Internal discussions of the subject reflected several basic outlooks echoing the general view of Christianity as a whole and the Catholic Church in particular.

The predominant argument was that this pilgrimage phenomenon contained within it the threat of political confrontation between the Catholic world and Israel, particularly on the question of the internationalization of Jerusalem and the future of the Holy Places. Logistically speaking, the situation was problematic: these sites were in poor condition due to the damage inflicted on them during the war, damage which Israel "had concealed from the world"[3] and which could not easily be repaired; passage between Israel and Jordan was fraught with problems because of Jordan's refusal in 1949 to permit movement of tourists in both directions (and from December 1949 only from Israel to the Old City), and administrative restrictions in Israel (including food rationing) which made it difficult to tackle an influx of tourists of as yet unknown scope.[4]

However, the Israeli minister in Brussels was echoing the deeper fears of many of his colleagues when he wrote:

> It seems likely that, in particular during the Easter season, masses of pilgrims will flock to Jerusalem, perhaps even tens of thousands. The religious ecstasy of these pilgrims, in that Jerusalem landscape where their savior lived, suffered, and sacrificed himself, will be tremendous; it will be heightened by the atrocity propaganda spread by the Christian press lately, accusing Israel of acts of desecration, which aggravates the tension by claiming that the Holy Places have been at risk since the war. This prevailing mood among the masses will be fertile ground for all kinds of tall stories and false rumors, and we face the danger of undesirable outbreaks and demonstrations. The pilgrims will encounter a Crusades atmosphere, and there will certainly be agitators ready to exploit the tension in order to transform the spark into a flame, particularly among the local Christians, who have always been hostile toward us: such demonstrations and outbursts will force us to intervene. . . . There will be a worldwide outcry if, in order to restore order, Jewish policemen are obliged to intervene.[5]

Such a confrontation was, of course, totally at odds with Israeli interests at the time. An influx of Christian Arab pilgrims also posed a potential threat, and Ben-Gurion instructed the relevant authorities "not to allow Christian Arabs in. Let them go to the Old City; they will not enter Israel."[6]

Theoretically, there were points in favor of wide-scale pilgrimage tourism, since it would imply de facto Vatican recognition of Israel, it would demonstrate that Israel maintained a liberal attitude on religious matters and Holy Places, and it would bring foreign currency into the country. The files, however, reveal that these considerations were regarded as minor and secondary.[7] High-level consultations in Israel clearly emphasized the negative and dangerous aspects of the situation, and, as Eytan said, with typical understatement, although a positive official decision had been made, there was no consensus on the question of "whether pilgrims are welcome here or not" and the extent to which "the government desires to encourage pilgrimage."[8] It was decided eventually neither to hand out too many invitations nor to encourage the phenomenon, so as to keep the number of pilgrims down.[9] It was also decided to do everything possible in terms of hosting tourists, conducting essential repairs in Christian Holy Places, and barring entry to other unrepaired sites on security and safety pretexts in order to reduce the risk of undesirable scenarios.[10] All this was to be done, as Israeli diplomats in Europe were briefed "since the pilgrimage to Israel will take place, whether we like it or not, because the Holy See has ordered it as a political move relating to Jerusalem and the Holy Places . . . and the die has been cast."[11] The only bans eventually imposed were against the entry of German nationals, apart from clerics and pilgrims from the Arab countries or Arabs who had left Israel during the 1948 war.[12]

At the same time, the Israelis plainly considered pilgrims to be a potentially hostile element, and this view was reflected in the report of the Governmental Coordinating Committee for Tourism in December 1949. It assigned a series of tasks to the General Security Service on such specifically tourist-related subjects as escorting pilgrims, selecting tourist guides and briefing them, choosing sites for visits, instructing Arab guides in Nazareth, and "general supervision of pilgrims on such matters as infiltration of agents, conveying information, espionage, etc."[13] It was also decided to attach a Ministry of Religious Affairs representative to each group of pilgrims "not just as a guide, but in particular as an observer and official representative in whose presence clerics will be reluctant to make inflammatory remarks."[14] In the end, Israeli fears proved ungrounded. Only 1,400 pilgrims, the great majority of them Catholics, visited Israel in 1950.[15] Not a single clash between the visitors and their hosts was recorded, nor did significantly hostile articles appear in the Vatican press. No "Crusade" occurred, and the Israeli authorities were apparently free of anxiety on this point throughout the 1950s and 1960s, particularly after the pope's visit, when tens of thousands of pilgrims visited the country each year.[16]

The Jewish historical reckoning with Christianity was a significant factor in other, perhaps unexpected areas. In late 1959, the deputy director of the West European Desk at the Foreign Ministry criticized the IDF's chief education officer for his "hostile views," as reflected in a monthly report on the Vatican that he produced. The response of the head of the IDF's Information Division, Ephraim Halevi (later head of the Mossad), echoed the general public attitude toward the subject in the 1950s:

> The "attitude" toward the Catholic Church could not be omitted from the reports. Do not forget that they are aimed at IDF officers—*Jews*—who belong

Bishops visiting Israel after the Ecumenical Council meeting at the New Grand Hotel in Nazareth, December 12, 1962. *Courtesy of the National Photo Collection of the Israel Government Press Office, Prime Minister's Office. Photo D796–071. Photographer Moshe Pridan.*

to a nation with a long and tortuous history. In the annals of this nation there have been numerous encounters between the Church and the Jews (the Inquisition immediately comes to mind), and these encounters, in addition to their immediate impact, joined together and left a considerable residue. To ignore this residue would have lent a false note to the article and would have evoked skepticism. I believe that it would have also constituted factual and historical disinformation. I have mentioned the Inquisition. There were another two affairs familiar to many of us—the relations between the Church and the regimes of Mussolini in Italy and Hitler in Germany, and the Church's attitude toward the State of Israel (including the question of internationalization of Jerusalem). These affairs are still alive in the hearts of many Israelis, and I think that we would not have been justified in ignoring them, and when it was decided to tackle them, there was no justification for deviating from the facts.[17]

As noted above, several factors prevented the adoption of a less emotional and more instrumental attitude toward the Catholic Church and helped to fix a fundamentally historical approach. Beyond the uncompromising hostility of this Church toward Israel, the country's leaders were concerned by the fact that other churches in Israel (such as the Greek and Russian Orthodox) lacked sufficient local and international weight to provide a political counterbalance to the Catholic Church, that the attitude some of them adopted toward Israel in the international arena was not categorically different from that of the Holy

See, and that most of them posed an internal challenge because of their missionary zeal. Israel's difficulties in this area were expressed in internal talks on the proposal to recruit the aid of Christians in the Middle East as part of what was termed "the periphery policy" aimed at cultivating political ties with non-Muslims in the region. The main issue addressed was the theoretical possibility raised by attempts by Maronites, which began prior to 1948, to establish contact with the Zionist leadership and then with the State of Israel. Jerusalem was skeptical, to say the least. Twenty-six years before the war in Lebanon, where for the first time an abortive attempt was made to implement this idea, Gideon Rafael represented the prevailing view when he said:

> Anyone who has studied the Maronites and their proposals closey . . . knows that one must not speak of them in generalized terms, because they are divided among themselves, and also knows that when the Maronites refer to Israeli aid they expect Israel to do the work for them, to rid Lebanon of the Muslims, to guarantee the exclusive rule of the "rebels," and until this job is done, they will stand idly by and wait to see what transpires. If the operation does not succeed, the Maronites will be the first to betray those they invited in to help them."[18]

It is not surprising, therefore, that this objective and conceptual reality helped foster an Israeli attitude of political fatalism toward the Christian world, particularly the Catholic Church, which explains why Israel neglected to collect and process information about the Church for most of the period discussed in this book. For example, in discussions in the Foreign Ministry in 1953, Herzog admitted that "for the past two years we have not known what is going on there [in the Vatican]."[19] Four years later, Fischer listed a number of political and intelligence tasks that needed to be carried out, and pointed out significant lacunae in this sphere, particularly where the Catholic Church was concerned.[20] The situation deteriorated further after his death.

Whatever the reasons, documents in various archives in Israel and elsewhere clearly indicate that Israel's approach toward the Christian world and especially toward the Catholic Church in the first few years of statehood was dictated not only by distinct elements of rational realpolitik and by the characteristic calculations of a state confronting the Church but also by the unique historical-emotional-religious burden it bore. Only an in-depth study of the churches in contact with Israel can supply the answer to the question of the extent to which this combination of motives served Israel well up to 1967, and whether it changed significantly after 1967 as a result of Israel's increased power, which affected its relations with the Christian world.

Most of the literature dealing with the Christian world's relations with Israel focuses on the theological perspectives and on the attitudes and policies of the Catholic Church. The present study, in contrast, focuses on the Israeli political perspective, which has hitherto been almost totally neglected. It offers a new interpretation of the complicated issues relating to Israel's relations with the Christian world in general and the Catholic Church in particular in those early years. Scholars have noted the intricate nature of the latter's approach toward Israel, which stemmed, to a large extent, from its dual character, as defined by Michael Perko: "On the one hand [the Vatican] is a sovereign power with particular policy goals [which] have included a desire to 'do good' by alleviating suffering, advocating causes of national and social justice, and setting an example for moral leadership in the political arena. On the other hand, the Holy See exercises a pastoral and teaching role for the world's Catholics and is a major vehicle by which the Church projects itself into the public sphere."[21]

These characteristics have had a significant impact on other Vatican activities in the international arena. The present study shows that Israel's basic approach in important spheres of foreign policy was also marked by duality because of its self-definition as a state but also to a considerable degree because of a national-religious system. Thus the confrontation between Israel and the Catholic Church was a clash between two complex and unique systems, which undoubtedly made it difficult for the Vatican to initiate attempts at rapprochement.[22] The newly opened files in the Israel State Archives provide, however, resounding proof that Israel also found it difficult, though to a lesser degree.[23] The text of the political agreement establishing formal ties between the two sides on 30 December 1993, known as the "Fundamental Agreement," provides only a glimpse about the problem, combining as it did theological and diplomatic elements.[24] As the deputy foreign minister of Israel at that time put it, "Behind this document are thousands of years of history characterized by hatred, fear, ignorance, and scant dialogue."[25] It is thus hardly surprising to learn that after more than ten years of intermittent negotiations, the two sides have not yet secured a mutually agreed implementation of crucial articles of the agreement.[26] It seems, therefore, that both the Vatican and Israel are fully mindful of the long path that each still needs to travel if this accord is to augur a radical change in their bilateral relations.

notes

Abbreviations

BGD   Ben-Gurion Diary, Ben-Gurion Archive, Sde Boker
CZA   Central Zionist Archives
FO   British Foreign Office Records
IILA   *Information for Israeli Legations Abroad*
ISA   Israel State Archives
NA   United States National Archives
PRO   Public Record Office, London

Introduction

1. See Kazin 1999.
2. See Bialer 2002, 1–80.
3. For a recent analysis of the subject, see Weber 2004.
4. Paul Charles Merkley, "Christian Attitudes toward the State of Israel—A Bird's Eye View," info@IsraelNationalNews.com, 14 March 2004, which is a synopsis of his detailed study. Merkley had hardly underestimated that hostility for the post-1948 period when speculating that "had the voting on the partition of the Palestine Mandate taken place five or ten years later, the Jewish state would not have come into existence." Merkley 2001, 6, 9–50.

1. The Sense of Threat Emerges

1. See Bein 1962, 672. For the early contacts between the Vatican and the Zionist movement, see Minerbi 1985. For later periods, see Fischer 1987, 191–211; Perko 1997, 1–21; and Mendes 1990.
2. See Stegemann 1999, 121–22.
3. Quoted in Paul Blanshard, "The Vatican and Israel," Rome, June 1950, ISA 2396\15. For a thorough biography of Moshe Sharett, see Sheffer 1996.
4. See, e.g., Phayer 2000, Zuccotti 2001, and Cornwell 1999. For the defense of Pius XII, see Sanchez 2002. For the Zionist perspective, see Friling 1998, 215–16, 660. The Church claims that the pope could have made the situation worse for the victims themselves by issuing declarations. One wonders how much worse their situation could

have been than death in the gas chambers. It is unclear why Pius XII chose to remain silent when he knew in 1940 that Nazis were killing Jews systematically in Poland and elsewhere. Perhaps it was due to the pope's fear of provoking a schism within the Catholic Church in Germany. In addition, he may have considered Bolshevism to be the major danger to Christianity, thus regarding Nazism as the lesser of two evils. Another reason could be that he wanted to remain absolutely neutral in order to preserve the possibility of becoming a mediator during or after the war. Whatever his reasons, it is clear that when he had to choose between the moral duty of denouncing genocide in order to save Jewish lives, and what he deemed to be the supreme interest of the Catholic Church, he preferred the latter.

5. See Fraenkel 1995, 114. For an extended account, see Melloni 1992.

6. See Ferrari 1991, 41.

7. Fraenkel 1995, 121.

8. See Lapide 1967, 282.

9. The above is based on Moshe Sneh's dispatches to Ben-Gurion, 6 October 1947, Central Zionist Archives, Jerusalem, CZA S25/1698, and 18 September 1947, CZA S25/1696, Sheleg 2003, and my interview with Yair Zaban, 28 July 2003. On Glasberg see Lazare 1990 and Hillel 1985, 154–59. For the foreign policy of the Jewish Agency at the United Nations during the late 1940s see Freundlich 1994 and Heller 2000. Roncalli's recently declassified diaries for the period 1945–48 (edited by the French historian Etienne Fouilloux and published by the Bologna Institute for Religious Studies) document his efforts to help reunite Jews whose families had been torn apart by the war and whose children had been taken under the wing of the Catholic Church. The new documents also shed light on the pope's reservations. In 1946 Yitzhak Herzog, the second chief rabbi of Palestine, came to see Roncalli in Paris to ask that Jewish children rescued during the war and placed in Catholic convents be returned to the Jewish community. The archbishop was pleased to oblige and on July 19 wrote a letter authorizing Herzog to "use his authority with the relevant institutions, so . . . these children may be returned to their original environment." But three months later Roncalli received the orders from the Holy Office to impede the return of the children. See Popham 2004, Barkat 2004, Palmieri-Billig 2004, and Melloni 2004.

10. Knesset Foreign Affairs and Defense Committee minutes, 11 July 1950, ISA. On Sharett's perception of the Vatican in 1947–49, see a retrospective elaboration in Bashan 1965, 135.

11. *IILA*, no. 545, 12 September 1952, ISA 7536/3. On Herzog, see Bar-Zohar 2003.

12. Ferrari 1984, 1985, and 1991. For the Vatican's general policy on the Arab-Israeli conflict, see Kreutz 1990, Rokach 1987, and Irani 1986. For other aspects of its relations with that region, see Ellis 1987.

13. The following is based on *IILA*, no. 408, 28 November 1951, ISA 7536/3.

14. Moshe Sharett to Leo Kohn, 11 June 1948, ISA 2397/3.

15. Yehoshua Prawer to Chaim Berman, 13 June 1948, ISA 2413/12.

16. Yaacov Herzog to Walter Eytan, 9 August 1948, ISA 2397/7. On Mount Zion as a holy site for Jews during the early years of Israel, see Bar 2004.

17. December 1948, ISA 5823/19.

18. Cabinet meeting minutes, 8 September 1948, ISA.

19. Shaul Colbi to Gershon Avner, 10 October 1948, ISA 5817/6.

20. Ben-Gurion to "Etzioni," 15 July 1948, ISA 2397/3.

21. See Morris 1989, 201.

22. Yosef Barpal to Yaacov Shimoni, 18 July 1948, ISA 5811/10.

23. Herzog to Eliyahu Ben-Horin, 8 September 1948, ISA 5812/3.

24. *IILA*, no. 128, 16 October 1950, ISA 7854/4

25. Michael Comay to Maurice Fischer, 3 September 1948, ISA 183/6.

26. *IILA*, no. 128, 16 October 1950, ISA 7854/4. On McMahon, see Carroll 1993. On the Christian community in Israel during the 1948 war, see Giovannelli 2000, 184–97.

27. Memo, 8 June 1948, ISA 2396/15. For the multifaceted interpretation of the term *holy places* in the context of the Jerusalem question, see Ma'oz and Nusseibeh 2000, 95–164. For a useful survey of Christian holy places in Israel, see Schiller 1992.

28. On Bernadotte's mission, see Ilan 1989.

29. Herzog to Ben-Horin, 8 September 1948, ISA 5812/3. On the attitudes of American Catholics toward Zionism and the State of Israel, see Feldblum 1977.

30. The following is based on Herzog to Michael Arnon, 2 September 1953, ISA 2578/20, and Eytan to Fischer, 4 October 1950, ISA 5823/2.

31. See Giovannelli 2000. The author of this book had access to classified documents at the Terra Santa Historical Archives in Jerusalem.

32. Herzog to Eytan, 4 October 1950, ISA 5823/2. Kuehn arrived at Palestine in 1945 and became the headmaster of the Terra Santa College in Jerusalem (see the *Palestine Post*, 27 November 1945). In 1949 he was made patriarchal vicar in the south of Israel, a position that was soon abolished. On Kuehn's opinions at that time, see Levin 1949, and "Memorandum Presented to the Conciliation Commission of the United Nations by the Catholic Religious Communities of the Jewish Sector of Jerusalem," 8 July 1949, http://domino.un.org/unispal.nsf. See also Giovannelli 2000, 198–200. For an analysis of the Catholic administration in Israel and in Palestine by the Foreign Ministry Research Division, see Raya Cagan to Mordechai Kidron, 1 November 1959, ISA 273/16.

33. See Colbi to Herzog, 28 August 1953, and Shmuel Tolkovsky to the Ministry for Foreign Affairs, 14 August 1953, ISA 5820/3.

34. Herzog to Ben-Horin, 8 September 1948, ISA 5812/3.

35. *IILA*, no. 128, 16 October 1950, ISA 7356/3.

36. The Congregatio pro Ecclesus Orientalibus (Congregation for Oriental Churches) was a unique formation in the Catholic Church, forming in some respects "a State within a State." It was the only congregation in the Vatican whose authority was not restricted to certain functional or ritual matters, but possessed full jurisdiction over certain territories as well as over all the Oriental Christian communities throughout the world. The territory was the Middle East, in a liberal interpretation of the term: from the Balkans in the West to India in the East and to Abyssinia in Africa. The Oriental Christian Communities included the Maronites, Melkhites, Greek Catholics, Armenian Catholics, etc., wherever they were to be found in the world. The importance of the Oriental Congregation was reflected in the fact that the pope himself was the "prefect," or the titular chief of the congregation, and that Cardinal Tisserant, who actually conducted its affairs, held the title of "secretary." The cardinal visited Palestine in 1904, then twice with the French army in 1917–19, and finally in 1926. See Ben-Horin's memorandum dated 17 January 1949, ISA 2396/15. It should be noted that Tisserant's positive attitude toward Israel, which found important expressions well into the mid-1950s, stood in marked contrast with that of the Custodia Terrae Sanctae. Further research is needed to establish to what extent this difference was somehow connected to the cardinal's efforts at the time to curtail the independence of the Custodia. See Giovannelli 2000, 222.

37. Knesset Foreign Affairs and Defense Committee minutes, 28 December 1949, ISA.

38. Herzog's cable, 29 September 1948, ISA 2396/15, and his dispatches on 7 October 1948 and 27 February 1949, ISA 2523/17.

39. Herzog to Arnon, 2 September 1953, ISA 2576/20.

40. Herzog to Tuvia Arazi, 3 December 1948, ISA 5823/1.

41. Arie Sternberg to Eytan, 20 December 1948, ISA 2396/15.

42. See *IILA*, no. 128, 16 October 1950, ISA 7854/4, McDonald 1951, 206, and Ben-Horin 2002, 999.

43. Herzog to Esther Herlitz, 20 January 1949, ISA 5823/1, and Ben-Horin to Sharett, 18 January 1949, ISA 2396/15.

44. Herzog to Herlitz, 17 March 1949, ISA 5812/3.

45. For an extended and perceptive analysis of the *Redemptoris Nostri* by an Israeli expert, see Chaim Vardi to Herzog, 2 May 1949, ISA 5823/9. See also a retrospective account in Herzog to Eytan, 5 July 1951, ISA 2393/23.

46. Vardi to Herzog, 2 May 1949, ISA 5823/9.

47. Herzog to Abba Eban, 13 October 1949, ISA 38/4.

48. Herzog to Eytan, 5 July 1951, ISA 2393/23.

49. Eytan to Shlomo Ginosar, 4 April 1950, ISA 2550/5.

50. Ibid.

51. Vardi to Herzog, 2 May 1949, ISA 5823/9.

52. Eytan to Ginosar, 4 April 1950, ISA 2550/5.

53. See Sharett's analysis at the cabinet meeting on 21 April 1949 and at the Knesset Foreign Affairs and Defense Committee meeting on 28 December 1949, ISA.

54. Sharett, June 1949, ISA.

55. Cabinet meeting minutes, 2 August 1949, ISA.

56. Sharett to Eban, 15 August 1949, ISA 2396/5.

57. Herzog to Eban, 13 October 1949, ISA 38/4.

58. Herzog's dispatch to Ben-Gurion, 7 September 1949, ISA 7854/6.

59. Hahn 1999, 569–82. See also Slonim 1998.

60. Quoted in Ben-Horin 2002, 1001.

61. Sharett to Yaacov Blaustein, 28 September 1949, ISA 2397/3.

62. Sharett to Eban, 15 August 1949, ISA 2396/5.

63. Ginosar to the Ministry for Foreign Affairs, 4 August 1949, ISA 2396/15.

64. Ginosar to Eytan, 10 October 1949, ISA 2396/15.

65. Herzog to Eban, 13 October 1949, ISA 38/4.

66. Knesset Foreign Affairs and Defense Committee meeting, 15 June 1949, ISA 170/12.

67. Gideon Rafael to Maurice Fischer, June 1949, ISA 170/12.

68. Fischer to Avner, 16 October 1949, ISA 2396/15.

69. Minutes dated 29 October 1949.

70. Sharett at the Knesset Foreign Affairs and Defense Committee meeting, 28 December 1949, ISA. Vittorino Veronese (1910–86), who conveyed the Vatican attitude to Herzog, was an antifascist lawyer who took up a senior post in banking after World War II and served as chairman of the Catholic Institute for Social Activity and Italy's Catholic Action between 1944 and 1952. He became director-general of UNESCO in 1958, but resigned three years later for health reasons. See http://portal.unesco.org.

71. See a report on that meeting in the U.S. National Archives (hereafter NA) Tel Aviv consulate files RG84/350/61/33.

72. Herzog to Arnon, 2 September 1953, ISA 2576/20. See also Mendes 1983, 53–55.

73. See note 71. On other plans concerning the Vatican and Jerusalem, see Eordegian 2003.

74. Yehoshafat Harkabi to Herzog, 7 November 1949, ISA 2396/15.

75. Benzion Kedourie's memorandum dated 7 December 1949, ISA 2523/17.

76. See Bialer 1984, 273–96. For the internal political pressures on the question of Jerusalem, see Katz and Paz 2004.

77. Boris Guriel's analysis dated 17 April 1950, ISA 175/11.

78. Quoted in Ben-Horin 2002, 1000.

2. The Struggle for Jerusalem

1. Cabinet meeting minutes, 27 December 1949, ISA. It should be noted that Israeli intelligence was very active at that time at the UN. See Gelber 1992, 658–59.

2. Knesset Foreign Affairs and Defense Committee minutes, 12 December 1949, ISA.

3. Ibid. For the prime minister's attitudes toward the Arabs, see Shalom 1995.

4. Cabinet meeting minutes, 20 December 1949, ISA.

5. Ambassadorial conference, 12 July 1950, ISA 2458/4.

6. Cabinet meeting minutes, 27 December 1949, ISA.

7. Cabinet meeting minutes, 20 January 1952, ISA.

8. "The Jerusalem Problem," memo, 24 December 1949, ISA 2602/10.

9. Sharett to Eytan, 29 December 1949, ISA 2316/15.

10. Cabinet meeting minutes, 2 February 1950, ISA.

11. Ambassadorial conference, 12 July 1950, ISA 2584/4.

12. Herzog to Shiloah, April 1951, ISA 7854/4.

13. Cabinet meeting minutes, 12 April 1950, ISA.

14. Knesset Foreign Affairs and Defense Committee minutes, 1 November 1950, ISA.

15. *IILA*, no. 761, 17 November 1953, ISA 2523/15.

16. Eytan to the director-general of the Ministry of Defense, 11 January 1950, ISA 2396/18.

17. *IILA*, no. 128, 16 October 1950, ISA 7854/4.

18. Herzog's report, 17 November 1953, ISA 2468/13. In a letter to Cardinal Spellman in early 1955, thanking him for notification of McMahon's impending resignation, Cardinal Tisserant noted that "he literally was on fire for the cause of Christ." See Carroll 1993, 19.

19. Herzog's report, 17 November 1953, ISA 2468/13.

20. Tsur to the director-general of the Ministry for Foreign Affairs, 25 November 1953, ISA 41/8.

21. Gideon Rafael at a meeting dated 11 June 1953, ISA 2458/7. See also Herzog to Shmuel Bendor, 4 May 1951, ISA 2468/9.

22. Eytan's memorandum, 24 December 1949, ISA 2602/10.

23. Herzog to Shlomo Kaddar, 28 December 1953, ISA 7854/5. See also an unsigned memorandum dated 9 January 1950, ISA 347/20.

24. Meeting on the Jerusalem question, 6 January 1950, ISA 7854/4.

25. Cabinet meeting minutes, 29 March 1950, ISA.

26. Cabinet meeting minutes, 12 April 1950, ISA.

27. Gershon Avner to the Israeli legation, Rome, 27 May 1951, ISA 277/17.

28. Herzog to Arnon, 2 September 1953, ISA 2576/20.

29. Herzog to Sharett, 9 August 1953, ISA 7854/4.
30. Sharett to Knesset Foreign Affairs and Defense Committee, 11 July 1950, ISA.
31. Sharett, ambassadorial conference, 12 July 1950, ISA 2458/4.
32. See Mendes 1983, 54–55.
33. First secretary, Israeli legation, Rome, to Avner, 16 May 1951, ISA 277/17.
34. Moshe Yishai to the Ministry for Foreign Affairs, 20 July 1952, ISA 2526/20.
35. Kohn to Reuven Shiloah, 4 November 1952, ISA 2395/15.
36. Herzog to Eytan, 4 September 1952, ISA 2396/15.
37. See Sharett's comments, 4 November 1952, ISA 2396/15.
38. Sharett to Eytan, 10 January 1950, ISA 2393/23.
39. *IILA*, no. 128, 16 October 1950, ISA 7854/4.
40. See Malachy 1978, Ariel 1991, Merkley 1998, and Conway 1999, 459–72.
41. Ginosar's memorandum, 23 January 1950, ISA 2550/5.
42. Sharett, ambassadorial conference, 12 July 1950, ISA 2458/4.
43. Meetings dated 11–12 April 1950, ISA 7854/4. For a recent in-depth analysis of one of these plans, see Eordegian 2003.
44. Sharett's dispatch to Israeli minister in Stockholm, 9 November 1950, ISA 175/11.
45. Sharett to Eban, 15 February 1950, ISA 2015/9.
46. *IILA*, no. 346, 27 August 1951, ISA 7526/3.
47. Cabinet meeting minutes, 12 April 1950, ISA.
48. Cabinet meeting minutes, 20 January 1952, ISA.
49. Herzog to Eliahu Sasson, 18 February 1954, ISA 2397/4.
50. Sharett to the Knesset Foreign Affairs and Defense Committee, 11 July 1950, ISA.
51. Meeting, 11 June 1953, ISA 2458/7.
52. Knesset Foreign Affairs and Defense Committee minutes, 1 November 1950, ISA.
53. *IILA*, no. 346, 27 August 1951, ISA 7526/3.
54. Cabinet meeting minutes, 18 January 1951, ISA. See also Herzog to Sasson, 18 February 1954, ISA 354/27.
55. Cabinet meeting minutes, 18 January 1951, ISA.
56. Eban at the Knesset Foreign Affairs and Defense Committee, 7 August 1950, ISA.
57. Consultation at the Ministry for Foreign Affairs, 11 June 1953, ISA 2457/8.
58. Knesset Foreign Affairs and Defense Committee, 22 January 1951, ISA. See also Golani 1999.
59. Herzog to Eytan, 17 September 1951, ISA 7854/4.
60. Sharett at the Knesset Foreign Affairs and Defense Committee, 30 July 1952, ISA. See also Brecher 1978.
61. Sharett at a Ministry for Foreign Affairs meeting, 31 August 1953, ISA 2404/12, and Vardi to Herzog, 8 May 1951, ISA 5816/5.
62. *IILA*, no. 408, 28 November 1951, ISA 7536/3.
63. Shimon Amir to Eytan, 7 February 1951, ISA 2397/4.
64. Herzog to Shiloah, 19 April 1951, ISA 7811/4.
65. Ginosar to the Ministry for Foreign Affairs, 29 January 1951, ISA 2397/4.
66. Avraham Nissan to the Ministry for Foreign Affairs, 22 February 1951, ISA 2550/12.
67. Ibid. See also consultation on Jerusalem dated 15 June 1951, ISA 7854/4.

68. Avner to Amir, 20 February 1951, ISA 2550/11.
69. Sharett to Maimon, 4 August 1953, ISA 2397/4.
70. Herzog to Shiloah, 19 April 1951, ISA 7854/4.
71. *IILA*, no. 346, 27 August 1951, ISA 7526/3 and consultation at the Ministry for Foreign Affairs, 11 June 1953, ISA 2458/7.
72. *IILA*, no. 408, 28 November 1951, ISA 7536/3.
73. A consultation at the Ministry for Foreign Affairs, 11 June 1953, ISA 2458/7.
74. The following is based on a report of the Research Division of the Ministry for Foreign Affairs, no. 194, 8 March 1954, ISA 7854/5.
75. David Shaltiel to the Ministry for Foreign Affairs, 23 October 1953, ISA 41/8.
76. Herzog to Kaddar, 28 December 1953, ISA 7584/5.
77. *IILA*, no. 761, 17 November 1953, ISA 2523/15.
78. Herzog to Shaltiel, 17 November 1953, ISA 136/6.
79. Shaltiel to Herzog, 4 December 1953, ISA 2581/4.
80. The following is based on a report of the Israeli Military Intelligence dated 3 March 1955, ISA 2498/25, on Avraham Biran to Eytan, 5 July 1954, ISA 2397/4, and on Herzog to Israeli minister in Stockholm, 26 July 1954, ISA 136/6. On Israel's relations with Jordan during this period, see Israeli 2002a and Tal 1998).
81. Biran to Eytan, 15 December 1952, ISA 2396/12.
82. Ambassadorial conference, 12 July 1950, ISA 2458/4. For a historical analysis, see Abadi 2002.
83. Fischer to Sharett, 16 October 1950, ISA 2550/8, and cabinet meeting minutes, 31 December 1951, ISA.
84. Herzog at meetings dated 11 June 1953, ISA 2458/7, and 20 July 1953, ISA 2458/8.
85. Eban's comments at the Knesset Foreign Affairs and Defense Committee, 7 August 1950, ISA.
86. Ambassadorial conference, 12 July 1950, ISA 2458/4.
87. Eban's comments at the Knesset Foreign Affairs and Defense Committee, 7 August 1950, ISA.
88. Herzog to Shiloah, 19 April 1951, ISA 7854/4, and Moshe Tov to Eytan, 2 February 1951, ISA 2384/21.
89. A meeting dated 31 August 1953, ISA 2458/8.
90. Herzog to Arnon, 2 September 1953, ISA 2576/20.
91. Eban to the Ministry for Foreign Affairs, 21 September 1953, ISA 136/6.
92. A memorandum dated 31 December 1950, ISA 5816/5.
93. Ibid.
94. Gershon Pappe to Sasson, 3 March 1950, ISA 2396/15.
95. Pappe to Daniel Levin, 18 March 1952, ISA 117/2.
96. See correspondence in ISA 117/2.
97. Sharett's report at the Knesset Foreign Affairs and Defense Committee, 1 September 1950, ISA.
98. Sharett at a meeting dated 20 July 1953, ISA 2458/8.
99. Consultation on Jerusalem, 20 July 1953, ISA 2458/8. See also a memorandum dated 2 August 1952, ISA 2526/20.
100. Cabinet meeting minutes, 20 January 1952, ISA.
101. A memorandum dated 2 August 1952, ISA 2526/20.
102. On the World Council of Churches, see Hudson 1977 and Lodberg 1999. On its attitude toward Israel, see Merkley 2001, 44–50.

103. On this subject, see Fishman 1973.
104. On the Scottish Church, see Proctor 1997, 613–29.
105. Vardi to Sharett, 2 September 1950, ISA 5816/5.
106. See correspondence in ISA 5816/5 and Hahn 1999, 569–82.
107. Colbi to Zerach Warhaftig, 20 April 1956, ISA 5806/11. Jacobus served as the Coptic archbishop of Jerusalem between 1946 and 1956. See Meinardus 1960, 81, and Colbi 1988, 137. For a general analysis, see Watson 2003, 115–29.
108. Colbi to the Finance Ministry, 20 March 1953, ISA 2396/11. On the Armenians in Jerusalem, see Azarya 1984 and Sanjian 2003.
109. October 1950, ISA 7854/4.
110. Sharett at a cabinet meeting, 2 February 1950, ISA.
111. Quoted in Avraham Drapkin to Yaacov Tsur, 19 January 1950, ISA 2396/15.
112. Tsur to the Ministry for Foreign Affairs, 17 December 1950, ISA 2581/4.
113. Tsur to the Ministry for Foreign Affairs, 25 January 1951, ISA 2581/4.
114. Sharett at a meeting, 31 August 1953, ISA 2458/8.
115. Eban at the Knesset Foreign Affairs and Defense Committee, 6 October 1952, ISA. For the debates on Jerusalem at the United Nations, see Le Morzellec 1979.
116. Herzog to Tsur, 23 August 1954, ISA 193/23; Herzog to Sharett, 26 November 1954, ISA 7854/5.
117. Herzog to Sharett, 27 December 1955, ISA 2523/12. For a retrospective analysis, see Kagan to Yehonatan Prato, 26 February 1964, ISA 968/2.

3. At the Gates of the Vatican

1. Sharett, cabinet meeting, 6 April 1952, ISA.
2. Herzog to Sharett, 18 March 1952, and correspondence in ISA 2396/15.
3. Avner to Yishai, Israel's minister in Rome, 18 June 1951, ISA 2523/17.
4. Yishai to the director of research for the Ministry for Foreign Affairs, 4 December 1951, ISA 2523/18.
5. Eytan to Eliahu Sasson, 1 March 1953, ISA 2396/15. See also Emil Najar to Sasson, 18 August 1953, ISA 2523/18.
6. See Sasson to Eytan, 9 August 1953, ISA 2526/20.
7. Herzog to Eytan, 28 April 1953, ISA 2396/15. See also his comments at a meeting dated 11 June 1953, ISA 2497/7.
8. The following is based on *IILA*, no. 408, 28 November 1951, ISA 7536/3.
9. Katriel Katz to Sharett, 5 December 1951, ISA 2523/6.
10. First secretary, Israeli legation Rome to Avner, 16 May 1951, ISA 277/17.
11. Sasson to Eytan, 16 October 1955, ISA 273/22.
12. Tsur as quoted in Herzog to Tsur, 27 October 1955, ISA 2523/18. See also Yosef Ariel to the Ministry for Foreign Affairs, 25 November 1955, ISA 193/23, and Sasson to the Ministry for Foreign Affairs, 29 January 1956, ISA 192/37.
13. Eytan to Sasson, 26 October 1955, ISA 273/22.
14. Herzog to Tsur, 27 October 1955, ISA 2523/18.
15. Ibid.
16. See Herzog's undated memorandum (probably of late November 1955), ISA 193/23.
17. Sasson to the Ministry for Foreign Affairs, 16 November 1955, ISA 2523/18.
18. Tsur to Eytan, 22 October 1955, ISA 273/22, and an undated memorandum (probably of late November 1955), ISA 193/23. Alphone Dupront (1905–90) was a pro-

fessor of history at the Sorbonne and became the founding president of the University of Paris—Sorbonne (Paris IV). The writings of Alphone Dupront included *Du sacre: croisades et pelerinages, images et langages, Le mythe de croisade, Qu'est-ce que les Lumieres?* and *Saint-Jacques de Compostelle*. On his work see Iogna-Prat 1998.

19. See a meeting dated 25 October 1956, ISA 2523/18.

20. See Kagan's report, 19 November 1956, ISA 273/22, and Yechiel Ilsar's dispatches to Israel's minister in Bern, 20 November 1956 (ISA 2523/18), and to the director-general of the Ministry for Foreign Affairs, 6 December 1956, ISA 3102/18.

21. Prato to the director-general of the Ministry for Foreign Affairs, 25 November 1956, ISA 2581/4.

22. See Bar-On 1992.

23. Tsur's dispatch to the Ministry for Foreign Affairs, 1 March 1956, and Dan Avni's dispatch to Herzog, 26 April 1956, both in ISA 192/37.

24. Ilsar's dispatches to the director-general of the Ministry for Foreign Affairs, 6 December 1956, ISA 3102/18. The following is based on Fischer's report dated 18 December 1957, ISA 273/15.

25. See a dispatch from Britain's representative to the Vatican to the Foreign Office, 13 March 1959, British Public Record Office (PRO) Foreign Office Records (FO) file FO 371/142295.

26. Yitzhak Ben-Yaacov to the Ministry for Foreign Affairs, 12 March 1957, ISA 273/15.

27. See a dispatch from Britain's representative to the Vatican to the Foreign Office, 20 August 1957, PRO FO 371/128104.

28. Fischer to Herzog, 1 August 1957, ISA 3102/19.

29. Fischer to Kohn, 15 November 1957, ISA 273/15.

30. Kagan to Fischer, 9 December 1958, ISA 237/18.

31. Sasson to Fischer, 29 November 1957, ISA 273/15.

32. Sasson to Mordechai Gazit, 3 February 1957, ISA 273/18.

33. Sasson to Fischer, 6 June 1958, ISA 273/18.

34. See Fraenkel 1995, and Herzog to Golda Meir, 3 November 1957, ISA 3102/21. On Roncalli, see Peter Hebblethwaite 1985, and the thoughtful biographical observations by Melloni 1996.

35. Sasson to Fischer, 20 November 1958, ISA 273/18.

36. Fischer to Meir, 30 October 1958, and to Sasson, 16 November 1958, ISA 273/18 and ISA 3102/20, respectively.

37. Kagan to Fischer, 28 November 1958, ISA 3102/21.

38. Sasson to Meir, 6 November 1958, ISA 272/18 and correspondence in ISA 3102/20.

39. Meir to Nahum Goldmann, 17 November 1958, ISA 3102/20.

40. Sasson to Fischer, 3 December 1958, ISA 3102/20.

41. Sasson to the director-general of the Ministry for Foreign Affairs, 12 November 1958, ISA 273/18.

42. Sasson to the Ministry for Foreign Affairs, 10 February 1957, ISA 204/19.

43. Sasson to Fischer, 21 November 1958, ISA 3102/20.

44. See the text in ISA 273/18.

45. Vardi to Fischer, 30 November 1958, ISA 3102/20.

46. Sasson to Fischer, 2 April 1959, ISA 273/18.

47. Fischer to Meir, 10 February 1959, ISA 334/18.

48. See Kagan's retrospective analysis dated 26 February 1964, ISA 217/13.

49. Fischer to Meir, 15 February 1959, ISA 334/18.

50. Kohn to the Ministry for Foreign Affairs, 27 February 1959, ISA 3102/20.

51. See Colbi's report, 27 June 1961, ISA 3314/4.

52. See a dispatch from Britain's representative to the Vatican to the Foreign Office, 13 March 1959, PRO FO 371/142295.

53. Tsur to Fischer, 18 February 1959, ISA 3102/20.

54. Fischer's memorandum, 25 February 1959.

55. Kohn to the director-general of the Ministry for Foreign Affairs, 27 February 1959.

56. Fischer to Meir, 5 November 1959.

57. Hagai Dikan to Fischer, 20 November 1959, ISA 3102/24; Fischer to Meir, 25 February 1960, ISA 3314/4.

58. Fischer to Meir, 5 November 1959, ISA 3102/20.

59. Dikan to Fischer, 6 December 1959.

60. Tsur to Sasson, 21 September 1959, ISA 273/17.

61. Fischer to Meir, 30 November 1959, ISA 3102/20.

62. Fischer to Sasson, 16 December 1959.

63. Fischer to the minister for religious affairs, 30 June 1959, and to Meir.

64. Haim Yahil to Sasson, 8 May 1960, 287/7.

65. Fischer to Meir, 25 February 1960, ISA 3314/4.

66. See Fischer to Arie Levavi, 11 July 1963, ISA 217/11.

67. Sasson to Haim Yahil, 11 May 1960, ISA 287/7.

68. Sasson to Fischer, 19 January 1960, ISA 287/6.

69. Sasson to the Ministry for Foreign Affairs, 10 March 1960.

70. Sasson to Fischer, 26 February 1960.

71. Sasson to the Ministry for Foreign Affairs, 10 March 1960.

72. Ibid. See also Sasson to Fischer.

73. Ben-Gurion Diary, Ben-Gurion Archive, Sde Boker (hereafter BGD) entry for 23 March 1960.

74. Fischer to Levavi, 31 July 1962, ISA 3404/32.

75. Sasson to Fischer, 6 April 1960, 25 April 1960, ISA 287/6. On Adenauer's multi-faceted attitude toward Israel, see Jelinek 2002.

76. Yahil to Sasson, 8 May 1960, ISA 287/7.

77. Sasson to Fischer, 30 March 1960.

78. Sasson to Fischer, 28 April 1960.

79. Sasson to Fischer, 31 March 1960.

80. Sasson to Fischer, 25 April 1960.

81. Sasson to Meir, 15 April 1960.

82. Sasson to Fischer, 27 April 1960.

83. Yahil to Sasson, 8 May 1960.

84. Ibid.

85. Sasson to Yahil, 29 April 1960.

86. Sasson to Yahil, 11 May 1960.

87. The semiofficial history of Israel's Ministry for Foreign Affairs totally ignores the above story. See Ben-Horin 2002, 1004.

88. Meir to Fischer, 22 December 1960, ISA 3314/4.

89. The bishop maintained contacts only with the Ministry for Religious Affairs. See Fischer to Meir, 26 June 1960, and to Levavi, 5 December 1961, ISA 3314/4. See also Fischer to Meir, 22 May 1964, ISA 217/9.

90. Fischer to Levavi, 16 March 1962, ISA 3404/32, and Kagan's memorandum, 26 February 1964, ISA 217/13. Tardini died in the summer of 1961.

91. Fischer to Yohanan Meroz, 13 March 1962, ISA 272/12.

4. Theology and Diplomacy

1. Kagan to Prato, 26 February 1964, ISA 217/13.
2. See Phayer 2000, and Wigoder 1988.
3. On Vatican II, see Alberigo 1995, 1997, 2000, 2003. See also Melloni 2000.
4. Phayer 2000, 204–08.
5. On the man see Leeming 1964 and Schmidt 1992.
6. Dikan to Fischer, 19 June 1960, ISA 287/7; Vardi to Eytan, 4 July 1960, ISA 3314/4.
7. Zwi Werblowsky to Fischer, 10 July 1960.
8. Fischer to Meir, 22 December 1960; correspondence in CZA Z6/1544; Werblowsky's report, 30 November 1961, ISA 280/8.
9. The following is based on Werblowsky to Fischer, 19 October 1961, ISA 280/8.
10. Werblowvsky's report, 30 November 1961, ibid.
11. Werblowsky to Fischer, 10 November 1961, ibid.
12. Werblovsky's report, 30 November 1961, ibid.
13. Fischer to Levavi, 27 November 1961, ibid.
14. Fischer to Levavi, 5 December 1961, ISA 3314/4.
15. Fischer to Meroz, 13 March 1962, ISA 217/12.
16. Goldmann to Vardi, 31 May 1962, ISA 3404/32.
17. Vardi to Fischer, 8 July, ISA 217/12.
18. Otto Ron to Fischer, 18 July 1962, ISA 3404/32.
19. Fischer to Levavi, 5 July 1962 ISA 217/12.
20. Ron to Fischer, 18 July 1962, ISA 3404/32.
21. Fischer to Levavi, 6 July 1962 ISA 217/12.
22. Levavi to Fischer, 12 July 1962, ISA 3404/32.
23. Fischer to Levavi, 31 July 1962.
24. Ibid.
25. Israeli legation New York to the Ministry for Foreign Affairs, 26 July 1962.
26. Levavi to Fischer, 23 August 1962.
27. Fischer to Levavi, 7 August 1962.
28. Colbi to the Ministry for Religious Affairs, 10 October 1962, ISA 5822/13, and Fischer to Levavi, 17 October 1962, ISA 3402/32.
29. Levavi to Katz, 6 January 1963, ISA 3045/6.
30. Fischer to Levavi, 15 November 1962, ISA 3404/32, and Katz to Levavi, 7 March 1963, ISA 3045/6.
31. Moshe Avidor to Fischer, 13 March 1963, ISA 3404/32; Levavi to Katz, 19 November 1962.
32. Fischer to Avidor 20 February 1963, and Avidor to Fischer, 13 March 1963.
33. Fischer to Levavi, 7 December 1961.
34. Fischer to Levavi, 10 February 1962, ISA 217/10.
35. Fischer to Levavi 18 March 1963. See also Vardi to Fischer, 19 May 1963, ISA 217/8.
36. Fischer to Levavi, 8 May 1963.
37. Fischer to Levavi, 25 September 1963, ISA 3404/32.

38. Vardi to Fischer, 19 May 1963, ISA 217/8. The play went on stage in late June 1964.

39. Fischer to Levavi, 22 May 1963.

40. Fischer to Levavi, 22 May 1963.

41. Kagan to Levavi, 8 July 1963, ISA 3404/32.

42. See Phayer 2000, 209–10.

43. Fischer to Avidor, 2 August 1963, ISA 217/11.

44. Fischer to Levavi, 10 November 1963.

45. Fischer to Levavi, 10 July 1963, ISA 3404/32.

46. Fischer to Levavi, 6 August 1963, ISA 217/11.

47. Fischer to Levavi, 25 September 1963, ISA 3404/32.

48. Fischer to Meir, 4 November 1963, ISA 217/5.

49. For the document, see ISA 6533/10.

50. Fischer to Levavi, 15 November 1963, ISA 217/5.

51. Fischer to Levavi, 13 November 1963.

52. Prato to Fischer, 14 November 1963.

53. Meir Argov to Arad, 29 November 1963, ISA 3404/32.

54. Victor Eliashar to Levavi, 17 December 1963.

55. Werblowsky to Fischer, 31 May 1964, ISA 217/9.

56. Ben-Horin to Prato, 29 January 1964, ISA 3544/4.

57. Prato to Meir, 26 May 1964, ISA 217/7.

58. Prato to Fischer, 23 August 1963, ISA 217/7.

59. Fischer to Levavi, 9 June 1964.

60. *IILA*, no. 2109, 5 December 1965, ISA 3544/6.

61. For a report on the hostile reactions within the Christian communities in the Middle East, see ISA 968/2.

62. For an extended analysis, see Phayer 2000, 208–16.

63. See correspondence in ISA 217/4, 6 and ISA 3544/8.

64. Prato to Nissim Yaish, 5 September 1965, ISA 218/3.

65. See Phayer 2000, 213.

66. *IILA*, no. 2109, 5 December 1965, ISA 3544/6. For two conflicting contemporary assessments of the significance of *Nostra Aetate*, see Bea 1966 and Blanshard 1966.

67. Levavi to Katz, 6 January 1963, ISA 3045/6.

68. *IILA*, no. 2109, 5 December 1965, ISA 3544/6.

69. Fischer to Levavi, 16 March 1962, ISA 3404/32.

70. Fischer to Levavi, 31 July 1962.

71. Fischer to Meir, 4 November 1963, ISA 217/5, Levavi to Fischer, 10 November 1963, ISA 3404/3.

72. See a report on consultation held on 12 December 1963, ISA 7934/8.

73. Fischer to Levavi, 5 December 1963, ISA 218/15.

74. See "Weekly Report," 184, 10 January 1964, ISA 6385/3661.

75. Fischer to Meir, 22 May 1964, ISA 217/9, Prato to Levavi, 26 May 1964, ISA 3544/4, Fischer to Prato, 25 April 1965, ISA 217/4 and Prato to Ehud Avriel, 12 January 1966, ISA 4024/7.

76. Fischer to Prato, 25 April 1965, ISA 217/4.

77. See report of a meeting, 12 December 1963, ISA 7934/8.

78. Avriel to Levavi, 20 April 1966, ISA 4024/7.

79. Herzog to Eban, 5 October 1969, ISA 7854/6.

80. September 1968, PRO FO 371/171659 M3/1/(17). On Israel and the Vatican

from the mid-1960s to the early 1990s, see Weiman 1996. The thorough thesis does not make use of declassified Israeli documents.

81. See Aumann 2002, 1034.

82. Fischer to Meir, 26 June 1960, ISA 3314/4.

83. Eytan to Levavi, 17 July 1963, ISA 3404/32.

84. Fischer to Levavi, 18 September 1963 ISA 217/11, and to Meir, 22 May 1964, ISA 217/9.

85. Fischer to Levavi, 5 December 1961, ISA 3314/4.

86. See correspondence in ISA 3404/32.

87. Fischer to Levavi, 15 January 1963.

88. Prato to Avriel, 12 January 1966, ISA 4024/7.

89. Fischer to Levavi, 15 January 1963, ISA 3404/32.

90. Yaish to Prato, 13 December 1965, ISA 3544/5, Prato to Avriel, 12 January 1966, ISA 4024/7.

91. Colbi's memorandum, 4 October 1965, ISA 3544/9.

92. Ilsar to the director-general of the Ministry for Foreign Affairs, 6 January 1967, ISA 4088/3.

93. Avriel to Ilsar, 26 June 1967, ISA 4089/11.

5. Missionary Activity

1. The following analysis is based on Colbi's undated (probably from late 1951) memorandum, ISA 8002/15, and on a memorandum written at the Ministry for Religious Affairs during 1965 entitled "The Christian Mission among Jews in Israel— Changes and New Developments," ISA 6258/2.

2. The thirty Catholic educational organizations operating in Israel in the early 1950s were Priests of the Patriarchate, Franciscan Fathers, Father of Zion, Assumptionists, Lazarists, Salisians, Benedictins of Bourons, Benedictins (French), Jesuits, Brothers of the Christian Schools, Brothers of St John of God (Austrian), Fathers of the Sacred Heart, Carmelites, Sisters of St Joseph, Polish Sisters of St. Elizabeth, Sisters of St. Claire, Sisters of the Holy Rosary, Tertiary Franciscans, Sisters of Charity of St. Vincent de Paul, Sisters of St. Charles of Borromeus, Franciscans Sisters, Sisters of Sion, Sisters of St. Dorothy, Sisters of St. Mary Auxiliatrix, Dame of Nazareth, Carmelite Sisters, Sisters of St. Anne, Tertiary Carmelite Sisters of St. Joseph, Tertiary Carmelite Sisters of St. Therese, and Little Sisters of Jesus. The eighteen active Protestant educational organizations in Israel at that time were Adventists of the Seventh Day, American Board of Missions to the Jews (New York), Israel Baptists' Fellowship, Christian Brethren in Israel, British Evangelistic Mission of the Pentecostal Movement, British and Foreign Bible Society, Bethel Jewish Mission (Los Angeles), British Jewish Society for the Propagation of the Gospel among Jews (Anglican Church), Church of Scotland, Chicago Hebrew Mission, Christian and Missionary Alliance, Finnish Mission to the Jews, Hebrew Evangelization Society (Los Angeles), Norwegian Israeli Mission, Svenska Israel's Missions, Svenska Jerusalem Foreningen, Watchtower Bible and Tract Society, and Witnesses of Jehovah. See Toren's memorandum, 9 July 1953, ISA 6337/10 and *IILA* 889, 2 June 1954, ISA 2523/15.

3. In the fall of 1960, during an official visit to Holland, the minister of trade and Industry, Pinhas Sapir, was approached by a group of Christians with a request to establish a Christian village in Israel. Their aim, they said, was to promote understanding and cooperation between Christian and Jews, and they assured him that they would

not engage in missionary activity. The necessary permits were granted by Sapir's Ministry, the Ministry of Finance, and the Jewish Agency and the village was set up on land near Ga'aton purchased from a Druze landowner. The religious parties raised the issue in the Knesset and various ministerial committees in 1962 and 1963, and conflicting views were voiced. Despite the objections, the government did not rescind its decision for reasons related to international relations. In September 1963 only three families were living in the village in caravans, working on the construction of permanent housing. See Yaish to Meroz, 26 September 1963, ISA 948/7. On the settlement, see Greenberg 1999. On the activities of other organizations, see Ariel 1998, Ariel and Kark, 1996, and Schmidgall 1996.

  4. Zeev Swift to Israeli embassy in Washington, 28 April 1954, ISA 172/12. For Catholic attitudes on this subject, see Racionzer 2004.

  5. Fischer to Levavi, 29 July 1963, ISA 217/11.

  6. See correspondence in ISA 2468/7.

  7. See a memorandum written by the cabinet legal adviser, dated 17 February 1952, ISA 8002/15, Eliahu Toren's report, 9 July 1953, ISA 6331/10, and Colbi's notes, 10 February 1965, ISA 3354/3.

  8. See Tibawi 1956, 271.

  9. See Colbi to the Ministry for Foreign Affairs, 27 January 1953, ISA 5817/19, and Malachi to Kalman Kahana, 14 July 1963, ISA 3413/1.

  10. Colbi to the Ministry for Foreign Affairs, 27 January 1953, ISA 5817/19.

  11. See, inter alia, Lang 1996, Eliav 1995, Shouval 1996, and Okkenhaug 2002.

  12. See a report by "Our Childrens' Fund," 11 March 1963, ISA 3045/6.

  13. See a memorandum written at the Ministry for Religious Affairs during 1965 entitled "The Christian Mission among Jews in Israel—Changes and New Developments," ISA 6258/2.

  14. Malachi to Kahana, 14 July 1963, ISA 3413/1.

  15. Ilsar circular letter to Israeli legations, 10 February 1967, ISA 4032/10.

  16. Malachi to Kahana, 14 July 1963, ISA 3413/1.

  17. A report dated 30 September 1966, ISA 4032/10.

  18. A cable dated 2 March 1963, ISA 217/9.

  19. A dispatch to the prime minister, 3 May 1964, ISA 6405/4226.

  20. Eshkol to Israel Brodie, 23 April 1963, ISA 6405/4226.

  21. Yehuda Benor to Colbi, 22 September 1958, ISA 3107/4.

  22. See correspondence in ISA 5807/7.

  23. Biran to the minister for interior affairs, 24 August 1950, ISA 5818/5.

  24. See correspondence in ISA 5814/8 and Benor's memorandum dated 23 June 1950, ISA 2524/12.

  25. Colbi to Biran, 28 August 1949, ISA 5828/5.

  26. See, e.g., cabinet meeting minutes, 3 May 1949 ISA.

  27. Moshe Keren to Bendor, 8 March 1951, ISA 338/27.

  28. Eytan to the cabinet's secretary, 26 May 1952, ISA 2396/25.

  29. ISA 2468/17.

  30. Eshkol to Brodie, 23 April 1963, ISA 6405/4226.

  31. Benor to the cabinet's secretary, 10 June 1952, ISA 2396/25.

  32. November 1950, ISA 5811/11.

  33. Vardi to Warhaftig, 17 March 1953, ISA 5822/2.

  34. Herzog to the cabinet's secretary, 13 May 1952, ISA 2396/15.

  35. Ishai to the Ministry for Foreign Affairs, 20 July 1952, ISA 2526/20.

36. Avraham Elmaliach at the Knesset Education Committee, 4 January 1950, ISA.

37. Colbi's memorandum, 27 January 1953, ISA 5817/19.

38. Colbi's undated (probably late December 1951) memorandum, ISA 8802/15.

39. Colbi's notes, 9 August 1952, ISA 5815/7.

40. Eytan to Ginosar, 4 April 1950, ISA 2550/5.

41. See Yehuda Leib Levin to Haim Shapira, 4 November 1951, ISA 5817/20.

42. Herzog to Bendor, 25 January 1951, ISA 2468/17.

43. See a dispatch from the Ministry for Foreign Affairs to Israeli embassy in Washington, 14 February 1951, ISA 338/27, and Keren to Bendor, 8 March 1951, ibid.

44. Herzog's notes, 6 September 1951, ISA 5824/4.

45. Michael Pragai to the Ministry for Welfare, 24 September 1950, ISA 2396/25.

46. Y. L. Levin to the cabinet secretary, 16 December 1951, ISA 5593/4686.

47. Cabinet meeting minutes, 23 December 1951, ISA.

48. See correspondence in ISA 2396/25.

49. The cabinet legal adviser to the cabinet secretary, 17 February 1952, ISA 8002/15.

50. The representative of the Ministry for Education defined missionary activities among adults as both "insult and danger" for the State of Israel. See Herzog to the cabinet secretary, 13 May 1952, and Benor to the cabinet secretary, 10 June 1952, ISA 2396/15.

51. See report of a meeting, 16 February 1954, ibid.

52. Tsur to the prime minister, 22 February 1954, ibid.

53. Avraham Harman to Bendor, 9 March 1954, and Shimoni to the Ministry for Foreign Affairs, 28 April 1955, ISA 394/11.

54. See a memorandum dated 3 February 1954, ISA 2396/25.

55. See correspondence in ISA 5816/17.

56. Sharett to Rafael, 17 May 1954, ISA 5593/4686.

57. Ben-Yaacov to the European Division of the Ministry for Foreign Affairs, 13 May 1954, ISA 2396/25.

58. Kahana to Ben-Gurion, 30 August 1956, ISA 5593/4686.

59. Shlomo Tsidon to Eshkol, 23 July 1964, ISA 6405/4226.

60. See a memorandum dated 26 February 1964, ISA 6405/4227.

61. See his dispatch to the Chief Rabbi of Great Britain, 23 April 1964, ISA 6405/4226.

62. See Prato's circular dispatch to Israeli diplomatic legations, 22 May 1964, ISA 217/9.

63. See correspondence in ISA 4632/16.

64. Shimoni to the Ministry for Foreign Affairs legal adviser, 16 January 1967, ISA 4632/10.

65. Eban to the minister of justice, 15 February 1967, ISA 4032/10.

66. See correspondence in ISA 4032/10. For an analysis of the broader issue, see Zameret 2002.

67. The following is based on a report written by the government legal adviser, 14 May 1963, ISA 6405/4226. On Israel's education system at that time, see Zameret 1997.

68. The following is based on Zalman Aranne to the prime minister, 12 September 1963.

69. For a reflection of the prevalent attitude, see Meir to Israel's ambassador in Rome, 31 July 1963, ISA 217/11.

70. Undated memorandum (probably late 1967), ISA 6258/17.

71. Aranne to the prime minister, 12 September 1963, ISA 6405/4226.

72. See a memorandum submitted by the government legal adviser to the prime minister, 9 May 1964.

73. Moshe Ben-Zeev to Aranne, 15 May 1963.

74. Aharon Yadlin to Adi Yafe, 9 October 1967.

75. Eshkol to Brodie, 23 April 1964.

76. Aranne to the prime minister, 12 September 1963.

77. For an early manifestation of this attitude, see Colbi to Biran, 28 August 1949, ISA 5825/5.

78. See Herzog to the Immigration Office, 12 May 1950, and Colbi to the Ministry for Foreign Affairs, 11 October 1950, ISA 5825/9.

79. Colbi's notes 22 November 1950, ISA 5817/20.

80. See correspondence in ISA 6331/10.

81. Colbi to the Division of Import and Export, Transportation Ministry, 26 May 1952, ISA 5807/4.

82. Yehoshua Shai to Eytan, 4 January 1951, ISA 2396/25.

83. Herzog to Bendor, 25 January 1951, ISA 2468/17.

84. Bendor to the Israeli embassy, Washington, 14 February 1951, ISA 338/27.

85. See correspondence in ISA 2469/17.

86. Malachi's notes, 4 December 1963, ISA 5826/10.

87. The Franciscan Custody employed seventy-six clergymen in 1947. Ten years later their number dropped to forty-eight. The Ministry for Religious affairs refused to grant permit entrance to more claiming that the number 76 relates to the end of the British Mandate and "is irrelevant now." Colbi to the Interior Ministry, 14 November 1958, ISA 5826/2. See also Herzog's notes, 20 March 1949, ISA 5832/2.

88. Shai to the Consular Division of the Ministry for Foreign Affairs, 21 December 1956, ISA 5825/14.

89. See correspondence during late 1966 in ISA 6258/2.

90. Herzog to the cabinet secretary, 13 May 1952, ISA 2396/25.

91. Colbi's notes 28 June 1956, ISA 5818/1.

92. ISA 6258/2.

93. Ibid.

94. Ibid.

95. See note 3.

96. See Herzog to the director-general of the Ministry for Religious Affairs, 16 March 1951, ISA 5817/20.

97. Colbi to Herzog, 12 January 1951, ISA 5817/20, and report of a meeting, 9. February 1954, ISA 5593/4686.

98. Herzog to the director-general of the Ministry for Religious Affairs, 16 March 1951, ISA 5817/20.

99. See a memorandum dated 17 February 1953, ISA 5593/4686, and correspondence in ISA 5451/1784 and ISA 2396/25.

100. See correspondence in ISA 8802/18, ISA 6305/27–8, and ISA 6306/14.

101. See a report dated 13 June 1955, ISA 2396/15.

102. Eytan to the cabinet secretary, 26 May 1952.

103. See Zeev Sharef's dispatch to the chairman of the committee, 7 October 1953, ISA 5593/4686.

104. See report of the committee, 23 February 1954.

105. See Toren to Warhaftig, 22 January 1954. For personal accounts illustrating this topic, see correspondence in ISA 3107/11.

106. See a report dated 9 February 1954, ISA 5593/4686, correspondence in ISA 2396/25.

107. See correspondence in ISA 5810/7.

108. Tsur to Eytan, 22 January 1954, and Eytan to Warhaftig, 29 January 1954, both documents in ISA 2396/25.

109. See report of a meeting dated 9 February 1954, ISA 5593/4686.

110. See conclusion of a meeting, 13 June 1955, ISA 2396/25.

111. See Colbi to "The Voice of Israel," 23 October 1952, ISA 5816/13.

112. Ilsar to Israel's minister in Berne, 1 May 1957, ISA 3102/23.

113. See correspondence in ISA 139/13.

114. See Ferrari 1991, 91–93.

115. See Ben-Horin 2002, 1002.

116. Fischer's to Reuven Barkat, 6 March 1958, ISA 3107/11.

117. See Zeev Shek to the foreign minister's secretary, 15 October 1964, ISA 968/2, and Shimoni to the Consular Division, 21 April 1955, ISA 349/11.

118. Meroz to the American Division, 30 April 1958, ISA 394/6.

119. Maurice Fischer was the initiator of the organization. See his letter to the Secretary General of the Ministry for Foreign Affairs, 23 June 1958, ISA 3107/11, Fischer to Yitzhak Navon, 28 August 1958, ISA 5593/4682, and correspondence in ISA 3085/10.

120. The chairman of the Knesset agreed to join the governing committee only after receiving a report from the General Security Service that "Catholic missionaries are not posing a danger to Jews in Israel." See Fischer to Levavi, 29 July 1963, ISA 217/11.

121. See Fischer to Avidor, 1 December 1957, ISA 3085/10.

122. See Robert Davis's dispatch to the State Department, 11 March 1955. Davis served as American deputy consul in Tel Aviv. NA, American Mission in Tel Aviv, NNO 959373, box 08. See also Avner to Israel's ambassadors in Paris and Rome, 26 July 1961, ISA 937/3.

123. On the British Mandatory government's general policy toward religious communities in Palestine, see Tsimhoni 1996.

124. See Hershco 2000, 154–69.

125. See Sharett to Eytan, 23 August 1948, ISA 2413/11.

126. See correspondence in ISA 5817/15.

127. Eytan to Fischer, 1 September 1948, ISA 2382/12.

128. See report of a meeting with the French consul, 9 December 1948, ISA 5823/25, and cabinet meeting minutes, 23 January 1949 ISA.

129. Sharett at a cabinet meeting, 23 January 1949 ISA.

130. Sharet to Eliash, 23 January 1949, ISA 2391/24.

131. Zeev Argaman to Levavi, 5 March 1963, ISA 3413/1.

132. Freundlich 1984, 395.

133. A meeting dated 11 February 1949, ISA 5817/11.

134. Shek to the Israeli minister in Paris, 5 December 1963, ISA 3413/15.

135. See correspondence in ISA 968/2.

136. Eytan to Shek, 10 December 1963, ISA 3413/15.

137. See correspondence in ISA 968/2 and 5809/5.

138. Shmuel Hadas to the Division of Western Europe, 8 October 1963, ISA 948/7.

139. Biran to Sharett, 1 November 1950, ISA 5816/5.

140. Shek to the Israeli minister in Paris, 5 December 1963, ISA 3413/15.

141. See correspondence in ISA 3413/15..

142. Yaish to the director-general of the Ministry for Foreign Affairs, 13 October 1963, ISA 3413/1.

143. Eytan to the Division of Western Europe, 6 November 1963, ISA 3412/2.

144. See correspondence in ISA 3413/15.

145. Eytan to Shek, 10 December 1963.

146. Shek to Israel's minister in Paris, 15 November 1963, ISA 3413/15.

147. Shek to Levavi, 3 December 1963.

148. A dispatch from the Ministry for Foreign Affairs to the Israeli embassy in Paris, 27 November 1963.

149. Shaul Kariv to the Israeli ambassador in Rome, 26 April 1964, ISA 217/9.

150. Shek to Meroz, 5 December 1963, ISA 948/7.

151. Arie Lapid to Levavi, 28 June 1963, ISA 3413/1.

152. See correspondence ISA 968/2; Hanoch Rinot to the education minister, 21 April 1966, ISA 4032/3.

153. Report on a meeting, 10 July 1969, ISA 4199/7.

154. See correspondence in ISA 4199/7.

155. See correspondence in ISA 2393/23.

156. Colbi to the Jerusalem District Commissioner, 16 October 1950, ISA 2393/23.

157. Ben-Gurion Diary, entry for 29 June 1948, BGD.

158. For an example, see Davis's dispatch from the American consulate in Tel Aviv to the State Department, 11 March 1955, NA, American Mission in Tel Aviv, NNO 959373, box 08.

159. See Osterbye 1970. It should be noted that there were dissenting voices among missionaries working in Israel at that time. See, e.g., the 1954 article by Rev. Robert Smith of the Church of Scotland. These, however, were clearly exceptions, which for obvious reasons had been greatly cherished by Israeli authorities.

6. Goat and Chicken Diplomacy

1. Shaul Colbi's memorandum, 9 October 1956, ISA 3107/7.

2. Colbi's memorandum, 10 February 1965, ISA 3354/3.

3. Yegar, Oded, and Govrin 2002, 1038. For a retrospective analysis of a former Israeli director of the Division of Christian Communities at the Ministry for Religious Affairs, see Colbi 1988. For the Christian communities under the Jordanian rule, see Tsimhoni 1993.

4. Chaim Vardi to the minister for religious affairs, 1 January 1954, ISA 5818/10.

5. The decision was confirmed at a cabinet meeting on 14 June 1948, ISA. See also Ben-Ami to the director of the Division of Christian Communities at the Ministry for Religious Affairs, 13 February 1963, ISA 5818/11, correspondence in ISA 5832/2, Eytan to the director-general of the Ministry for Religious Affairs, 22 July 1948, ISA 5812/12, and Kohn to the director of the Division for International Organizations at the Ministry for Foreign Affairs, 27 July 1949, ISA 2393/23.

6. Eytan to Sharett, 23 January 1950, ISA 2395. The Foreign Ministry was almost totally disconnected from the issue of ecclesiastical property in Israel, which as will be demonstrated later was one of the central issues in its relations with the Christian world. See correspondence in ISA 5811/6.

7. Vardi to the minister for religious affairs, 3 March 1952, ISA 2396/22.

8. Ben-Ami to the director of the Division of Christian Communities at the Ministry for Religious Affairs, 13 February 1963, ISA 5818/11.

9. Vardi to the minister for religious affairs, 1 January 1954, ISA 5818/10.

10. Colbi to the deputy minister for religious affairs, 20 September 1960.

11. Cabinet meeting minutes, 15 September 1949, ISA.

12. Vardi to the minister for religious affairs, 1 January 1954, ISA 5818/10.

13. Vardi to the minister for religious affairs, 3 March 1952, ISA 2396/22.

14. Fischer to the director-general of the Ministry for Foreign Affairs, 15 May 1957, ISA 3107/4.

15. From a Ministry of Religious Affairs report dated July 1952, ISA 5815/10.

16. Colbi's memorandum, 9 October 1956, ISA 2523/6.

17. From a press release of the Israeli Bureau of Statistics, 24 July 1963, ISA 5820/4.

18. Tsimhoni 1989, 140.

19. See Palmon's memorandum, 5 August 1952, ISA 2402/29, and Boymal 2002, 71–73.

20. On the emerging government attitude toward non-Jews in Israel, see report of a meeting dated 5 May 1949, ISA 5593/4682.

21. Herzog to Eytan, 27 April 1953, ISA 2402/29.

22. Boymal 2002, XI.

23. Quoted in Lustik 1985, 78.

24. Cabinet meeting minutes, 20 January 1952, ISA. For two historical interpretations of Israel's policies toward the Druze, see Avivi 2002 and Firro 1999.

25. Avner to the Israeli minister in Rome, 12 December 1950, ISA 2523/6. Emphasis in the original.

26. A memorandum for the foreign minister, 21 September 1949, ISA 2393/23.

27. See Palmon's comments on George Hakim's open letter in *Alyawm*, 23 May 1951, ISA 2523/4.

28. See correspondence in ISA 4088/3.

29. "The Catholics in Israel," 11 March 1951, ISA 5811/15. See also Reuven Dafni to Herzog, 15 July 1951, ISA 4088/3.

30. Colbi's memorandum, 21 October 1956, ISA 5810/12.

31. Palmon to the Ministry for Foreign Affairs, 11 November 1949, ISA 2395/24.

32. Colbi to Yoel Barromi, 29 March 1953, ISA 2523/6.

33. Sharett to Israel's ministers in Stockholm and the Hague, 9 November 1950, ISA 175/11.

34. Fritz Simon to Colbi, 19 July 1955, ISA 5820/7.

35. Palmon's comments, 23 May 1951, ISA 2523/4. On incidents where Christian clergymen in Israel were involved in espionage and crimes, see correspondence in ISA 3107/4, and Colbi to the minister for religious affairs, 11 June 1961, ISA 5819/7.

36. Tsimhoni 1989, 140.

37. Colbi to the minister for religious affairs, 16 April 1953, ISA 5811/9, and 8 December 1949, ISA 5824/10.

38. See Davis' dispatch to the State Department, 11 March 1955, NA, American Mission in Tel Aviv, NNO 959373, box 08.

39. On the role of the prime minister's adviser for Arab affairs at that time, see Boymal 2002, 118–26.

40. It should be noted that local Christian leaders declined for political reasons to publicize in this publication their letters of support for Israel. See Kariv to the Information Division, 18 November 1952, ISA 117/3. The *Christian News from Israel* was de-

signed to serve a clear political purpose and was therefore carefully planned by the authorities. See Herzog to Avner, 9 January 1951, ISA 2523/17.

41. Ginosar to Sharett, 12 October 1950, ISA 2523/6.

42. See Ozaky-Lazer 1996, and Boymal 2002. See also Oren-Nordheim 1999 and Ozaky-Lazer 2002. For a detailed analysis of the emergence of the government's policy toward the Arab population in Israel and its 1948 war context, see Gelber 2004, 397–429.

43. Byomal 2002, 442–43.

44. Lustik 1985.

45. Y. Landman to the director-general of the Ministry for the Interior, 10 March 1958, ISA 2216/13.

46. Landman to the minister for the interior, 31 August 1955.

47. Landman to the counselor for Arab affairs, 30 January 1956.

48. Yosef Somech to the Haifa district commissioner, September 1955, ISA2216/12, and report of a meeting dated 14 August 1956.

49. Joseph Goldin to the Jerusalem District Commissioner, 18 November 1959, ISA 2216/11.

50. Uri Lubrani to Goldin, 4 August 1959. On the Jordanian attitude, see a memorandum dated 13 October 1958, ISA 2393/23.

51. Biran to Sharett, 6 March 1951, ISA 2396/24.

52. See Eytan's notes, 11 March 1951, ISA 2396/24.

53. See Meir Mendes to David Anat, 16 December 1952, ISA 5816/17.

54. See Yitzhak Shani to Herzog, 11 November 1953, ISA 2391/1.

55. Herzog to Sharett, 12 October 1950, ISA 2523/6.

56. Khouri to the prime minister, 15 January 1959, ISA 5804/11.

57. Colbi to Avner, 27 June 1951, ISA 2540/9.

58. Notes of a meeting dated 6 May 1951, ISA 7536/5.

59. Colbi to Aharon Levi, 28 October 1959, ISA 5826/4.

60. Colbi to the Ministry of the Interior, 7 February 1954, ISA 5825/10.

61. Colbi to Levi, 22 March 1959, and Lubrani to Colbi, 14 June 1959, ISA 5804/4.

62. See Palmon to Herzog, 29 October 1954, and Herzog to Palmon, 21 November 1950, ISA 2563/22, and Shani to Herzog, 11 November 1953, ISA 2396/1.

63. Colbi to Eli Natan, 4 August 1953, ISA 5813/3.

64. Colbi to the Jerusalem District Commissioner, 14 August 1953.

65. Colbi to Shai, 23 Septemer 1953, ISA 5816/4.

66. Colbi to the deputy minister for religious affairs, 18 August 1955.

67. Levi to the Ministry for Religious Affairs, 29 March 1961, ISA 5826/5.

68. Shaul Bar-Haim to the Ministry for Religious Affairs, 4 November 1952, ISA 5816/13. It should be noted that Herzog's recommendation to outlaw Christian broadcasting was not accepted. Pappe to Harry Beilin, 12 January 1953, ISA 394/1.

69. Bar-Haim to the Ministry for Religious Affairs, 18 October 1951.

70. Sharett at a cabinet meeting, 4 July 1954, ISA.

71. See correspondence concerning George Hakim's application for building permits for a new church in Ilabun, ISA 5819/9.

72. Director of the Eastern Europe Division to Shek, 27 January 1955, ISA 2396/18. The following analysis is based on Halevi 2004.

73. Colbi to Warhaftig, 29 August 1954, ISA 5817/6.

74. Colbi to the Ministry for Industry, 19 February 1958, ISA 5815/7.

75. Colbi to the Ministry for Industry, 16 March 1953, ISA 5818/9.

76. Colbi to the Ministry for Industry, 28 September 1951, ISA 5811/10.

77. Colbi to the minister for religious affairs, 14 February 1963, ISA 5804/20.

78. Colbi to K. Kadish, 23 June 1960, and Kadish to Colbi, 31 July 1960, ISA 5819/9.

79. Warhaftig to Ben-Gurion, 27 June 1954, and Zalman Divon to the director of the Prime Minister's Office, 10 October 1954, ISA 5804/16. On the Ikrit and Biram affair, see Ozaky-Lazer 1993.

80. Moshe Pearlman to Bechor Shitrit, 7 December 1948, ISA 308/11.

81. Moshe Yetach to the director of the Food Division, 3 August 1948, ISA 309/47.

82. The following is based on Colbi's memorandum, 5 March 1954, and his letter to Haim Pozner, 22 March 1954, ISA 2396/22.

83. See notes on the subject dated 30 May 1963, ISA 5822/13.

84. The Greek Catholic community was an exception. Notwithstanding nominal dependence on headquarters located in Lebanon, it enjoyed considerable freedom of action within Israel.

85. Palmon to the Ministry for Religious Affairs, 22 March 1950 and 22 June 1950, ISA 3925/24. See also Ilsar to the director-general of the Ministry for Foreign Affairs, 6 January 1967, ISA 4088/3.

86. Vardi to Palmon, 4 June 1950, ISA 5812/10.

87. The Latin Catholic, the Armenian, the Greek Catholic, the Maronite, and the Syrian Orthodox. See correspondence in ISA 5811/20. During the 1950s, only two of them had juridical systems: the Greek Orthodox and the Catholic. See correspondence in ISA 5820/8.

88. There were between 2,000 and 4,000 Protestants in Israel during the late 1950s including 1,000 Arabs who belonged to the Anglican Church. The others were divided among twenty religious organizations. See Colbi to Leo Savir, 27 September 1959, ISA 5810/2.

89. Colbi to Vardi, 5 June 1959.

90. Colbi to Savir, 12 August 1959, ISA 5810/2.

91. Colbi to the director-general of the Ministry for Religious Affairs, 21 August 1958, ISA 5820/9.

92. Moshe Hess to the Israeli chargé d'affaires in Berne, 4 September 1957, ISA 3319/22.

93. See correspondence in ISA 5810/7.

94. Harel to Eytan, 7 July 1954, and Warhaftig to Sharett, 10 August 1954, ISA 2524/14.

95. Colbi to the minister for religious affairs, 18 February 1964, ISA 5820/9.

96. See correspondence in ISA 3413/1.

97. See notes of a meeting dated 9 December 1962, ISA 5819/6.

98. See correspondence in ISA 3413/1. For Israel's policy toward the conflict between Christians and Muslims over holy places in Nazareth during a later period, see Israeli 2002b.

99. See Hochman 1988, 125.

100. Colbi's memorandum dated 15 October 1957, ISA 5817/8. The ongoing gravity of the situation made it necessary for the Israeli cabinet to discuss the issue two years later. See cabinet meeting, 21 June 1959, ISA.

101. Colbi to the Finance Ministry, 12 June 1951, ISA 5816/17.

102. See Vergani's article dated 29 February 1952, ISA 117/2.

103. On the official policy, see Colbi to the Defense Ministry, 9 September 1953, ISA 5814/10. Between 1948 and 1962 100 Christians served in the Israeli army. See Ben-Gurion Diary, entry for 9 February 1962, BGD.

104. Fischer to Haim Laskov, 10 March 1959, ISA 3107/4.

105. Colbi to the Ministry for Foreign Affairs, 24 September 1959, ISA 5806/11.

106. Herzog to the Israeli minister in London, 1 April 1952, ISA 5805/15. The sums of money involved were significant due to the austerity in Israel and the acute shortage of foreign currency. Thus the Assyrian Orthodox received 8,800 pounds sterling between 1955 and 1958, the Coptic Church 45,000 between 1951 and 1956, and the Armenian Church 12,500. See correspondence in ISA 5805/15.

107. Colbi to the Finance Ministry, 17 February 1954, ISA 2403/1.

108. Colbi to Shimon Sirkin, 6 February 1955, Comay to Kessler, 23 January 1953, ISA 5807/4, Colbi to Eileen Barkai, 6 November 1955, ISA 5807/5.

109. See reference to the document in ISA 3413, which deals with the subject and was reclassified during 1991 "at least until 2013."

110. Report of a meeting, 5 March 1963, ISA 3413/1.

111. See an illuminating retrospective analysis of the subject in an undated memorandum (probably June 1968), PRO FO 371/171659.

112. Michael Williams to Anthony Moore, 30 July 1968, PRO FO 371/171661.

113. Ilsar to the director-general of the Ministry for Foreign Affairs, 6 January 1967, ISA 4088/3.

114. Herzog to Eytan, 16 September 1954, ISA 2396/20. On Hakim, see Zameret and Yablonka 2000, 212–14.

115. Colbi's notes, 20 April 1952, ISA 2396/3, and 18 March 1953, ISA 2396/1.

116. See correspondence in ISA 5804/71. The following analysis is based on an undated memorandum (probably early 1964) and on a memorandum by the counselor for Arab affairs that Laish enclosed to Yael Vered, 24 May 1964, ISA 3728/23.

117. Colbi's notes, 23 July 1956, ISA 5804/17.

118. Sasson to Eytan, 12 May 1954, ISA 2396/1.

119. Colbi to Kariv, 31 July 1956, ISA 5804/17.

120. *IILA*, no. 408, 28 November 1951, ISA 7536/3.

121. Palmon to Sharett, 8 May 1956, ISA 3782/23.

122. Kohn to Colbi, 23 April 1956, and Colbi to Kohn, 30 April 1956, ISA 5804/17.

123. See correspondence in ISA 5804/17.

124. Kagan to Fischer, 8 June 1960, ISA 5804/20.

125. See an undated (probably 1953) intelligence report, ISA 2396/18.

126. Harry Odel to Ivan White, 17 May 1954, NA, American mission in Tel Aviv, NND 959373, box 06.

127. See, e.g., Eytan to Herzog, 17 March 1952, ISA 2526/2.

128. Herzog to Sharett, 12 October 1950, ISA 2523/6.

129. Tsimhoni 2001, 31–42. For detailed analysis of the Christian communities in Jerusalem, see Zeldin 1992 and O'Mahony 2003. For a broader perspective, see Kreutz 1992 and Sennott 2001.

130. See Ginosar to the Western Europe Division, 1 December 1950, ISA 2523/17.

131. The Catholic press often blamed Israel during the 1950s that "under the cover of insignificant gestures" it aimed at "suffocating Christian life in the country." See reference to such writings in Avner's dispatch to Herzog, 22 May 1951, ISA 5813/13.

132. A typical example can be found in the references to the subject during Dean Acheson's meeting with Sharett during late 1951 as reported to the cabinet by Sharett on 31 December 1951, ISA.

133. See Kamen 1985, and Haidar 1988.

134. My thesis is indirectly supported by findings of a very critical account of Is-

rael's handling of holy places for Christians and Muslims from its establishment until the mid-1950s. See Peled 1994, 120.

7. Israel and the Question of the Russian Ecclesiastical Assets

1. On the subject, see Kark 1995, Golan 2001, and Oren-Nordheim 1999. For the historical background, see Doukhan-Landau 1979, Stein 1984, Kark 1990, and Katz 2001.

2. See Golan 2001, 12–19, and Oren-Nordheim 1999, 65.

3. See references to this subject by the Israeli finance minister during a meeting with the Lutheran World Federation, 26 January 1950, ISA 2468/8.

4. Haim Kadmon to the finance minister, 28 November 1951, ISA 2395/24.

5. The following is based on *IILA*, no. 562, 22 October 1952, ISA 3044/5.

6. See circular letter to Israeli legations, 6 December 1955, ISA 139/7.

7. See undated (probably mid-1950) memorandum, ISA 2564/13.

8. For references to various handling of ecclesiastical properties, see Herzog to Sharett, 29 November 1950, ISA 2396/11, Colbi to the Jerusalem district commissioner, 17 August 1955, ISA 6895/14, Colbi to Barkai, 6 November 1955, ISA 5807/5, and Colbi to the Finance Ministry, 17 December 1954, ISA 2403/1.

9. See Kark 1984. On the Russian presence, see Hopwood 1969 and Stavrou 1963. For the Christian activities in Palestine during this period, see Carmel 1983.

10. See Ro'i, Freundlich, and Yaroshevski 2000 (hereafter *Israeli-Soviet Documents*), 575.

11. The following analysis is based on a memorandum dated 3 August 1949, ISA 2396/9. For more information, see two memoranda written by Moshe Levin, 12, 15 November 1946, PRO FO 371/52591.

12. The Ottoman authorities barred sale of properties to foreign governments but allowed purchase by individuals or organizations. This practice created many complications for the British and Israeli authorities when they tried to decide about legal ownership of real estate bought before the First World War. See correspondence in ISA 5656/26.

13. See Degani 1999.

14. On the Russian Church under Communist rule, see Pospielovsky 1984.

15. See M. Levin's memorandum, 15 November 1946, PRO FO 371/52591.

16. See M. Levin's memorandum, 12 November 1946, PRO FO 371/52591.

17. See a memorandum written by the legal adviser of the Mandatory government of Palestine, 17 November 1945, PRO FO 371/52591, and the British high commissioner to the Permanent permanent undersecretary of state for the Colonial Office, 31 January 1946.

18. See Zander 1971, 90.

19. See an undated report (probably 1946) in PRO FO 525/91371.

20. Rabinovitch's notes, 9 August 1948, CZA A386/106.

21. On the subject, see Zander 1973, 331–66.

22. Zander 1973, 356.

23. PRO FO 371/52591, 18.

24. Zander 1973, 363–64.

25. Ibid., 361–62.

26. See correspondence in PRO FO 371/52591, 47–48.

27. Rabinovitch's notes, 9 August 1948, CZA A386/106, and his dispatch to Sharett, 30 August 1948, ISA 2501/16.

28. See a dispatch from the British high commissioner to the Colonial Office, 31 January 1946, PRO FO 371/52591.

29. See his comments dated 1 April 1945, PRO CO/733/466/3.

30. Harold Beeley's notes, 2 July 1946, in PRO FO 371/52591.

31. The Israeli government legal adviser to Shmuel Friedman, 5 January 1949, ISA 2501/16.

32. See a memorandum dated 25 November 1944, *Israeli-Soviet Documents*, 90–92.

33. *Israeli-Soviet Documents*, 95. For the Russian ecclesiastical activities in Palestine, see Zifroni 1977, 162–95.

34. See correspondence in ISA 2501/16 and ISA 2396/9.

35. Yitzhak Rabinovitch to the Political Department, 9 May 1948, ISA 2501/16.

36. Rabinovitch to Sharett, 30 August 1948. See also his notes, 8 August 1948, CZA A386/106.

37. *Israeli-Soviet Documents*, 282.

38. See Gorodetsky 2003. For the Soviet Union's policy toward the Zionist movement and the State of Israel, see Ro'i 1980.

39. See a dispatch from the Czech consul to the Jewish Agency, 28 May 1948, ISA 2501/16.

40. Rabinovitch to Eliahu Dobkin, 14 July 1948, ISA 2501/16.

41. See report of the committee preparing negotiations on the Russian ecclesiastical properties, 6 April 1960, ISA 6382/3630.

42. The file PRO CO/733/490/3 at the Public Record Office in London, which deals specifically with British activities concerning Russian ecclesiastical properties in early 1948, has been formally declassified but in fact is being held by the authorities apparently for reasons that are not difficult to understand.

43. See Alan Cunningham to the Colonial Office, 1 April 1948, PRO CO/733 /490/2.

44. See Rabinovitch's notes, 9 August 1948, CZA A386/106.

45. *Israeli-Soviet Documents*, 345. Israeli authorities got hold of the drafts.

46. The law was later published. See an undated report (January 1949), ISA 2501/19.

47. See report of the committee preparing negotiations on the Russian ecclesiastical properties, 6 April 1960, ISA 6382/3630. See also Yaroshevski 2003.

48. Rabinovitch to Sharett, 30 August 1948, ISA 2501/16.

49. See Colbi 1988, 91.

50. Rabinovitch to the Political Department of the Jewish Agency, 22 June 1948, ISA 2501/6, and Alexander Helm to the Foreign Office in London, 3 March 1950, PRO FO 371/82629.

51. There is reliable testimony on the expulsion from Israel of "White" Russian mission personnel who were suspected of collaboration with the Arab enemy in Jordan. See undated memorandum (probably May 1948), CZA A386/99, and Rabinovitch's dispatch to the "military authorities in the occupied area of North Jerusalem," 8 July 1948, CZA A386/63.

52. Levavi to the Ministry for Justice, 28 July 1948, ISA 2501/16.

53. Rabinovitch to Sharett, 30 August 1948, ISA 2501/16. On the Soviet diplomatic mission in Israel, see Freundlich 2003.

54. Dov Joseph to Sharett, 21 December 1948.

55. *Israeli-Soviet Documents*, 338.

56. Rabinovitch to Sharett, 28 October 1948, ISA 2501/16.

57. *Israeli-Soviet Documents*, 344.

58. Rabinovitch to Sharett, 28 October 1948, ISA 2501/16.
59. Friedman comments on Rabinovitch's letter dated 28 October 1948.
60. *Israeli-Soviet Documents*, 420–21.
61. Government legal adviser to Friedman, 5 January 1949, ISA 2501/16.
62. See cabinet meeting minutes, 2 August 1949, ISA.
63. See Richard Ford to the State Department, 12 November 1949, NA, American mission in Tel Aviv, 84/350/61/33 RG.
64. See cabinet meeting minutes, 2 August 1949, ISA.
65. Helms to the British Foreign Office, 3 March 1950, PRO FO 371/82629.
66. Friedman to the Israeli legation, Moscow, 9 February 1949, ISA 2501/16, and Ford to the State Department, 12 November 1949, NA, American mission in Tel Aviv, 84/350/61/33 RG.
67. Friedman to Eliahu Elath, 19 April 1949, ISA 2501/16.
68. Friedman to the Israeli legation, Moscow, 22 February 1949.
69. Friedman undated note (probably mid-September 1951) to Sharett, ISA 2501/19.
70. Helms to the British Foreign Office, 3 March 1950, PRO FO 371/82629.
71. Friedman to Mikhail Mukhin, 29 May 1949, CZA A386–99.
72. Memorandum, 30 November 1951, ISA 2501/8.
73. See an exchange of notes between the Russian consulate in Israel and the Ministry for Foreign Affairs on negotiations concerning the ecclesiastic properties since 1948, ISA 6382/3630.
74. Friedman to Israel's minister in Prague, 19 July 1949, ISA 2501/17.
75. Friedman to Yaacov Shapira, 28 July 1949.
76. An undated memorandum (probably August 1949), ISA 2396/9.
77. See an intelligence report, 27 July 1949, ISA 2501/17.
78. Friedman to Mordechai Namir, 2 March 1949, ISA 2501/16.
79. *Israeli-Soviet Documents*, 534.
80. Friedman to the Israeli legation, Moscow, 14 November 1949, ISA 2501/19, and a memorandum dated 1 January 1950, ISA 2501/19.
81. *Israeli-Soviet Documents*, 556, 574–75, 559.
82. Friedman to the Israeli consulate in Moscow, 31 January 1950, ISA 2501/17, and *Haboker* 6 January 1950 (Hebrew).
83. Levavi to Namir, 13 October 1950, ISA 2325/3.
84. Note of a conversation, 20 October 1950, ISA 2396/9.
85. See Helms dispatch to the Foreign Office, 3 March 1950, PRO FO 371/82629. The British diplomat referred to American pressure exerted on Israel. However, such pressure has not been recorded in Israeli documents.
86. *Israeli-Soviet Documents*, 674.
87. Ibid., 605.
88. Cabinet meeting minutes, 8 February 1951, ISA. The following analysis is based on a memorandum dated 18 February 1951, ISA 2501/19.
89. See the minister for justice to the foreign minister, 18 February 1951, ISA 2396/9.
90. See a memorandum dated 8 April 1952, ISA 2501/18.
91. It was located mainly in what was commonly referred to as the "Russian Compound." See Walter to Efraim Evron, 14 November 1951.
92. See a memorandum by the Foreign Office legal adviser, 8 April 1952.
93. Baron Horace Gunzburg was the unofficial leader of the integrationist current within Russian-Jewish society in the second half of the nineteenth century. On his archives and collections, see Nathans 2002, 12, 128–29, and Stanislawski 1987.

94. Cabinet meeting minutes, 8 March 1951, ISA.

95. *Israeli-Soviet Documents*, 720–21, 729–30, 734.

96. Yael Uzai to Reuven Gal, 11 October 1951, ISA 2396/9, and Friedman to the custodian-general, 26 March 1952, ISA 2501/18.

97. See a memorandum by the Foreign Office legal adviser, 8 April 1952. Israel declined to transfer the function of dealing with the Russian property to a government official for fear of adverse reaction by the Soviets and therefore left Rabinovitch to handle the matter on its behalf. See Gal's memorandum, 8 April 1952.

98. Friedman's dispatch to the Israeli consulate in Moscow, 16 October 1951. See also *Israeli-Soviet Documents*, 753.

99. See Zander 1971, 91, *Israeli-Soviet Documents*, 800, and the legal adviser to the Foreign Ministry, 23 April 1952, ISA 2396/9.

100. Friedman's dispatch to the Israeli consulate in Moscow, 3 March 1952, ISA 2501/18.

101. *Israeli-Soviet Documents*, 786–90.

102. Friedman to the custodian-general, 26 March 1952, ISA 2501/18, and *Israeli-Soviet Documents*, 801.

103. See a memorandum dated 8 April 1952, ISA 2501/8.

104. Legal adviser to the Foreign Ministry, 23 April 1952, ISA 2396/9.

105. *Israeli-Soviet Documents*, 800.

106. ISA. See also Kadmon to the Ministry for Foreign Affairs, 6 August 1952, ISA 2501/20.

107. *Israeli-Soviet Documents*, 803, and Kadmon to Rabinovitch, 30 June 1952, CZA A386/79.

108. Notes of a meeting, 22 March 1953, ISA 2369/9.

109. *Israeli-Soviet Documents*, 839.

110. Notes of a meeting, 22 March 1953, ISA 2369/9.

111. Shabtai Rosenne to Levavi, 26 July 1953, ISA 2501/18.

112. For details about the Russian ecclesiastic properties, see report of a meeting, 6 April 1960, ISA 6382/3630.

113. See, e.g., dispatches from the Soviet embassy to the Ministry for Foreign Affairs, 16 March 1955 and 14 March 1956, ISA 2507/11. See also notes of a meeting, 9 June 1956.

114. See correspondence in ISA 2507/11.

115. See report of a meeting, 6 April 1960, ISA 6382/3630.

116. See correspondence in ISA 2507/11.

117. See the Ministry for Foreign Affairs to Israeli embassy, Moscow, 12 July 1956, Meir to the cabinet secretary, 12 September 1956, 2410/29, and Teddy Kollek to Meir, 18 September 1956, ISA 5726/19.

118. See a report dated 6 April 1960, ISA 6382/3630.

119. Ibid.

120. Argaman to the cabinet secretary, 5 May 1960.

121. William Lockling to the State Department, 13 June 1960, American Tel Aviv consulate files, NA 661.842/6–1360.

122. Theodor Frye to the State Department, 6 December 1960, American Tel Aviv consulate files, NA 661.884A/12–660.

123. Fragmented evidence is found in notes of meetings during 1960 and in a meeting between the Soviet ambassador and the Israeli general custodian, 12 January 1962, ISA 6382/3630.

124. See notes of meetings 30 October 1963 and 13 November 1963, ISA 6382/30.

125. See the text of the agreement in ISA 3152/8.

126. See notes of a meeting, 2 August 1960, ISA 4049/14.

127. See notes of a meeting, 23 January 1964, ISA 4049/14.

128. See correspondence in ISA 450/7.

129. See correspondence in ISA 6382/3130, ISA 6382/3630, and ISA 4049/14.

130. See Joseph to the Land Registry Office, 31 August 1964, ISA 5726/19. For Israeli official position, see Colbi 1988, 177. See also Uriel Doron to Yosef Carmil, 27 January 1966 ISA 4049/14.

131. Doron to the director-general of the Ministry for Foreign Affairs, 15 September 1964, ISA 3754/4.

132. Zak 1988, 279–82.

133. See correspondence in ISA 3574/4 and ISA 5726/19.

134. See *Ma'ariv*, 20 October 1964 (Hebrew).

135. On the topic, see Govrin 1998.

136. For a retrospective analysis of the British ambassador in Israel, see his undated (May 1966) dispatch to the Foreign Office, PRO FO 371/186812. See also a report on Eban's meeting at the State Department on 4 March 1964, NA Political Affairs, box 1964–6 2358 RG59.

137. Dov Satat to Carmil, 10 October 1966, ISA 4049/23.

138. Shlomo Hillel to the minister for religious affairs, 7 November 1967, ISA 4200/10.

139. See a report in the *Jerusalem Post*, 29 March 1991.

140. See Nadav Shragai's report in *Ha'aretz*, 31 March 1995 (Hebrew).

141. Private information.

8. Land in the Shadow of the Cross

1. Oren-Nordheim 1999, 119–24.

2. Katz 2001, 256–64.

3. See an undated (probably late 1951) report on the Templars' property, PRO Treasury papers, file T 317/775.

4. See correspondence in PRO FO 371/182184.

5. On the Templars' settlements in Palestine, see Ben Artzi 1996.

6. See report of a meeting, 12 August 1949, ISA 2396/5, Haim Kadmon to Eliezer Kaplan, 23 August 1949, and Oren-Nordheim 1999, 136. For a Lutheran perspective, see Schiotz 1980, 89–93.

7. See Evron's memorandum, 23 December 1949, ISA 2468/8. The Syrian Orphanage in Jerusalem was founded in 1860 by Johann Ludwig Schneller, born in Wurttemberg, Germany. In 1948 Elias al-Haddad came to Lebanon with twelve Palestinian schoolchildren, and Rev. Hermann Schneller, Johann's grandson, was deported to Australia by the authorities. In 1951 Hermann Schneller returned to Lebanon and after several sojourns rented a place in Zahle, a main city in the Bekaa. At the end of 1952, he moved with the children into the newly opened school at Khirbet Kanafar, where to the present day socially underprivileged youths and orphans are given a home, schooling, and vocational training. The school is owned and operated by the National Evangelical Church of Beirut. See http://www.jlss.org/About.htm.

8. Notes of a meeting, 15 August 1949, ISA 2468/8.

9. See correspondence in ISA 5811/11.

10. January 1950, ISA 2396/5.

11. See correspondence in ISA 2396/5.

12. The document upon which the following account is based is in ISA 2468/7.

13. See report of a meeting, 26 November 1950, ISA 2468/8.

14. See Kadmon to the finance minister, 25 January 1950. On Anglo-Israeli financial talks at that time, see Bialer 1992.

15. See notes of a meeting, 14 February 1951, ISA 56811/6.

16. See a report dated 27 January 1950, ISA 2468/8, and a dispatch to Arthur Lurie, 20 February 1950, ISA 5811/11.

17. See correspondence in ISA 2468/8, a dispatch from Britain's UN representative to the Foreign Office, 24 February 1950, PRO FO 371/182184, and a dispatch from U.S. United Nations delegation to the State Department, 18 February 1950, NA Tel Aviv consulate files, RG/84/350/61/33.

18. Eban to Kollek, 3 March 1950, ISA 2468/8.

19. Avner to Sharett, 15 April 1950, ISA 2490/11, and Herlitz to Eban, 15 June 1950, ISA 372/18.

20. Kadmon to Kaplan, 7 May 1950, ISA 1859/8.

21. Kadmon to Max Habicht, 12 June 1950, ISA 372/18.

22. See a memorandum dated 7 July 1950, ISA 2396/5, and Kadmon to Kaplan, 25 July 1950, ISA 2468/9.

23. See correspondence in ISA 119/5.

24. See Kadmon to Kaplan, 7 May 1950, ISA 1859/8.

25. See reference to a meeting dated 29 January 1950 in Oren-Nordheim 1999, 131.

26. See a memorandum dated 16 October 1950, ISA 2468/9.

27. Kadmon to the finance minister, 7 January 1951, and notes of meetings dated 21 January 1951, ISA 5811/11, and 1 February 1951, ISA 2396/5.

28. See Herzog to Shmuel Bendor, 4 May 1951, ISA 2468/9.

29. See the finance minister to the cabinet secretary, 15 April 1951, ISA 5567/4067.

30. See the cabinet secretary to the finance minister, 1 April 1951, ISA 6331/13.

31. See the finance minister to the cabinet secretary, 4 March 1951, ISA 2468/9.

32. See Kadmon to Sharett, 16 October 1951, ISA 2396/5.

33. See *IILA*, no. 408, 28 November 1951, ISA 7536/3.

34. See Oren-Nordheim 1999, 134.

35. Kadmon to Eytan, 17 July 1952, ISA 2488/9.

36. See Oren-Nordheim 1999, 135.

37. Kadmon to the finance minister, 19 June 1951, ISA 2396/5.

38. See correspondence in ISA 2468/9.

39. Kadmon to the finance minister, 19 June 1951, ISA 2396/5.

40. It should be noted that the agreement was considered at the time extremely sensitive for both sides. The limitations on publicity were therefore raised only five years later. See Uri Gordon to Israeli embassy in Washington, 6 May 1956, ISA 2468/15.

41. See Yehuda Gideon to Levin, 27 February 1952.

42. Zeldin 1992, 95.

43. See Colbi to the Ministry for Foreign Affairs, 13 June 1952, ISA 2542/12.

44. See Najar to Yahil, 31 August 1953, ISA 2416/15.

45. See report of a meeting dated 15 November 1950, ISA 5811/11, and Bendor to Eytan, 9 February 1951, ISA 2396/5.

46. See correspondence in ISA 2396/17 and ISA 2771/13.

47. See correspondence in ISA 2416/15.

48. See an unsigned dispatch to Comay, 27 August 1952, ISA 2542/12.

49. See correspondence in ISA 5656/26 and ISA 2542/12.

50. See A. Levhar to Avner, 3 November 1950, ISA 5811/11.

51. See Kadmon to the finance minister, 7 January 1951.

52. For Israel's efforts to put pressure on Vergani, see Eli Natan to the Finance Minister Bureau, 10 January 1951, ISA 5656/26, and notes of a meeting dated 21 March 1951, ISA 2396/5.

53. See notes of a meeting, 25 April 1951, ISA 5811/11, and 27 June 1951, ISA 2468/9.

54. See Kadmon to the finance minister, 13 August 1951, ISA 5656/26.

55. Notes of a meeting, 1 July 1951, ISA 5811/6, and Kurt Livne to the Ministry for Foreign Affairs, 18 July 1951, ISA 2542/12.

56. The following is based on Kadmon's diary, ISA 2468/4, and his dispatch to the Finance Ministry, 13 August 1951, ISA 5656/26.

57. On the Benedicts in Palestine and in Israel, see Degani 1999, 190–91.

58. See note 61.

59. See *Ma'ariv*, 24 May 1951 (Hebrew).

60. See correspondence in ISA 2542/12.

61. *IILA*, no. 430, 13 January 1952, ISA 2523/14.

62. On Israel's cooperation with Father Rudloff, see Levhar to Kadmon, 25 January 1951, ISA 5811/11.

63. Kadmon's memorandum, 8 April 1952.

64. Notes of a conversation, 19 May 1952, ISA 354/22.

65. Kadmon to Herzog, 26 January 1952, ISA 5811/11.

66. Kadmon to Felix Shinar, 12 February 1952, ISA 2523/12.

67. Harel to Israel's consul in Munich, 11 August 1952, ISA 2523/6.

68. See a report dated 14 April 1953, ISA 2542/12. For the negotiations concerning the Templars' property which ended in agreement in June 1962, see Oren-Nordheim 1999, 141–43, and Rutland, 2005.

69. See notes of a meeting, 13 March 1953, ISA 2542/12, Sharef to Eytan, 13 April 1953, ISA 1859/4, and undated (probably April 1953) memorandum.

70. For full details, see ISA 1859/4.

71. Private information.

72. See Ilsar to the Foreign Minister's Bureau, 24 December 1953, ISA 2542/13.

73. See Sharef to Sharett, 30 November 1953, ISA 1859/4.

74. See correspondence in ISA 1859/4 and ISA 2542/13.

75. Notes of a meeting, 22 October 1953, ISA 1859/4.

76. See notes of a meeting with Rudloff, 11 March 1954, ISA 2542/13.

77. See Zeldin 1992, 96, and Kadmon to Yahil, 7 May 1954, ISA 2542/13.

78. Ilsar to the Foreign Ministry, 23 August 1955, ISA 295/2.

79. See Arad to the Israeli embassy in Washington, 2 February 1954, ISA 354/22, and Yehuda Blum to Raphael Israeli, 10 October 1962, ISA 2967/17.

80. See, inter alia, Bertram and Harry 1921, Tsimhoni 1978, Roussos 2003, Biger 1974, Kark and Oren-Nordheim 1985, Ben Arieh 2001.

81. On the subject, see an illuminating memorandum, dated 21 January 1958, PRO FO 371/133893.

82. For the negotiations during the mid-1930s between the Jewish Agency and the Greek Orthodox Church concerning land purchases, see CZA L18/827.

83. For an ownership map of lands in Jerusalem on the wake of the British Mandate, see Reichman 1989.

84. See a memorandum dated 21 January 1958, PRO FO 371/133893.

85. See correspondence in CZA L18/827, CZA L18/689, and ISA 8023/17.

86. See Hugh Dow's notes, 8 January 1951, PRO FO 371/91398. On the Christian Greek Orthodox community, see Tsimhoni 1982.

87. See correspondence during November 1951, PRO FO 371/91398.

88. For information on Greek Orthodox property, see Colbi to Avner, 6 June 1950, ISA 2411/16, and his memorandum, dated 10 January 1950, ISA 2395/28.

89. See the cabinet secretary to the finance minister, 25 July 1950.

90. See correspondence in ISA 2395/24.

91. For illustration, see Colbi to Herzog, 13 March 1950, ISA 5823/9.

92. See Israel Zipper's report, 23 May 1950, ISA 5803/6.

93. See Bialer 1984 and Golani 1995.

94. See Reichman 1989.

95. For an early expression of this effort, see Herzog to Avner, 22 September 1949, ISA 5824/4. On Greece's policy toward Israel, see Gilboa 2002. For the beginnings of these relations, see Nachmani 1987.

96. See Herzog to the prime minister, 7 September 1949, ISA 7854/6.

97. See minutes of the Knesset Foreign Affairs and Defense Committee, 6 May 1950, ISA.

98. See a dispatch from Dow to the Foreign Office, 9 February 1950, PRO FO 371/182183.

99. See Colbi's memorandum, 19 January 1950, ISA 2395/28, and Herzog to the prime minister, 7 September 1949, ISA 7854/6.

100. See Colbi to Eytan, 2 December 1949, ISA 2396/2, Rosenne to the Finance Minister's Bureau, 29 December 1949, ISA 2395/24, and Colbi's memorandum, 19 January 1950, ISA 2395/28.

101. The following is based on Dow's dispatch to the Foreign Office, 20 September 1950, PRO FO 371/82189, Herzog's undated dispatch to Kadmon (probably November 1951), and Herzog to Avner, 12 November 1950, both in ISA 2395/24.

102. See *IILA*, no. 128, 16 October 1950, ISA 7854/4.

103. Herzog to Sharett, 29 November 1950, ISA 2395/24.

104. Ibid.

105. The following is based on Dow's dispatch to Geoffrey Furlonge, 8 January 1951, PRO FO 371/91398.

106. See Herzog to Avner, 17 May 1951, ISA 2523/8.

107. See Herzog to Avraham Granot, 15 July 1951.

108. April 1951, ISA 2523/8.

109. Asher Moisis to the Ministry for Foreign Affairs, 25 July 1951, ISA 5803/10.

110. See Herzog to Avner, 5 August 1951, ISA 2523/8.

111. See Herzog's dispatch to Lourie, 5 April 1951, ISA 2396/2.

112. The following is based on Dow to the Foreign Office, 15 October 1951, PRO FO 371/91398, and correspondence in CZA KKL/23237.

113. See *IILA*, no. 408, 28 November 1951, ISA 7536/3.

114. See a dispatch from the British consul in Jerusalem to the Foreign Office, 16 November 1951, PRO FO 371/91398.

115. British consul's dispatch of 5 August 1952, PRO FO 371/98501.

116. See Herzog to the Ministry for Religious Affairs, 18 November 1951, ISA 7536/5.

117. Dispatch from the British consul in Jerusalem to the Foreign Office, 16 November 1951, PRO FO 371/91398.

118. See Colbi to the director-general of the Ministry for Religious Affairs, 21 November 1955, ISA 5803/13.

119. Colbi to the Division of Western Europe, 15 July 1954, ISA 2523/8.

120. July 1952, ISA 2396/2.

121. See *IILA*, no. 408, 28 November 1951, ISA 7536/3.

122. Colbi to David Reif, 28 December 1952, ISA 5803/12.

123. Meir to the minister for religious affairs, 19 November 1959, ISA 3107/9.

124. See Zipper's memorandum, 23 May 1950, ISA 5803/6.

Epilogue

1. The following is based on Aumann 2002, 1033–38. See also Aumann 2003.

2. The following is based on Vardi to Herzog, 16 May 1949, ISA 2396/17.

3. See notes of a meeting dated 19 October 1949, ISA 2771/13.

4. Notes of meetings dated 20 September 1949 and 23 December 1949, ISA 2396/17.

5. Michael Amir to the Ministry for Foreign Affairs, 5 December 1949, ISA 2523/3.

6. Avner to the Israeli counselor in Rome, 29 September 1949, ISA 277/13, Eytan to Sharett and Sharett's response in ISA 2396/18.

7. The cabinet secretary to the ministers, 24 July 1949, ISA 2396/17.

8. Eytan to Sharett, 29 October 1949, ISA 2396/18.

9. See cabinet meeting minutes, 6 December 1949, ISA.

10. See correspondence in ISA 2396/17.

11. Avner to Israel's representative in Benelux, 19 December 1949, ISA 2521/13.

12. See correspondence in ISA 5807/9.

13. Shiloah to Avner, 22 December 1949, ISA 2524/3.

14. Aharon Propes to Colbi, 27 March 1950, ISA 5807/9.

15. The first Protestant group arrived at the end of January 1951. See correspondence in ISA 2524/3 and ISA 2396/18.

16. See a report dated 8 March 1962, ISA 5826/12.

17. Ephraim Halevi to Savir, 3 December 1959, ISA 3102/24.

18. Rafael to Biniamin Gibli, 5 May 1956, ISA 2396/6. See also Eshed 1988, 258–66, Ehrlich 2000, and Eisenberg 1994.

19. Report of a meeting, 11 June 1953, ISA 2458/7.

20. See a report on his mission to the Vatican, ISA 273/15.

21. See Perko 1997, 1.

22. On other obstacles, see Minerbi 2003.

23. On the general subject, see Inbar 1990.

24. For the lengthy negotiations leading to the agreement, its text, and its conflicting interpretations by both sides, see Berger 2004. It is highly significant that the preamble to that agreement relates pointedly to "the unique nature of the relationship between the Catholic Church and the Jewish people." As Eugene Fisher, a former consultant to the Holy See's Commission for Religious Relations with the Jews and a member of the International Catholic-Jewish Liaison Committee, said recently in a retrospective interview on *Nostra Aetate*, "a major issue that will be with us for this

generation, and perhaps the next, is coming to terms with our respective historical memories, not only of the Shoah, but of events in the centuries preceding it" (Rome, 27 June 2003; Zenit.org, http://www.zenit.org).

25. See Lorenzo Cremonesi's analysis in Berger 2004, 43. It should be noted that the non-official line of the Israeli Foreign Ministry at the beginning of the Third Millennium was to underrate the significance of the Vatican's conciliatory diplomacy. Concluding a long analysis of Pope John Paul II's visit to Israel in March 2000, Sergio Minerbi, a leading official authority on the subject at the Ministry, wrote, "Even when the pope says: 'We must work for a new era of reconciliation and peace between Jews and Christians,' we should ask a cardinal question. Does the pope mean 'reconciliation' as Paul meant it? Paul wrote that Jesus' purpose 'was to create in himself one new man, out of the two [the Jews and Pagans], thus making peace, and in this one body to reconcile both of them to God through the Cross' (Ephesians 2:15–16). It is interesting to note that in all his speeches to a predominantly Moslem public in Jordan or in the territory of the Palestinian Authority, the pope never used the word 'reconciliation,' preferring 'understanding and cooperation.' For example, at the Mass in Bethlehem the pope said: 'I greet the Muslim Community of Bethlehem and pray for a new era of understanding and cooperation among all the peoples of the Holy Land.' This reinforces the feeling that 'reconciliation' is constantly taken in the meaning given to this word by Paul, expressing the necessity to convert the Jews to Christianity." See http://www.mfa.gov.il/MFA/MFAArchive, under "The Pope's Visit to the Holy Land."

26. Sinai 2004.

bibliography

Unpublished Primary Sources

Ben-Gurion Archive, Sdeh Boker. Ben-Gurion Diary. General Correspondence.
Central Zionist Archives, Jerusalem. Papers of the Political Department. Moshe Sharett
    Papers. Yitzhak Rabinovitch Papers.
Israel State Archive, Jerusalem. Papers of the Ministry of Foreign Affairs. Cabinet Pa-
    pers. Papers of the Finance Ministry, Ministry of Religious Affairs, Ministry of
    Justice, Ministry of the Interior, Prime Minister's Office, Ministry of Education,
    Knesset Papers.
National Archives, Washington, D.C. State Department Files.
Public Record Office, London. Foreign Office Papers.

Secondary Sources

Abadi, Jacob. 2002. "Constraints and Adjustments in Italy's Policy towards Israel." *Middle Eastern Studies* 38, no. 4: 63–94.
Alberigo, Giuseppe, ed. 1995. *History of Vatican II.* Vol. 1: *Announcing and Preparing Vatican Council II: Toward a New Era in Catholicism.* New York: Orbis.
———. 1997. *History of Vatican II.* Vol. 2: *The Formation of the Council's Identity: First Period and Intersession, October 1962–September 1963.* New York: Orbis.
———. 2000. *History of Vatican II.* Vol. 3: *The Mature Council: Second Period and Intersession, September 1963–September 1964.* New York: Orbis.
———. 2003. *History of Vatican II.* Vol. 4: *Church as Communion: Third Period and Intercession, September 1964–September 1965.* New York: Orbis.
Ariel, Yaacov. 1991. *On Behalf of Israel: American Fundamentalist Attitudes towards Jews, Judaism, and Zionism, 1865–1945.* New York: Carlson.
———. 1998. "Evangelists in a Strange Land: American Missionaries in Israel, 1948–1967." *Studies in Contemporary Jewry* 14: 195–213.
Ariel, Yaacov, and Kark, Ruth. 1996. "Messianism, Holiness, Charisma, and Community: The American-Swedish Colony in Jerusalem, 1881–1933." *Church History* 65, no. 4: 641–57.
Aumann, Moshe. 2002. "Israel and the Christian World: A Turn." In Moshe Yegar, Arie

Oded, and Yosef Govrin, eds., *The Ministry for Foreign Affairs: The First Fifty Years*, 1033–38. Jerusalem: Keter Press. (Hebrew)

———. 2003. *Conflict and Connection: The Jewish-Christian-Israel Triangle.* New York: Gefen.

Avivi, Shimon. 2002. "Policy towards the Druze in Israel and Its Implementation: Consistency and Lapses (1948–1967)." Ph.D. dissertation, Haifa University. (Hebrew)

Azarya, Victor. 1984. *The Armenian Quarter of Jerusalem: Urban Life behind Monastery Walls.* Berkeley: University of California Press.

Bar, Doron. 2004. "Re-creating Jewish Sanctity in Jerusalem: Mount Zion and David's Tomb, 1948–67." *Journal of Israeli History* 23, no. 2: 260–78.

Barkat, Amiram. 2004. "Pius XII Told Churches Not to Return Holocaust War Babies." *Haaretz*, 30 December. (Hebrew)

Bar-On, Mordechai. 1992. *The Gates of Gaza: Israel's Security Policy and Foreign Policy, 1955–1957.* Tel-Aviv: Am Oved. (Hebrew)

Bar-On, Mordechai, and Zvi Zameret, eds. 2002. *On Both Sides of the Bridge: Religion and State in the Early Years of Israel.* Jerusalem: Yad Ben Zvi. (Hebrew)

Bar-Zohar, Michael. 2003. *The Life and Times of a Jewish Prince: A Biography of Yaacov Herzog.* Tel Aviv: Yediot Aharonot. (Hebrew)

Bashan, Refael. 1965. *I Have an Interview.* Tel Aviv: Am Oved. (Hebrew)

Bea, Augustin. 1966. *The Church and the Jewish People.* New York: Harper and Row.

Bein, Alex. 1962. *Theodor Herzl.* Cleveland: World.

Ben Arieh, Yehoshua. 2001. *A Land Reflected in Its Past.* Edited by Ran Aahronsohn and Lavsky Hagit. Jerusalem: Magness Press. (Hebrew)

Ben Artzi, Yossi. 1996. *From Germany to the Holy Land.* Jerusalem: Yad Ben Zvi. (Hebrew)

Ben-Horin, Nathan. 2002. "Israel's Relations with the Vatican in the Maze of Theology and Political-Religious Interests." In Moshe Yegar, Arie Oded, and Yosef Govrin, eds., *The Ministry for Foreign Affairs: The First Fifty Years*, 993–1032. Jerusalem: Keter Press. (Hebrew)

Berger, Marshall, ed. 2004. *The Vatican–Israel Accords: Political, Legal, and Theological Contexts.* Notre Dame: University of Notre Dame Press.

Bertram, Anton, and Luke, Harry Charles. 1921. *Report of the Commission Appointed by the Government of Palestine to Inquire into Affairs of the Orthodox Patriarchate of Jerusalem.* London: Oxford University Press.

Bialer, Uri. 1984. "The Road to the Capital: The Establishment of Jerusalem as the Official Seat of the Israeli Government in 1949." *Studies in Zionism* 5, no. 2: 273–96.

———. 1992. "Sterling Balances and Claims Negotiations: Britain and Israel, 1947–1952." *Middle Eastern Studies* 28, no. 1: 157–77.

———. 2002. "Top Hat, Tuxedo, and Cannons: Israeli Foreign Policy from 1948 to 1956 as a Field of Study." *Israel Studies* 7, no. 1: 1–80.

Biger, Gideon. 1974. "The Policy and Activity of Jews and British in the Development of Jerusalem, 1918–1925." MA thesis, Hebrew University, Jerusalem.

Blanshard, Paul. 1966. *Paul Blanshard on Vatican II.* Boston: Beacon Press.

Boymal, Yair. 2002. "The Attitude of the Israeli Establishment towards the Arabs in Israel: Policy, Principles, and Activities—The Second Decade, 1958–1968." Ph.D. dissertation, Haifa University. (Hebrew)

Brecher, Michael. 1978. "Jerusalem: Israel's Political Decisions, 1947–1977." *Middle East Journal* 32 (Winter): 13–34.

Carmel, Alex. 1983. "Competition, Penetration, and Presence: The Christian Activity and Its Influence in the Land of Israel." In Ben Arieh Yehoshua and Bartal Israel, eds., *The History of Eretz Israel: The Last Phase of Ottoman Rule, 1799–1917*, 109–54. Jerusalem: Yad Ben Zvi. (Hebrew)

Carroll, David. 1993. "On Fire for the Cause of Christ." *Catholic Middle East* 19, no. 6: 15–19.

Colbi, Saul. 1988. *A History of the Christian Presence in the Holy Land.* Lanham, Md.: University Press of America.

Cornwell, John. 1999. *Hitler's Pope: The Secret History of Pius XII.* New York: Penguin.

Conway, John. 1999. "The Founding of the State of Israel and the Response of the Christian Churches." *Kirchliche Zeitgeschichte* 12: 459–72.

Degani, Rami, ed. 1999. *Christian Churches Orders and Communities in Israel.* Jerusalem: Ariel. (Hebrew)

Doukhan-Landau, Lea. 1979. *The Zionist Companies for Land Purchase in Palestine, 1897–1914.* Jerusalem: Yad Ben Zvi. (Hebrew)

Ehrlich, Reuven. 2000. *The Lebanon Triangle: The Policy of the Zionist Movement and the State of Israel towards Lebanon, 1918–1958.* Tel Aviv: Ma'arachot. (Hebrew)

Eisenberg Laura. 1994. *My Enemy's Enemy: Lebanon in Early Zionist Imagination, 1900–1948.* Detroit: Wayne State University Press.

Eliav, Mordechai. 1995. "By Virtue of Women: The Role of Women in the Conversion Attempts by the British Mission." *Cathedra* 76: 96–115. (Hebrew)

Ellis, Kail. 1987. *The Vatican, Islam, and the Middle East.* Syracuse: Syracuse University Press.

Eordegian, Marilyn. 2003. "British and Israeli Maintenance of the Status Quo in the Holy Places of Christendom." *International Journal of Middle East Studies* 35, no. 2: 307–28.

Eshed, Hagai. 1988. *Reuven Shiloah: Father of Israel's Intelligence Services.* Tel Aviv: Idanim. (Hebrew)

Feldblum, Esther. 1977. *The American Catholic Press and the Jewish State, 1917–1959.* New York: Ktav.

Ferrari, Silvio. 1984. "The Holy See and the Postwar Palestine Issue: The Internationalisation of Jerusalem and the Protection of the Holy Places." *International Affairs* 60, no. 2: 261–83.

———. 1985. "The Vatican and the Jerusalem Question, 1943–1984." Middle East Journal 39, no. 2: 316–32.

———. 1991. *Vaticano e Israele: dal secondo conflitto mondiale alla guerra del golfo.* Florence: Sansoni.

———. 1998. "The Fundamental Agreement between the Holy See and Israel and the Conventions between States and the Church since the Vatican II Council." *Catholic University Law Review* 47: 385–406.

Firro, Kais. 1999. *The Druzes in the Jewish State.* Leiden: Brill.

Fischer, Eugene. 1987. "The Holy See and the State of Israel: The Evolution of Attitudes and Policies." *Journal of Ecumenical Studies* 24, no. 2: 191–211.

Fishman, Hertzel. 1973. *American Protestantism and a Jewish State.* Detroit: Wayne State University Press.

Fraenkel, Yuval. 1995. "The Activity of Monsignor Angelo Roncalli during the Holocaust." *Yalkut Moreshet* (April): 109–36. (Hebrew)

Freundlich, Yehoshua, ed. 1984. *Documents on the Foreign Policy of Israel.* Vol. 2: *October 1948–April 1949.* Jerusalem: Keter Press.

———. 1994. *From Destruction to Birth: The Zionist Policy from the End of World War II until the Birth of the State of Israel.* Tel-Aviv: Universities Enterprises. (Hebrew)

———. 2003. "A Soviet Outpost in Tel Aviv: the Soviet Legation in Israel, 1948–53." *Journal of Israeli History*. 22, no. 1: 37–55.

Friling, Tuvia. 1998. *An Arrow in the Dark: Ben-Gurion, the Yishuv's Leadership, and the Attempts to Rescue European Jews during the Holocaust*. Sde Boker: Ben-Gurion Research Center. (Hebrew)

Gelber, Yoav. 1992. *Growing a Fleur-de-Lis: The Intelligence Services of the Jewish Yishuv in Palestine, 1918–1947*. Tel Aviv: Ministry of Defense Press. (Hebrew)

———. 2004. *Independence versus Nakba*. Or Yehuda: Kineret, Zmora Bitan, Dvir. (Hebrew)

Gilboa, Moshe. 2002. "The Background and Activity towards Greece's Recognition of Israel." In Moshe Yegar, Arie Oded, and Yosef Govrin, eds., *The Ministry for Foreign Affairs: The First Fifty Years*, 377–97. Jerusalem: Keter Press.

Giovannelli, Andrea. 2000. *La Santa Sede e La Palestina: La Custodia di Terra Santa tra la fine dell'impero ottomano e la guerra dei sei giorni*. Roma: Studium.

Golan, Arnon. 2001. *Wartime Spatial Changes: Former Arab Territories within the State of Israel, 1948–1950*. Sde Boker: Ben-Gurion Research Institute. (Hebrew)

Golani, Motti. 1995. "Zionist without Zion: The Jerusalem Question, 1947–1949." *Journal of Israeli History* 16, no. 1: 39–52.

———. 1999. "Jerusalem's Hope Lies Only in Partition: Israeli Policy on the Jerusalem Question, 1948–1967." *International Journal of Middle Eastern Studies* 31, no. 4: 577–604.

Gorodetsky, Gabriel. 2003. "The Soviet Union's Role in the Creation of the State of Israel." *Journal of Israeli History* 22, no. 1: 4–20.

Govrin, Yosef. 1998. *Israeli-Soviet Relations, 1953–67*. London: Frank Cass.

Greenberg, Ofra. 1999. *Nes Amim: Life under Contradiction: The Story of a Christian Village in Israel*. Ramat Efal: Yad Tabenkin. (Hebrew)

Hahn, Peter. 1999. "Alignment by Coincidence: Israel, The United States and the Partition of Jerusalem, 1949–1953." *International History Review* 21, no. 3: 569–82.

Haidar, Aziz. 1988. "The Different Levels of Palestinian Ethnicity." In Esman Milton and Rabinovich Itamar, eds., *Ethnicity, Pluralism, and the State in the Middle East*, 95–120. Ithaca, N.Y.: Cornell University Press.

Halevi, Masha. 2004. "Religion, Symbolism, and Politics: Symbolic and Political Aspects of the Buildup of the New Church of the Annunciation in Nazareth." Master's dissertation, Hebrew University. (Hebrew)

Hebblethwaite, Peter. 1985. *Pope John XXIII: Shepherd of the Modern World*. Garden City, N.Y.: Doubleday.

Heller, Joseph. 2000. *The Birth of Israel, 1945–1949: Ben-Gurion and His Critics*. Gainesville: University Press of Florida.

Hershco, Tslila. 2000. *Between Paris and Jerusalem: France, Zionism, and the Establishment of Israel, 1945–1949*. Tel Aviv: Ministry of Defense Press. (Hebrew)

Hillel, Shlomo. 1985. *Operation Babylon*. Tel Aviv: Yediot Aharonot. (Hebrew)

Hochman, Rami, ed. 1988. *Jews and Arabs in Israel*. Jerusalem: Hebrew University. (Hebrew)

Hopwood, Derek. 1969. *The Russian Presence in Syria and Palestine, 1843–1914* Oxford: Clarendon.

Hudson, Darril, 1977. *The World Council of Churches in International Affairs*. London: Royal Institute of International Affairs.

Ilan, Amitzur. 1989. *Bernadotte in Palestine 1948*. London: Macmillan.

Inbar, Efraim. 1990. "Jews, Jewishness, and Israel's Foreign Policy." *Jewish Political Studies Review* 2 (Fall): 165–83.

Iogna-Prat, Dominique. 1998. "Alphonse Dupront ou la poetisation de l'Histoire." *Revue Historique* 608 (October/December): 887–910.

Irani, George. 1986. *The Papacy and the Middle East: The Role of the Holy See in the Arab-Israeli Conflict, 1962–1984.* Notre Dame: University of Notre Dame Press.

Israeli, Raphael. 2002a. *Jerusalem Divided: The Armistice Regime, 1947–1967.* London: Frank Cass.

———. 2002b. *Green Crescent over Nazareth: The Displacement of Christians by Muslims in the Holy Land.* London: Frank Cass.

Jelinek, Yeshayahu. 2002. "Konrad Adenauer and the State of Israel: Between Friendship and Realpolitik, 1953–1963." *Orient* 43, no. 1: 41–57.

Kamen, Charles. 1985. "After the Catastrophe: The Arabs in the State of Israel." *Notebooks on Research and Criticism* 10: 3–91.

Kark, Ruth. 1984. "Changing Patterns of Land Ownership in Nineteenth-Century Palestine: The European Influence." *Journal of Historical Geography* 10, no. 4: 357–84.

———. 1995. "Planning, Housing, and Land Policy, 1948–1952: The Formation of Concepts and Government Frameworks." In Troen Ilan and Lucas Noha, eds., *Israel: The First Decade of Independence*, 461–94. New York: State University of New York Press.

Kark, Ruth, ed. 1990. *Redeeming Land in Israel: Idea and Practice.* Jerusalem: Yad Ben Zvi. (Hebrew)

Kark, Ruth, and Michal Oren-Nordheim. 1985. *Jerusalem and Its Environs: Quarters, Neighborhoods, 1800–1948.* Jerusalem: Academon. (Hebrew)

Katz, Yossi. 2001. *The Battle for the Land: The Jewish National Fund (KKL) before the Establishment of the State of Israel.* Jerusalem: Magnes.

Katz, Yossi, and Paz Yair. 2004. "The Transfer of Government Ministries to Jerusalem, 1948–49: Continuity or Change in the Zionist Attitude to Jerusalem?" *Journal of Israeli History* 23, no. 2: 232–59.

Kazin, Orna. 1999. "There Is No Prophet in His Town." *Ha'aretz*, 23 December. (Hebrew)

Kreutz, Andrej. 1990. *Vatican Policy on the Palestinian Conflict: The Struggle for the Middle East.* New York: Greenwood Press.

———. 1992. "Arab Christian Communities of the Holy Land: A Minority in Crisis." *British Society for Middle Eastern Studies, Proceedings.* Edinburgh: 263–78.

Lang, Joseph. 1996. "The Struggle against Missionary Activity at the Beginning of the First Aliyah and Its Reflection in the Jerusalem Press." *Cathedra* 80: 63–87. (Hebrew)

Lapide, Pinchas. 1967. *Three Popes and the Jews.* New York: Hawthorn Books.

Lazare, Lucien. 1990. *L'abbe Glasberg.* Paris: Cerf.

Leeming, Bernard. 1964. *Agostino Cardinal Bea.* Notre Dame: University of Notre Dame Press.

Le Morzellec, Joelle. 1979. *La Question de Jerusalem devant l'organization des Nations Unies.* Bruxelles: Bruylant.

Levin, Marlin. 1949. "Israel and the Churches," *Jerusalem Post*, 26 July, 4.

Lodberg, Peter. 1999. "World Council of Churches." *Kirchliche Zeitgeschichte* 12: 527–36.

Lustik, Ian. 1985. *Arabs in the Jewish State: Israel Control of a National Minority.* Haifa: Mifras. (Hebrew)

Malachy, Yona. 1978. *American Fundamentalism and Israel.* Jerusalem: Institute of Contemporary Jewry, Hebrew University of Jerusalem.

Ma'oz, Moshe, and Sari Nusseibeh, eds. 2000. *Jerusalem: Points of Friction—and Beyond.* The Hague: Kluwer Law International.

McDonald, James. 1951. *My Mission in Israel, 1948–51.* New York: Simon and Schuster.

Meinardus, Otto Friedrich. 1960. *The Copts in Jerusalem.* Cairo: Commission on Oecumenical Affairs of the See of Alexandria.

Melloni, Alberto. 1992. *Fra Istanbul, Atene e la gueree: La missione di A. G. Roncalli, 1935–1944.* Genoa: Marietti.

———. 1996. "Pope John XXIII: Open Questions for a Biography." *Catholic Historical Review* 72: 51–67.

———. 2000. *L'altra Roma. Politica e S. Sede durante il Concilio Vaticano II (1959–1965).* Bologna: Mulino.

———. 2004. "Pio XII a Roncalli: non restituite i bimbi ebrei." *Corriere della Sera*, 28 December.

Mendes, Meir. 1983. *The Vatican and Israel.* Jerusalem: Hebrew University.

———. 1990. *Le Vatican et Israel.* Paris: Cerf.

Merkley, Paul. 1998. *The Politics of Christian Zionism, 1891–1948.* London: Frank Cass.

———. 2001. *Christians Attitudes towards the State of Israel.* Montreal: McGill-Queen's University Press.

Minerbi, Sergio. 1985. *The Vatican, the Holy Land, and Zionism, 1895–1925.* Jerusalem: Yad Ben Zvi. (Hebrew)

———. 2003. "Palestinian Christians Putting on Fire Religious Controversy." *Kivunim Hadashim* 8: 70–82. (Hebrew)

Morris, Benny. 1989. *The Birth of the Palestine Refugee Problem, 1947–1949.* Cambridge: Cambridge University Press.

Nachmani, Amikam. 1987. *Israel, Turkey, and Greece: Uneasy Relations in the Eastern Mediterranean.* London: Frank Cass.

Nathans, Benjamin. 2002. *Beyond the Pale: The Jewish Encounter with Late Imperial Russia.* Berkeley: University of California Press.

Okkenhaug, Inger Marie. 2002. *The Quality of Heroic Living, of Higher Endeavour and Adventure: Anglican Mission, Women, and Education in Palestine, 1888–1948.* Leiden: Brill.

O'Mahony, Anthony, ed. 2003. *The Christian Communities of Jerusalem and the Holy Land: Studies in History, Religion, and Politics.* Cardiff: University of Wales Press.

Oren-Nordheim, Michal. 1999. "The Crystallization of Settlement Land Policy in the State of Israel from Its Establishment and during the First Years of the Israel Land Administration, 1948–1965." Ph.D. dissertation, Hebrew University. (Hebrew)

Osterbye, Per. 1970. *The Church in Israel.* Lund: Gleerup

Ozaky-Lazer, Sarah. 1993. *Ikrit and Biram: The Full Story.* Givat Haviva: The Institute for Arab Studies. (Hebrew)

———. 1996. "The Crystallization of Arab-Jews Relations in Israel: The First Decade, 1948–1958." Ph.D. dissertation, Haifa University. (Hebrew)

———. 2002. "The Military Government as an Apparatus of Control of the Arab Citizens of Israel: The First Decade, 1948–1958." *New East* 42: 103–32. (Hebrew)

Palmieri-Billig, Lisa. 2004. "Pope Pius XII Wanted to Keep Baptized Jewish Children after the War." *Jerusalem Post*, 29 December.

Peled, Alisa. 1994. "The Crystallization of an Israeli Policy towards Muslim and Christian Holy Places, 1948–1955." *Muslim World* 84: 95–126.

Perko, Michael. 1997. "Towards a 'Sound and Lasting Basis': Relations between the Holy See, the Zionist Movement, and Israel, 1896–1996." *Israel Studies* 2: 1–21.

Phayer, Michael. 2000. *The Catholic Church and the Holocaust, 1930–1965.* Bloomington: Indiana University Press.

Popham, Peter. 2004. "Pius XII Barred Jewish Children Returning Home." *Independent* (online edition), 31 December.

Pospielovsky, Dimitry. 1984. *The Russian Church under the Soviet Regime, 1917–1982.* New York: Crestwood.

Proctor, J. 1997. "Scottish Missionaries and the Struggle for Palestine, 1917–48." *Middle Eastern Studies* 33: 613–29.

Racionzer, Leon. 2004. "Hebrew Catholicism: Theology and Politics in Modern Israel." *Heythrop Journal* 45: 405–15.

Reichman, Shalom. 1989. "A Map of Land Ownership in Jerusalem 1947." In Lavsky Hagit, ed., *Jerusalem in Zionist Vision and Realization*, 303–11. Jerusalem, Merkaz Shazar. (Hebrew)

Ro'i, Yaacov. 1980. *Soviet Decision Making in Practice: The USSR and Israel, 1947–1954.* New Brunswick: Transaction Books.

Ro'i, Yaacov, Yehoshua Freundlich, and Dov Yaroshevski, eds. 2000. *Documents on Israeli-Soviet Relations, 1941–1953.* London: Frank Cass.

Rokach, Livia. 1987. *The Catholic Church and the Question of Palestine.* London: Saqi.

Roussos, Storis. 2003. "The Greek Orthodox Patriarchate and Community of Jerusalem: Church, State and Identity." In Anthony O'Mahony, ed., *The Christian Communities of Jerusalem and the Holy Land*, 38–56. Cardiff: University of Wales Press.

Rutland, Suzanne. 2005. "Buying Out of the Matter: Australia's Role in Restitution for the Templer Property in Israel." *The Journal of Israeli History* 24, 1: 135–54.

Sanchez, Jose. 2002. *Pius XII and the Holocaust: Understanding the Controversy.* Washington, D.C.: Catholic University of America Press.

Sanjian, Ara. 2003. "The Armenian Church and Community of Jerusalem." In Anthony O'Mahony, ed., *The Christian Communities of Jerusalem and the Holy Land*, 57–89. Cardiff: University of Wales Press.

Schiller, Ely. 1992. *Guide to Christian Historical Sites and Holy Places in Israel.* Jerusalem: Ariel. (Hebrew)

Schiotz, Fredrik. 1980. *One Man's Story.* Minneapolis: Augsburg.

Schmidgall, Paul. 1996. "American Holiness: Churches in the Holy Land, 1890–1990—Mission to Jews, Arabs, Armenians." Ph.D. dissertation, Hebrew University.

Schmidt, Stjepan. 1992. *Augustin Bea, the Cardinal of Unity.* New Rochelle: New City Press.

Sennott, Charles. 2001. *The Body and Blood: The Holy Land's Christians and the Turn of the Millennium.* New York: Public Affairs.

Shalom, Zaki. 1995. *David Ben-Gurion, the State of Israel, and the Arab World, 1949–1956.* Sde Boker: Ben-Gurion Research Center.

Sheffer, Gabriel. 1996. *Moshe Sharett: Biography of a Political Moderate.* Oxford: Oxford University Press.

Sheleg, Yair. 2003. "He Was the Priest Who Saved Jews." *Haaretz*, 11 July.

Shouval, Noam. 1996. "Swedish Activities in and around Jerusalem at the Beginning of the Twentieth Century." *Cathedra* 81: 61–74. (Hebrew)

Sinai, Ruthie. 2004. "The Churches against Israel." *Ha'aretz*, 30 March. (Hebrew)

Slonim, Shlomo. 1998. *Jerusalem in America's Foreign Policy, 1947–1997.* Boston: Kluwer Law International.

Smith, Robert. 1954. "The Church and the Jews in Israel." *East and West Review* (April): 60–64.

Stanislawski, Michael. 1987. "An Unperformed Contract: The Sale of Baron Gunzburg's Library to the Jewish Theological Seminary of America." In *Transition and Change in Modern Jewish History: Essays Presented in Honor of Shmuel Ettinger,* lxxiii–xciii. Jerusalem: Merkaz Shazar.

Stavrou, Theofanis. 1963. *Russian Interests in Palestine, 1882–1914: A Study of Religious and Educational Enterprise.* Thessaloniki: Institute for Balkan Studies.

Stegemann, Ekkhard. 1999. "The Dual Attitude of the Church towards Zionism and the State of Israel." *Kivunim Hadashim* (December): 119–30. (Hebrew)

Stein, Kenneth. 1984. *The Land Question in Palestine, 1917–1939.* Chapel Hill: University of North Carolina Press.

Tal, David. 1998. *Israel's Day-to-Day Security Conception: Its Origins and Development, 1949–1956.* Sde Boker: Ben-Gurion Research Center. (Hebrew)

Tibawi, Abdul Latif. 1956. *Arab Education in Mandatory Palestine: A Study in Three Decades of British Administration.* London: Luzac.

Tsimhoni, Daphne. 1978. "The Greek Orthodox Patriarch of Jerusalem during the Formative Years of the British Mandate in Palestine." *Asian and African Studies* 12: 77–127.

———. 1982. "The Greek Orthodox Community in Jerusalem and the West Bank, 1948–1978: Profile of a Religious Community in a Nation-State." *Orient* 23: 275–98.

———. 1989. "The Political System of the Christians in Israel." *New East* 32. (Hebrew)

———. 1993. *Christian Communities in Jerusalem and the West Bank since 1948.* Westport, Conn.: Praeger.

———. 1996. "The British Mandate and the Status of Religious Communities in Palestine." *Cathedra* 80: 150–74. (Hebrew)

———. 2001. "Christians of Israel and the Territories: Disappearance." *Middle East Quarterly* (Winter): 31–42.

Watson, John. 2003. "Egypt and the Holy Land: The Coptic Church and Community." In Anthony O'Mahony, ed., *The Christian Communities of Jerusalem and the Holy Land: Studies in History, Religion, and Politics,* 115–29. Cardiff: University of Wales Press.

Weber, Timothy. 2004. *On the Road to Armageddon: How Evangelicals Became Israel's Best Friend.* Grand Rapids, Mich.: Baker Academic.

Weiman, Rachel. 1996. "From Recognition to Reconciliation: The Catholic Church and the Jewish People." Ph.D. dissertation, Temple University.

Wigoder, Geoffrey. 1988. *Jewish-Christian Relations since the Second World War.* Manchester: Manchester University Press.

Yaroshevski, Dov. 2003. "Beyond the 'Russian Property' Discourse, 1917–1953." *Journal of Israeli History* 22: 56–70.

Yegar, Moshe, Arie Oded, and Yosef Govrin, eds. 2002. *The Ministry for Foreign Affairs: The First Fifty Years.* Jerusalem: Keter Press. (Hebrew)

Zak, Moshe. 1988. *A Forty Years Dialogue with Moscow.* Tel Aviv: Ma'ariv. (Hebrew)

Zameret, Zvi. 1997. *Across a Narrow Bridge: The Education System during the Great Aliya.* Sde Boker: Ben-Gurion Research Institute. (Hebrew)

———. 2002. "Yes to a Jewish State, No to a Clerical State: The Mapai Leadership and Its Attitude to Religion and Religious Jews." In Mordechai Bar-On and Zvi Zameret, eds., *On Both Sides of the Bridge: Religion and State in the Early Years of Israel,* 175–244. Jerusalem: Yad Ben Zvi. (Hebrew)

Zameret, Zvi, and Hana Yablonka, eds. 2000. *The Second Decade, 1958–68.* Jerusalem: Yad Ben Zvi. (Hebrew)

Zander, Walter. 1971. *Israel and the Holy Places of Christendom.* London: Weidenfeld and Nicholson.

———. 1973. "On the Settlement of Disputes about the Christian Holy Places." *Israel Law Review* 8: 331–66.

Zeldin, Gabriel. 1992. "Catholics and Protestants in Jerusalem and 'the Return of the Jews to Zion,' 1948–1988: A Historical, Sociological, and Ideological Study." Ph.D. dissertation, Hebrew University. (Hebrew)

Zifroni, Gavriel. 1977. "'Red' Russians and 'White' Russians in Jerusalem." *Cathedra* 5: 162–95. (Hebrew)

Zuccotti, Susan. 2001. *Under His Very Windows: The Vatican and the Holocaust in Italy.* New Haven, Conn.: Yale University Press.

index

URI BIALER holds the Maurice B. Hexter chair in International Relations—
Middle East Studies in the Department of International Relations at Hebrew University. He is author of *Oil and the Arab-Israeli Conflict* and *Between East and West: Israel's Foreign Policy Orientation, 1948–1956*. He is a member of the editorial board of *Israel Studies*.